BISON
BOOKS

Women in the West

THE
COWBOY GIRL

THE LIFE OF
CAROLINE LOCKHART

John Clayton

University of Nebraska Press ☞ Lincoln and London

Library of Congress Cataloging-in-Publication Data
Clayton, John, 1964–
The cowboy girl : the life of Caroline Lockhart /
John Clayton.
p. cm.—(Women in the West)
Includes bibliographical references and index.
ISBN-13: 978-0-8032-5990-4 (pbk. : alk. paper)
ISBN-10: 0-8032-5990-5 (pbk. : alk. paper)
1. Lockhart, Caroline, 1871–1962. 2. Novelists,
American—20th century—Biography.
3. Women ranchers—Wyoming—Biography.
I. Title.
PS3523.O237Z6 2007
813'.52—dc22
[B]
2006029802

Set in Bulmer by Kim Essman.
Designed by A. Shahan.

To Kari

CONTENTS

ILLUSTRATIONS

AUTHOR'S NOTE

This is a work of nonfiction. All characters are real; nothing has been disguised or embellished. Where I have used dialogue, it is based on the recollection of at least one participant, as documented in the endnotes.

I was drawn to this story by landscape and language. I stumbled across Caroline Lockhart's old ranch (a few hours' drive from my home) one May when spring turns it heavenly. Then I tracked down some of her novels and was surprised at how much I enjoyed them. That prompted one of my driving questions: Why had so few people heard of this woman? When I later learned her full story, that question only intensified.

Obsessed with cowboys and romanticizing the old West, Caroline Lockhart came to Montana and Wyoming long after the frontier had been "closed." So she tried to do something about that situation, to reinhabit a cowboy West. Can a single individual, no matter how ornery, turn back the march of time and progress? That's not just the classic question of Western literature. It's also, I found, the arc of Caroline Lockhart's life.

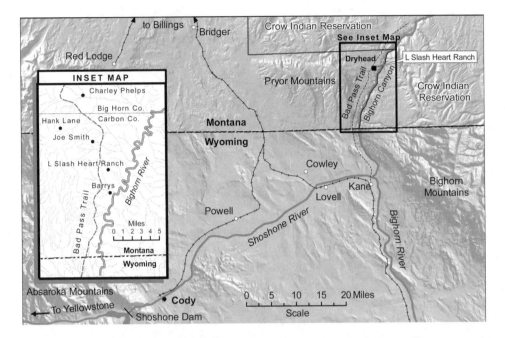

In 1926 Caroline Lockhart moved from Cody, Wyoming, to the remote Dryhead area of southern Montana. Inset is an approximation based on information provided by Tuffy Abbott in *Trails and Tales South of the Yellowstone*. Map by Tom Kohley, © 2006 by John Clayton.

THE COWBOY GIRL

Prologue

In late summer of 1901, Philadelphia's celebrity female journalist, pen named "Suzette," got off a train in Blackfoot, Montana. She was alone.

Dwarfed by the Montana prairie and sky, in the middle of an Indian reservation, Blackfoot was not much of a town. Suzette quickly arranged an overnight fifty-mile journey northwest to a place along the Swiftcurrent River where a few dozen people lived in log cabins and white tents. Boosters of this village, called Altyn, liked to claim that it sat in the center of a natural amphitheater, "fringed with majestic forests of pine and surrounded by titanic mountains, rugged canyons and azure lakes, the whole country being a masterpiece of beauty and sublimity." For once the boosters weren't much exaggerating: the place is now part of Glacier National Park, not far from the stunning Many Glacier Hotel.

Suzette's arrival represented major news for Altyn, which had been born less than three years previously, when a strip of land was taken from the Blackfeet Indians and thrown open to mining. Altyn's prospectors believed that within a few years its destiny would be decided: "the richest and biggest camp on earth or nothing." A writer from *Lippincott's Magazine* could help alert the forces of capital to Altyn's glorious potential.

What's more, in a rough-and-tumble camp filled mostly with males, the writer from *Lippincott's* was a gorgeous female. Possessed of an hourglass figure; long, thick, dark blonde hair often tied in a ponytail; sultry eyes; and a toothy, winning smile, Suzette was thirty years old but looked far younger. The fact that she was unmarried, and unchaperoned, further heightened local attention.

Women were still a novelty in the news-gathering business. There were women writers—novelists, essayists, society columnists—but few who traveled the country in search of insight or adventure. Nellie Bly had been the first, just twelve years previously. Writing for a New York newspaper, Bly had gone on adventures culminating in a trip around the world (designed to make the circuit in less than eighty days, beating the record set by Jules Verne's fictional character). On that trip Bly, an unmarried twenty-five-year-old, had been accompanied by her mother.

3

Suzette, by contrast, simply bought a train ticket to Montana and once there hired an old horse packer named McNeill. She told him she wanted to see some scenery, so he took her to Altyn and next perhaps they would go "across the summit to MacDonald Lake," noted a local newspaper. "The opinion of the boys is that Mack will keep going as the lady is quite attractive."

Who was this woman, and why had she come to this wilderness? Suzette's real name was Caroline Lockhart, and she'd been in journalism for about six years. In the aftermath of Nellie Bly's success, several major newspapers had hired women to write about feats of daring—"stunt girls," they were called. Lockhart had filled that role on the lurid *Boston Post*. Later she'd moved to the more staid *Philadelphia Bulletin*, where she'd turned from stunts to interviews and travel, covering the 1900 World's Fair in Paris. Now she was on a tour of the West. But in a fashion typical of her character, she refused to visit well-developed resorts. She wanted adventures: Indian reservations, remote mining camps, wilderness mountain trails.

It was partly her personality, out for adventure and fun, interested in the escapades and lingo of common folk rather than blue bloods. And it was partly ambition. She wanted to be famous, and she intended to achieve her fame through writing. Already readers and editors had admired her breezy style. She was making the step up from newspapers to magazines such as *Lippincott's*. She'd even started writing a novel.

In those days the road to literary fame generally led through exotic locations. Readers hungered for stories of places they hadn't been, especially romantic places like the western frontier. As a journalist, Lockhart had the goal of researching those places and people, then writing about them. She would soak in the character of Altyn and use it as a setting for stories and novels. She would meet lots of unusual people and turn them into characters. She would have adventures and recycle them as plots.

McNeill, for example, she later depicted as "a spry old man in a woolen shirt and ragged overalls. . . . He had a deeply lined face which looked like an old leather glove that had lain out in the weather and his mild blue eyes bespoke both honesty and friendliness." She liked that he had achieved local fame as a bear hunter and had once hunted and trapped for the Hudson's Bay Company. She also liked the way he took care of his horses, the fact that he called his blankets "soogans," and the way he let her call him "Sourdough Sam."

West of Altyn, the terrain soared more than two thousand feet to peaks along the continental divide. A rugged pass led through them to McDonald Lake, which was so scenic that it had already become something of a tourist destination (it would later become the heart of the national park). Suzette met more than one man in Altyn who told her quietly, "It's a rough trail." One told her that no woman had ever made it across. Such challenges only egged her on.

On horseback she and McNeill forded the Swiftcurrent River at the edge of Altyn and easily covered the first four miles, the relatively flat entry to a steep-sided bowl. At the far end of it McNeill stopped his horse and said, "Thar's yer trail."

"What!" It looked almost perpendicular.

"That's it. Want to go back?"

"No."

Today the route is a popular, if grueling, overnight hike. The bottom of the wall is a forbidding but also inspirational spot, with waterfalls tumbling over sheer mountain cliffs. It's the sort of scene that could convince a person to (a) leave Philadelphia for good, or (b) get the hell back there as soon as possible. Ahead, Park Service materials warn, the trail has been notched into the rock and is not for those who fear heights. In 1901 the trail had not yet been notched into the rock.

Lockhart was comfortable on horseback. She'd ridden horses since she was a very young girl. She didn't get much chance to now, living in the city, but on the occasions she did, she delighted in others' admiration of her skills. Horses were not just transportation to her. They stood for independence and freedom. She loved the act of riding and the skill of riding well; she found beauty in the paraphernalia of riders and in the animals themselves. A few years earlier she'd summered in Maine, where she had a horse of her own, and it may have always been in the back of her mind to return to a place where she could be a horsewoman.

This horse, however, was not to her liking. McNeill rode "a sturdy little mountain horse that dug in its toes and climbed slowly while my mount was a long-legged sorrel from the plains country. He was high-strung and took the climb in jumps." She fell far behind her guide. Finally she decided to get off the horse and hang onto his tail as he walked, letting him pull her up the slope. But the horse didn't cooperate. He moved too quickly for her and kicked dirt in her eyes.

Soon the horse jerked free of her and ran to the edge of a cliff. She saw him tremble there. She saw a fear come into his eyes that she thought was almost human. Then she saw him snort, whirl, and tear off up the mountainside, leaving her behind.

She had to trudge on afoot. She claimed later that she was mostly "on my hands and knees, grabbing at bushes, tufts of grass, anything that would keep me from slipping back. It was like trying to climb the side of a steep roof and getting steeper inch by inch as I neared the summit." Then she realized the rock underneath her had changed. She was now climbing on shale, far more slippery and unstable than the previous limestone. Every time she moved, she started a small slide. Any rock she dislodged "dropped over the edge of a precipice into a canyon so deep that I couldn't hear when it landed. It was the same spot where the pack horses had gone over and whose bleached bones were still lying where they fell."

She was now utterly alone. As much as she liked Sourdough Sam—the crusty old-timer full of the wisdom of a rough outdoor life, so different from the dull society types back East—he may not have been the most trustworthy choice for a guide. As much as she loved horses, this one had left her in a bad spot. As much as she loved wilderness exploration, she was now literally nauseated with fear.

Of course, adventurers thrive on such emotions. The fear, the individual challenge, the sense of pushing a perimeter—Lockhart would hardly be the last person to find these thrills in the natural wonders of the West. (Nor was she the first: the adventure, as much the economic opportunity, had always driven Americans to the frontier.) With both horse and guide gone, she was now truly alone on a dangerous precipice: "I couldn't go ahead, I couldn't go back, so with arms and legs outstretched I laid flat on my face and waited. I tried to call but nothing came out but a squeak while shale rattled with the violent trembling of my body. Though I laid as still as possible, at intervals the slide started of itself and I felt cautiously with my foot for an embedded rock that would hold but they all gave way and each slide brought me a little closer to the edge."

Caroline Lockhart had arrived in the West. It may have been crumbling away beneath her, but she was determined to hold on. Her ambition would land her here in the Rockies, amidst the scenery and colorful characters and powerful legends. She intended to find her footing, make a success of herself. Getting off this slate would be only the first step.

I

Born on a Horse

In April 1861 Joe Lockhart bought his first piece of land. He was twenty-three years old, five-foot-nine, with black eyes, thick black hair, and a bushy black moustache. He may have known then that it was only the first of hundreds of pieces of land he would buy in his lifetime, but if so he did not broadcast the fact. He was a taciturn man who rarely talked about business.

The land was in northwest Illinois in a place called Elkhorn Grove. Twenty years earlier Elkhorn Grove had been a primeval forest, with towering maples, oaks, and black walnuts, with herds of deer and flocks of birds. The first white settlers built a mill to harvest those trees. The trees became houses in nearby villages, tables and chairs and bureaus, fork handles and wooden rakes and spinning wheels. They became beams for plows built by the nearby Grand Detour Plow Company, owned by a man named John Deere. The forest was an untapped resource, waiting for a frontiersman to apply the hard work to turn it into profit. Once the forest was cleared, another frontiersman could start a farm. Lockhart purchased his 1¼ acres from the owner of the lumber mill.

Lockhart had grown up in northeast Pennsylvania, where his Scottish ancestors had lived for several generations. His father, a merchant, had died young, and as soon as Joe graduated from high school in 1856, he joined the flood of pioneers moving to Illinois. During the decade the once-frontier state's population grew to 1.7 million, making it the fourth largest in the union. Joe moved to the town of Polo, seven miles east of Elkhorn Grove, where he called himself a merchant.

He was probably a jack-of-all-trades, as many such young men were. He may have traveled around the state trading horses and mules. He probably worked cutting trees and sowing crops. After purchasing his property he likely grew wheat, corn, oats, or pumpkins, and raised cattle or hogs. His widowed mother soon purchased a nearby farm with a brick mansion and eighty acres of land. He undoubtedly spent a good deal of time at her place and must have met a neighboring family, the Woodruffs, and their fifteen-year-old daughter, Sarah.

But 1861 was a troubled year, the beginning of war. In October, Polo town founder Zenas Aplington organized the Seventh Illinois Cavalry, signing up Joe Lockhart for a three-year hitch. Lockhart spent his army days in Missouri, Tennessee, and Mississippi, where his unit's rampages slowed the Confederate response as Grant's army crossed the river at Vicksburg. But in later years he talked as little about the war as he did about business.

Mustering out, Lockhart returned to Elkhorn Grove. Over the next eight years he engaged in a bewildering series of real estate transactions, most of them involving farmland near Polo or Elkhorn Grove, most of them proving shrewd investments. In 1867 he married the now-matured Sarah Woodruff, and by 1870 they had amassed $8,000 worth of property ($111,000 in 2005 dollars), a considerable amount for the neighborhood, especially for a man of just thirty-two.

On February 25, 1871, Sarah gave birth to their first child, Caroline Cameron Lockhart. Soon after the birth Joe apparently got restless. His ancestors had always been merchants, traders, moneymakers; his uncles were making lots of money back in the Pennsylvania coal country. Joe himself apparently preferred the frontier, but that description was increasingly hard to apply to Elkhorn Grove. In February 1872 the sawmill burned. Not that there was much wood left to mill—the forest was dwindling to the point where little wildlife remained. A year later the last deer in the grove was killed. Soon after that folks started referring to the nearby settlement of Hitt as Stumptown. The black walnuts were gone, the maples and oaks and birds, the opportunity to tame wilderness. A few years later the Joliet Match Company would come in to take the useless basswood, the stuff nobody wanted, and chop it up into tiny fire starters.

But by then the Lockharts would have set off for a new frontier.

The landscape of eastern Kansas, where the Lockharts settled, was actually quite similar to what they'd left in Illinois. Its prairies of tall bluestem grasses were cut by small streams, with wooded bottomlands up to a halfmile on either side of each stream. As in Elkhorn Grove, you could grow hay, corn, and wheat in the valleys while running cattle on the upland plains. You probably had a garden, maybe an orchard or some specialty crops. The difference was that here land was cheaper, railroads newer, nature wilder, and money-making opportunities more lucrative.

This wasn't the dry open plains of western Kansas, where Texas cattlemen drove their product to railheads. This part of the state had a much more midwestern influence and was home to lots of migrants from northern Illinois. The Polo newspaper featured regular reports from Kansas on the ease of raising stock there. The Lockharts settled on Wakarusa Creek, halfway between the towns of Topeka and Burlingame. Topeka was the state capital, and Burlingame was on the route of the old Santa Fe Trail, now a bustling railroad.

The Lockhart family headed to Kansas just four years after another young midwestern family. In 1868 Charles and Caroline Ingalls and their two daughters moved from Pepin, Wisconsin, to Independence, Kansas, about one hundred miles south of Burlingame. The second daughter, named Laura, would later write a series of books based on her childhood experiences, the most famous of which was *Little House on the Prairie*. Though the Ingallses lived only two years in Kansas, returning to Wisconsin in 1870, their experiences on homesteads throughout Minnesota, Iowa, Kansas, and South Dakota all had common themes. We can assume with some confidence that their lifestyle applied to the Lockharts as well. Like the Ingallses' various houses, the Lockharts' house was doubtless a log cabin, which Sarah may have tried to make homey with quilts and red check tablecloths. She might have likewise made a lamp from a button and axle grease, or prepared foods such as blackbird pie or green pumpkin pie. Sarah and little Caddie, once she was old enough, would have helped milk the cow, churn butter, and carry wood and water.

The Lockharts themselves didn't leave much record of this time on the Wakarusa. They spent five or six years there, from about 1873 to 1878. Sarah, doubtless busy running the household, never kept any journals. Caddie was aged just two to seven, and her later memories were decidedly fuzzy. Joe, whose real estate transactions left the family's most enduring records, sold off his Illinois land by the end of 1873 and didn't buy any more in Kansas during this time. An 1875 census taker found Joe, Sarah, Caroline, and George (born 1873) living with the Akers sisters, two Pennsylvania-born teenagers who were probably servants. The Lockharts claimed just forty-five hundred dollars of real estate—far less than what they'd had in Illinois five years earlier, but still better than average for the area, and not bad given the drought and recession of those years. By the end of their tenure, at least, the farm was stable enough for Joe to get back to his favorite activity, trading. A Burlingame newspaper noted in February 1878 that "J.C. Lockhart, living on the Wakarusa, claims the largest mule in the state of its age. It is a last spring's foal, is 14 hands high, is well built proportionally. Mr. Lockhart purchased him about two months ago of George Lee for $50."

Based on Caddie's later attitudes, as well as the experiences of Laura Ingalls and others, we can imagine that this was an idyllic time for the youngster. Whether working or playing, she was usually outside, on the open prairies, under the wide skies. Like Laura Ingalls, she was probably a tomboy, Dad's right-hand man, energetic, passionate, and stubborn. She was close to animals: horses, mules, cows, chickens, and pigs. She likely felt an affinity to wild animals as well. Most girls of the times, even at such young ages, played key roles on the farm: herding, gathering, even hunting. Especially since her father presumably left on frequent trading trips to upgrade the quality of his cattle stock and acquire abnormally large mules, Caddie likely gained a feeling of accomplishment, independence, and self-confidence from helping with the men's work. By age four or five, she was probably on the back of a horse, helping to herd or deliver messages.

That was the greatest joy of all. In later years she would tell anyone who would listen: "I was born on a horse."

In late 1878 the family relocated to the town of Burlingame. They rented the large home of a newspaper editor who was moving to a bigger town. Their first activity worthy of public note centered on Caddie's eighth birthday the following February: "A children's party, with some 16 being present, was given at J.C. Lockhart's on last Saturday. The affair was highly relished by the juveniles."

It is not entirely clear why the Lockharts traded farm for town. Joe occasionally implied that he'd homesteaded the plot on the Wakarusa; if so, he would have had to spend five years to "prove up" and then could have sold it for a profit. But homestead records don't really support this claim, so it could be that he simply realized he liked business better than farming, or even that he failed at farming. And it's quite likely that Sarah wanted the refinements of town, including a quality education for Caddie and George. In many rural areas the cheap land diminished the tax base that supported the local school, and all the farmwork cut into studying time. Like Laura Ingalls's mother, Sarah Lockhart expressed herself through church, the temperance movement, and the education of her offspring. It was surely through her mother's prodding that seven-year-old Caddie, in December 1878, recited a speech at a meeting of the Youth Temperance Alliance.

Whatever the reason, the Lockharts had picked the right time to move to Burlingame, the Osage County seat with about one thousand residents. Coal was discovered that year on the east side of town. Coal fueled the trains that brought the Texas longhorns from railhead to market, and the rail company especially valued a source along its route. Several new coal shafts required miners. New jobs meant new money as well, and Burlingame residents started replacing their older frame buildings with more expensive brick and stone. Two new newspapers sprang up, as well as several new men's and women's clubs.

Joe Lockhart built houses for the miners. He'd taken a step up now: not just trading mules and land with pioneers, but working with banks and governments. He got himself appointed to the board of directors at the Burlingame Savings Bank and, with a partner, bought some land east of the city and had it platted and annexed. By spring of 1880 he was busy hauling lumber to the new neighborhood, which was known as Thomson and Lockhart's addition. He could sell you a house he'd built or an empty lot for you to build your own. He advertised that he had sixteen lots, "terms and prices reasonable." For the year in Burlingame as a whole, sixty-five new residences were added. Lockhart sold some, sold land on which others were built, and leased land for new mining shafts that created demand for more.

He also built a house of his own in the brick and stone neighborhood. Sarah birthed a third child, named Grace. The 1880 census taker found the family, along with Westly Acres and two other servants, living in the city, though Joe still called himself a farmer. In later years Caddie would say she spent her girlhood in Burlingame. Actually it was less than four years, but she was aged seven to eleven during those years, so it must have indeed felt like her girlhood, which she spent with her favorite animals. In a 1912 newspaper story, a Burlingame historian wrote, "Our earliest recollection of 'Cad' was that she seemed always to be astride a horse."

When she was in her midtwenties, Caroline Lockhart recalled that girlhood, writing, "I lived in a Western town on the old Santa Fe trail. The embers of the Indian campfires still burned along the creeks and ravines. A boom had struck the town, a typical Western boom, the three-card monte man flourished, the man who doled out fire-water to the thirsty speculators grew fat and corpulent. The minister guarded his little flock and grew more hungry and discouraged looking every day. Cowboys from the surrounding ranches added to the general interest of the place in their pensive way."

By the time she published this sketch, in the 1890s, Lockhart was already a mythmaker, stretching facts to fit the romantic notions of her audience. She talked about the West, the ravines, and the Santa Fe trail without noting that her town was in Kansas (indeed, the green valleys of eastern Kansas). In addition to the cowboys and Indians, she claimed the streets were full of "covered wagons, embellished with such mottoes as 'Busted—Going Home to My Wife's Father,' etc." She said many of those failed homesteaders were committing suicide.

But her article neglected two key elements of Kansas in the 1880s: first, the cowboys were failing worse than the homesteaders. Second, many area homesteaders who did fail were selling out to her father.

At the time the word "cowboy" referred to a man employed on one of the big Texas cattle drives, which had had their heyday in the 1870s. Anglo-Texan cattle ranchers kept longhorn cattle, tough cows accustomed to finding their own feed. Longhorns could be left on the open range all winter and rounded up just twice a year. Cowboys herded them on horseback, using lassos and the large hats they adapted from their Mexican neighbors. Beginning after the Civil War, cowboys drove those cattle across the open plains to the Kansas railheads, which provided an easy route to the slaughterhouses of Chicago and the Midwest.

Starting in 1870, some of these Texans tried to winter their herds in western Kansas. But longhorns didn't take well to the cold, dry winters. They got cold and sick and couldn't find enough to eat. While various ranchers continually tried the Texan "cowboy" system in the plains until the disastrous winter of 1886–87, it never worked well north of Texas. And as farmers and ranchers increasingly fenced off the open range, the era of the long cattle drives ended as well.

In the meantime, however, Kansas was filling up with midwesterners. People like Joe Lockhart had raised cattle in Illinois using a very different system. They fed their cattle all winter using hay they'd grown all summer. They depended more on stock pens, herding dogs, and pasture fences than lassos and horses. They also paid a lot of attention to breeding. No longhorns for these folks: through selective breeding they developed cattle that could handle blizzards, drought, overstocking, and market fluctuations. Durhams, Devons, Herefords, and mixtures generically referred to as "shorthorns" came to dominate the plains. They were housed in small-scale operations, places that frequently also had dairy cows, and perhaps crops, pigs, and/or sheep. In other words, they weren't really ranches; they were more often called stock farms, mixed farms, or improved ranches.

The "cowboy" had been hired for those long Texas cattle drives largely because he was unattached: with no family, he could leave home for long periods of time and work cheap. He could ride a horse and wield a lasso. But in Kansas the stock farms were making those skills irrelevant. It may not be so odd that Lockhart's reminiscence doesn't give the cowboy anything to do (he "added to the general interest of the place"): she'd probably never seen one working.

She had seen homesteaders galore, however. The Homestead Act of 1862 offered 160 acres of free land to a farmer who improved the property and stayed five years; in the act's first thirteen years, one hundred million acres nationwide were claimed this way. During that same period another five hundred million acres went from the government into corporate hands, mostly to railroads around proposed routes. Though not technically homesteaders, the eventual buyers of this land likewise sought to farm it. And after the recession of the mid-1870s, they did well. By the early 1880s farms like the Lockharts' Wakarusa place sprouted everywhere, abetted by what proved to be abnormally wet weather.

But the late 1880s were dry. On the high plains of western Kansas, half the residents departed between 1886 and 1890, devastated by drought. Similar problems affected areas of eastern Kansas, including the Flint Hills, southwest of Burlingame. Its thin, rocky soil couldn't support mixed farming. It could support cattle grazing, but only on a scale far bigger than 160 acres. Homesteaders were forced to sell. And Joe Lockhart—taking his profits out of Burlingame city real estate at the height of its short-lived boom—bought them out.

Joe Lockhart was no longer a farmer, nor was he exactly a rancher or a cowboy. He lived in town, buying and selling land and cattle, leaving the daily chores to hired hands. He called himself (in an occupation far more common to the time than *cowboy*) a *stock dealer*. The stock dealer straddled the peak of the Kansas economy: he was wealthy and admired; he dealt with cows and horses but rarely had to get dirty; in bargaining with buyers and developing breeding programs he didn't necessarily have to work hard, just smart. Joe's phenomenal success as a stock dealer influenced not only his family's fortunes but also their view of how to succeed in the West.

As a child, however, Caddie appreciated few of these political and economic dynamics. On the rare occasions that she later offered specifics about her childhood, they involved her adventures on horseback.

"Who's that boy that carries your books home every day?" Joe Lockhart asked his daughter one day at dinner.

Caddie, aged perhaps thirteen, squirmed in her chair. Finally she stammered, "Oh, a boy." In fact his name was Jim. He sat in front of her at school. He was the first boy, she recalled later, whom it had not occurred to her to fight with.

Joe didn't like that answer, so her brother George helped out. "It's the felly whose father has the running horses down at the track."

Caddie scowled. George just liked making trouble for her. Jim had given her a crawfish claw and a handful of colored chalk. She felt that she loved him, especially after the crawfish claw. Jim insisted on calling her his "Gypsy Queen." She didn't think she resembled such a person at all, with her tow hair in two little pigtails, a snub nose, and freckles. But Jim would talk about wading through blood and slaying Caddie's enemies for her. She told him she could do her own fighting, could "thrash any boy in the room," but she admired the sentiment. He devoured nickel novels, hiding them inside his geography book at school, so he talked and acted like the hero of such a book.

"I don't want it to occur again," said her father at the dinner table, speaking of Jim carrying her books. "I don't think he is a proper playmate."

George giggled.

Caddie felt miserable but soon realized that such misery was the stuff of nickel novels. She was an oppressed heroine. She decided to enjoy it.

The next day she told Jim about it. He beat himself on the chest and cried, "Alas! And will a stern parent separate two lovin' souls?" He asked, "Wilt thou fly with me and be my bride?"

She could not resist. They plotted to leave on their ponies the next morning. Though she claimed to be going for just a short ride, she astonished her mother with a touching farewell. Then, after just a few miles, the sun came out scorching and hot. Her pony kicked up dust to his knees. Caddie grew thirsty and cross and her head ached. She and Jim quarreled before they even reached the next town.

There they dismounted in front of a butcher's shop. "What you going to do?" Jim asked.

"Buy bologny." She pulled out the pennies she'd emptied out of her little iron bank. Where was the boy who would wade through gore for her? Jim was so humble he was irritating. She bought a huge ring of bologna, broke it in two, and stood on the steps eating alternately from each end.

He watched her wistfully.

She finally threw him a piece, while she wondered at its odd taste. The piece she threw fell on the sidewalk, but he ate it anyway.

She felt worse than she had before the bologna. "I don't want to fly any further," she said, and climbed back on her pony. Jim followed, and they rode back home across the prairie. She was hot, the dust was hot, the wind was hot. They didn't speak the whole way. The bologna had made her sick. Finally, as the sun was going down, they came in sight of her house. She made a pronouncement.

"If you ever ask me to be your bride again I'll lick you."

That story, from her perspective about twelve years later, is surely overdramatized. But it does illuminate several key features of her childhood.

First, she indeed lived on horseback. A horse was not only a means of transportation but also a symbol of freedom. On a horse you could run away, set up a new life. You could even think of it as flying.

Second, she chafed at her father's stern hand. Their relationship would worsen through her life, as she felt that his generosity did not grow with his fortune. One of her novels began with her hero similarly running away as a boy. The boy's father didn't "care about anything but horses and cattle. Certainly his father did not care about *him*. He could not remember when the stern man had given him a pat on the head or a good-night kiss. . . . It seemed to him that his father seldom spoke to him except to reprimand or ridicule him."

Third, she was intimately familiar with cheap paperback novels. Invented just after the Civil War, they were popular with children until the turn of the century. Like the comic books of later generations, they were seen as immoral, perhaps because they took kids away from their chores. Many were set in the West and starred road agents and scouts. Others were set in the city or the jungle. But whatever the exotic landscape, they featured adventure, heroes, larger-than-life characters engaged in struggles that stood for key elements of American society. It wasn't spelled out, of course, but kids learned about success from Horatio Alger, about individualism from Davy

Crockett or Deadwood Dick, and about adventure from Nick Carter or Buffalo Bill. Some of these heroes had the names of real people, but their characters were always completely fictionalized, idealized to the standards of the culture. Few of those heroes were women, but when they were—Calamity Jane being the prime example—their heroism arose from their ability to ride and shoot like a man.

Finally, note the behavior of the first man Lockhart ever claimed to love. He talks like a storybook hero, but in a crisis he wilts. She is the stronger one. She provides bologna and the money to pay for it, though the butcher takes advantage of her by selling her bad meat. Bewildered at first, Jim even comes to depend on her handouts, thus earning even more of her contempt.

How *should* a man react to a strong woman? Caddie's ambivalence may have been tied to her ambivalent feelings about her father. In another reminiscence, she wrote of the time her mother bought a bustle (a wire frame that extended the back of a woman's skirt). Joe told her, "If you wear that thing I won't go out with you."

"They're the fashion." Sarah's tone implied that her words settled the argument. And soon they did. He agreed to go downtown with her and her bustle.

Caddie and George giggled. "Privately," she recalled, "we thought that papa wasn't very bright if he thought he could out-smart mamma—ever."

In 1882 Joe delivered a blow to the young frontier girl: he took her off the frontier. The Lockharts moved to Sterling, Illinois, a growing city about twenty miles south of Elkhorn Grove. Sarah probably drove the decision, with her interest in the children's education, her fondness for fashion, and her relatives nearby. But in later years Caroline placed the blame (and to her it was *blame*) squarely on her father, saying he was concerned about schooling and also "thought the frontier no place to raise a genteel lady."

Sterling, by contrast, had a population of about eight thousand (including its sister city Rock Falls), with an academy of music, an opera house, and a symphony club. It also boasted one of the best schools in the state. The Second Ward School was run by Alfred Bayliss, a respected educator whose wife was a scientist and writer. Clara Kern Bayliss, the first-ever female graduate of Michigan's Hillsdale College, did not teach after her marriage, but wrote grammar textbooks and articles for national newspapers and magazines. In the 1880s she must have already been investigating the sloughs and bayous around Sterling that she covered in her first children's book a few years later. So at a time when most girls had few career role models, Lockhart had one who was literary.

Joe Lockhart returned to Illinois in relative wealth. He purchased the home of Sterling's first mayor, a two-story brick Italianate jumble of gables and towers. In July 1882 Sarah bore their fourth child, a boy named Robert, and in the fall of that year Caddie enrolled in Miss Trowe's class at the Second Ward School. Her grades were mostly in the eighties, though it was later claimed that her teachers "found that she was a natural writer." Others said she had a "'nose for news,' although in those days they called it 'inquisitiveness.'" Her friends remembered her as a bit of a tomboy, a little husky, an outdoor girl, likeable and full of spirit. She regularly fought with an African American boy named George Clark. "George and I were evenly matched and with no holds barred our frequent encounters never failed to draw an audience. The only trouble was that the cheers of our partisans always attracted some grown up who insisted on pulling one or the other of us off and thus spoiled our enjoyment."

A typical teenager, the fighter also craved romance. Once town beau Johnny Crawford took her for a ride in his buggy, behind his trotting horses. The buggy top was laid back, with a linen lap robe on the seat. She admired the buggy whip tied in a bow. "What a thrill I got when he helped me in," she wrote later, "although I could easily have stood on the ground flat-footed and jumped onto the seat. It made me feel grown up to be helped."

One way she differed from other teenagers was her vivid sense of humor, one that bit hard.

"Your father is seldom home," the old lady sitting across the table said to the teenaged Caddie.

Joe Lockhart still had all of his land in Kansas; indeed, while living in Sterling he kept acquiring more. He spent plenty of time on the frontier, buying, selling, and inspecting cattle and land. An 1885 state census records him as living alone in Burlingame (though 1883 and 1887 directories—the only ones still existing—list him in Sterling). The arrangement made sense to the Lockharts, but not necessarily to their neighbors. Sterling was full of midwestern busybodies, wagging their tongues at the infrequency of Joe's visits. Now one was trying to pump the girl for information, in exchange for a piece of cake.

"Uh-huh." Caddie couldn't respond coherently since her mouth was overstuffed with cake.

"And yet he always has money and pays his bills with cash."

"Yes'm." Caddie continued eating. Joe was a taciturn man, which was part of the old lady's problem; he was not forthcoming with much information himself. Caroline claimed she inherited at least some of that reticence.

"He has no visible means of support. Just what business is he in?" the woman finally demanded.

"My dad," Caddie said without batting an eyelash, "is a train robber. But the family would rather you didn't mention it to anyone."

～

Captain Mortlake has been strung up by outlaws. They are going to lynch him, hang him from a tree. Suddenly they are interrupted by a lone man, a government scout named Buffalo Bill on a twenty-day leave of absence from his army duties. The handsome scout cuts the rope to liberate the captain.

This was no dime novel. It was a live play, performed in a theater in Clinton, Iowa, not far from Sterling. The crowd whooped in delight.

Many critics found the play abominable: melodramatic, sensationalistic trash. One suggested that the best actor in the troupe was Jerry the Trick Donkey. Another, foolishly trying to analyze the plot, asked why Bill didn't shoot the outlaws a lot earlier, thus saving himself a deathbed rescue. And a third said the star was "laboring under a severe disposition, superinduced by a too free indulgence of intoxicants."

But the crowd loved it. They were seeing a legend in person. For the actor playing Buffalo Bill was William F. Cody himself.

Cody had indeed been a government scout, had gained fame as a tracker and buffalo hunter, and had then found his name attached to an idealized dime-novel hero. That hero was always fighting villains, performing deathbed rescues, helping virtue triumph. So the real Buffalo Bill decided to get in on the action. In 1872, the year after Lockhart was born, he had dime novelist Ned Buntline write a play for him to star in.

Great theater it was not. Buntline wrote the entire play in four hours. Its beautiful Indian maiden spoke with a bad Italian accent. Cody, who to this date had seen maybe a dozen plays in his life, couldn't remember any of his lines, and in fact looked comfortable on stage only when he totally departed from the script and just told stories. But there was lots of pistol and rifle shooting, blood and thunder. The plot featured massive Indian slaughters—so massive that one actor allegedly died sixteen times during the course of the night. Like today's professional wrestling, Buffalo Bill's entertainment achieved widespread appeal through its outsized characters, oversimplified morality, and lots and lots of violence.

The play had another advantage: authenticity. Other plays featured "Buffalo Bill" portrayed by an actor, but this one had the real thing. (It was also advertised as having live Indians, but the marketing people forgot to tell the casting people in time.) "Imagine Julius Caesar playing his own part in the tragedy named after him," one critic wrote, in apparent approval of that notion. Again like professional wrestling, the entertainment's great charm lay in the stars' insistence that such obvious make-believe was real.

William F. Cody polished this formula over the next dozen years. He improved his acting. He got real Indians to show up. He figured out the logistics of leading a troupe on a railroad tour of one-night stands all over the country. He brought current events into his metaphoric world; for example, he produced *The Red Right Hand, or the First Scalp for Custer* just three months after the general's 1876 fiasco at the Little Bighorn. (The script had little to do with Custer—it was just more wild shooting and Indian slaughter—but nobody seemed to care.) He also started including trick shooting and other exhibitions of skill, previewing his later move to a Wild West show that made no pretenses at theater.

Thus, Buffalo Bill helped invent a mythic Old West—larger than life, full of action and violence, a fantasy world with claims to authenticity—long before anyone had thought to label the West as old. In the 1870s and 1880s, his audiences could go west themselves. His theatricality encouraged them to seek adventure, moral certainty, larger-than-life characters, and great stories.

Caddie Lockhart must have been in that crowd in 1882 in Clinton, Iowa (or maybe Rockford or Rock Island, Illinois—each a short train ride from Sterling). Loving dime novels, outdoors, theater, and the West, how could she have resisted? Wherever Buffalo Bill's carriage stopped, children thronged around the door. Every boy who saw the performance wanted to start carrying a long knife and shiny pistol in imitation of his hero. If young Caddie, headstrong and tomboyish, was not present physically at the show, she certainly was in spirit. She had loved the particulars of her childhood in the West; now Buffalo Bill was adding a set of romantic ideals to match.

When school let out in May 1887, Caddie was granted her longtime wish to leave Illinois. Joe packed up two cars of goods and loaded the family for a trip to Kansas. After five years away they were moving to Topeka, thirty miles north of Burlingame. Their house was at 1211 West Sixth St., near downtown. Caddie would attend Bethany College, which despite its name and ivy-covered campus was a high school. It focused on music and art, as well as elocution (reading aloud words written by others), but also insisted girls spend forty minutes a day in active exercise in open air. It was run by Episcopalians, including on its board of trustees the wonderfully named S. S. Prouty, editor of the *Kansas Cowboy*, a newspaper that covered the cattle business. From Topeka, Caddie would also have plenty of time to visit friends in Burlingame. It should have been a delightful time for the sixteen-year-old. But tragedy was a little more than a year away.

In the middle of July 1888, Sarah Lockhart developed a fever. She lost her appetite, felt weak, had stomach pains. Joe traveled back and forth to Burlingame and his outlying ranches all summer, but Sarah stayed at home in Topeka. Somehow she managed to care for the children through the illness, even though the youngest, Robert, was just six. It was a quiet illness, about four weeks in duration. She was able to keep it from most of her friends. By mid-August she was feeling better, and she let Caddie spend a week visiting friends in Burlingame.

But on the first Sunday in September, Sarah took a turn for the worse. A doctor was called in, but he could not help her. It wasn't even clear whether the fever had been typhoid or malaria, though at the time there was little a doctor could do for either one. (Later in life, Caroline would claim that the doctor was a drug addict who gave Sarah an accidental overdose. No one else ever voiced such an opinion, though even if it was imagined, it could well have clouded Caroline's view of the profession for years to come.)

The death was a shock to everyone. "Few knew she was ill; of them, none thought she would die," wrote the Burlingame newspaper. She was just forty years old. "No lady was more highly esteemed in Burlingame than Mrs. Lockhart." Her remains were taken back to Polo for internment, where the sadness was equally great.

The household scattered. Gracie, aged eleven, stayed in Polo. George, fifteen, was in Topeka, perhaps boarding at school. But Caddie wouldn't go back to school. She and little Robert spent most of the autumn in Burlingame, where they must have been rather difficult for Joe to manage. He had cattle, he had land, and now he had headstrong children to take care of in his taciturn way while mourning the loss of his true love. It soon proved more than he could handle. On January 3, 1889, he packed up Caddie and George and took off for northeast Pennsylvania, where his wealthy relatives might be able to help.

～

My feet sunk deep in priceless rugs. A huge brilliantly lighted crystal chandelier hung from the ceiling, heavy damask curtains at the long windows fell to the floor while oil paintings in gilt frames, which even in my colossal ignorance I recognized as good, adorned the walls. I noted that Uncle Bob watched my face as I stared. Perhaps he was thinking that I might not be as hopeless as I looked.

Reminiscing in later years, Caroline often portrayed herself in Pennsylvania as a frontier rube intimidated by such heights of wealth and privilege. Certainly she was entering a far different landscape: three of her father's uncles had intermarried with the Packer family, one of the richest in Pennsylvania, founders of Lehigh University. Though Uncle Bob's wife and the two other Lockhart brothers had died young, Uncle Bob was still well connected.

"The next day my papa took me and my telescope to the old Female Seminary at the end of the street. It was a drab building looking all of its hundred or more years. It was surrounded by a high board fence and resembled an out-size calaboose." The word *calaboose*, which meant *jail*, was a favorite of hers. "When papa, with visible relief, turned me over to the Principal, gave me a quick kiss, admonished me to be a good girl, and left, I felt like a convict sentenced to do a long stretch."

The Moravian Seminary was indeed an older, more formal place than anywhere on the frontier. Actually 140 years old, the school boasted that its objectives were, in order of importance, "the formation of a proper character and *proper habits* of life; the development and discipline of mental faculties; and advancement in learning." As a junior, Caddie had to take algebra, literature, and intellectual philosophy; she could also choose from Greek, Latin, French, German, history (Greece and Rome), criticism, or trigonometry. She boarded with other students in a "family" overseen by a resident teacher, an arrangement designed to promote the "courtesy, discretion, self-restraint and ease of manner so necessary to a successful intercourse with the world at large." Based on her later behavior, the arrangement was not terribly successful.

"The girls I met were all from the South and East. They didn't even know where Kansas was until I showed them on the map. Nor did they seem too friendly—just curious. But I noted that when I mentioned the fact that I was Uncle Bob's niece they seemed impressed."

By her own account, Lockhart was something of a troublemaker. Once she was caught dangling out of a second-story window in a harness designed as a fire escape that she tried out on a dare. Another time she stuffed stockings in the Lehigh colors and hung them from a third-floor dorm window, as if a boy was climbing into her room. The faculty gave her tight-lipped, accusing looks, and the principal suggested Caddie was disorganizing the school.

The relatives, meanwhile, tried to civilize her. One weekend they sent her to visit her cousin Augusta Packer, a young childless widow who lived in a mansion overlooking the village of Mauch Chunk. Lockhart remembered that she and Gussie had very different ways of introducing themselves: Caddie was shown portraits of their ancestors, while Gussie was informed of Caddie's pony, her tame coyote, and her ability to outrun any boy in school. Something in Gussie's elegance prompted a smidgen of self-doubt in Caddie, a sense that maybe there was more to life than tomboy hijinks. As much as Caddie hated people who put on airs, Gussie didn't have to. Gussie was the real thing: high class, well bred, refined, and respectable. Gussie had been to Europe—she had a maid who spoke only French—and lived without a man, having no interest in remarrying after her husband's death. In other words, she was somewhat independent and adventurous, in the ways Caddie craved. Yet Gussie was also a lady, whom everyone treated with respect. The combination set up an ambition and internal struggle that would influence Caddie for the rest of her life.

She spent that summer at Asbury Park, a New Jersey seaside resort, "with cousins and aunts by the score." Home to a dozen hotels and a thousand guest cottages, it was known for its grandeur, with a sanitary sewer system, outstanding trolleys, and electric lights. It and neighboring Long Branch attracted upper-class vacationers to resorts where women were expected to change clothes often, put on formalwear for dinner, and pass their time playing croquet or cards, or reading and chatting on the porch. For an outdoorsy Kansas girl, there simply wasn't much to do. Caddie's frustration was reflected in a story she later told about that summer.

"Sa-ay, do you know, I should like to kiss you?" He was the only son of a Pennsylvania coal baron, immaculate and driving a stunning horse and carriage. The other girls envied Caddie when he came over from Long Branch.

"I should advise you not to," Caddie said, astonished. She'd been thinking that he wasn't particularly brilliant, that she did not enjoy his conversation especially, that she was only out with him because she liked to drive and she liked the other girls to envy her. She wondered what was ailing him.

They were both silent for some time. She got the odd impression that he actually seemed to be thinking deeply.

"Sa-ay, do you know, I like you better than anyone I know?"

She felt fidgety. She knew something was about to happen. She buttoned and unbuttoned her gloves a half-dozen times.

More silence.

Caddie found it ghastly. She coughed and said something about the warm weather. But he didn't respond.

"Sa-ay, would you marry me?" As he said this, she reflected that it was the first time since she'd met him that he actually looked interested in something.

She gasped. "What for?"

Returning to Moravian for her senior year, Caddie took logic, geology, chemistry, domestic economy, and evidences of Christianity/ethics. She later claimed, "I learned to make Vassar fudge and worry the teachers, but not much else."

In her memoirs she said that when cousin Gussie asked what she wanted to do after graduation, she responded "that I guessed I'd have to go back to Kansas and teach . . . so that I could help Papa pay taxes and keep us out of the poor house." That was what many girls were doing—in fact, it was exactly what Laura Ingalls had done. Laura had started her teaching career at age fifteen; by this comparison, Caddie's extra four years in school were a luxury. But the comparison is not entirely appropriate: Caddie's family had a lot more money than Laura's. It seems unlikely they would have forced her into the difficult and ill-paying role of frontier schoolteacher.

But that fear—even if Lockhart was later exaggerating it—illuminated a very real dilemma. A young woman of 1890 faced few career options, especially a woman in this odd position of frontier wealth. Poorer and less-educated girls were going to work in factories, or even operating the newly invented business machines called typewriters. High-society East Coast girls had their own world of travel and arts. Caddie didn't fit in either world.

Worse, she was a little bit headstrong, a little bit vain, bold, adventuresome, ambitious, and comfortable in the spotlight. She began to think about the stage. In March or April 1890, her senior year, she wrote to her father that she wanted to go to school in Boston the following year. She had in mind the Moses True Brown School of Oratory—elocution being somewhere between literature and theater—but she may not have even told him that much.

"I opened the letter eagerly when the answer finally came and received a stunning shock. It stated briefly that he had remarried; that if I wished to go to Boston I could do so; that he would send me money for my ticket, pay my tuition and give me an allowance of $35 a month until I was graduated, after that I should be able to take care of myself and need expect nothing further from him."

Joe's bride was Kate Reed, a thirty-six-year-old woman who with her parents had been renting the old Lockhart home in Sterling. Their wedding was a brief, quiet ceremony at Kate's sister's home in Iowa. The Reeds were respectable—Kate's father had retired from a farm outside of Sterling—but as a spinster in a family that was renting rather than owning property, she was several steps down in class from the posh relatives Caddie had newly met in Pennsylvania. And as a substitute mother, coming into the family just eighteen months after Sarah's death, she was not likely to have quickly gained Caddie's admiration.

In fact, she earned Caddie's scorn. Caddie claimed Kate had been the family seamstress—a dull, lowly occupation—"and with a child's intuition I knew that she did not like me when she first came to sew at our house." There is little other record of Kate Reed the person—even her obituary, published ten years after the death of her husband, never uses her first name, referring only to "Mrs. J.C. Lockhart." But it must have been difficult for her: coming into the marriage knowing that Caddie and George would resent her and at least suspecting (as we suspect now) that Joe had married her mainly to take care of the younger kids. There may not have been much love in the relationship. Though he never spoke publicly against her, when he died in 1927, his remains were taken back to Polo to be buried next to Sarah's; in Kansas Kate would have to fend for herself.

But for now Joe allied with Kate against his daughter. He added a postscript to the letter: George and Caddie would be welcome to come home to visit, but only if they were prepared to treat Kate with proper respect. Throughout Caroline's life (she would soon drop the youthful "Caddie"), she was unable to mask her feelings when she disliked a person. Her hatred for the woman she called "Steppy" was as strong as any force in her life, so she saw this ultimatum from her father as an insurmountable barrier.

The break forged her independence. She was a bright, rebellious young woman. She had a talent for, and an interest in, literature and elocution. She had a bit of money (thirty-five dollars in 1890 would be just over seven hundred dollars a month in 2005—a substantial supplement to a salary, though maybe not enough to feel rich on). She had brains, spunk, and good looks. No longer welcome in her father's home, she became determined to make her own way in the world.

Stunt Girl

Here's a description of Boston in about 1892:

There is not a city in the United States so full of young girls away from home as Boston is. They flock here from all parts of the country, each with her own particular hobby. With one it is the ambition of her life to study for the stage. With another it is elocution [or music or painting]. . . . There are very few among these girls, these readers, vocalists, instrumentalists, artists and actresses, that have not come from comfortable, quiet, conventional homes. They have money for their tuition in the various schools; they pay anywhere from $5 to $6.50 a week for their board, a few not so much as $5. The rest of their monthly allowance, not a large sum in the beginning, they have to spend as they like. For the first time in their lives they are away from their parents, without restraint of any kind beyond the words of warning and caution that come in the form of letters from home.

The voice belongs to Caroline Lockhart, writing just a few years after she'd entered this world she called an "innocent Bohemia." If it sounds a bit like the student culture of the 1960s, that may be because the youth culture of the 1890s similarly arose from increasing middle-class wealth, which freed young people from the need to immediately make money, allowing them to explore the arts and their own boundaries. Young men of the time might go west to find adventure on the frontier. For example, Owen Wister, born eleven years before Lockhart but delayed by college and law school, spent much of the late 1880s and early 1890s in Wyoming; O. Henry, born nine years before Lockhart, spent that time in Texas, where he got in trouble with the law. Caroline's own brother George, equally dismayed at his father's remarriage, went off looking for gold in Old Mexico. But the frontier wasn't well set up for an unmarried woman. She would be required to have a chaperone, a husband, a job, a society—precisely the elements these youths were escaping. A girl seeking that freedom went to the city.

And so these girls—perhaps less chastely than Lockhart's newspaper account describes—would have fun. At the theater for a Saturday matinee, "They feel that it is such an extraordinary and unconventional thing to do that they are in the wildest spirits. They eat caramels and butter scotch, they giggle to their hearts' content and have the best time imaginable." Likewise they go to the symphony and the opera. They delight in coming home late. "The writer knew a girl who used to seem to extract the most exquisite pleasure Sunday from sitting up in bed grinning from ear to ear and listening to the church bells ring. The wickedness of absenting herself from church seemed to delight her beyond words." (This anonymous girl is the only source Lockhart quotes in the lengthy article, suggesting that it may all be a thinly veiled Caroline Lockhart experience.)

Settling in a boardinghouse with friends, and getting permission to cook in the room, "they make coffee and chocolate, boil eggs, cook oyster stews and all sorts of things in the same dish. . . . They cover the bare floors with rugs. They drape their walls with fish nets, half finished sketches and paintings are everywhere. They like joss sticks [incense], portieres [doorway curtains], huge sofa pillows and easy couches. They like everything, in fact, that suggests comfort, cosiness, and Oriental indulgence."

The only problem with this large collection of similar girls is that most of them have to face up to their relative lack of talent. The budding elocutionist "is rather surprised to find that there are two or three hundred other girls in the school who recite just as well as she does." The young musician who so impressed people in her country village now discovers "seven hundred other girls who can play the Black Hawk waltz and the Beautiful Blue Danube." The aspiring actress "has the thorniest road of all to travel. If she has sense enough to know in the beginning that schools of oratory will never help her on the stage, she will save herself two or three wasted years."

Again, Lockhart's voice speaks from experience: she herself aspired to the stage, and thus must have viewed her time at elocution school as wasted, except for how much glorious fun it had been. "They forget how poor they are; they forget their disappointments and troubles; they are the merriest girls in the world over their chocolate and tea. They are bright and witty, for there is no room for stupid people in the girl artists' Bohemia." Coming off those starched summers in Asbury Park, Lockhart must have especially relished these girls, who prized cleverness over money, disdained propriety, and celebrated daredevils. "They are merry-hearted, jolly good fellows, these girl Bohemians, and when their student days are over and they are ready for the career for which they have been preparing themselves they go back to the cross-roads in Ohio or anywhere else with knowledge of the world and human nature [and] with a broad and generous sympathy for others that their Bohemian student life has developed in them."

Except that Lockhart didn't go home. Perhaps she was more talented than the others, more ambitious, or more stubborn. Perhaps she felt that her father's remarriage had robbed her of a home to return to. (She was already claiming to have been born in Kansas, and though numerous relatives remained in Illinois, she would not return there until her old age.)

In her memoirs Lockhart downplayed the role of theater in her young life. "My enthusiasm for a career as an elocutionist waned daily," she wrote. "There was only one girl in the school who had a thimbleful of talent to my way of thinking. Her name was Louise Closser and in [1903] she verified my opinion by making notable success in one of Bernard Shaw's plays when it appeared on Broadway."

Her acting career, Lockhart said in the memoirs, began and ended with a night as an extra in the Grand Opera Company, when she had to sit down and take off a slipper that didn't fit—on stage in the middle of the star's grand aria. She realized she would not be the next Sarah Bernhardt, and "it was clear that I must [find] some other way of achieving fame and fortune."

In fact, Lockhart's theatrical career met with a small degree of success. Her scrapbooks contain a clipping about a comedy called *Rosedale* performed on January 12, 1894, at least eight months after its premiere. The clipping provides a line drawing and biography of actress Caroline Lockhart. The drawing shows an attractive, well-dressed woman with hair piled elegantly atop her head. She looks perhaps older than her twenty-two years, and a bit husky through the shoulders, but she has a well-proportioned face, smooth cheeks, and large eyes. "The casual observer, even, would know to look at Miss Lockhart, that she belonged to the dashing style of women rather than the meek and subdued. Her western bringing up may in part account for this, for from her earliest childhood, she was accustomed to ride on horseback across the prairies in her native state of Kansas and shoot Jack rabbits with a revolver. A feat many a full grown man might envy her in doing."

Whatever its duration or success, Lockhart eventually tired of her theatrical career. And in every later account, she explains her next move as an idea that "came out of clear sky: why couldn't I write for a newspaper?" Or, more to the point, "Nellie Bly was making history at the time so why couldn't I? To think was to act at this stage of my development and I selected the new Boston Post as my target."

Nowhere does Lockhart suggest that her ambition to write came from a love of reading, from favorite childhood escapes through literature, from parents passing along a passion, or even from her apparent natural felicity with language. She wanted fame, fortune, and adventure; she saw writing as a way to achieve those goals. And she was correct: the world of journalism was desperately seeking attractive, self-assured girls with such ambitions.

A newspaper of the early 1890s was far different from what we know today, but also far different from what it had been just ten years previously. For decades newspapers had been bland repositories of dry text, generally lacking illustrations, humor, or personality. But technology and wealth had created a boom in working-class newspapers. Now came tabloid-style headlines, more lurid stories, signed columns, illustrations, crusades, and contests. Now came intense competition, publicity stunts, and rapid-fire innovation. Soon would come comic strips, advice columns, and more. Joseph Pulitzer's *New York World* led the revolution that purists derided as "yellow journalism," but his style was wildly effective. In Pulitzer's first four years at the *World*, 1883 to 1887, he increased Sunday circulation from twenty thousand to two hundred thousand. Furthermore, despite its sensationalism, the competitive environment he fostered produced some outstanding journalists and writers, such as Jacob Riis, Albert Payson Terhune, Richard Harding Davis, and H. L. Mencken.

Massachusetts-reared Edwin Grozier climbed the ranks of Pulitzer's *World* to become editor in chief by 1891, at which point he decided to strike out on his own. He returned to Boston to buy the moribund *Post*, with plans to turn it into "the People's paper," Boston's version of the *World*. His publicity schemes included elephants, traveling movie scouts, prizes for randomly selected readers, and a Santa Claus Fund charity that still operates today.

At the *World*, while Grozier was city editor, one of Pulitzer's major innovations had been to hire the girl reporter Nellie Bly. With a few exceptions, most previous female journalists had covered women's stories, such as fashion or recipes. If lucky, they might get to critique drama or music. But they didn't enter the newsroom, instead sending in their essays by mail. They didn't even use their own names, so as not to sully their families with the taint of newspaperdom. Thus, for her first byline Elizabeth Cochrane was rechristened with the misspelled name of an 1850s Stephen Foster song.

Bly entered journalism in Pittsburgh in 1885, exhibited so much talent that she temporarily broke out of the women's beat, but became frustrated when she was repeatedly relegated to theater critic. So she moved to New York and badgered the *World* editors until they gave her an assignment: feign insanity and get committed to an asylum, in order to write an exposé. The two-part series included a byline and attention-grabbing layout—unusual for any newcomer, much less a woman. Bly herself became a celebrity, and her name synonymous with this sort of "stunt reporting," in which a reporter donned a disguise to get a sensational story of crime, scandal, or shocking circumstance. In subsequent stories Bly posed as a maid to expose employment agencies, an unwed mother to expose a baby-selling racket, and a sinner to expose conditions at the Magdalen Home for Unfortunate Women. She joined a chorus line, asked a lobbyist for a bribe, and learned to fence; she visited the training camp of heavyweight boxer John L. Sullivan; and she explored Buffalo Bill's Wild West, where she found the women riders much more interesting than the cowboys. But other papers could hire women reporters, send them on stunts, and promote them as celebrities. In a competitive environment, Bly always had to go one better. This led to her most famous escapade, the 1889-90 trip around the world.

When he took over the *Post*, Grozier applied all the lessons he'd learned at the *World*, including the use of women beyond the traditional society pages. For example, the February 11, 1894, issue of the *Post* boasted that it was the product of women alone. But Caroline Lockhart was not involved—she was not yet on the staff.

"Cub in," said the elocution teacher in answer to Lockhart's timid knock.

She entered. He was "a beardless youth, who looked as though the balmy zephyrs of perhaps twenty-two summers had fanned his brow." He glared at her, then went back to his writing. She stood in the middle of his room, embarrassed. Had she offended him somehow? And here Lockhart fully gets into her story:

Once more he cast a withering glance upon me that frizzled my very soul, and asked, "Well, young woben, what cad I do for you?" He had a terrific cold in his head which no doubt accounted for his pronunciation and the habit he had of keeping his mouth open.

"That's what I don't know," I replied laughing. But he frowned so upon this frivolous remark that I immediately subsided.

"I came to study for the stage," I added, "if you have any hours left at all."

"Well," he said, after a few moments' deep thought, "I will try ad work you id just to accobodate you." I was deeply grateful and told him I should like to begin immediately on the balcony scene from "Romeo and Juliet."

He did not likc Shakspere, but he "accobodated" me again.

"Dow, I hope you are idtelligent," he said as he handed me a book.

"Not very," I replied, for I thought it might not be well to appear to overestimate myself in the beginning.

"Dow this chair will be the balcudy, ad after I say a couple of lides you cub out."

I waited nervously behind the desk for him to begin, and finally he started.

"But soft! What light through yonder breaks?"

I looked to see if someone was coming with a lantern, but no—he meant me. I was coming from behind the desk.

"It is the east, ad Juliet is the sud. Arise, fair sud, and kill the envious bood."

I arose at this point and stood on the chair to kill the "envious bood."

He continued till he came to the line: "Oh, that I were a glove upod that had that I bight kiss that cheek."

The book said that I must sigh: "Ah, me." Which I did, greatly agitated, but still, it was a very rational sigh, I thought.

"No, not that way," he shouted, angrily. "Like this"—and he gave a sigh that scattered the papers on his desk.

And so we struggled on, he shouting out his love for me in a manner that would have brought the whole Capulet family about his ears. He tore his hair, strode up and down the room and smote his chest. I became aroused myself. I made up my mind I was not going to let him beat me, if all I needed was lung power, so we shouted, gestured, and waved in a fashion that would have made Shakspere turn over in his grave. It was a wonderful scene; there never was such a Romeo, such a lusty Romeo, and I am positive there was never such a Juliet.

I was handicapped a little by my balcony. It did not seem to me I did myself justice, but all went well till I came to the line, "Good night, good night, parting is such sweet sorrow." I wafted him a resounding kiss and stepped backward. Parting was not such sweet sorrow after all, for I almost dashed my brains out against the wall, and Romeo did not look particularly sorry for me, considering his recent ardent words. He only gathered me up in an absent-minded sort of way and asked me to pay my $2, please.

These words are not a reminiscence but a piece of journalism—likely one of Lockhart's first major features for the *Post*. As a stunt girl, she presented herself to four private theater teachers who advertised their ability to obtain positions for students in first-class companies. Then she published the article to expose them.

As an exposé, the article has some drawbacks: notably, it doesn't name the teachers. (It could hardly have been news that such quackery existed.) But as entertainment, it shines. Lockhart's attitude carries the piece. She's bold and self-confident, cynical but amused more than outraged. She indeed already has enough acting ability to pull off the stunt, and in doing so she's having the time of her life.

Furthermore, the writing captures that. You get the sense that she dashed the story off but still managed to capture it perfectly. You might call it, as subsequent critics would, a "breezy style." Her personality comes through; it reads just like it would have sounded were she telling it to her girlfriends over chocolate and tea. She's a natural storyteller.

She also has a wonderful ear for accent, for expressing on paper the way someone sounds with a head cold, and making it funny. This was a popular form of humor at the time; for example, Finley Peter Dunne's "Mr. Dooley" was a heavily accented Chicago saloonkeeper who offered humorous philosophical tidbits. Later in the same piece Lockhart depicts one of the incompetent instructors trying to talk western: "now let on yer jollying the bartender."

The article is bylined "The Post Woman," and that pen name also appears in a subhead: "The Post Woman Takes Half a Dozen Lessons . . . "It's unclear what happened to the producers of February's all-women's issue, but this moniker suggests that by the fall of 1894 Lockhart was the only female the paper was publishing. Furthermore, she was being marketed as a sort of Nellie Bly, a celebrity whose article was worth reading not because it was news, but because it was hers.

She apparently got the job by working her way up through the ranks. In one of her scrapbooks is pasted an undated ad, for Fancy Slippers and Shoes: "Monday will be the day to buy satin slippers. Just think of it! Slippers that cost $4.50 on Saturday can be bought for $1 on Monday at H.H. Tuttle's." The adjacent handwriting, unmistakably Lockhart's, says, "First ad." Below it are clippings labeled "First criticism" and "First music criticism." These showed enough talent that she was turned loose on bigger stories, and eventually became one herself.

Lockhart clearly took to that arrangement. She got to write about herself. She got to tell stories. She didn't necessarily have to do a lot of homework, since the articles would rarely inform. She just had to be witty, charming, and flirtatious—qualities that came to her easily. Assigned to spend a day with a mounted policeman, she first discussed how she got permission, then where she got her horse, then how the cop reacted when she suggested they start galloping. Assigned to interview Russian Prince Serge Wolkowsky, she spent more than half the article amusingly recounting her preparation for and travel to the appointment. Assigned to interview three bachelor politicians, she expressed surprise that none of them had heard of her.

Her stunts included taking the wheel of a full-rigged ship, spending Christmas Eve on the street in Boston's most squalid neighborhood, posing as a servant girl to hire out of an employment office, working as a cranberry picker, wearing bloomers for a day, and going down a toboggan chute. After heading out on a sailboat during a blizzard, she wrote, "If the boat had not been so strong my story would not have been so long. And it would not have been written by me, since the managing editor does not think my style stiff enough for use in the obituary department."

She did not have the responsibility of coming up with the stunts, but that meant she was at the mercy of the editor who did. The Sunday editor, whom she called Johnny Tincup, made a lasting impression, as did the sporting editor, who sat across the hall from her once she was given her own cubbyhole with a table and chair ("I felt very happy and important"). The name of the sporting editor was Andrew McKenzie, and he would become the first love of her adult life.

Little information survives about how their relationship started. There are hints, such as the way McKenzie gets light-heavyweight champ Spike Sullivan to deck a man who'd been hassling Lockhart, or the way she pastes into her scrapbook boxing articles she clearly did not write, or the affectionate tone of an article in which she's riding on a tandem with the "bicycle editor" of the *Post*.

McKenzie, the same age as Lockhart, had been raised in suburban Boston, the son of a Baptist clergyman. He'd attended Brown University, but his taste for adventure took him far beyond the standard Ivy League fare. In 1894 he left his job as an editor for a Baptist newspaper to join Coxey's Army, a group of unemployed workers who marched from all around the country to Washington, D.C., to demand that the government create more jobs. It was one of the first significant popular protests in American history, and McKenzie made his reputation corresponding on it for the *Post*.

McKenzie plays a prominent role in Lockhart's article "Hunting for the Festive Rabbit" in which Lockhart, informed that thousands of rabbits are overrunning the country town of Lexington, gets a young man to take them hunting there. "He is a great wing shot. I know it, for he told me so himself, but I did not think this particular talent of his would be of much use in rabbit hunting, so another sportsman [obviously McKenzie], who said he was a great ground shot, was invited to join the party. I am what might be called a good all round shot. By this I mean that I can shoot things all around me, behind me just as well as in front. I could hit a rabbit on the fly just as well as though he were running or walking. I am also famous for quick, unexpected shots, shots that are as great a surprise to me as any one else. This is the reason that upon previous hunting expeditions I have been so much alone." Lockhart discovers that her cartridges are too big for her shotgun and suspects the Great Ground Shot of bribing the sporting goods clerk to keep her safely unarmed. Thus, she's delighted to report that he spends hours tracking a "quail" that turns out to be an old widow's hen. They find no rabbits whatsoever, and indeed a farmer informs them that there has not been a rabbit in the woods for fifty years.

At some point her articles started appearing with the byline "Caroline Lockhart" rather than "The Post Woman." This development may have come after a Boston city council meeting in which councilman William Woods said that women should not be allowed to vote on the school board, and she wrote, "That may all be; I am not a suffragist, but if any 19-year-old girl of my acquaintance could not vanquish Brother Woods in an argument, and in better language than Brother Woods ever dreamed of in his wildest flights, I am much mistaken."

Woods fired back, accusing the *Post* of having an ill-tempered man masquerade as its "Post Woman." Always delighted to sell papers through a fracas it had mostly invented, the *Post* played up the story, insisting he apologize for his "slanders" against "a most estimable and talented young woman." In so doing it had to name her.

Lockhart's work was not all stunts. She profiled politicians, society ladies, prizefighters, philanthropic groups, women artists, a blind architect, and an opium fiend known as the queen of Chinatown. In these stories Lockhart rarely shows much knowledge or appreciation for their work—her questions for famed radical orator Robert Ingersoll, for example, are obviously scripted—but she does show surprisingly real and moving empathy.

Even a story titled "Champion Fat Boy of the World" condescends to thirteen-year-old, 193-pound Michael Corrigan of Waltham far less than his family and community seem to. The *Post* had previously reported that Harry Gutterman was fattest boy in America or even the world, but the city of Waltham protested, and the Post Woman is sent to investigate. She meets Corrigan at home, interviews him with his mother, and takes him to a grocery store for weighing. He is indeed plump, she says, "so plump that when he falls down he bounces back on his feet again." But she actually takes the time to get to know him, and her report should have deflated Michael's promoters more than himself: "He seemed to be a great favorite with all and he should be, for Michael is not only fat, but a well-mannered and obliging boy as well." The story was so well done that a week later Howard Tibbets of Malden, who weighed 210 pounds, asked for similar treatment.

She similarly rises above the stunt when profiling some freaks on display at a museum. "I thought it would be funny, and I had laughed merely at the thought of dining with the man with the cast-iron stomach." But once she sits down at the dinner table, "I never felt less like laughing in my life. There was nothing funny about 'the lady with the elastic skin,' with her thin, tired face, and her tired blue eyes." The blue man "not only looked blue, but he seemed to feel blue, for during almost the entire meal he kept his head bowed, his thoughts apparently miles away. He seldom spoke, and when he did his voice was low and full of a sort of lonely, homesick feeling." Indeed, few of them speak much, though they are achingly polite. She captures the unique loneliness of each and subtly contrasts them with the fatuous promoter, who talks all dinner about money. She concludes the article with a final scene: "The pretty little girl who kept the boarding house dropped into a chair exhausted with a long day's work, and as I went out of the dining room I saw the blue man leaning silent and alone against a window which looked down upon the museum hall below."

Lockhart's story on Buffalo Bill, published in the summer of 1895, is particularly interesting in hindsight. At age twenty-four, Lockhart has already become a confident writer and strong storyteller, and she also has heartfelt, well-reasoned opinions about the cowboy culture of the West.

Most of the article, a lengthy Sunday feature, discusses her experiences with Buffalo Bill's horsemen. Of course the stunt girl will ride a horse, though "I had ridden only once in four years, and that was with the Boston mounted police" on a trotting horse, which she had not been familiar with. Despite the fact that her stirrups are too long and she loses her "gallant cowboy's sombrero," she runs her horse like a greyhound. "Some of the bystanders who had expressed grave doubts as to my horsemanship said I was 'all right,' and having earned their approval I was willing to get off, although I should have liked to ride for a week."

She thoroughly likes the horsemen, especially bucking-horse rider Angus McPhee ("only 20 years of age, with a fine physique and a frank, honest face that is thoroughly likeable") and manager William Brace ("He is a tall, manly fellow, kind and courteous to women, as are all typical western men"). She repeats her point about Brace four paragraphs later: "The cowboys helped me in every way they could; every one was kind; and, in fact, not once among all these rough riders of the plains did I hear a single unpleasant comment, and nothing but the greatest courtesy was shown me, from the stable boy to Colonel Cody himself."

To modern ears, these sound like typical descriptions of the chivalrous cowboy. But Lockhart penned it six years *before* Owen Wister basically invented that stereotype in his novel *The Virginian*. Pre-Wister, cowboys were generally seen as drifters, as socially crude and morally suspect. They visited whores and never invested their wages. They weren't honorable any more than they were well scrubbed. In the nickel and dime novels of the West up to that time, the heroes were more likely road agents, scouts, or miners than cattle tenders. By the 1890s the reputation of the cowboy was improving (an 1898 newspaper said, "now only in the South—for instance, Arizona—is the term cowboy equivalent to desperado"), but only in comparison to how poor it had once been.

But for Lockhart the West was about horses. The West was where she'd grown up riding horses; riding horses was what she missed about being an East Coast celebrity. So naturally she is drawn to these men who work with horses, to their attitudes and philosophies, to their braveness. A difficult horse is part of the adventure of the frontier, one that she shares with them. "Every man who rides the bronchos takes his life in his hands, for they are the genuine buckers, wild and unmanageable as when they first left the plains." As charmingly self-absorbed as ever, she adds, "I ought to know, for I was born out West myself, in a place the natives call 'Topekee,' Kan."

Certainly Buffalo Bill, too, understood the magic of horses: that's what Brace and his boys were doing in the show. Horses were a far bigger draw than theatrical melodramas—they and their riders represented the *authentic* West. In this article Lockhart, claiming herself to be a transplanted westerner, is in a unique position to confirm that authenticity, proclaiming these showmen real. And she proclaims them not only real but also honorable.

Indeed, her defense of the cowboy hints at her own ambitions, as well as her understanding of her unique qualifications. "Both Mr. Brace and [Mr. McPhee] are the kind of men that Western people recognize as the real Western type. They are not the horse-stealing, thieving, uneducated barbarians, one degree above the Digger Indians, that the 10-cent novelist who has never been out of his own country would have us believe. The Western cowboy is kindness and gentleness itself to women. He is honest, straightforward and brave, and I know what I am talking about, which is a great deal more than can be said of the writers of some of the wild articles which appear at stated intervals in some of the Eastern papers."

In the article she also admires a cowboy's lasso skills (after an explanation of ropesmanship, she writes, presaging a linguistic trend by one hundred years, "Easy isn't it—not!"), eats lunch with the crew, and rides in the Deadwood coach for the afternoon matinee. And she briefly describes a meeting with Buffalo Bill himself: "He is a tall, large man, with keen but kindly eyes. He is a very busy man, as well, for he does all his own writing, and he receives on an average fifty letters a day. He showed me the picture of his ranch in Nebraska, and quantities of relics and souvenirs which he has collected during his travels. He is a very interesting conversationalist and an extremely pleasant man to meet." (In subsequent reminiscences, she would claim either that they became such close friends that she later had to move to Cody's town in Wyoming, or that he was so hung over he did not speak at all. This account, however, shows that their relationship was cordial if distant.)

The great man, however, is a mere sidelight for her. She is more taken with the horses, the cowboys, and the characters. She both opens and closes the article by recounting conversations with an alleged old friend of hers, an Indian named Yellow Bird. Their dialogue is so self-mocking that one has to assume she invented all of it: their words, their shared Kansas history, their names (she is "Lilly-Walk-On-Water-Foot-Just-Like-A-Board"), and his "savage" status (he sobs, "I haven't seen a gopher for months"). But one theme seems real, or at least seems like she wants to make it real. As they say goodbye, she closes the article, "Thus we parted, changed and saddened by civilization."

The fog rolled in, a thick gray blanket. The mist was so wet it dampened Lockhart's face and hair. This was bad news, she knew: fog this wet wasn't going away soon.

From her tiny rowboat, she could no longer see any of the surrounding islands. "Now, I want to go in a slanting northeasterly direction," she said aloud, but there was nobody there to hear her. The only reply was the caw of a solitary crow.

Lockhart was off Naskeag Point, on the coast of Maine, where she was taking a working vacation during the summer of 1895. At 2:00 p.m. on a bright afternoon she'd decided to row to Crow's Island to pick some strawberries. The island was barely visible from the shore, and the journey had taken her two hours. But as soon as she arrived she noticed the heavy fog bank to the east starting to move toward her. She had no time to pick strawberries, only to catch her breath. Yet as she set off for the mainland the fog was already upon her.

"It must have been about twenty minutes from the time I had started when suddenly an island loomed up. . . . I thought there was something familiar-looking about it and as I rowed nearer I discovered to my horror that it was the same island I had started from. The tide had turned me completely around. Then for the first time I realized how really serious it was. I leaned quietly on my oars and tried to determine what to do."

Newspaper correspondents commonly parlayed success into travel. Stephen Crane, who'd been born the same year as Lockhart and had started writing for New York newspapers in 1891, leveraged the success of his 1895 novel *The Red Badge of Courage* into journalistic assignments in the West. Nellie Bly, the first time she'd been demoted in Pittsburgh, had taken off for Mexico, where her freelance stories reestablished her reputation.

But Lockhart didn't travel like most correspondents. She didn't go to the fashionable resort of Bar Harbor, as a friend had recommended. (She may have remembered from Asbury Park how stifling such a resort could be for an adventurous woman.) And she didn't travel with a chaperone, as Nellie Bly did. She went alone to a remote village where she could have outdoor adventures.

Though now she was worried she'd gotten in over her head. Remembering that old-timers would steer by the wind, she set out again with the breeze against her cheek. She rowed for another hour, heart skipping occasionally as the breeze would appear to die off. She saw no landforms as she continued:

I rowed on and on, hoping and watching. Blisters were coming on my hand, so every stroke was painful, the moisture was dripping from my hair and wetting my clothes. I had no wrap and wore only a boating skirt and blue sweater. I stopped rowing to listen, thinking I might hear the surf breaking on some of the rocks. But not a sound, only that awful maddening stillness; the fog had shut down till its thickness was almost past belief. I could hardly see a dozen feet from me. Suddenly I realized that either the boat had drifted around while I had been resting on my oars or the wind had shifted. Now it was blowing in my face, and the tide was coming in the opposite direction. All my courage and presence of mind seemed to leave me. I seemed hopelessly bewildered.

The little boat danced up and down with the waves, while I sat there simply drifting. It was no use to row, I might be rowing myself out to sea, and for the first time in my life that I can remember I was terribly frightened. I was as scared as it is possible for anyone to be.

She eventually landed on another island, searched all over it for wood dry enough to make a fire, answered several calls that turned out to be just crows or seals, and finally heard the voices of villagers who had realized she was missing and taken a larger boat out to rescue her.

She'd had a rocky start with the villagers, who were not accustomed to tourists; mistrusted the young, single woman as a "furriner"; and initially struck her as inbred and illiterate. But along with the compassion of the rescue, she came to appreciate their vast knowledge of winds, tides, and fog. She came to think of them as "a quaint type of folk of whom little was known."

Another draw of spending the summer in rural Maine was that she could have a horse. At Buffalo Bill's show she'd bought a homesick-looking pony named Kid. "'He is thinking of his life on the prairies,' I said to myself, 'and contrasting his happy childhood days with the present. Then he ate buffalo grass and roamed at his own sweet will; now he eats baled hay and chases Indians around a sawdust ring.'" She named him after McPhee and Brace and put him on a boat for Maine. He turned out to be more than she could handle—actually more than she and seven neighbors could handle—as she recounted with amusement later that summer. She had to get him more exercise, but wrote, "There are times when I have ridden Kid-Angus-William-Brace-McPhee many weary miles in the hot sun, merely for his breath—not mine. Then I almost wish I was just a 'summer girl' sitting somewhere in the shade with my parasol, my drooping white hat and pink roses over my left ear."

Almost was the operative word. She had no such wishes whatsoever. In fact, though she returned to her reporting duties in Boston over the winter, by the summer of 1896 she had left New England for good.

What happened to Lockhart's stunt girl career? Though it sounds glamorous, and though the tone of her articles suggests she was loving it, all was not fun and games. Stunt girls got little respect: traditional female writers were scandalized, and male reporters were condescending. A stunt girl would never rise through the editorial ranks.

Worse, the stunt girl phenomenon was a fad that was running its course. As early as 1894 the *New York World*'s Sunday female stunt slot behaved like an assembly line: Find a girl, give her a stunt, have her write it up, and publish it under a one-size-fits-all byline ("The Post Woman" may have been the *Post*'s way of copying the *World*'s generic byline "Meg Merrilies") so she doesn't become a celebrity and thus gain power.

Nellie Bly had left the *World* just a month after her return from her round-the-world trip, because they'd offered her little pay or thanks. (Failing as a novelist, she returned a few years later and bounced in and out of journalism throughout the 1890s, bored but unable to make a living any other way.) Furthermore, Bly's career had taken a toll on her personal life. After her trip she was an unmarried twenty-seven-year-old, at a time when that was perilously close to being an old maid. Young, she hadn't felt successful enough to find a mate she would consider suitable; successful, she feared she was too old.

By 1896 Lockhart was similarly an unmarried twenty-five-year-old (though, like Bly, she continually lied about her age). Most other female journalists left their career for marriage, and Lockhart may have hoped for that fate, or despaired of ever finding it. Lockhart said nothing in her memoirs about how or why she left the *Post*, and no diary of that time survives. A magazine article, however, does give a clue.

"There is no vocation into which women have entered where disillusions materialize so rapidly as they do in journalism," writes Haryot Holt Cahoon in an 1897 Boston magazine article titled "Women in Gutter Journalism." Cahoon describes the typical career path of a young, idealistic girl, usually from the West or South, who brings "her education, her personal attractions, her youth, her illusions, her energy, her ambition, and her enthusiasm" to the city. She is tempted to seek her fame as an actress, but conservative family members view the stage with horror. So she pursues journalism, not knowing that this job will ruin her worse than the stage.

Cahoon's composite stunt girl has youth, cleverness, enthusiasm, and love of adventure, but most of all "she is impressionable; everything interests her because she sees everything." Because of her good looks, she has a naïveté that creates a charming if unpolished writing style. As an early assignment, her editor sends her to interview a prizefighter. Then she goes to the police court, the slums, and a Chinese immigrant neighborhood; she poses as a Sunday-school teacher, a sufferer from an incurable disease, and an unwed mother. "She sold what is rarely offered at $10 per day: her word, her honor, and her self-respect."

Soon her illusions and idealism wane, as do the editor's ideas for stunts. The editor sends her onto the streets in hopes she will be propositioned. "I have it from her own lips that she was not molested," Cahoon writes, but the girl produces the story as if she was, because truth has become less important than controversy. After just a few years, "She has lost all the capital she had when she began,—youth, health, credulity, her ideals, her self-respect, her enthusiasm, and her ambition. . . . She realizes that what she took to be fame was only vulgar notoriety, and that it was unworthy of her."

Although there is no proof that Cahoon knew Lockhart, it's not unreasonable to imagine. And Cahoon's "composite" fits Lockhart to a T. If Lockhart was indeed Cahoon's unnamed source, the story suggests how dramatically she failed in the first campaign of her consuming quest for fame.

Lockhart sought adventure as well, and for the next eight years she pursued travel opportunities that took her farther than most people of her generation traveled in a lifetime. She did little contemporary writing about the experiences, however (she told a friend at the time that she never began writing until her money ran out), so they come to us in brief glimpses.

One account has her in Mexico, spurning an offer of marriage from a wealthy but cowardly nobleman. Another report has her in western North Carolina, admiring a man named Vance Galloway who is riding a bull. A third has her in coastal Labrador, bragging that she has now gone farther north than any white woman other than Josephine Peary, who accompanied her explorer husband, Admiral Robert E. Peary, on his second try for the North Pole.

A sporadic diary recounts episodes from a trip to New Mexico Territory in the spring of 1898. Lockhart and Andrew McKenzie, the sporting editor who left the *Post* about the same time she did, visited the tiny mining town of Hillsboro, where they stayed at an old adobe hotel. McKenzie was sick—he would be sickly for the rest of his life, apparently from something he caught on an adventure in South America—and they were running out of money. Later they rented a ranch in the area from a Mr. Hopewell, who at one point propositioned her. By June McKenzie "sold his story to the *Watchman* for $10 and his mother sent him $10. We have $55 in the bank. We celebrate the check from the *Watchman* by buying a ham. So poetical." She would go for weeks without writing in the diary, and then write grumpily, as if it was therapy. Presumably the trip also had joyous experiences, ones that better matched her idealization of the Bohemian lifestyle. Uninterrupted misery might have prompted her to scurry back to a resort such as Asbury Park. But instead she merely unburdened herself to the diary.

Lockhart and McKenzie were obviously traveling together, despite not being married. Sex in Victorian times is an exceedingly difficult topic to research, because nobody ever talked about it. But did they do it? Or did even young rebels like Lockhart internalize the era's prudent morality? In Lockhart's case, her later diaries indicate that McKenzie *was* her lover—her first. Given that they probably didn't meet until she was twenty-four, she was by modern standards remarkably chaste. Presumably, she consummated this relationship only after accepting that she would not find true love in time to marry so young as most of her contemporaries.

∾

Lockhart stood at the massive door to an old-fashioned mansion on Walnut Street, Philadelphia's most exclusive neighborhood. An English butler, in livery, opened the door and gave her the once-over. He reluctantly let her into the reception room. She was impressed. The mansion was handsome, the room tastefully furnished, with a ceiling of astonishing height.

Lockhart explained that she was there to see the lady of the house. Ava Willing was a grande dame of Philadelphia society, scion of wealth, married to the codeveloper of New York's Waldorf-Astoria Hotel, John Jacob Astor IV (whom Ava didn't like very much). Lockhart wanted to interview her. She was back in the newspaper business.

The butler appeared startled. She waited for him to recover, feeling a bit like a Fuller Brush man. "I'll take up your card," he finally said. Lockhart admitted she didn't have an engraved visiting card. He finally found a plain card on which she scribbled her name in pencil. He put the card on a silver plate and ascended the steep, old-fashioned staircase. He looked back at her, and she thought he "half-wished he had locked up the silver."

He soon returned with a note. He hadn't even talked to Miss Willing, only a secretary, who had written, "Miss Ava Willing would not be able to see a reporter from the *Bulletin*." Lockhart tried to hide her disappointment. Shouldn't the name of the *Bulletin* have gotten her in this door? She hadn't been crazy about the idea of interviewing socialites, but that's what the *Bulletin* editor had wanted. Now she had to go back to him empty handed.

Such a paper—the newsroom felt to Lockhart like a Quaker meeting-house—was far different from the wild *Post*, where reporters had always been getting doors slammed in their faces, and editors were always coming up with crazy new schemes. Apparently the single rebuff had exhausted her editor's creativity.

He said, "I can't think of an assignment for you just now."

"I can," she responded.

"Yes?"

"I'm going to crawl out on the brim of Billy Penn's hat and take a look-see at the town from there." A thirty-seven-foot-tall bronze statue of city founder William Penn stood atop City Hall. It had just been finished a few years earlier and was by far the highest point in Center City. The statue wore a hat twenty-three feet in circumference.

"What!"

She nodded. "Yes, I've got it all fixed. There are ladders all the way up, through the statue with an opening in the top of his hat."

It may not have happened this way—Lockhart told this story in her memoirs, which tended to telescope and overdramatize—but somehow she reentered the newspaper field, with a promotion. Philadelphia was the nation's third-largest city, and the evening *Bulletin* was a "correct, conservative, and noncommittal" paper.

She started in the spring of 1899. Just a few months earlier, and just a hundred miles south, another writer started a journalism career, calling it "the maddest, gladdest, damnedest existence ever enjoyed by mortal youth." Though nine years younger than Lockhart—he was just eighteen when he got the job—their attitudes and careers were remarkably similar. Their paths would cross only briefly, but with mutual admiration. The young journalist's name was Henry L. Mencken.

The enthusiasm Mencken brought to his early working days resembled that of Lockhart in Boston. So did the opportunities. Mencken the police reporter, like Lockhart the stunt girl, got to meet a wide range of characters whom his upper-middle-class background would not otherwise have exposed him to. He was charmed by their antics, if also disappointed in their character. He was fascinated by their creative use of language, mixing it with his own high-powered vocabulary to help create a uniquely American literary voice. Lockhart, while not as gifted or driven as Mencken, was doing the same.

Exposure to the seamy side of life turned some journalists into muckrakers, others into cynics. Mencken and Lockhart were both in the cynic camp, though not yet embittered. Both were chiefly amused by people's flaws. They could feel compassion as well, but they tended to view most predicaments as self-inflicted. They were not moved to anger at an unjust system. Then again, neither were they moved to anger at people's stupidity. (In both cases, this would change with age.) Life was funny, especially if you could depict it in high language. Lockhart did a story on a twenty-one-year-old girl named Dora Cooperstein, who "believes she has been bewitched. So does Dora's careworn father and her excitable mother, and the dozen howling little Coopersteins who roll on the floor and gaily bang each other over the head." She ended up finding some sympathy and admiration for Cooperstein's father, a weary tailor. But her overall attitude was laughter. She was delighted to have stepped out of the closed drawing rooms of the wealthy, to encounter these wacky if often dim-witted characters.

In Philadelphia, to judge by the output, the twenty-eight-year-old Lockhart no longer approached journalism with the same gusto she had in Boston. But she did approach it with a bit more maturity. She had apparently concluded that she would make her career as a writer—not merely as a stunt girl, not even merely as a journalist. Like Mencken, her ambition propelled her beyond the life of the day-to-day news gatherer. She still wanted fame, of a more literary sort, and she started building her career toward that goal.

One step was a new pen name. Newspapers still weren't ready for a woman writing under her own byline, so Lockhart became "Suzette." No record exists of how the name came about, but it appears to have been a remarkable shift in the traditional power structure, away from management and toward the writer. The name "Suzette" did not belong to the *Bulletin* (like "Meg Merrilies" belonged to the *World*). Lockhart wrote as Suzette for other publications, and when she left the *Bulletin* they did not plug another woman into that byline.

Another step was to move beyond stunts. Despite adventures like climbing out on Billy Penn's hat brim or swimming the Delaware River, Lockhart was no longer a stunt girl. That fad was passing, and other female reporters were similarly moving into newer fads. One such fad was Christmas coverage, coming on the heels of the *New York Sun*'s famed 1897 editorial "Yes, Virginia, there is a Santa Claus." So Lockhart took the Santa beat. For example, she told the story of Rosie, the only one of forty-six child actors in a production of *Beauty and the Beast* to still believe in Santa. Lockhart was also made "celebrity in chief" of the *Bulletin*'s Christmas party, in which the paper served three thousand newsboys a turkey dinner. In regular letters addressed to "My dear newsboys" but published in the paper for all to read, she promised "Big Time Coming Christmas Day" and "Newsboys' Dinner the Biggest of All."

The tone of the newsboy articles was still personal and chatty, using first person, as in "The other day in my letter to you I spelled Iky Segerman's name wrong, and Iky says everybody is talking about it. I did not do it on purpose, and I'm awfully sorry it happened, so I thought I would better explain that it was a mistake." But they were no longer so personally revealing as her earlier work, no longer the young naïf spilling her guts in public. She was learning reserve and distance. She was building her craft.

Another fad was the advice column. At the *Bulletin*, when questions arrived asking if girls should play kissing games, if a boy should kiss a girl who dared him to, or how a man should break with the girl who loves him, Suzette provided the answers (no, yes, and "any time that you are out with her and it rains do not say anything about getting a hansom cab. Just scud her along and reproach her for wearing thin shoes and no rubbers.")

She'd always interviewed news makers, but her stories for the *Bulletin*—including interviews with presidential candidate William Jennings Bryan and aged financier Jay Cooke—weren't so self-absorbed and worked harder at describing their subjects. For example, Bryan "has a strong face and dark, earnest eyes that look squarely into those of the person he is addressing. . . . He is a natural orator, a rich, well-turned sentence seems to give him actual pleasure."

Given the *Bulletin*'s respectability, this was news that was really happening, rather than sensations the paper created. When the women working at a cigar factory went on strike (cigar making was an industry quite open to women at the time, though many of the workers were under sixteen), the two sides' public statements disagreed about working conditions and wages. So Lockhart applied for a job to find out for herself. Not revealing that she was a reporter, she talked with some of her strikebreaking coworkers about wages and conditions, finding that she agreed with the company's arguments more than the strikers'. "I was not tired," she said toward the end of her day, "for I grew interested in the work. It is like embroidery—it is fascinating to see how much one can get done."

The story created such a stir that the union boycotted the *Bulletin*. In her memoirs, Lockhart claimed that a cigar had once been named after Suzette—if so, it was surely the company's way of thanking her for the exposé.

In addition to news, she also wrote little vignettes, miniature stories of regular folks that sought an emotional rather than intellectual response, in an occasional column titled "Suzette's Stories of Everyday Life." These stories, in truth, were not very good. Many were self-indulgent, such as her complaints of the silly things that unidentified women hoped she would print in the paper. Others were both cloying and condescending, such as the streetcar scene where society ladies move up to provide a seat for a "stout colored woman with a basket of laundered clothes on her arm and a black baby of two gripping the other hand," or the restaurant scene where the ugly but prosperous businessman presents the plain and uninteresting cashier with a bundle of violets, just to brighten her day. The subject matter of these pieces is indicative of her interests: with the circus freaks and fat boys of the world, not the Ava Willings. However, the quality of these pieces is not necessarily indicative of her best work. By this point her top-drawer material was going elsewhere.

Suzette got out of the cab at the hotel and found a bit more than she'd bargained for. One uniformed man opened the cab door, and then another led her to a third, "who stood waiting in fearful dignity in the broad corridor." She had just arrived in Paris, France, where she had expected relatives to meet her at the train station. But they weren't there, so she'd taken a stranger's advice on hotels. Now a fourth uniformed attendant showed her to the hotel office, where a fat man with a pen behind his ear bowed profoundly. "The only room vacant, according to the fat gentleman, was on the first floor. He could not tell me this until he had examined the plan of the hotel and consulted with three other persons, also with pens behind their ears. Hardened as he was, I think even his conscience smote him as he told me the price of the room."

A day or two later she checked out. "Two people came up with my bill. One was able to carry it, being strong for a Frenchman, but the other—I think the other was a physician, who came in case I fainted."

Throughout the summer of 1900, the *Bulletin* published Suzette's letters from Europe. Several of her dispatches followed the time-honored tradition of discussing how difficult the French were. Her next stop after the too-expensive hotel was a too-cheap guesthouse, where she was forced to share a room with a French girl who snored. It had an international clientele, with just one other American, "who, having been in Paris since October, spoke English with an accent unless she forgot it." After a few days Suzette checked out of this place as well, to what she believed was the landlady's regret, since "the American girl and myself were the only ones in the house who seemed to take baths, which daily added a franc to her income."

Lockhart was hitting her stride as a humorist: tossing off caricatures, describing through creative metaphors, poking bloated egos, and turning the exasperating experiences of her own life into humorous vignettes. Like Mencken's ("No one ever went broke underestimating the taste of the American public") and some of Twain's ("Wagner's music is better than it sounds"), it was slightly haughty humor, surprising in the brevity of its thorough dismissal. A few days later she reported on the dedication of a statue of Lafayette in Paris, donated by the self-important American Ferdinand Peck, "whose speech was frequently interrupted by applause from his family and his appointees, the latter with great forethought having stationed themselves where he could witness their enthusiasm."

Her sympathies went out to animals, especially horses. She was horrified by the way cabmen treated their horses, with revolting sores under their harnesses, and sides striped with welts from lashing. She also commented on a sickly old man lying in front of the Place de l'Opera, blood dripping from his mouth—and only a passing foreign girl taking pity on him with a donation of coins.

She filed stories that summer from around the continent. In Oberammergau, Germany, she saw the famed *Passion Play*. At Ostend, Belgium, she swam in the ocean and poked fun at her own modesty about wearing a skimpy rented bathing suit.

But Paris with its World's Fair was the star of the trip. She returned later in the summer for an experience she turned into one of her favorite stories. After dining at a nice restaurant, she and an unidentified companion hail a cab and ask to go to the Casino de Paris. The *cocher*, or cabman, agrees, but instead takes them to the Opera Comique, insisting it is the Casino. She refuses to get out, and he finally takes them to a theater, claiming it is the Casino. She disagrees again. Eventually their argument attracts a crowd. Fearing the crowd, Lockhart finally decides to get out of the cab and pay the man, but not give him a tip. Enraged, he "danced up and down and swore till he was black in the face. The crowd grew denser and surrounded us. Then a gendarme made his way into the crowd." A fat man bulls his way to the front of the crowd as if to translate for the police, but speaks no English. ("I do not know what led him to believe we could understand his French any better than that of the other.") The cabman insists that she had asked to go first to the Opera Comique, and then the theater, and thus he deserves three francs plus tip. The policeman tells Lockhart if she doesn't pay, she'd be arrested. So, crowd and all, they go to the stationhouse.

They go directly to a magistrate, where the cabman makes his case with great vehemence. Then the judge frowns at the Americans. Lockhart's companion knows no French, so Lockhart pleads their case in what little French she learned at the Moravian Seminary. When she argues that the mess was the fault of the cabman, she accidentally uses not the word *cocher* but *cochon*—the obscene word for pig.

Lockhart always despised vulgar language, so she may have loved this story because it showed her mistakenly using it. The rest was anticlimactic: eventually a translator was found who pled their case successfully.

As she had since arriving in Boston, Lockhart in Philadelphia lived in hotels and boardinghouses. A 1900 census taker found her boarding with a couple named Harry and Nina Peebles at 4836 Hazel Avenue. Later she published a story about moving into an actual house with a friend named Elizabeth, where "we had pigs feet, and tripe, and corned beef and cabbage, and all the ignoble dishes which we were ashamed to order in hotels." Elizabeth took a bath without other tenants rattling at the door. The two women argued about how often to clean dishes, and whether the bed should be turned down or up, and how to deal with peddlers at the door. Lockhart finally put up a sign: "Don't want to buy any apples or oranges/needles or pins/my life insured . . . don't want nuthin' of nobody, so please don't ring." But of course the whole neighborhood came to read the sign, so Elizabeth said she was just going to move back to a hotel, and Lockhart had to follow suit.

McKenzie may now have moved to New York, where he at some point served as Sunday editor of the *New York Press*, but Lockhart was never at a loss for male companionship. Even turning thirty, she held her stunning looks. She also held romantic notions of marriage. She wrote, "There are women of brains and character, and womanliness, too, whose pride and self-respect will not let them marry some insignificant, rabbit-hearted little creature who may admire them." She would not be tied down doing domestic chores for some rich idiot. Rather, "Each woman has, or has had, her own little romantic dream, which she hopes may come true, and the central figure in the romance is always a man to love and respect, to be proud of and rely upon, a man who brings with him contentment and happiness." She would not settle for anything less.

Though she apparently was willing to play around. Indeed, her opinion that so many marriages failed to live up to her ideal may have helped her conclude that it was OK to dally with married men. It was almost surely during this time that she met Jack Painter, a family man ten years her senior. He owned a large store on Chestnut Street, the fashionable business district, where he sold imported Swiss music boxes. But his heart wasn't in business as much as it was in big-game hunting and mining. In 1895 he made his first hunting trip to Montana and by 1897 he was spending summers there. In 1901 he sold the business and permanently moved his family to the West.

"I have a plan which may prove advantageous to both of us." With this air of conspiracy, the Sunday editor of the *Philadelphia Press* wrote to Lockhart. His note is preserved, though undated, in Lockhart's scrapbook, evidence of her career success. By 1903 she had stopped writing for the *Bulletin* (the clipping of her advice on how to break up is labeled, in her handwriting, "Last Bulletin story"), and in the spring of 1904 she and a cartoonist filled a page of each Sunday's *Press*.

Even better, she was breaking into magazines. *Lippincott's* sought to be a national literary journal, just a few rungs below today's *New Yorker*. Based in Philadelphia and associated with a major publishing house, it included a section of unsigned vignettes called "Walnuts and Wine," comparable to the *New Yorker*'s "Talk of the Town." As stories of everyday life, they needed to be entertaining and literary rather than newsworthy or literally true. This was an ideal situation for Lockhart to exercise her storytelling skills for better pay and prestige. She could draw on her unusual experiences, exotic travels, and the kooky characters she'd met. She may not have had the intellect of Bly or Mencken, but she did have one talent neither of them would ever master: spinning yarns.

Eventually, like many young writers moving up through the *Lippincott's* ranks, she graduated to bylined features and stories. In fact, a 1901 short story titled "Her Maiden Name" was highlighted on the cover as "'Suzette's' first fiction." It described a couple named Stanley forced to book separate staterooms for their return from a Paris vacation. For kicks, the wife books her room in her maiden name and insists her husband romance her as if they are unacquainted. Unfortunately her unattached status plays to her insecurities, which are worsened by the scorn she earns from gossipy passengers. Eventually the couple is reunited and the chief scandalmonger gets her comeuppance. Two themes in the story are indicative of Lockhart's future career. First is the use of personal experience: she herself had returned from Paris the previous autumn. She may well have had a sweetheart on board, sneaking kisses the way she portrays the Stanleys doing. Second is the disdain for gossipy high society, especially the way its women would seek to tear down women of independent and adventurous spirit.

Another note in her scrapbooks demonstrates the interest of the Lippincott publishing empire. On May 10, 1900, a Lippincott editor named Minz wrote that he had heard "that you are finishing a novel. Why not let me see it before you try for publication elsewhere? And, if you haven't finished it, why could you not stop at about forty thousand words and let me see it then?"

Some time thereafter a brief notice appeared: "Miss Caroline Lockhart, the young writer who has won a name for herself in journalism as 'Suzette,' and whose stories are coming to be recognized with pleasure by magazine readers, is building her first novel, a story of western life to which she has given the clever title, 'The Cowboy Girl.'"

3

Cowboy Novelist

When Lockhart went to Montana and asked "Sourdough Sam" McNeill to take her over the pass to McDonald Lake, she was prospecting just as much as the miners in Altyn. She was prospecting for stories.

The story about being stranded on the shale was a good one. After McNeill came back to rescue her, she wrote it up for *Lippincott's*. "A Girl in the Rockies" is a first-person account of her trip from Blackfoot over the pass, boasting a strong sense of place and several effective characterizations. The story is not labeled fiction or nonfiction—the distinction wasn't important in that era—and she appears to mix truth and make-believe throughout. Some events can be independently verified, as can the names of several characters, but at other times Lockhart clearly stretches the truth. For example, she portrays McNeill as a seventy-year-old who "went over the boulders and climbed the tallest peaks with the agility of a mountain goat" and who scoffs at prospecting as "commonplace." But, in fact, he was an Altyn prospector who was not yet sixty.

But back to her own prospecting: Lockhart was sifting through the lives of Montanans, looking for nuggets (characters, settings, plots) that would lead to her success. Her prospecting differed from the miners' in that she was seeking fame more than fortune and working with words rather than pickaxes. But she was similarly seeking opportunity in the West, and seeing it through the eyes of a decades-old mythology. Prospectors came West following the myth of the mother lode. Lockhart came following the myth of the frontier.

Americans' self-image had always been wrapped up in the frontier, the boundary of wilderness continually being tamed and civilized. The frontier myth generally incorporated several key elements. One was *nature*, which by 1901 was wedded to the rugged landscapes of the greater Rocky Mountains. A second was *individualism*, the notion that each man faced down nature's challenges by himself. A third was the *equality* these first two suggested: if each man went into the wilderness alone, then his success depended on his character, rather than his nobility, money, or connections. Nature was the great leveler, offering fantastic untapped resources to those strong enough to conquer them.

These mythic elements had come together repeatedly in American history, literature, and oral tradition, especially in the West. For example, most of the men in Altyn followed the gold rush myth, a version of the frontier myth in which the lone prospector overcomes the challenges of the wilderness and eventually finds gold in his pan. This story's structure was not all that different from the homesteading myth, in which the lone family overcomes similar challenges to build a successful farm, or even the Horatio Alger myth, in which the lone orphan overcomes the slums to achieve success in business. These types of stories kept popping up in different environments because they so effectively captured American character.

Obviously, however, the myth was not necessarily true nor fair. Plenty of homesteaders and prospectors failed, and most mines paid off far better for large corporations than for lone prospectors. Furthermore, we note today, the myth was horrifically and falsely white-male-centric. But its elements were both powerful and malleable. For example, Indians often came to stand for nature—usually savage, sometimes noble. Women (especially society women) came to stand for civilization as the opposite of nature. Outlaws came to stand for individualism gone bad. A hero's interactions with nature, Indians, outlaws, and women—firm or even violent with the first three, respectful toward the last—came to stand for his character. As the century turned and the frontier became harder to pinpoint, the myths only intensified. Those who bought into them would search harder and farther for the setting in which they would come true.

Altyn, thus, was full of dreamers and romantics. More than fifty years after the initial California gold rush, these prospectors still hoped to cash in the way they believed the '49ers had. (Indeed, many Altyn residents had fled from Butte, Montana, a few hundred miles south, where the large copper mines and labor-management struggles made mining more resemble a city than their legendary frontier.) They were thus a natural fit for Lockhart, who also hated the stratifying society of the East, sought adventures to prove her toughness, and loved the romantic stories that floated around the camp.

For example, in another feature based on her experiences in Altyn, Lockhart discusses a night atop the pass, where she and Sourdough Sam are forced to share a cabin with a dangerous-looking fellow who turns out to be a train robber on the lam. According to her article, he and Sam discuss the legend of Liver-Eatin' Johnston and agree that the famed mountain man did *not* eat an Indian's liver, but merely cut it out and threw it on the fire. They then discuss Johnston's funeral, which was so big it even featured a preacher from Billings. Lockhart might have turned her journalistic skepticism on these stories. (Liver-Eatin' Johnston, who denied ever cutting out any Indian's liver, had died just the previous year in a Los Angeles veterans' hospital, without any big funeral.) But she prefers to embrace them. She admires Sourdough Sam—so much so that she would keep his picture on a wall in her house for the rest of her life. So she admires the stories he tells, and repeats the tall tales in her own work. In another half-dozen sketches and short stories based on her Altyn experiences, she populates the real-life Montana landscapes with horse thieves and killers who sound more like dime-novel inventions than actual Montanans.

She brings in Indians, too—but these she had actually met.

"I'm going to see my grandma," said the schoolgirl. "Would you like to go 'long?" The girl, as Lockhart described her, was "an attractive half-breed who had been to boarding school."

Though she used the term "half-breed," she didn't apply as much scorn to it as some did. It was merely a statement of ethnicity, as "mixed-blood" might be today. Priding herself on her westernness, Lockhart knew that the area was full of mixed-bloods, and that in real life they didn't necessarily carry the symbolic baggage they did for some easterners. (Because most easterners of the time did not believe in racial mixing, they preferred to view ethnically mixed characters as deficient. Writers—especially those who had not visited the West—played to those sensibilities in inventing the stereotypically evil "half-breed.") Lockhart was tremendously curious about Indian lifestyles and at various points in her life found empathy for Native Americans (a generosity she rarely extended to other ethnicities). Perhaps she was moved by the exoticism and sense of adventure; probably she associated them with nature and the frontier. She eagerly accepted the girl's invitation.

The girl's name was Jennifer Kathleen LaMott and she was about fifteen years old. Jennie and her sister attended an Indian boarding school at Fort Shaw, and she occasionally cooked for Joe Kipp, whose trading post was the chief business in Blackfoot. Her extended family lived on the Two Medicine River about thirty miles south.

Lockhart expected a ranch house, perhaps infected by bedbugs, as a previous place she had stayed on this trip had been. She was shocked to ride up to a field dotted with Indian lodges. ("Do they live—that is—I mean—are they camping out?" she asked Jennie.) Lockhart slept with a dozen other people in a tepee and attended a feast where she reluctantly ate several pieces of meat she couldn't identify.

It was just the sort of exotic adventure Lockhart had been hoping for, and she made the most of it in another set of articles and stories written when she returned to Philadelphia. Now Lockhart, with her western upbringing and journalism training, could counter the wild western stories she'd critiqued as far back as her 1895 article on Buffalo Bill. Indians were alive and well and living in tepees, and that was proof enough to Lockhart that Montana was still a wild frontier.

But even more than the adventure, she seemed taken with her guide. Lockhart wrote of LaMott: "She uses the best of English and knows more about the latest styles according to the fashion books than I do. She is beautiful in her dusky way. Her coal black hair falls to her waist. When excited her cheeks crimson and her black eyes shine like stars. Her teeth are beautifully white, and, with her cigarette between her red lips, . . . [and] a Mexican sash about her waist, she is a picture to fill an artist with delight."

LaMott later married, bore two children, suffered from tuberculosis, and became known in her community as an expert in healing herbs, gardening, and cooking. She died in 1946, and there is no record that she and Lockhart ever spoke or wrote again after their horseback trip to see LaMott's grandmother. But the brief encounter affected Lockhart profoundly. Ten years later her artistry with language would focus the country's delight on a picture of Jennie LaMott.

Lockhart made her trip to Montana in the summer and fall of 1901. She published stories and essays about it in 1902. But the next logical step, publication of a book or at least another trip West, didn't materialize. Lockhart remained in Philadelphia, writing for newspapers and magazines, until 1904. What went wrong?

In all likelihood, writing a novel proved more difficult than she expected. (Her diaries for the time no longer exist, so we can't say for sure.) Plotting had never been her strong point—she'd always just had adventures and written them down. Her short fiction from this era is generally melodramatic and draws its power not from plot but from dialogue, characterizations, and descriptions of landscape. For example, the 1902 story "Straight as a String" features a Montana prospector named McNeal pining after his wife in Massachusetts. Wintering at Iceberg Lake, getting his claim in good shape to sell so he can return to the East, McNeal repeats to himself that his wife is smart, educated, straight as a string. She'll stick with him. So when she writes that she's going away with someone else, he vows to return immediately to save the marriage. He must hurry across the plains to the town of Blackfoot to catch the train, but he gets caught in a blizzard. He doesn't make it. At the end of the story, his "dog licked his cold face and howled, then the dog and the pony wandered off together for shelter under a willow in a nearby coulee, and the snow covered McNeal, who slept to wake no more."

To some extent, Lockhart's lame plots worked in her favor. Almost all women writers of the time were pigeonholed as "popular" novelists, generating contrived, melodramatic fluff for an audience consisting entirely of women. The analogous situation today might be if all women writers were pigeonholed as Harlequin-style romance novelists—the formula is potentially lucrative to those willing to follow it, but horribly restrictive to anybody who wants to do something else. Lockhart's problem was that she wanted to do something else.

In this regard she resembled literary novelists such as Edith Wharton and Willa Cather, who sought to get out of the "woman writer" trap by becoming self-consciously highbrow. They made a firm break with sentimental contrivance, instead emphasizing their literary professionalism. But then again Lockhart didn't quite resemble these novelists, because Lockhart—whose surviving papers never mention Wharton or Cather—had ambition of a different sort. She had no interest in the highbrow New York literary scene. She had no problem with contrivance or sentimentality—she just didn't want to write it for the female audience of formula "popular fiction." She wanted to write action-filled male adventure stories in realistic frontier settings, featuring strong-willed western heroines like herself.

Lockhart apparently had few writer friends to advise her. She was still close to Andrew McKenzie, the journalist-adventurer, but he had no better understanding of the literary game than she. She never maintained any close female friendships, and her other boyfriends of the time—the music box salesman Jack Painter and Philadelphia district attorney Harry Scott—weren't into literature either. She did develop a lifelong working relationship with a *Lippincott's* editor named J. Berg Esenwein, but in later years she lamented the lack of guidance she'd received early in her writing career.

She faced another obstacle as well. This frontier she so loved, where she wanted to set her adventures, was disappearing. In 1893 the historian Frederick Jackson Turner had declared that the frontier was now closed, the West settled, nature vanquished, a long period of American history done. Turner used census data to prove his point, but you could see it in other developments as well. Indians (including LaMott's family) were everywhere confined to reservations. Western cities such as Butte and Denver were as urban as anywhere in the East. Large cattle ranches had been decimated by the winter of 1887-88, and with them went any notion that the West could develop in a unique way. In the Turnerian view, the West would fill up with small farmers just like the East and Midwest had; its forests would be tamed just like Elkhorn Grove had; its economies would mature just like Sterling and Topeka had. Thirty years previously Joe Lockhart had been able to escape to Kansas when it was still frontier. But now civilization was catching up to his daughter. How could she write a book called "The Cowboy Girl"— how could she *be* a cowboy girl—after the end of the frontier?

⤳

The following note appeared in a Cody, Wyoming, newspaper in October 1904: "Miss Lockhart, who has recently resigned from the staff of the Philadelphia *Bulletin* and *Press*, and who is now interested in general literary work, contributing to *The Century* and *Lippincott's* magazines, is in Cody for several weeks stay."

The clipping suggests Lockhart's celebrity, though it provides no explanation as to what has brought her back West. But farther down the page is a pretty good hint. "Mr. A. C. McKenzie, formerly editor of the Sunday edition of the *New York Press*, who has been in Wyoming for several months, is now trying tent life on the Irma grounds."

In later years Lockhart never sufficiently explained how she got to Cody. She wouldn't mention McKenzie, either out of fear of scandal or to emphasize her own independence. She eventually started claiming that she had come because she admired Buffalo Bill, even claiming that they had become fast friends during her Boston interview. But she and the showman were little better than acquaintances.

McKenzie had come in hopes that Cody's hot springs would aid his health. It's likely Lockhart came to visit him and did not necessarily plan to stay. In Kansas the following April, she told a reporter she'd "spent the winter" in Cody, as if she might spend the summer somewhere else. But Cody had become her permanent home.

At age thirty-three, Lockhart still had a fine figure, buxom yet slim waisted. Her gold-burnished hair caught the sun; her intelligent eyes watched the people watching her. She first arrived in Cody by train, taking a four-horse stage from the station to town.

Cody was a dusty, nearly treeless burg centered around the Irma Hotel, "Buffalo Bill's Hotel in the Rockies," named after the showman's daughter. Buffalo Bill's imprint was all over his namesake town: he owned the Cody Trading Company, a livery stable, and the *Enterprise* newspaper. He owned two large ranches in the cattle country south of town and two resorts (the Wapiti Inn and Pahaska Tepee Lodge) on the road west to Yellowstone. His friends and business associates had platted and built the town and owned the irrigation company that provided its reason for existence.

A surveying party in 1895 had looked into damming the Stinkingwater River in a narrow canyon above Cody, using the water to irrigate land for many miles downstream. Irrigation was part of the maturing frontier economy: rather than merely letting cattle graze, you could apply labor and technology to make the land bloom. An 1894 federal law, the Carey Act, encouraged such irrigation systems by providing free land to the companies that built them. Buffalo Bill's son-in-law, who'd been part of that surveying party, soon convinced the showman to invest in the Stinkingwater scheme.

Cody's first building was constructed in 1896, the railroad arrived in 1901, and the Irma opened in 1902. That same year the Stinkingwater was renamed the Shoshone so as to better entice farmers and tourists. By the time Lockhart arrived in 1904, the town had boomed to several hundred residents. It had the Irma and another hotel at the DeMaris Hot Springs, a lumber company, two bakeries, a hardware store, drug store, horseshoer, taxidermist, train station, and thirteen saloons. But there wasn't much female commerce unless you counted the whorehouse. The Ladies Emporium was run by a woman named Poker Nell, a former card dealer with a diamond embedded in her front tooth. Along the four dirt blocks of the main street, a lady generally walked on the north side. (And if in the dirt, mud, slush, and horse droppings she wore a long, sweeping skirt, she did so at her own peril.) The south side, with its male-only saloons and gambling halls, was not really safe.

Lockhart later described Cody as "a typically frontier town with board sidewalks, hitching racks, kerosene lamps on the two blocks of main street, [and] stores with false fronts." Encountering that description today, we might forget how unique that situation was in 1904. As the West entered a new century of progress—paved streets and sidewalks, automobiles, electric lights, and buildings with genuine second stories—there were few "typically frontier" towns left. Lockhart's description suggests her delight at finding one.

Though the town itself was new, cattle ranches had dotted nearby mountain valleys for more than twenty years. The folks who had worked those ranches possessed the same sort of veteran outdoor wisdom Lockhart had admired in Sourdough Sam. Furthermore, because the town was new and still retaining that "frontier" character, it (like Altyn) attracted romantics and adventurers. As other cities in the West followed their apparently inevitable path toward civilization, Cody attracted a subculture of people who wanted to get off that fast track. There were old sourdoughs, sheepherders, prospectors, unemployed cowboys, drunks, and various other social misfits, some of whom might even be called borderline outlaws.

"I like this country," Lockhart said a few years later, explaining why she stayed, "the mountains and the sagebrush plains, the stimulating air, and the amusing episodes of the town." Furthermore, she liked those characters and set out to capture them on paper.

In October 1905—one year after arriving—Lockhart purchased a house. One block north and half a block west of the Irma Hotel, it was a white wood frame house on a stone foundation. A shallow porch trimmed the front, with a door in the middle and a window on each side. From the porch, Rattlesnake Mountain marked the bright western sky.

Andrew McKenzie moved on. In 1907 he sent Lockhart a postcard from Las Cruces, New Mexico. In 1908, in Guadalajara, Mexico, he finally succumbed to his illnesses, dying at the age of thirty-seven.

But Lockhart stayed and wrote. "Suzette Tells about the Man Hunt and Hold Up at Cody" says the headline on her piece in November 1904, just a month after arriving. It describes the middle of a sleepy afternoon, when two men ride into town and hold up the Wall Bank, across the street from the Irma. The cashier, Ira Middaugh, is killed, and the outlaws escape to the south, pursued by a quickly organized posse.

Here was news of the "real West"—and it followed the legends of dime novels. Holdups, outlaws, posses, manhunts: most writers waited a lifetime for such events. *Century* magazine had once asked a veteran western correspondent to draw a picture of a posse, and received this response: "The artist, in the course of many rides over these mountain pastures, by daylight or twilight or moonrise, has never yet encountered anything so sensational as a troop of armed men on the track of a criminal." But in Cody, Lockhart hit the jackpot as soon as she arrived.

Lockhart's story uses the names of real people, including Middaugh, Judge and Mrs. Wall, Mayor Jakie Schwoob, and town cofounder George Beck. She had probably already met all of these individuals and may have believed she was having some lighthearted fun with them. But her humor bites hard. She describes the "fearless Colonel of the Forest Rangers" who hides behind a radiator and an Englishman who hides behind a safe but says that he is "merely guarding it." The clerk of the Irma "leaped nimbly over the office desk and leaped nimbly back." Two other men run out of the bank "like two jackrabbits" while several bystanders, including a dentist and the judge's wife, grab guns and start shooting wildly. Schwoob yells, "Five hundred dollars, boys, dead or alive!" and Beck counters, "Two hundred and fifty more!" Another two thousand dollars soon comes into the pot, but, Lockhart concludes, "the Codyites will have to ride faster and shoot truer than they do at present to get it."

She doesn't ridicule everybody. Her chief targets are cowards and blowhards in positions of power. She sketches other portraits that merely provide local color. Thus, in passing she mentions Frances Lane, "the little woman doctor, who puts into place the broken bones of the cowboys and ranchmen for a hundred miles around." Trying to reach the injured Middaugh, Lane scurries through the crossfire, "ducking bullets like a sage hen."

Within a few months the satirist Lockhart struck again. "Suzette Goes on a Hunt with Buffalo Bill," says the headline in the *Philadelphia Press*. The article again mentions the bank robbery, and then summarizes Buffalo Bill's hunting expedition: "Thirty men hunted ten days, with the following result: Elk: 0. Bear: 0. Deer: 0. Mountain sheep: 0. Mountain goats: 0. Wildcats: 0. Mountain lions: 0. Wolves: 0. Coyotes: 0. Snowshoe rabbits: 0. Pack rats (rooked and clubbed): 13." It then describes the night of

Buffalo Bill's Thanksgiving ball, when a man is shot in the leg and Dr. Lane, in an evening gown and engaged for the next waltz, sends regrets that she cannot pull out the bullet.

Again Lockhart is mixing fact and fiction to make her stories both "better" and "more western." For example, despite the headline, she was not actually *on* the hunt; furthermore, the reference to the robbery seems an overly forced attempt to make the village feel as lively as something in a dime novel. However, this story also shows her great humor and timing. Indeed, she's willing to mock the hunting skills of the great Buffalo Bill. Readers in Philadelphia must have loved it, and Cody old-timers may have as well (there's evidence that several saw Buffalo Bill as a drunk, womanizer, and fraud). But the showman had a loyal entourage that did not like to see any chinks in their hero's armor.

Lockhart especially enjoyed telling tales of progress through the eyes of old-timers skeptical of change. She mocked them, but with affection. For example, she told the story of "When Autymobile Struck Town" (as well as several others) through two semifictional characters: bartender "Mine Albert" Heimer and his customer, the Old Cattleman of the Southfork.

"Cody has gone plumb to the dogs," says the Old Cattleman, plucking an icicle from his overhanging eyebrow. "I just met something I take for an autymobile as I was comin' up the street, and my cayuse clum a telegraft pole. It took thirty minutes' coaxin' with a pair of spurs to git him down."

Albert comments on the size of the Cattleman's spurs ("I thought they was phonygraph records") and summarizes the havoc caused by the car's first trip down Cody's streets.

The Cattleman asks of the new contraption, "Do it come under the head of furniture and stay in the house, or is it livestock and boards at the livery stable?"

The two characters allow Lockhart to indulge in her talent for capturing accents. They also allow her to conflate her images of old-timers in Cody and Altyn into a near-mythic Old West character. The Old Cattleman says,

It were a mercy that Two-Dog Jack and Sour-Dough-Sam were took off to their everlastin' punishment by that rise in the crick before they lived to see a autymobile whoopin' down the streets of Cody. 'Twould a broke their hearts to see what the old town is comin' to. . . . 'Twant half a dozen years ago that we used to ride into Red's place of a Sab-

bath afternoon, four abreast, and shoot holes in the ceilin' in our innocent glee; and now females, with high foreheads and purposes, is gallo-
pin' from house to house with petitions to close up the dancehalls and
stop gamblin'. The church bells is a ringin' of a Sunday and a proces-
sion of hard biled hats and biled shirts goes trompin' off to church.

She had put her finger on (and in this example surely exaggerated) the
key element of western literature: the clash between frontier and progress,
adventure and civilization, taverns and churches. But it wasn't just literature: this was her life.

Finally Lockhart had a horse of her own, and country to ride in. One of her
riding friends was Daisy Beck, the wife of town cofounder George Beck.
Four years younger than Lockhart, Daisy had come west as a ten-year-old
orphan in the mid-1880s. A slim, dark-haired woman, she was an outstanding rider; her beauty atop a horse had been what attracted her husband. The
Becks worked together at the irrigation company, oversaw a three-story sand-
stone mansion in town, and loved to camp in the mountains. Another companion was Frances Lane, the lady doctor. Riding, sometimes on multiday
pack trips, was a popular pastime for Cody women who could afford a horse
and time off. In 1906 Lockhart and two other women took a long trip south
and east through Thermopolis, Shoshoni, Copper Mountain, Lost Cabin,
Jackpot Ranch, Hole-in-the-Wall, Tensleep, and Hyattville. They crossed
the Big Horn Mountains and swam their ponies across raging Owl Creek.
Both Thermopolis and Hole-in-the-Wall were notorious outlaw hangouts,
good for another set of exotic locations for Lockhart's stories.

Sadly, Lockhart's diaries for this period no longer exist, and we have to
imagine the delight with which the writer took to her new western life. In
these first years she was quite popular in Cody, apparently worshiped by
men and women alike. A glimpse comes from an outside observer, a college kid named Bill Leaphart, one of the first individuals to go from Cody
into Yellowstone on a bicycle. He wrote in his diary that he'd seen a group
of women on horseback west of Cody. "They are all pretty good riders and
don't hesitate to pass the time of day with you in pleasant fashion. One of
the ladies, we met this morning. Mrs. Thompson [the innkeeper at Wapiti]
said she is a fairly well-known writer of stories of a certain sort. Her name
is Lockhart. Gee, but was she pretty! Mrs. Thompson was muchly stuck

on Western women and Western ways; especially in the way they did their own work and their independence combined with their friendliness for each other. For instance, she was short of help at the Inn and Miss Lockhart, the night she was there, helped her with the dishes."

When Lockhart wasn't riding, she was writing. Over her first six years in Cody, she published almost twenty short stories in national magazines. The stories were generally humorous and domestic, set in the West but featuring more romance than violence, with sharply drawn, unusual characters. For example, in "The Second Star: A Mormon Story," a Mormon woman urges her husband to take a second wife so that she "will have a second star in heaven like the bishop said."

> "Maybe Esther won't have me," broke in Cropsey, grasping at straws.
> A swift rage leaped into Mrs. Cropsey's hard, gray eyes. "What!" she shouted. "That holler-chested, pie-faced thing, with teeth like a wood-rat's and a hump like a buffalo-gnat, not have you?"

He finally relents, and when he returns from Esther's, he finds his wife praying: she wants that star, but she dislikes Esther, and "Cropsey wouldn't be nothin' to her, and he's everything to me!" Since Esther has rejected him and he only ever wanted one wife anyway, they live happily ever after.

Today we see the story's prejudice, especially knowing that by its 1905 publication the Mormon church had long disavowed polygamy. But the subject was of continuing fascination to eastern readers, and despite the scornful humor, Lockhart's characters gain some dignity when they are redeemed by love.

That story is set in southern Alberta, fitting a literary trend known as "local color," which sought to provide intimate details about exotic settings. As a local-colorist, Lockhart set some of her stories in Cody and others in obvious fictional stand-ins for Cody, such as "Beartooth" or "Wind River City," Wyoming. She also returned to places she'd written about before, such as New Mexico and Altyn. Even if she'd only visited a place, she usually retained enough of a vision of its landscape to put lots of specifics in her stories. In a time when people did little traveling, such specifics were what readers craved.

It's difficult to judge today how popular the stories were, except to note that the publishing opportunities kept coming. Lockhart gradually evolved from newspaper sketches to magazine fiction, with at least two appearances in *Century*, which was in the nation's top two or three magazines, and at least one in *McClure's*, where stories by O. Henry and Willa Cather also appeared. In other words, Lockhart made it into the nation's most successful general-circulation magazines, rather than merely the women's magazines, and she did so writing about women.

For example, "Doc's Beau" stars a female doctor in the small-town West who idealizes her absent eastern boyfriend. But when Mr. Stotesbury finally arrives, he finds both Doc and the town far too unrefined. She's not receptive to his ideas of improvement, nor he to hers. "When Doc finally saw Mr. Stotesbury dressed according to her taste she realized that she had considerably overestimated the power of clothes." So she dumps him in favor of a well-bred but more earthy and outdoorsy local man.

"The Woman Who Gave No Quarter" also features a western woman who is neither schoolmarm, farm wife, nor whore. Bronco Bess, a single mother, breaks and sells horses for a living but holds herself back from society. She harbors an odd hatred for the new schoolteacher, a married man who can't quite bring himself to flunk Bess's daughter out of school. We eventually learn that he is her husband, who abandoned her on a Nebraska homestead years before. In a role that most authors would have saved for a man, Bess dies saving a runaway wagon full of schoolkids, and in her last breath asks the teacher to treat her daughter "as your own."

As that summary suggests, Lockhart's stories were still marred by clichés and contrivances. (That was common for local-color fiction. Even female authors usually contrived happy endings in which the heroine married a dominating man.) But humor abounded. In "His Own Medicine," a bartender and supposed bad man cynically advises lovelorn cowboys—until his wife shows up to henpeck him. In "The Pin-Head," Lockhart summarizes one character this way: "If Harrison had had a brain to educate, he would have been a man of some learning; as it was, he had only a vocabulary." In "The Dude Wrangler," a garrulous westerner brings in ten eastern vacationers, nine of whom eventually abandon him as ignorant and useless. But one overweight spinster decides to marry him, and the story concludes with him launching into a typical monologue: "I'll sell this dudin'-outfit and go in for sheep. I can wrangle sheep to a fare-ye-well. We'll buy a ranch on the Graybull and then—"

Despite McKenzie's departure, Lockhart in Cody had an active love life. She was linked to Harry Thurston, Cody's first federal forest supervisor, but in 1906 he jilted her and married another woman. That same year Jack Painter, the Philadelphian who had moved his family to the remote Sunlight Basin area northwest of Cody, purchased a house in town—adjacent to Lockhart's. But any affair with Painter must have been off and on, because Lockhart was soon also linked to a man named Smith.

John L. Smith was bigger than any one nickname. "Red-Eyed" Smith, "Two-Gun" Smith, or (because he was once married to a Crow woman) "Squaw" Smith, he'd come to the West in 1878. Just two years after Custer's defeat, Smith settled in southern Montana not far from the Little Bighorn. He had frontier skills—he hunted and trapped—and old-timers described him as a "man of nerve." Soon the city of Billings sprouted around him, and he served as a deputy sheriff between 1887 and 1893. But he also had a frontier temperament: he was nomadic and violent. In 1897 or 1898 he'd shot a Billings man in a quarrel, though authorities hadn't prosecuted. Soon, like many frontier characters, he made his way to Cody.

Cleaned up for a photograph, he looks the camera straight in the eye. He's a big man: tall, broad, with a bushy gray beard to match. A tall, narrow-brimmed hat, slightly askew, accentuates his height. His teeth are surprisingly white. His expression is curious and thoughtful, if not necessarily intelligent.

Later, after their romance was over and she was writing a sketch for an eastern publication, Lockhart gave this description: "Smith is somewhere near six feet tall, with a rather formidable breadth and thickness of shoulder, and like the South American animal whose ugliness is its defense, Smith's best protection is his face, though he habitually packs a gun in a holster under his arm." She calls him "the local Bad Man," because a "Bad Man" was what he called himself.

"I never packs a gun fer looks," she has him say. "I'm no yeller-back, and I can handle the iron some. I made Livereatin' Johnson squeak, and the way I shot up Chiny Clark's nephew over in Muntany didn't trouble me." With a four-horse team, he hauls logs to the dam site, driving through the canyon where Italian immigrants are building a road. "Guess I'll have to drive over a few of them dagoes," he says. "I'm one of the most notorious dago wranglers that ever jumped up, and I can wrangle railroad hoboes to a fare-ye-well. I'll do any old thing. I'm a game one. I'm a killer—me, Smith!"

Did she enlarge his alleged badness, either out of spite at the end of the relationship or because it better fit the dime novel legends? Evidence suggests Smith indeed lacked morals—years later in Billings he killed an unarmed man and pled self-defense. He himself may well have been a romantic who had read dime novels and decided to act them out, but choosing the villain's role. Furthermore, that "badness"—along with old-time frontier wisdom and a brash masculinity—may have been what attracted Lockhart in the first place. It was only in hindsight that she decided to ridicule him. The highlight of her sketch comes when the tiniest of the Italian immigrants throws a rock at him, and Smith runs away, saved only by the noon whistle calling the Italians to dinner.

She may have found this character bigger than any one sketch. Or she may have decided that she'd had great fun doing it, combining writing with revenge. Whatever the motivation, by about 1910 she set aside her continual struggles with "The Cowboy Girl" and finally hammered her way to a novel-length plot featuring her ex-boyfriend. She titled it after his refrain "Me—Smith!"

⤳

Me-Smith was serialized in the *New York World*, Nellie Bly's old paper. It was the Lippincott publishing house's lead spring title for 1911. It was reviewed, and made best-seller lists, all over the country. Caroline Lockhart's first published novel brought immediate success.

In the first chapter of the book, a drifter named Smith "trades" horses with a dude while holding him at gunpoint, and then shoots an Indian in the back to steal his blanket. He boasts, "I'm a killer, me—Smith!" and heads for a nearby ranch owned by a widowed Indian woman. On the way he runs into a visiting archaeologist and his driver, stuck in a mud hole. To their rescue, as Smith watches, comes a girl on a galloping horse: "She sat her sturdy, spirited pony like a cowboy. She was about sixteen, with a suggestion of boyishness in her appearance. Her brown hair, worn in a single braid, was bleached to a lighter shade on top, as if she rode always with bared head. Her eyes were gray, in curious contrast to a tawny skin." With no help from Smith, the girl, named Susie MacDonald, orchestrates a rescue from the mud hole, bossing around the driver Tubbs in a way that gives him confidence in her skill. Then she turns to Smith and asks dryly, "Awful tired, ain't you, Mister?"

Their conversation has the spark and wit of banter, except that on her side it is fueled by instant hatred. She implies that he is a Missourian and a sheepherder—both, Lockhart informs us, terrible insults. They continue:

"Say, girl, can you tell me where I can find that fat Injun woman's tepee who lives around here?"

"You mean my mother?"

He looked at her with new interest.

"Does she live in a log cabin on a crick?"

"She did about an hour ago."

"Is your mother a widder?"

"Lookin' for widders?"

"I likes widders. It happens frequent that widders are sociable inclined—especially if they are hard up."

So Smith invades Susie's house, along with the archaeologist Peter, whom she likes. Through the rest of the book, Smith tries to marry and/or swindle the widow, rustle all the area cattle, and pin the murder and rustling on Peter.

Reviewers loved it. The *New York Times* wrote, "The author has humor and dramatic force, an infallible ear for local vernacular and a keen eye for types. As a delineation of western life at once realistic and picturesque, it compares favorably with Mr. Wister's 'the Virginian.'" The *New York Globe* elaborated on what made *Me-Smith* better: "It is a story of a cowboy who is not a college graduate, and who, moreover, is not in the end reformed and refined by a woman's love."

Owen Wister's *The Virginian* was indeed the standard against which stories of the West had to be judged. Published in 1902, it was a huge national best seller that was also admired by critics. Wister invented an entire genre.

A well-born Philadelphia lawyer, Wister had gone west for his health. He'd fallen in love with Wyoming's vanishing cattle culture, and the young men who worked that open range. In this book he gave those cowpunchers the traits of classical mythic heroes such as King Arthur. The Virginian, handsome and virile, is a natural aristocrat who happened to have been born poor and who overcomes that obstacle by proving himself through acts of managerial expertise as well as physical and moral courage. (Ironically, such fulfillments of the requirements of myth leave the Virginian little time for roping, branding, or dehorning—the more typical activities of genuine cowboys.) He has a strong sense of honor and eventually must act on it through a gunfight, the ultimate test of manhood.

That tie between masculinity and violence mirrored a cultural trend embodied by Wister's friend Teddy Roosevelt. Previously, Victorians had equated manhood with restraint, sobriety, self-denial, and respectability. Roosevelt, however, built his reputation as a tough, straight-talking man of the people by emphasizing his wilderness exploits on a North Dakota ranch. The Rooseveltian man, increasingly celebrated in a school of literature known as "red-blooded realism," was strong and adventuresome rather than domestic or idealistic. Roosevelt was also a social Darwinist, believing that only the fittest would be able to survive such adventures, and only the well bred would have that fitness. (Wister fudged a bit on the social Darwinist formula by making his Virginian a "natural" aristocrat even though he couldn't trace his breeding, a move that probably helped his sales to the masses.) Like Jack London's heroes in Alaska, and like Edgar Rice Burroughs's Tarzan in Africa, the Virginian showed superior character triumphing over wilderness and savagery.

The Virginian also tapped into nostalgia over the closing frontier. Wister equated the *frontier* (previously defined as any border between wilderness and civilization) with open range cattle drives. (There are few Indians in Wister's work, few miners, loggers, or even stock dealers.) Though the West was a varied place, Wister encapsulated it in the cowboy. He thus put a human face on Turner's thesis: the frontier was over because the open range had passed; its evolution into "civilization" was, if inevitable, nevertheless tragic.

None of this was exactly true: the open-range cattle system, always economically marginal, failed due to overgrazing and the terrible winter of 1887-88 rather than the encroachment of homesteaders or arrival of civilizing women; cowboys were not necessarily more honorable than miners, lawyers, or factory workers; and the gunfight sprung from the novelist's imagination as a stylized way to conclude a mythic conflict. Nevertheless, it was all quite powerful. Soon large numbers of less-talented authors were churning out stories of natural-aristocrat cowboys polished to their true potential by the civilizing influences of education and love.

What readers loved about *Me-Smith*, then, was that its cowboy hero was irredeemable. Throughout the book Smith continually does horrible things, and each time readers who'd grown sick of facile cowboy fables swooned with delight.

Lockhart played to these expectations with a subplot involving a school-marm who becomes another target for Smith's (and the other cowboys') amorous advances. Dora, product of "the limited experiences of a small, Middle West town," careens all over the place: attracted to Smith in hopes of reforming him; attracted to the courage and looks of the fast-drawing but dim-witted cowboy Babe Britt; and attracted to the tall, golden-tongued deputy Dick Ralston, who comes to investigate the rustling.

The deputy's visit interrupts a scene where Dora tries to teach Smith grammar. It's not successful; Smith tells her, "Say, I can tie a fancy knot in a bridle-rein that can't be beat by any puncher in the country, but *darn* me if I can see the difference between a adjective and one of these here adverbs!" Nor does she get far with Tubbs, who confuses prepositions with mining propositions. Nor does Peter, the eastern scientist, succeed in a later effort to teach the cowboys about evolution ("Look here, Doc, if that's so why ain't all these ponds and cricks around here a-hatchin' out children?") or the science of phrenology, in which the shape of Tubbs's skull should indicate his personality characteristics ("That's where a mule kicked me and put his laig out of joint").

Lockhart's humor, then, comes from a contrast of East and West where both deserve to be mocked. She pokes fun at Peter's big words, such as when he defines evolution as a passage "from an indefinite heterogeneity to a definite, incoherent heterogeneity." What's the use of such education, or of Dora's grammar, in a world where Smith "judged by the standards of the plains: namely, gameness, skill, resourcefulness"? Lockhart's affection for the place-based knowledge of the uneducated creates not only the humor but also a meaningful tension throughout the book. Whatever his faults, Smith has those plainsman's skills. His heroic courage is evidenced by the final line of the book: "Tell *her*, you damned Injuns—tell the Schoolmarm I died game, me—Smith!"

Other reviewers rejoiced at the relative realism of the characters and plot— again in contrast to the many dime novels and imitation-*Virginians* that had come to define writing about the West. One wrote, "In fiction that country has been almost absurdly melodramatized. It may have been the romantic Bret Harte who sowed the first seeds of misrepresentation." But Lockhart, he said, was different. She was real, and she represented the West the way it really was. (Though the anonymous reviewer for the New York–based publication gave no indication of how he knew what was authentic.) Another suggested that the characters were actually quite stereotypical—Susie wild but good hearted, Smith a killer, Ralston handsomely heroic, the cowboys ingenuous. "However," he concluded, "in some wonderful way, Caroline Lockhart has evolved a story that holds one's interest, that fascinates, that is different."

Today we can be especially appreciative of Susie. This cowboy girl is not limited to feats of sharpshooting, like Annie Oakley, nor even to horsemanship. She entraps Smith in his own rustling scheme, playing her part so well that he never suspects. ("Hatin' makes you smart," she explains to Ralston, "and I hate Smith so hard I can't sleep nights.") Furthermore, as a half-Sioux, she is one of the first female mixed-blood heroes in American literature. And at the end of the book, by happy contrivance, Peter turns out to be a long-lost uncle who offers to board her while she attends school in the East. The heroine thus achieves her happiness not through marriage to a dominant man, but education.

At the time, however, reviewers noted not so much the gender of the hero as the gender of the author. The *New York Tribune* wrote, "It is worth noticing that this story is the work of a woman, for it deals with a phase of frontier life that has hitherto been practically monopolized by American writers of the other sex."

In fact, there was at least one other writer of that sex successfully covering this territory. Bertha Muzzy Bower had been born in Minnesota in 1871, the same year as Lockhart. At age eighteen Bower moved to Big Sandy, Montana, where she worked as a schoolteacher and got married. She started writing in 1900 to earn enough money to get divorced. In 1904 she published her first short story, in *Lippincott's*. Later that year she published another story about a cowboy named Chip who lived on a Montana ranch called the Flying U.

That led to Bower's first novel, *Chip of the Flying U*, published in 1905 and also favorably compared to *The Virginian*. (The comparisons always went one way: critics never compared works with Lockhart's or Bower's.) It was a much more domestic novel than Wister's, with no rustling or killing. In fact, in his spare time Chip painted landscape scenes. He may have been based on cowboy artist Charlie Russell, who was a neighbor of Bower and provided illustrations for the book.

Chip of the Flying U was the first cowboy character since the Virginian to achieve national celebrity. Bower quickly grasped the value of her franchise and wrote numerous sequels (she would eventually publish sixty-seven books in a thirty-five-year career). Her Flying U was a big happy family, and plot developments typically centered on weather and horses rather than shootouts. Bower included plenty of female characters, mostly ranchers, cooks, and boardinghouse keepers; when Bower tried to write delicate heroines, she was generally less successful. But she was empowered by her intimate knowledge of the Montana plains landscape, which she skillfully incorporated into her narratives.

But in contrast to Lockhart, most people didn't know Bower was a woman. She wrote under the name B. M. Bower, because her publishers believed that sales depended on hiding her gender.

How much sexism existed in publishing at the time? Certainly all aspects of society were more skewed toward males than they are today. Yet, from Harriet Beecher Stowe (*Uncle Tom's Cabin*) to Helen Hunt Jackson (*Ramona*) to Charlotte Perkins Gilman (*Women and Economics*), plenty of feminists had been able to publish works that made an impact in their day. Meanwhile, writers like Kate Chopin and Sarah Orne Jewett achieved income if not literary prestige through their local color stories. Edith Wharton was achieving some literary success, and Willa Cather was on her way. It was not easy for them, but then it's rarely easy for writers of any sex.

When it came to novels of the West, however, the gender issue may have been more acute. Though Owen Wister often gets credit for inventing the western, he arrived long after a woman named Mary Hallock Foote. Trained as an illustrator, Foote had reluctantly gone west with her mining engineer husband in 1876. For the next thirty years, leading magazines published her sketches, stories, and novel excerpts set in the West (and this income often supported her family as her husband suffered financial failures). Her 1883 novel *The Led-Horse Claim* centers on a woman whose brother and lover own competing mines, building to a fatal confrontation. "Maverick" features a shootout on the Idaho plains; like *The Virginian*, this 1894 story is narrated by an educated easterner fascinated by the title character's frontier skills. Another 1894 Foote story, "In Exile," concerns the romance between a cultured girl and a boy of rough manners but high integrity. It was that same year that Foote welcomed Wister to the western-writing scene. She said there were subjects that she couldn't, or shouldn't, write—but a man could.

If Foote's themes sound similar to Wister's, consider Frances McElrath's 1902 novel *The Rustler*. It was a romance of a rugged cowboy and an eastern gentlewoman set against a backdrop based on the events of Wyoming's Johnson County War of 1892. In other words, McElrath covered exactly the same events and themes as *The Virginian*—in a book that came out at the same time and was utterly ignored.

On the one hand, maybe Wister was a better writer than McElrath or Foote or Lockhart, with richer metaphors, better rhythm, deeper characters, and less melodrama. He'd studied the classics at Harvard, whereas the women tended to rely on the "local color" style, emphasizing specifics about exotic locations over characterizations or plot. On the other hand, maybe the women's sex held them from a "legitimacy" that readers insisted on. The red-blooded realism school was all about a hero realistically proving his masculinity. His exploits might mirror those of mythic heroes, but they also had a specificity and currency of landscape, dialogue, and physical action to mark them as authentic. Readers, wanting to validate their own masculinity, wanted these stories to be true. So publishers marketed their authors' legitimacy. For example, *Popular* magazine, the biggest all-fiction magazine in the country, liked to run biographies of its authors that established them as legitimate experts in the subject they were writing about. But since Lockhart and Bower were women, it never did so for them. How could readers accept such a story written by a woman as truth?

There's no indication that Lockhart ever considered writing under a pen name to hide her sex, or that anyone ever asked her to.

For *Me-Smith* at least, there seemed little penalty for it. No reviewers panned the book because it was written by a woman. Instead, her sex gave Lockhart a unique celebrity in the way of one who first crosses a societal boundary. Lippincott distributed a publicity photo of her in Indian dress, with a feather rising from her long braided hair. The *Boston Globe* noted, "Once upon a time, so long ago that it would be unfair to tell, a merry girl by the name of Caroline Lockhart . . . wore the first suit of bicycle bloomers seen in these parts—pretty, light gray bloomers they were, and a quill in her hat. . . . She wrote so well, and did her work of observation and analysis so thoroughly, that it is no surprise now to receive books from her that bear the same characteristics." And the *Denver Times* ran a fawning profile citing her ready smile and describing her writing room decorated with Navajo rugs, leopard skins, Russian wolves, and skins of pythons from the Nile.

Lockhart had become a minor national celebrity, though her taste of fame left her wanting more. Additionally, however, she had found one of her life's great passions. She had settled into a career, if not a domestic life. After all the rewrites of the previous ten years, she had figured out how to do novels— humorous yet realistic novels of cowboys and girls. For the next ten years, that passion would be her avid pursuit.

∽

Lockhart also had interests beyond writing. They'd been occupying her in Cody for several years, during the time she was writing *Me-Smith*. Her interest in local medical care had been spurred by a dramatic accident.

In September 1907 a young Austrian immigrant named Marko Ferko hung from a rope fifty feet in the air. The Shoshone River canyon loomed below him, along with the half-constructed dam that would soon irrigate the farmland for miles around. Ferko was a bright, active kid, the most daring and efficient worker on the dam's high cliff abutments. On this day he was setting a dynamite charge high in one of those cliffs. Then the dynamite exploded before it should have.

The explosion tossed Ferko off the cliff. It practically tore off his thumb, and broke his leg in two places. He landed on the rocks at the bottom of the canyon, except that he didn't really land. A rod had blown through his neck and actually kept his head off the ground. "His escape from instantaneous death was miraculous," a supervisor later said.

Coworkers pulled the rod out of Ferko's neck, bandaged him, took him to a bunkhouse, and called Dr. James Bradbury. What happened next was the source of a good deal of controversy. Ferko and his cousin Martin believed that Bradbury and other doctors provided poor care. They said Bradbury at first claimed the leg wasn't broken, then said he would set it at the hospital. At the hospital, Martin later explained, "I say, 'What about the leg?' and Bradbury say, 'No use troubling with the leg, probably he die by morning.'"

The hospital was run by Bradbury and his medical partner, Dr. Frances

Lane. They had a contract with the federal government—which had taken over dam construction from Buffalo Bill's partnership—to treat injured workers. A dollar a month was deducted from each worker's paycheck to pay the doctors. But were they competent?

Bradbury and Lane failed to ever set, wash, or dress the leg, the Ferkos alleged, and wanted to amputate the entire hand rather than just the thumb. After amputating the thumb, they failed to drain the hand properly. Marko then languished several weeks in the Lane-Bradbury hospital, they said, and his leg became swollen, crooked, black, and very smelly. Bradbury told them it too had to be amputated. Incensed, Martin moved his cousin to a different hospital, but he was too late. Because of infection, the other doctor indeed had to amputate the hand and leg—due, the Ferkos believed, to Lane-Bradbury's incompetence.

But that was just the Ferkos' view. The frontier was a dangerous place, especially for a lower-class Austrian boy. Seven workers had been killed building the dam; you could argue that Marko was lucky to be alive. Ferko's boss had even visited him in the hospital and found the boy well cared for in a private room. Bradbury later explained that he'd set the leg three times—the first time right there in the canyon, an easy job because Ferko was still in shock—but it just wouldn't heal. Ferko had been paid a high wage precisely because of the danger of the work; luckily his dollar a month had also covered the cost of his medical care.

That was the way most people saw it. Only if you didn't trust Cody's distribution of power might you wonder about the poor kid, alone in a strange country and now maimed for life. You might then wonder why Cody's snobbish society-builders made lots of money administering the dam, while the laborers took all the risks. And if you ventured into the bars on the south side of the main street that served those workingmen, you might hear some other troubling stories suggesting this was not an isolated—or unavoidable—incident.

Lockhart the journalist did exactly that, prodding until she found specific names and cases. She uncovered a vast conspiracy. Folks died in the Lane-Bradbury hospital and were sloughed off to the graveyard as quickly as possible. Ninety percent of the cemetery's burials were from that hospital, though there was at least one other hospital in town. Lane and Bradbury always wanted to amputate rather than set any broken bones: one man went under anesthesia believing his broken arm would be set and woke up to find it amputated above the elbow. Another man, his leg broken when a wagon ran over it, never got the wound properly cleaned; months later "a piece of wool as long and so big as a big darning needle came out of the hole in my leg." A third man spent four months in the hospital but never received adequate treatment; meanwhile the doctors were cashing and keeping his paychecks. A dam employee named Billy Dunn, shot in the arm on the Fourth of July, was refused treatment because his injury wasn't work related. So Dunn's friends raised ninety dollars for his medical treatment, and then found it stolen out of his pillow, with Bradbury allegedly admitting taking some of it. Then the doctors tried to amputate Dunn's arm, botching the job and causing him to bleed to death.

Lockhart got all of the men telling these stories to sign affidavits. That proved they were true, having the stories recorded on paper in their own rough words. She bundled together the affidavits, editing them slightly and providing an introduction, and shipped the package to the *Denver News* to run as an exposé. As a doctor, her introduction said, Lane was incompetent: her medical school, Chicago's Hering College, specialized in homeopathy, which was a widely discredited approach to medicine. But worse than incompetent, Lane was greedy. When the government contract was approved, Lockhart wrote, Lane had exulted, "Well, I've got it. Now—I'm out for the stuff!"

Lockhart later described Frances Lane at the time as "youngish and not ill-looking. Her wide-brimmed Stetson sat at a rakish angle on the side of her head. The shirt-waist she wore was of a mannish cut, as were her stout, square-toed shoes. The only feminine garment was a bedraggled, soiled woolen skirt. She walked with a long stride, put her foot on the brass rail and did not hesitate to ask whoever chanced to be at the bar to buy her a drink." Clearly Lane had the assertiveness necessary for a woman to enter (and succeed in) medicine. She was two years younger than Lockhart, a native of Ohio whose sister was married to one of the dam's engineers. One of three or four doctors in town, she had quickly gained a reputation as one of the best. Her house calls regularly took her to the homes of Cody's wealthier residents, and her hobbies—including horses, tennis, golf, and fishing—regularly took her outdoors with them. She was also civic minded, active in the Cody Club, the Daughters of the American Revolution, and the Cody Women's Club, where she helped found the county library in 1906.

Thus, much of Cody's high society—the women whom both Lockhart and Lane counted as friends—refused to believe Lockhart's accusations. Since most medical care was delivered in the home, many of Lane's patients had never even set foot in the hospital (nor had they fraternized with the lower-class construction workers), so couldn't judge for themselves. They *did* know that there seemed to be some recent bad blood between Lockhart and Lane. The doctor's allies emphasized this personality dispute, suggesting that it, rather than muckraking, was Lockhart's chief motivation.

Mayor Frank Houx and town founder George Beck got wind of Lockhart's proposed *Denver News* article and wrote to the paper to stop it. Their letter said, "Before publishing anything of this nature, especially from her [Lockhart's] pen, please do us the favor to investigate the merits of the article, as we know the hospital is all right, and is run according to the principles of medical etiquette, and is doing a great work in this community. Miss Lockhart's venom is turned against it purely and simply to satisfy a personal spite which she holds towards the managing doctors."

The *News* backed away, refusing to run the story. So Lockhart, the enterprising freelancer, shopped it elsewhere. She succeeded with the *Billings (Montana) Gazette*, which ran it under the byline "a friend." Town leaders complained to the *Gazette* as well and persuaded it to print a retraction.

At one time Lockhart and Lane had been close. They rode horses together. Lockhart wrote stories about female doctors. They even acted together in a minstrel show: photographs survive of them locking umbrellas as if playfully clashing swords, then standing arm in arm. In the photos both wear hats and jackets, with scarves around their necks and long hair tied in a bun. Lane is in a long, dark skirt; Lockhart in white pants. Lockhart is taller, heftier, and shapelier than her companion, wearing a jacket tailored to show off her curves. Neither appears to show particular emotion, either affection or dislike—in the arm-in-arm shot, Lane looks straight ahead at the camera, while Lockhart looks away.

But now they were bitter enemies whose quarrel divided the town. Perhaps feeling abandoned, frustrated that her friends such as Daisy and George Beck supported Lane, furious that such incompetence could be so carelessly ignored, Lockhart decided to make a federal case out of it. Literally.

She wrote to an old friend named John Wilkie, a high-ranking official in the Secret Service division of the federal Treasury Department. Since the dam was a federal project, she reasoned, malpractice among its contractors deserved a thorough investigation.

Wilkie, who had known Lockhart when she was in Philadelphia, wrote back, "I know we all missed you when you dropped out of newspaper work, and I have often wondered where you had found a field for your activities. I felt sure, however, that we should hear from you some day, unless you had been stolen away by some mere man, dropped the pen and flourished in its stead the sceptre usually wielded by the queen of a domestic domain." He encouraged her to send along her story and affidavits.

The resulting investigation further stirred the controversy. Letters went flying back and forth. Ferko's boss wrote to describe the tragedy of Ferko's accident and the valor of his treatment. He noted that Lane was the most popular physician around, Bradbury was competent, and together "they offered the best facilities for treatment and care of the ill and injured, and . . . had the best local reputation for surgical work." The president of one of the construction firms wrote that he had "never yet heard a single complaint from a patient" about medical care. The doctors themselves wrote that previous inquiries into "alleged troubles and dissatisfaction about the hospital . . . have found Caroline Lockhart, a resident of Cody and a newspaper reporter, to be the instigator of the trouble. Because of the personal enmity and malice she has for the managing doctors. We note she is a witness to every signature in those affidavits."

Cody society closed its ranks against Lockhart. The investigation was carried out by local officials, so she felt they were basically investigating themselves. She suspected they were also intimidating witnesses, and the dam workers tended to be transients anyway. They were just laborers, many of them immigrants; they could be ignored or banished. She wrote Wilkie to warn him that the whole thing was a setup, but there was little he could do. In June he returned her material with the report, asking her to read it but not publish it.

She found it a defeat of epic proportions. She felt profoundly humiliated. As she later wrote, "The Reclamation Service whitewashed that pair of murderers and thieves and made me appear ridiculous and malicious. I suppose a keen lawyer could have checked up on them easily enough but I had not the experience nor the money to continue the fight. It left its mark on me, embittered me." She threw the report in the trash. The government had let her down.

Lockhart's crusade mirrored one on the national scale. In 1906 the American Medical Association conducted its first-ever inspection of the country's 160 medical schools, which had never faced any sort of accreditation procedure. It found many of them sorely lacking. Hering College was indeed one of the shabbier institutions of higher medical learning. By 1902 (just two years after Lane's graduation) it had been absorbed into another small college, and in 1917 that school closed as well.

Ferko's main objection, however—and that in most of Lockhart's affidavits—seemed to be the medical skills of Dr. Bradbury, not Dr. Lane. Bradbury had gone to a legitimate medical school. But Lockhart focused on Lane.

A newspaper reported the following February: "Marko Ferko, an Austrian boy, is suing the Lane-Bradbury hospital for $25,000 in damages for an arm and leg, the loss of which he alleges in his petition was due to gross neglect and unskillful treatment. His case will be heard in Sheridan on February 9."

Someone had hooked Ferko up with the Austro-Hungarian consul general in Chicago, who had found him a labor union attorney in Billings to file the lawsuit. The doctors kept trying to postpone the case. But the attorney argued "that witnesses had left the country under suspicious circumstances and others had been tampered with by interested parties, and if the case [was delayed] again it was doubtful if the plaintiff would have any witnesses left."

So the trial was held in Sheridan. And the unnamed reporter filing these stories about it—who seemed to know a great deal about other lawsuits "now in preparations" against the doctors—had a suspiciously familiar-sounding prose style: "For nearly two years a bitter feud has waged between the Lane-Bradbury sympathizers and those who have espoused the cause of the workingmen who were their patients, so the denoument in the Sheridan . . . courts is awaited with more than ordinary interest by the hundreds of people who comprise the two factions."

Lockhart was not the only journalist of the time to so delightedly violate impartiality—in the 1920s H. L. Mencken would similarly engineer and then report on the famous Scopes trial. She was an accomplished and entertaining writer; plenty of papers were willing to run her material. The stories allowed Lockhart the chance to make her case again: to review the affidavits and federal investigation, to refute the contractors' claims that workers had never complained about medical care, and to ridicule Frances Lane.

One midtrial article led off with a quote: "'Yes, we went at night to Waples' yard and dug up Ferko's leg.'" Then it explained what had happened long after Ferko's other doctor had finished the amputation: "Although Dr. Bradbury and Dr. Waples are both elders in the Presbyterian church of Cody, Dr. Bradbury had no hesitancy in admitting that he had trespassed upon the property of his brother elder and had pilfered the amputated leg of Dr. Waples' patient." Apparently as the furor rose, Lane and Bradbury had decided they wanted to look at the limb themselves. The incident may not have been terribly relevant to the lawsuit, but Lockhart knew a juicy tidbit when she heard one. In the story's only quote from Lane's testimony, the lady doc said this:

> "We took a pick and shovel . . . and dug below the frost line to the leg. It was in a sack so we carried it to the hospital and put it under the sidewalk. Then we moved it to Bradbury's coal house and a few days later made an incision in it in Bradbury's bath room."
>
> "Didn't you know you were trespassing?" demanded counsel for plaintiff.
>
> "It wasn't Waples' leg," replied the witness smartly.

By now the hatred between the two women was clear to all. Lane threatened to file a libel suit against Lockhart. She threatened to publish a letter that Lockhart had dropped in the courtroom, saying it was racy and written by a married man. The judge got the message: this fight was between rival doctors and rival hospitals, and most important between a couple of jealous women. He ruled against Ferko.

In later months circulars were distributed asking for money to support Ferko and an appeal. Ferko did get a sixteen-hundred-dollar insurance settlement and moved to Montana, where he lost most of the settlement money. In late 1909 he returned permanently to Austria.

Though she was also writing fiction during the time, Lockhart spent almost two years on her Ferko quest. What exactly had set her off? Why had she turned from self-absorbed essays to investigative journalism, from an elitist cynic to a muckraking friend of the workingman? And why didn't she fight equally for other workers' causes? Ferko wasn't an old-timer, a backwoods savant, or a "bad man," so what did she see in him?

And what on earth did she have against Frances Lane? Lockhart had now tried and failed to indict Lane through her journalism, through the government, and through the courts. But she did not give up. Instead she turned to her most powerful weapon.

Nationally, the hype over the new celebrity female western author continued into 1912, with Lippincott's announcement that Lockhart's new novel would lead its fall list. One quote, probably from the publisher, read, "No author to-day understands the far West better than Miss Lockhart does." Another, placed in a booksellers' magazine as prepublication publicity, said, "The publication this Fall of her new novel, *The Lady Doc*, will more fully establish her reputation as the greatest living writer of Western stories."

But most reviewers disagreed.

When readers of the novel first encounter Dr. Emma Harpe, she is in Nebraska filling out a death certificate:

> Dr. Harpe arose when the certificate was blotted and, thrusting her hands deep in the pockets of her loose, square-cut coat, made a turn or two the length of the office, walking with the long strides of a man. Unexpectedly her pallid, clear-cut features crumpled, the strained muscles relaxed, and she dropped into a chair, her elbows on her knees, her feet wide apart, her face buried in her hands. She was unfeminine even in her tears. . . . Alexander Freoff was away from home. What would he say when he learned that his wife had died of an operation which he had forbidden Dr. Harpe to attempt?

The operation Harpe has botched is not named in the novel, but one critic asserts, convincingly, that it is an abortion. Furthermore, it may be the first abortion to appear in hardcover American fiction, most notably the first performed by a woman.

Harpe's incompetence causes her to be run out of town, and she heads to a western boomtown. "Crowheart was platted on a sagebrush 'bench' on a spur of a branch railroad. The snow-covered peaks of a lofty range rose skyward in the west. To the north was the solitary butte from which the town received its name. To the south was a line of dimpled foothills, while eastward stretched a barren vista of cactus, sand, and sagebrush."

This is a precise description of Cody (the solitary butte is called Heart

Mountain), and not only the landscapes but also nearly all of the characters in the novel are similarly lifted directly from real life. George and Daisy Beck come in for especially vicious satire, but so do Frank Houx, Jakie Schwoob, and even Valentin Di Colonna, one of Lockhart's occasional sweethearts.

Again the humor comes from the clash of cultures, but this time the West is posed against the Midwest. Harpe's arrival in Crowheart symbolizes a transition for the town. Previously it had been wide open and friendly, a place without social stratification: "There were no covert glances of dislike or envy, no shrugs of disdain, no whispered innuendoes. The social lines which breed these things did not exist. Every man considered his neighbor and his neighbor's wife as good as himself and his genuine liking was in his frank glance, his hearty tones, his beaming, friendly smile. . . . Most were young, all were full of life and hope, and the world was far away, that world where clothes and money matter."

But Harpe epitomizes a type of newcomer from the middle class of the Middle West: "They were uninteresting and mediocre, these newcomers, yet the sort who thrive astonishingly upon new soil, who become prosperous and self-important in an atmosphere of equality."

Lockhart delights in mocking the social pretensions of these small-town strivers. The town founder invites people to a dinner based on their social status rather than their kind deeds. His wife, trying to show off her vocabulary in responding to a friend who "has a hankerin' for eggs," says, "We became quite surfeited with eggs, Phidias and I." Dr. Harpe pretends to be a churchgoer, prompting the hotel owner to say, "It makes a good impression upon strangers to come into a town and hear a church bell ringin', even if nobody goes."

Unlike *Me-Smith*, however, this book is almost completely social satire—there's very little violence. Such satire was a growing trend in American literature. Mencken loved it, wrote some of it as nonfiction, and in his book reviews made national stars out of satirists such as Sinclair Lewis. Revolts from the prudishness and snobbery of the American heartland were also central to the work of writers including Cather and Sherwood Anderson.

Lockhart takes it even further than some of those other, more well-known authors. Her Lady Doc is not only incompetent, duplicitous, snobbish, and greedy ("We're going to make money hand over fist," she tells herself). She is not only an abortion provider. She also has some unusual relationships with those of her own sex.

The late Alice Freoff was Harpe's "best friend"; Alexander "had not liked the intimacy between herself and his wife." In Crowheart, Harpe "felt lonely—inexpressibly lonely. She thought of Alice Freoff and the restlessness grew. Downstairs she heard Essie Tisdale's merry laughter and it changed the current of her thoughts." So when the young orphaned waitress knocks on her door, she says, "Come in Essie; I'm lonesome as the deuce!"

But soon a crimson-faced Essie nearly runs over her boss in the hallway. When asked what's the matter, she says, "Don't ask me! but don't expect me to be friends with that woman again!"

Meanwhile "Dr. Harpe was sitting by the window panic-stricken, sick with the fear of the one thing in the world of which she was most afraid, namely, Public Opinion."

Later Harpe deepens her friendship with Gussie Symes, a lowly black-smith's sister whom Harpe had helped to marry the town founder. With new clothes and hairdo Gussie is entering the town's striving class. Paying her a visit, Harpe says this:

> "That's a nifty way you have of doin' your hair and you walk as if you had some gumption. Come here, Gus."
>
> Dr. Harpe pushed her unpinned Stetson to the back of her head with a careless gesture; it was a man's gesture and her strong hand beneath the stiff cuff of her tailored shirtwaist strengthened the impression of masculinity.

Later in the conversation Harpe says this to Gussie:

> "I like women anyhow; men bore me mostly. I had a desperate 'crush' at boarding-school, but she quit me cold when she married. I've taken a great shine to you, Gus; and there's one thing you mustn't forget."
>
> "What's that?" Mrs. Symes asked, smiling.
>
> "I'm jealous—of your Phidias."

One critic argues that Dr. Harpe is "the first unambiguous delineation of a lesbian in hard-cover American fiction." Newspapers and pamphlets had featured homosexuals, and Henry James, Gertrude Stein, and Sarah Orne Jewett had implied ambivalent sexuality in some of their characters. But are these depictions unambiguous? (Or, for that matter, is Harpe's?) Marking any one incident as "the first" is nearly impossible, both because authors of a hundred years ago covered such taboo subjects circumspectly, and because today's literary critics are ingenious at finding symbolism in circumspect narratives. Without making too lengthy a debate, we can say at least that (a) Lockhart intended for readers to understand that Harpe was lesbian or bisexual, and (b) she did so with stronger implications and more obvious code than perhaps any previous American literary figure.

Part of the problem in analyzing this question is that society had not yet settled on a clear definition of homosexuality. Throughout the nineteenth century very fine lines separated friendship from romantic friendship from intimate relationship. Two women might hold hands, kiss, or caress each other (though rarely in front of men)—these "romantic friendships" were usually assumed not to be sexual. Though an act of sodomy was seen as a sin from which a man must repent, there was no comparable standard for women.

This attitude changed with the turn of the century and greater interest in psychology. With a new "more scientific" approach, many people decided that homosexuality must be a disease or a manifestation of a bodily or mental condition. It couldn't be merely a sin or spiritual failing—and so "sinners" became "perverts." Furthermore, if men could be classified as perverts (rather than people who occasionally sinned), then so could women.

Thus, for Lockhart, making Dr. Harpe a lesbian was not necessarily an act of literary ambition. It was one of character assassination, yet another arrow in her quiver to be used against Frances Lane. Dr. Harpe was greedy and duplicitous and an abortion provider and a pervert. And if she was obviously a fictionalization of Dr. Lane, then Lockhart could finally take pleasure in being able to attack her former friend without being constricted by facts or libel laws.

She did her job well—too well. This was precisely the critics' problem: Emma Harpe was such a horrible character that you didn't want to read about her. At least the villain Smith had been a cowboy, with those courageous frontier virtues and an attraction to the schoolmarm. Dr. Harpe was just brutal and sordid. She had no redeeming qualities, and readers especially wanted redeeming qualities in a *female* character. One reviewer called *The Lady Doc* "a disappointing story whose villainess-heroine is only superficially human." Another said, "A more unlovable character than the lady doc has seldom been portrayed . . . the result is something ludicrous and at the same time pitiful." And a third judged, "It is a bad and inhuman book that no plea of art can excuse."

Even the *Philadelphia Press*, Lockhart's part-time employer, was forced to warn readers that this was not the romp they might expect: "This is a very different book from *Me-Smith*. Miss Lockhart is no longer trying to write romantic melodrama. . . . For pitiless realism, yes, for sheer brutality, this book would be hard to match in all the range of American fiction. . . . It is a very strong book, much stronger than one would have expected Miss Lockhart to write. It is also a horrible book; one comes from it as from a physical encounter with a ruffian of the most degraded type. . . . It would almost seem as if Miss Lockhart, who has lived in the West, were taking her revenge on it."

In Cody the novel added to an already hostile atmosphere. "One could get a fight anywhere in town by bringing up the subject of Caroline and Dr. Lane," one historian wrote. Late in her life, obviously overdramatizing, Lockhart compared the situation to the McCoy-Hatfield feud and herself to "a modern Jean d'Arc who had the courage to tell the truth."

Cody newspapers made only brief mention of Lockhart that year. The social notes in both papers in November indicated that Lockhart had returned from traveling. The *Park County Herald*'s note referred to her as "authoress of *Me-Smith* and *The Lady Doc* and several other books of equal popularity." But the competing *Enterprise* did not discuss her career. No surprise: back in March an *Enterprise* editorial noted that "Cody has a decadent journalist," surely referring to Lockhart even though it used the male pronoun for its anonymous target. "In order to even up some old grudges and to turn a few thrifty pennies, he is willing to jeopardize the well being of the town and tear down its institutions. . . . He has already been repudiated in his public work in this city. He should also recognize that his presence is no longer desirable."

Even if it wasn't a public topic, privately Cody residents must have intensified their speculation about the source of the women's feud. Lane never spoke about it. Lockhart had laid it all out—she hated Lane because of the shoddy, greedy medical work on Ferko and others—but the explanation seems wanting. Could outrage at incompetence really drive such fury? *The Lady Doc* proved to be a serious derailment of Lockhart's career. Didn't it have to be caused by something bigger, deeper, more personal? But if so, what?

Seeking answers, Codyites would continue to ponder Lockhart for many years to come. Her behavior presented a real-life puzzle like those in old-fashioned mystery novels: can we determine from her later actions what must have been her motives? There were, certainly, obvious clues. But Lockhart remained silent until her final days—while most of the whispered innuendoes were dead wrong.

Not all reviews of *The Lady Doc* were negative. In fact, the book identified a fault line among literary critics. If the purpose of literature was to entertain, then the book failed because its main character was too unpleasant. But some critics argued that the purpose of literature was not escapism but realism: documenting the daily joys and sorrows of ordinary people, and showing humanity's base animal instincts. (In the case of *The Lady Doc*, a politically minded reviewer could trace the base animal instincts to feminism: once society lets women become doctors and wear cowboy hats, they will become as greedy and sordid as men—and perverts to boot.) The debate had been raging for decades, and in some forms rages still. *The Virginian* represented a turn away from realism, toward entertainment through more mythically resonant plotlines. Most popular critics embraced that turn, and so national reception for *The Lady Doc* may have had as much to do with societal trends as the novel's own merits.

One New York advocate of realism tried valiantly: "*The Lady Doc* I hail as one of the hopeful signs of an awakening of vitality in American fiction. Cowardice, sentimentality, sugared theology, conventionalism, tawdriness—these have long been the elements in our native novels. You will find not a trace of one of them in *The Lady Doc*. It is a vital and brutally faithful bit of realism."

But he was fighting a losing cause. The grand landscapes of the West begged for romantic interpretation. Maybe realism could work in urban settings, but people didn't read western novels to see the ugly underside of humanity. They read for grand, heroic tales. In 1912, the year *The Lady Doc* came out, another story of the West was published by a New York City dentist who'd been transfixed by a vacation in the Southwest. His name was Zane Grey, and the book was *Riders of the Purple Sage*.

Grey's hero, the mysterious Lassiter, first appears silhouetted against the sky:

"He's come from far," said one.
   "Thet's a fine hoss," said another.
   "A strange rider."

"Huh! He wears black leather," added a fourth. . . .

"Look!" hoarsely whispered one of Tull's companions. "He packs two black-butted guns—low down—they're hard to see—black agin them black chaps."

"A gun-man!" whispered another. "Fellers, careful now about movin' your hands."

Lassiter is the ultimate in Rooseveltian manhood, rising mysteriously from the wilderness to wreak honorable vengeance. He treats women with politeness ("'Evenin' ma'am,' he said to Jane, and removed his sombrero with quaint grace") and reverence ("Where I was raised a woman's word was law. I ain't quite outgrown that yet"); he treats men with confidence and certainty. A confrontation in this first chapter kicks off a blockbuster thriller, pulsing with tension and imagery on every page.

It's actually something of a formula, which Grey would eventually apply in more than fifty western novels. The formula features a conspiracy, a revenge-and-rescue plot, and a conclusion of sanctifying violence. It features nostalgic settings of a bygone West and detailed, loving descriptions of landscapes: "the grove of cottonwoods, the old stone house, the amber-tinted water, and the droves of shaggy, dusty horses and mustangs, the sleek, clean-limbed, blooded racers, and the browsing herds of cattle and the lean, sun-browned riders of the sage." Grey's novels are set in many different western states, but like the plots, the settings all boil down to some basic elements: desert, sage, weird rock formations, verdant cottonwood valleys, and lots of horses. Tensions—rustler/cattleman, Indian/white, Mormon/Gentile, and selflessness/individualism—are merely exotic backdrops for a mysterious stranger's righteous vengeance against a powerful conglomerate.

In short, Grey took Wister's concept of putting a King Arthur–style legend in the glorious setting of the American West and polished it to a gleaming perfection. Granted, such a gunfighter story now bore little resemblance to anything that had ever actually happened, but he wasn't writing history. He wasn't interested in realism. He was writing an updated sort of fairy tale, and in the West he'd found a landscape to fit it.

⌒

Riders of the Purple Sage sold more than a million copies in hardcover. Grey hurried to produce a follow-up, as did numerous imitators. Then Lockhart's third novel, *The Full of the Moon*, was published in early 1914. It included the following passage:

> "Let me out! Let me go!" Even with the imperious demand she realized hopelessly that he had no intention of doing either, as he purposely stood between her and the door.
>
> "Where?" He smiled in cynical amusement.
>
> "Somewhere on this ranch there must be a decent man!" she cried furiously.
>
> "My handsome foreman, perhaps?"
>
> "Yes—your foreman, then!" she flashed defiantly.
>
> "My foremen do not interfere in my affairs—new ones are too easy to get."

A wealthy but headstrong twenty-one-year-old easterner named Nan Galbraith has decided to venture to the Southwest alone, telling her family that before getting married and settling down, "I'm going to have my fling first!" But after she accepts the invitation of a rancher to visit his place, he attempts to force himself on her, and as this scene shows, her only hope for escape will be his good-looking cowboy foreman, Ben Evans. Instead, it is a Mexican-Apache mixed-blood woman, known only as Mrs. Gallagher, who interrupts to save Nan. The next morning, as Ben rides toward them in a cloud of dust, Nan figures that he is "coming to her aid. But her elation and relief were short, for he rode past the window without so much as a glance and stopped at the blacksmith-shop, near the men's bunk-house. He was only on an errand, and on one no more romantic and chivalrous than a half-dozen forgotten horseshoes."

Ben Evans may be a Zane Grey–style cowboy, but he's a coward under the thumb of his rich boss. Nan is stunned that this "towering, picturesque, six feet of manhood could not help a girl in her extremity because he might 'lose his job!' Again, Ben Evans, hero, fell from his pedestal with a crash."

The people who drive the action in the first half of this book are females: Nan, Mrs. Gallagher, and an impoverished girl named Edith. Eventually Ben and Bob (Nan's hometown sweetheart, who has followed her west) swing into action, and the evil ranch owner gets his comeuppance, but throughout the novel Lockhart's message is clear: cowboys are eye candy, lacking the substance and breeding to be genuine heroes. Bob, an upper-class easterner, must save Ben from a trumped-up rustling charge and save Edith from a flood in a box canyon. Nan then comes to the realization that "I thought I was in love with [Ben] because I am in love with the life which he typifies," but actually she loves Bob's loyalty and unselfishness. At the end of the book they marry and buy the ranch on which she was once held captive.

Like Teddy Roosevelt and other social Darwinists, Lockhart believed that only upper-class people would succeed in the West. You had to have the right breeding, the sort she knew about from her relatives in Pennsylvania. In *The Full of the Moon*, Bob and Nan have breeding, but Ben is "hopelessly plebian." Ben and Edith can marry and work, perhaps with Bob's backing run a small ranch. But Bob and Nan, who will split their time between East and West, are the true western heroes.

This view was evidenced not only in Lockhart's fiction but also in her life. Lucille Patrick, a Cody historian who knew Lockhart personally, said that Lockhart hated people addressing her as "Caroline" (it had to be "Miss Lockhart"). Though Lockhart had chosen the informality of the West, and a lifestyle that few considered ladylike, she felt she deserved adulation because of her birth and talents. To Patrick, Lockhart's wars with Cody society—including her enmity for Dr. Lane—arose because "she was a snob plain and simple."

Is *The Full of the Moon* the feminist, icon-busting western that critics today wish had been published in 1914? It's tempting to see Lockhart responding to Zane Grey, writing a story of the bygone Southwest with gender roles reversed. In fact, however, this was the New Mexico manuscript Lockhart had been working on for more than a decade (long before Grey had come on the scene), the one she'd first called "The Cowboy Girl" in description of Nan. The title was apparently a cause of great difficulty: for a 1913 copyright it was called "Moonlight," then it changed again before its publication the following February.

The title changes provide fodder for interesting speculation. For example, what makes Nan a "cowboy girl"? (Recall that Lockhart started writing the book in 1901, before Wister had transformed cowboys into legends. It's unclear, however, when Lockhart applied the title, or how closely early drafts resembled the published version.) Nan spends a lot of time on horseback—riding is her chief pastime during her New Mexico sojourn. Like the Virginian, she does little roping, branding, or dehorning. But she's independent and adventuresome, even fearless. For the time period, she controls a surprising amount of her own destiny, not only traveling to New Mexico but also choosing whom to marry and where (they marry in New Mexico, rather than back East, because she wants to shock her family). These traits Nan shared with her creator, who chose to travel to New Mexico and later move to Cody, whose chief pastime was riding, and who chose never to marry at all.

Despite behavior that we might today see as relatively bold feminism, *The Full of the Moon* is a very flawed novel, arguably Lockhart's weakest. Nan, the strongest character, disappears in the final third of the book. Lockhart's trademark humor shows up only occasionally. And a lengthy side plot involving Mexicans does nothing but show Lockhart's sickeningly racist attitudes (at one point a Mexican man drowns, but Ben saves his horse from the raging river and says in a way Lockhart means to be heroic, "I don't mind the greaser, but a good horse—well it would a set heavy on my conscience.")

It's not surprising that this novel languished unpublished for so long, that it was propelled to publication only by Lockhart's success with *Me-Smith*, and that critics found little to praise. One wrote, "The situations are impossible." Another said it "lacks the spontaneity and charm" of her previous work. And of the kind reviews, most seemed to be parroting a publisher's press release, since they nearly always referred to Lockhart's "breezy, outdoor style." Surprisingly, none questioned the final title: the text contains practically no references to moonlight, full or otherwise. We are left with the disheartening theory that Lippincott added the concept as a way of explaining Nan's behavior—during a full moon people will do all sorts of crazy things. Lockhart had conceived of Nan as a hero in her own image, but the world needed an excuse for why she was so loony.

Still, the book remains interesting today at least for its autobiographical tidbits. When you know that Lockhart's stepmother had first been the family seamstress, you cringe at the scene where Nan responds to her mother's warning about bringing the family its first-ever disgrace by saying, "Grandfather Maitlack married the sempstress." When you know that Lockhart had traveled to New Mexico in 1898, where she had recoiled from "uncouth and disrespectful" overtures from a rancher named Hopewell, you marvel at her capacity for revenge—villainizing a rancher who lives in a town named Hopedale. When you know that Lockhart had also published at least two short stories about a young woman traveling to New Mexico and encountering a Mexican/Apache woman who'd once been married to a man with an Irish name, you can picture the aspiring author continually rehashing her experiences, trying to learn how to turn them into successful fiction.

If Lockhart's pre-1918 diaries were still available, they might now reveal dozens of other slights that she avenged in her fiction. Sadly, only scraps have survived. So we are also left wondering how Lockhart reacted to the negative reviews of *The Full of the Moon* that she pasted carefully in her scrapbook. Could she have let herself enjoy the irony? Most critics found the plot (the rich girl leaving the sophisticated East to wander relatively unchaperoned through New Mexico) far too absurd. But that was the most truthful aspect of the book—precisely what Lockhart herself had done! Especially difficult for her must have been the *New York Times* review: "as for the young lady who holds center stage, she is the kind of person whom, as Richard Watson Gilder once said, 'one gets up in the middle of the night to hate,' and it is disconcerting to perceive that she finds favor in the eyes of her creator." Finds favor, indeed. In so many ways "the cowboy girl" was not just Nan but Lockhart herself.

For the last hundred years, the leading theory about the source of the rivalry between Lockhart and Dr. Frances Lane has been that they were both in love with the same man. Jack Painter, the Philadelphia music-box importer, had moved his wife and three children to the Sunlight Basin northwest of Cody. But he was already well on his way to abandoning them in pursuit of more glorious western adventures.

The dapper Painter, who wore a huge black moustache under an equally prominent nose, sometimes claimed to have been an orphan adopted by a wealthy New York family. In fact, however, he'd been born in Maryland in 1861, moving to Philadelphia when he was eighteen. He'd traveled domestically and in Europe, and he did know plenty of wealthy people through his memberships at the Philadelphia Yacht Club and two gun clubs. He was a marksman and trophy hunter and also a miner; in Sunlight Basin he pursued both hunting and mining. But as noted earlier, he also bought a house in Cody—right next door to Lockhart.

Was this when he gave Lockhart the ring of amethyst surrounded by diamonds that she wore for the rest of her life? Was he the married man who had written the letter Lane picked up in the courtroom? (Or, as some allege, did Lockhart have several other married lovers as well?) Had Lockhart really dropped it in the courtroom, or had Lane found it at his house during a visit of her own? We can easily imagine all sorts of scenarios for the two women to clash over Painter—and we can never really know about any of them.

A big problem with the Painter theory, however, is that Lockhart won this battle with Lane. She, not Lane, received the amethyst ring. She, not Lane, was invited to a lengthy stay at Painter's Sunlight Basin ranch while his wife was out of town—a visit that, when the wife returned, ended the marriage. She, not Lane, spent summers from 1911 through 1913 at his new digs in another state. Having won Painter's hand, why would Lockhart have continued to despise the woman who lost it?

May 1911 indeed marked the beginning of Lockhart's first full summer away from Cody. She was in Salmon City, Idaho, getting an old-timer to talk about the main fork of the Salmon River. She asked:

> "Honest, now, is it really so bad?"
> "I'll tell you about me, mum. I have fit Injuns and I ain't afraid of a gun, er a knife, er pizen, er grub in the Bismark Restauraw but you couldn't git me down that river 'thout tyin' and gaggin' me."
> "And the Pine Creek Rapids—you go through them—"
> "Like a bat out of hell, mum."

Roiling 150 miles through the rugged Bitter Root (now usually spelled Bitterroot) Mountains, even today the Salmon is one of the most challenging river-rafting trips in the country. In Lockhart's day, before the channel was smoothed and widened, it was called The River of No Return because boats could only go down it—never back up. This hazard of navigation was a benefit to the few hardy souls living in the gorge, who were delighted to dismantle any arriving supply boats for lumber.

The most competent, innovative, and daring boatman on the Salmon was Harry Guleke. He'd even designed his own flat-bottomed *scow*, a barge made of green boards just one inch thick and controlled by front and back oars called *sweeps*—a design quite similar to today's rafts. Lockhart described Guleke this way: "big as a bear and as strong, and with a bear's surprising agility as I afterwards learned—low-voiced, deliberate, with a slow, pleasant smile and a droll fashion of shaking his head and saying, 'Well, well, I declare!'" Guleke was so strong that to save a young girl's life, he had once broken a sweep—a fir tree twenty-five feet long and six inches in diameter—in half. His fame had been cemented in 1908 when he took a group of railroad surveyors—by reputation, some of the most adventuresome explorers of the West—from Salmon City through the gorge to Lewiston, Idaho, in a fruitless effort to find a viable rail route. Yet, Lockhart wrote, he "had the characteristics one likes to find in men who do brave things—namely, gentleness and modesty."

As Lockhart chatted up the old-timer about the Pine Creek Rapids, Guleke was returning from a river trip the only way anyone could return: by rail through Spokane, Washington, and Butte, Montana, a route more than twice as long as the straight shot downstream. He had led three scows of mining equipment—thirty-seven feet long, eight feet wide, ten thousand pounds on each barge—down the rapids to a mine. On that trip Guleke's scow had filled to within six inches of the top, and once he'd had to hang on to a rock in the middle of the river until after midnight. Another boat in the party hadn't even done that well. It had sunk, losing its cargo.

The Salmon River Mining Company paid for this wild and risky ride through one of the last remaining wilderness frontiers in the United States. Its manager was Jack Painter. Lockhart was inquiring about the rapids because as soon as Guleke returned, he would shoot the rapids with another set of scows full of mining equipment, and this time he would be taking with him an enterprising female writer.

Painter, after his wife kicked him out about 1909, had run the Salmon with Guleke. Falling in love with the country, he bought a sandbar about halfway down. He built a hunting lodge there: a large log building with a stone fireplace, French windows, a trophy room, a bar, mirrors, and a pool table. By far the most elegant building on the river, it was ironically referred to as the Bungalow. All of its furnishings were floated down on Guleke's scows. Painter planted some apricots to go with peaches planted by the previous owner (one legend has it that the apricot trees were intended for the governor of Idaho and sent to Painter by mistake—once they'd arrived at such a remote place, there was no sense trying to reship them anywhere else) and added some cattle that he let roam free since they were hemmed in by the mountains.

Painter chose this spot because of gold; there was dust in the sand at the bottom of the river, and a whole vein running along the left bank. An individual could accumulate the dust through "placer mining," the labor-intensive process of running water through sand until the heavier gold settles out. But Painter thought big. He wanted to develop a full-on industrial mine to dig out the source vein. He persuaded his wealthy eastern friends to invest sixty thousand dollars in a generator and a mill. The machines now sat on Guleke's scows in Salmon City, waiting for the final, wild leg of their long journey.

Guleke and his fellow boatmen finally arrived, told crazy stories of their trip, and spent a day making and adjusting the sweeps for their new scows. Two other captains would follow Guleke in identical boats. Each would also have a rear sweepman and a baler. Lockhart would ride next to the baler on Guleke's boat, while a couple named Symes would ride in the second boat. Lockhart claimed that she and Mrs. Symes were the first women ever to attempt this hazardous trip, though that distinction "was no solace to me at times when I was less than a foot from my Everlasting Punishment, and at such moments glory seemed a puny thing indeed."

Their first challenge came their second day on the river, at the notorious Pine Creek Rapids. This seven-mile stretch began three miles below the town of Shoup, the last full settlement on the shoreline, where a person could still get out on a rough road. Residents of Shoup came out to watch. Lockhart gave this account:

> There was something creepy, ominous, in the very quietness with which we glided from the stiller water of the eddy into the channel. Nobody spoke; it was silent as a graveyard, save for the occasional lap of a ripple against the boat. The big pilot, half-crouching over his sweep, made me think of a huge cat, a cougar waiting to grapple with an enemy as wily and formidable as himself, and, for a space, we crept forward with something of a cougar's stealth.
>
> Then the current caught us like some live thing. Faster and faster we moved. The rocks and bushes at the water's edge began to fly by. I thought I heard something. It sounded like the rumble of thunder far back in the hills. It grew louder with every beat of my heart. [The sweepman] dropped his eyes for an instant and grinned.
> "Hear 'em roar?"

Hear 'em roar? Oh, mother! Did I hear 'em roar! It sounded like a cloud-burst in a canyon—like the avalanche of water dropping over Niagara.

I stood up and stretched my neck to look ahead. What I saw made my heart miss four beats. I took a fresh grip on my life-preserver and wondered how long it would take me to shuck myself out of my khaki shirt.

As far as I could see there was a stretch of spray and foam, short intervals of wild, racing water, then more spray and foam where it churned itself to whiteness against a mass of rocks. And from it all came a steady boom! boom! . . .

For an instant it seemed as though the boat poised on the edge of a precipice with half her length in mid-air before she dropped into a curve of water that was like the hollow of a great green shell. The roar was deafening. When the sheet of water that drenched us broke over the boat it seemed to shut out the sun. The barge came up like a clumsy Newfoundland, with the water streaming from the platform and swishing through the machinery in the bottom. Guleke was there at his sweep, unshaken by the shock, throwing his great strength upon it first this way then that, to keep it in the center of the current—the tortuous channel through which we were tearing like mad. . . .

"Well, well, I declare, they didn't get us that time!"

"That's the worst, isn't it?" I hoped that he would not notice the quaver in my voice.

"Oh, no; it gets worse as you go further down."

At each of those subsequent rapids, Lockhart later described, the scenery grew "wilder," the mountains rising straight from the water's edge. At Big Mallard they got out to scout the rapids from the shore. She found it terrifying. "I looked in a horror I made no effort to conceal. It is no disgrace to be scared at the Big Mallard. . . . I have met rapids before—shot them and poled over them—but never anything like the rapids of this river, and he who makes the trip can assert with truth that he has taken the wildest boat ride in America."

The boatmen said only, "It's a lot worse than the first trip." The water was higher, which gave the captains less control over their boats—and hid the rocks they needed to avoid. They went back to the boats and nudged their way into the current:

As we whipped around the point I forgot something of my fear in look-ing at the pilot. The wind blew his hair straight back and the joy of battle was gleaming in his eyes as he laid down on the sweep. His face was alight with exultation; he looked a monument of courage, the per-sonification of human daring. Fearlessness is contagious, and a spirit of reckless indifference to consequences filled me as we took the final rush. It lasted only a second or two, but the sensations of many years were crowded into the tense moment when on that toboggan slide of water the boat shot past the rocks on the left and cut the hole on the right so close that half the stern hung over it and the baler stared into its dark depths with bulging eyes.

As in Altyn, she had sought out the wildest part of the frontier, for adventure. And unlike most previous westerners, she saw the challenge not as Indians, or lawlessness, or the difficulty of carving a living out of this wilderness. In a very twenty-first-century way, the challenge was nature's power—and the challenge was its own reward. The West was a place where she could crowd the sensations of many years into a moment of reckless ecstasy.

And she did it as a woman. In her Idaho experiences we see again her need for men—especially "men who do brave things"—to respect her cour-age, ideally without condescending to her sex. Though she tried to down-play it with humility, the article she wrote about the experience concluded:

"Your 'sand' is all right," said the boatman flatteringly when we parted. "You rode through rapids that the survey outfit of the Pittsburgh and Gilmore Railroad walked around."

I felt that it was something for which to be thankful that my coward-ice was not of the conspicuous kind.

Once she arrived at Painter's mine, Lockhart found it idyllic. She wrote her publisher, "I am trying to do a little work on a short story, but it is well-nigh impossible, as there are so many more fascinating things on hand like trout fishing, hunting grouse, killing rattle-snakes and panning dirt (this is a placer diggings)." During the three years when Lockhart spent summers on the Salmon, her output of short stories did indeed drop off, although she must have been putting final touches on *The Lady Doc* and *The Full of the Moon* during this time. She wasn't lying to her publishers about why: her scrapbooks contain pictures of her catching fish and rattlers, rowing a canoe, and posing with placer mining equipment. The pictures show her, at age forty, no longer thin. But she looks vigorous, outdoorsy, happy, and her weight is voluptuously distributed through her bust and hips.

Among the writing tasks she did complete were an article covering the boat ride for *The Outing* magazine (the *Outside* of its day) and a feature for a Philadelphia newspaper describing placer mining (though it somewhat resembled scrubbing floors in an office building, she said, the gambler's excitement proved alluring). In this piece she again delighted in depicting the old-time characters she had met floating the river. For example, Johnny McKay, an old-time boatman and miner,

> saw us coming and rushed to the water's edge shouting and waving his arms like a man in distress. When we were within hearing distance he yelled frantically:
>
> "Hi there! Hi! What month is it? Is this June?"
>
> It is told that the war with Spain was begun and ended before he found it out, and he was so greatly excited that he shortened his visit in Salmon City to hurry back and tell the news to his neighbors, a day's walk away, who are even less given to gadding than he.

During these winters, from 1911 to 1913, Lockhart did a lot of traveling. There's even some evidence that she avoided spending much time in Cody in the aftermath of *The Lady Doc*. After her second summer in Idaho, a newspaper covering a nearby settlement noted that the famous author "passed through Elk City this week for her home in Philadelphia." Also in 1912 she was able to get the autograph of *Lippincott's* editor Berg Esenwein on a copy of his new book *Studying the Short-story* (which suggests she was visiting Philadelphia at the time). She also visited some of her relatives in Kingston, Pennsylvania, probably in the same year.

It must have been during this time that Lockhart tried her hand at a different medium, penning "In the Bitter Roots: A One-Act Play." A melodrama just fifteen pages long, its plot is sentimental and silly, though the dialogue is not bad and the set description quite detailed and accurate sounding. The play is worth noting for a couple of features. First, its paper-thin characters are named Spivey (the name of the evil ranch owner in *The Full of the Moon*), Jennie LaMott (an innocent but educated half-Indian beauty), and

Bruce Burt (a name Lockhart would remember). Second, its author is listed as "Caroline Lockhart, New York City."

Nevertheless, Lockhart had not moved away from Cody, nor from her career as a novelist. Rather, she had entered a phase (much like 1898-1902) where she spent as much time traveling as she did in any one "home." Coupled with her unmarried status and talents as an author, these experiences made her a person who was frequently envied. Perhaps hesitant to dwell on the drawbacks of *The Full of the Moon*, a reviewer for the *Chicago Tribune* covered not the book but something easier to admire: "Miss Caroline Lockhart, who sprang into fame with her first novel, *Me-Smith*, is a most interesting young woman. She lives in Cody, Wyoming, when she is at home, but she is very seldom at home. Sometimes she runs on from Wyoming to New York or to visit her publishers in Philadelphia, but most of her time she spends in exploring strange places. I doubt if there is a young woman in this country who has been in more seemingly impossible situations than Miss Lockhart."

She was about to get in another one.

Late in her Idaho period, perhaps in 1912, Lockhart began working on another novel. This time she did not choose for her protagonist an anti-hero, nor a feminist. This time—after such dismal reception for her last two books—she played it safe. *The Man from the Bitter Roots* would be a rollicking adventure tale with a hero of the traditional western variety: uneducated, physically powerful, driven by honor, independent, and male.

Again, when looking for material, Lockhart simply drew on her own experiences. The title character, named Bruce Burt, builds a mine at the bottom of the Salmon River Canyon. His mining equipment has to be floated down the wild river. Passages from Lockhart's nonfiction account of her river trip made it into the novel almost unedited. Did Lockhart have real-life models for Bruce Burt and his love interest, a female journalist from Philadelphia? The more relevant question may be whether it pained Lockhart to have to shave so many years off her and Painter's ages.

Clearly, however, she had done her homework. The novel goes into great detail about the mining operation, and the depictions of Bruce dealing with industrial sabotage are particularly believable. In fact, Lockhart almost seems more interested in Bruce as a capitalist than a cowboy. While he must overcome nature in the form of a blizzard and the river, equally daunting are the challenges in fund-raising, engineering, and management.

If she is on new terrain by making her hero a likable miner, she covers familiar ground with her villain. Victor Sprudell is the richest man in a small Indiana town: dim witted, vain, amoral, overweight, and worst of all, self-important. Her depiction of him is exaggerated nearly to the point of ruining the story. As Sprudell torments Bruce so as to gain favor with his Indiana buddies, Lockhart again portrays the wild West threatened by the conformist values of the small-town Midwest. Sprudell lacks breeding, intelligence, and curiosity; he also lacks a sense of respect for natural wonders. She demonstrates his evil by showing him killing an entire family of majestic bighorn sheep that Bruce had adopted—not for food or even trophy but in "wanton slaughter."

Lockhart's resentment of the Midwest relates specifically to its value system. Bruce, too, is a native of the Midwest, born in Iowa. But he is a man *from* the Bitter Roots because he has adopted the values of the West: stubborn individualism, antigovernment capitalism, and admiration for physical prowess rather than parlor sophistication.

Bruce is an exaggerated ideal: a man who claims to not need friends, but who makes them easily; a man described as having little interest in the affairs of the world, but who makes lengthy antigovernment rants (which have a surprising focus on irrigation projects such as the one on the Shoshone); a man who wants to build an industrial mine in the wilderness, but who treats wildlife far better than any other character in the novel. The clashes of the twenty-first-century West—environmentalism vs. economic development, dependence on government vs. resentment of government, the need for untrammeled wilderness vs. the desire to trammel in it yourself—coexist peacefully within Bruce. Actually, the novel might be a little more exciting today if those conflicting impulses led to more tension, but then Lockhart may not have seen them as conflicting. The frontier had always represented open space, an unmarked canvas, which could be anything to anybody. In contrast to mournful nostalgics like Wister, Lockhart insisted that such a frontier still existed. There was still room to reinvent yourself and have your adventure, to both experience the wilderness and make your fortune. In the novel Lockhart has one of her old-time characters say, "There's a hundred square miles over there that I reckon there never was a white man's foot on, and they say that the West has been went over with a fine-tooth comb. Wouldn't it make you laugh?"

If *The Lady Doc* represented Lockhart's fatigue with the petty social niceties of the small-town West, the Idaho experiences reinvigorated her with the ideals that had first brought her to the region: rugged landscapes, unpeopled territory, outdoor exploits, and the tough individualists who loved all that. On one level, *The Man from the Bitter Roots* is a cartoonish adventure story, but on another level it captures that evolving notion of frontier.

In late 1913, as she left Idaho for Cody, her manuscript was in pretty good shape. She took it with her to do some final edits during her winter adventure. That December she left Cody for Denver, St. Louis, New Orleans, and points south.

After an overnight boat ride from New Orleans, Lockhart reached the port of La Ceiba on Honduras's mosquito coast. The town of large, airy, wooden houses bustled with a variety of characters: Honduran peasants, Caribbean islanders black and white, and European and North American adventurers and capitalists. Most of them were there because of bananas.

Fifteen years earlier three New Orleans brothers had arrived in Honduras to scout out banana plantations. By 1905 they established their headquarters and port in La Ceiba, a village formerly so small that it was named after a single ceiba tree growing on the beach. As bananas grew to 60 percent of Honduras's exports by 1913, La Ceiba grew as well.

As usual, Lockhart left no clear explanation of how she chose her destination. Certainly the banana phenomenon, combined with political instability and the impending opening of the Panama Canal, was giving Central America an increasing public profile. Furthermore, because Honduras had established an extradition treaty only in 1912, it had a sort of frontier atmosphere, attracting all sorts of North Americans on the lam (including the writer O. Henry, who had briefly escaped there in 1904). Lockhart went in midwinter, avoiding the Rocky Mountain cold. But there's no indication she knew any banana magnates, or that she had a magazine assignment in hand. And once again a man may have been hidden in her motivations.

Soon after Lockhart arrived she got a fever, perhaps from the *garrapatas* (ticks) she'd been warned about on the dock. The community's only doctor was an ex-Texas veterinarian who gave her pills she suspected were intended for horses. It was no fun being sick at the ill-painted Hotel Gran

Paris, with its wide archway full of mongrel dogs. A chicken laid an egg in the dining room during lunch; the ten-year-old houseboy's sole article of clothing was a fur cap he had acquired from a sailor.

If she'd gone to do political reporting, she soon realized this was not her strength. As she admitted a few years later, "It is my misfortune to have a piffling mind that takes notes of trifles rather than important happenings, and, plainer than I can see the advance of the conquering army . . . I can see the cook of the worst hotel in the world, a blotch of color in the salmon pink undershirt he affected, with a chunk of raw meat, unwrapped, and fresh from the abattoir, under an arm as he darted and dodged his perilous way among looting Caribs and drunken English negroes." The conquering army, she claimed, had consisted of "an American soldier of fortune with seven men and a machine gun." In fact, she had probably witnessed a minor skirmish in the banana wars, fought among mercenaries of rival fruit companies. But she lacked either the interest or the analytic skill to make sense of that broader story and was left instead with a pastiche of vibrant, long-lasting images.

She also spent time reworking her *Bitter Roots* manuscript, and then, she recalled in her memoirs, she took a boat trip to a historic town down the coast. Her return was troubling:

> We were still some distance from La Ceiba when we saw what looked like smoke drifting over the Gulf from about where La Ceiba should be.
>
> "They must have had a fire," someone remarked.
>
> A fire! The whole town had burned down in the night. . . . The Gran Hotel Paris was only a heap of smoking rubble and in it was my steamer trunk containing my manuscript, my clothes, my money. I had nothing left except what I was wearing and a few dollars in my purse.

When she returned to Philadelphia in April, she explained to a reporter, "It's disheartening to contemplate the loss of two whole years' work, but I intend to get busy and write that book again." But she told the newspaper that the manuscript, her other baggage, and that of other tourists off the coast of Nicaragua "went to the bottom of the sea when a small boat which was transporting it from the steamship to the coast capsized." It was a memorable scene, she said, because also on board was a "traveling salesman for a soap concern, who ran up and down the deck wringing his hands and crying, 'My samples! Oh, my samples!'"

Which was it? A fire in Honduras, or capsizing off Nicaragua? In her memoirs she mentioned nothing about Nicaragua—had she been there but later tried to hide it? That seems likely. Jack Painter's descendants believe that he too spent the winter of 1914 in Central America.

Nicaragua, just southeast of Honduras, boasted not only banana and coffee plantations but also gold mines. Nicaragua was also under the control of the U.S. Marines. The United States had long meddled in Nicaraguan politics, in part because a Nicaraguan canal was a potential alternative to the Panama Canal. Painter, perhaps using the clout of Idaho's expansionist-minded senator William Borah, may have gotten a government contract to do something in Nicaragua—though given Painter's history, he was probably mostly interested in gold.

There's a good chance that Lockhart traveled with Painter in Nicaragua and later pretended she didn't, instead emphasizing her time alone in La Ceiba. Again, she may have wanted to avoid the scandal of traveling with a man, or she may have preferred to depict herself as so independent that she always traveled abroad alone. Regardless, there is evidence that she did lose a manuscript and did witness both a capsizing and a fire—and in telling the story later she would change her mind as to which sounded more dramatic.

The Man from the Bitter Roots was serialized in August 1915 in *Popular*, the big fiction magazine, where an editor's note boasted that "it is one of the best long stories that has ever appeared in this magazine." The book came out later that fall, and reviewers were generally kind. Several called it her best work since *Me-Smith*. As usual, they were especially impressed with the reality of her western settings. "Miss Lockhart manages to get the real stuff into her stories of the West—the look, the very smell, of the land, the talk of the men, the sense of adventure and stress of life that belongs in the wild places," wrote one. "We have always maintained that Caroline Lockhart has an unfair advantage in the business of writing western stories. Her advantage is not in that she has lived in the west and knows it, but in that she has absorbed it. There is nothing staged about Miss Lockhart's narratives. . . . It is more panoramic than *Me-Smith* and not as depressing as *The Lady Doc*," wrote another. "There is no sentimentality about Miss Lockhart; she does not lather us with maundering drivel about life and love," said a third.

They were also impressed with the mining details, especially given the gender of the author. "Miss Lockhart has that happy faculty denied so many women who write—the ability to depict the life of a man so skillfully that the reader never once says, 'A woman wrote this.'" Indeed, the phrase "a man's book" appears in so many reviews that Lippincott may have used the phrase in its marketing. "For this is a man's book."; "Decidedly a man's book"; "Caroline Lockhart can tell a man's story a whole lot better than many man writers." So the good news for Lockhart was that she was back on the road to success. The bad news was that this road was labeled a man's road.

At least, however, the success was meaningful. Even Hollywood saluted Lockhart: the novel was turned into a 1916 movie. The project was adapted and directed by Oscar Apfel, a frequent collaborator of Cecil B. DeMille who had just left DeMille's Paramount studios for Fox. William Farnum, one of the highest-paid actors in the business, played Bruce. The movie focuses more on Bruce's alleged murder of his mining partner and less on the development of the mine itself. It even invents a dance-hall-girl-turned-detective, who clears Bruce's name and forces Sprudell to confess. In a turn of events that was perhaps symbolic of Lockhart's personal life, despite the Idaho setting the movie was filmed in Cody.

As Lockhart returned to Cody in 1916, another woman with a relatively high national profile moved there too. Her name was Marjory Ross, she was the secretary of the National Woman's Party, and by some accounts she was quite beautiful. A thirty-eight-year-old native of southwest Pennsylvania, she had taught Latin at girls' schools in Pittsburgh and Washington, D.C. But for the last four years, she'd spent most of her time making speeches about suffrage.

Women had advanced to where they could be journalists, best-selling novelists, and doctors. But they still weren't trusted with a voice in the political process, except in the West. Wyoming had allowed women to vote since its formation as a territory in 1869. Now the nation as a whole was experiencing a strong push for those rights. The National Woman's Party was a leading radical voice in that debate, and the face of that voice belonged in part to Marjory Ross.

Until she got to Cody. After coming to Cody, Ross stayed. She kept a low profile in town; she was generally admired but not very deeply known. She rarely spoke publicly any more, and left behind no journals. So in determining why she stayed in Cody, we can go only on facts of her public life.

Ross's work was in the office of Dr. Frances Lane. Ross's home was in the home of Frances Lane. She was known as Lane's companion until Lane's death twenty years later, when she inherited Lane's property.

Given the times, and their situation in small-town Wyoming, the women never came out as lesbians. Even today, one hesitates to contribute to the "outing" of historical figures, because they are no longer alive to define their own sexual orientations. But the story of Lane and Ross is important for at least two reasons. First, though they didn't exactly hide their relationship, Cody generally responded with tacit support. Both women held positions of leadership in church and community. Ross outlived her companion by more than twenty-five years, all of that in Cody, and in her old age she was looked after by several prominent families.

The more fundamental importance for this story is the impact of Lane's sexuality on her feud with Lockhart. No wonder Lockhart, who always wrote from experience, portrayed Dr. Emma Harpe as a lesbian. No wonder Lane never sued for libel. No wonder Lockhart pretended to have been offended solely by Lane's professional incompetence; no wonder Lane played along. In small-town Wyoming in the 1900s and 1910s, you didn't talk about sex, especially sex outside of marriage, especially sex with people of the same sex.

Unfortunately, however, the lesbian angle raises as many questions as it answers. What relevance, exactly, does Lane's sexuality have to the source of their feud? All those rumors about Lane and Lockhart fighting over a man—was Lane bisexual?

Or had the two clashed over a woman?

One day in the summer of 1916, Lockhart's horse, Sunny Joe, picked his way along the rocky slopes of Copper Mountain. She had ridden more than one hundred miles south of Cody to this slope of sagebrush, juniper, and grass. Most of Copper Mountain was still unfenced government land, open range. It was now late afternoon, and she turned her horse eastward to gain a view of upper Kirby Creek. The small stream ran through a level flat dotted with bands of sheep that reminded her of lice. Most cattlemen hated sheep, saying sheep and cattle could not exist on the same range. (In fact, overgrazing by both cattle *and* sheep had degraded the range; the cattlemen's disdain may have had more to do with the fact that sheepherders worked on foot rather than horseback.) At the center of the flat, several sheep wagons encircled a large canvas tent. That camp was her destination.

As Lockhart rode up, a half-dozen dogs barked her arrival. A woman climbed out of one of the sheep wagons. "She was sixty or thereabouts, with a clear, healthy complexion and hard, shrewd blue eyes. She was barefooted and the ready-made gingham dress she wore was fairly clean." The woman didn't smile. She looked like she never smiled. Her face was round and flat and her mouth naturally tended downward. The tanned face was none too wrinkled for all of its time outdoors, but none too pampered either. The firm jaw suggested tenacity; some called hers a fighting face.

This was Lucy Morrison Moore, widely known as the "Sheep Queen." That title had been bestowed in irony, years previously, by area cattlemen who sneered at her occupation. It was no longer ironic. Moore controlled twenty bands of sheep, managed the entire outfit, and owned a great deal of the surrounding land. She was known as a recluse, even a misanthrope. Legends about her abounded: that as a young shepherdess lacking a babysitter she had tied her children to sagebrush, that lacking poison or gun she'd once used ground-up glass to kill a mountain lion that threatened her sheep, that before marrying her second husband she'd given him two bands of sheep so she could say she'd married a sheepman instead of a lowly sheepherder, that for more than thirty years now she'd been living year-round in her sheep wagon despite her wealth. Lockhart, intending to write a new book, had come to hear these stories from the source.

The woman did not speak to greet her. She evinced no friendliness.

Still atop her horse, Lockhart explained that she was a writer. She wrote for newspapers. She wanted to learn about sheep, for a story. She wondered if she could stay for a short time.

"You can help Lavicy herd bucks," Moore said, referring to a band of male sheep. "Get off."

Though the command was preemptory, Lockhart saw a gleam in her eye. Moore was proud of her success. She would talk. Lockhart dismounted and untied the sack on the back of her saddle.

"Wanta sleep light or dark?" Moore asked. Eventually she explained that Lockhart could sleep under the stars (light) or in a sheep wagon (dark) with Lavicy, Moore's daughter.

Lockhart chose the wagon.

Moore jerked her thumb. "That's her'n. Stow your stuff and make yourself to home. Lavicy is down in the corral rasslin' sheep, but she'll be back soon."

When Lavicy appeared, Lockhart recalled, she turned out to be six feet tall with oxlike strength. She wore a high-crowned Stetson, a white silk blouse, a long brown denim skirt divided for easier riding, sheer pink silk stockings, and pink satin dancing slippers. Lockhart found Lavicy to be utterly without manners or tact yet paradoxically quite proud of her looks and accomplishments. Lavicy knew only mail-order catalogs and sheep. She knew a lot about sheep, and Lockhart respected such knowledge, but her mother's wealth made Lavicy conceited, a quality Lockhart could not stand.

It was a great story, Lockhart knew, but they were difficult women. The conflict inherent in that situation made for a memorable visit, one that Lockhart in her old age especially enjoyed retelling.

A cowbell rang for supper, and Lockhart sat down with several sheepherders. They discussed the progress of Moore's latest initiative, a series of scarecrows designed to keep coyotes away from bedded sheep at night. Moore had ordered dozens of men's longtailed nightshirts, painted them with a big black M for Moore, and put them over the scarecrow crossbeams. But, a herder reported, "every cowboy in the county was wearing a white shirt with the tail cut off and a large black M on the front."

At bedtime Lavicy asked, "Do you snore? Snorin' keeps me awake."

"I don't think so," Lockhart responded. She grimaced to realize they were sharing not only the wagon but a single bunk. She crawled in the back.

It turned out that Lavicy was the one who snored. Lockhart later wrote, "Flinging her arm across my face and pinning me down with her legs she opened her mouth and such snores came forth as must have reached the furthermost wagon in camp. Also she rolled and thrashed. It was like trying to sleep with a two-year-old steer with the colic."

Sleeping may have been difficult, but Lockhart loved how eccentric Lavicy and her mother were. For example, Lucy frequently referred to herself in the third person ("Mrs. Moore don't allow no rope throwed in her corral"). The women both fulfilled and confounded conventional notions of the Old West: They had made a fortune on the open range—but with the scorned sheep rather than cattle. They had lived through what Wister described as the golden age—but forty years later were still living in the wilderness as they had back in the 1880s. They had chosen the Old West way of life and sustained it through progress and wealth.

Lockhart reported Moore's story: a Utah widow with two small children, she decided to take a band of sheep to Copper Mountain. "She greased the wheels of a rickety covered wagon, purchased a scanty supply of corn-meal, flour, salt-pork, baking powder. . . . They endured every known hardship such as bitter cold, heavy snow and windstorms. They camped where there was no fuel except sagebrush or buffalo chips and often no water. They had sick horses and breakdowns. Frequently they were hungry and it was an occasion for rejoicing when the children killed a rabbit with a rock."

By 1916 Moore had male sheepherders and a male cook, but she still ran the outfit. When it came time to dip sheep into disinfectant to clean them before shearing, she could grab a full-grown ewe by the rump and the scruff of the neck and toss it in the dipping vat in one easy motion. "Though she could have lived in a mansion," Lockhart recalled, "she continued to follow her sheep in a wagon."

In addition to the physical courage of Moore the pioneer, two other characteristics of the Sheep Queen stuck out in Lockhart's memory. One was her contempt for "poor folks," especially the "poverty-stricken homesteaders from the Middle West" who fenced off the open range that both Moore and cattlemen had considered their domain. "Toward such she was both ruthless and adroit in the methods she used to frighten or starve them out." The other, however, was the flip side: how, as a woman, Moore was continually taken advantage of. When Moore's men went to town for supplies, another writer explained, they might order fancy fruits and jellies to eat on the ride, having them charged as peas or corn. The M shirts were another example: stealing from the Sheep Queen was a regional joke. Quick to side with an underdog, Lockhart saw that Moore's misanthropy and "fighting face" were necessary because everybody—from Indians to ranchers, townspeople to homesteaders, cattlemen to employees—was against her.

Her memories of the Sheep Queen come to us through Lockhart's late-life memoirs and show the writer at her mythologizing best. She mixes fact and fiction to reshape traditional cowboy myths, emphasizing the type of characters she herself appreciates—eccentrics, people averse to change, and lone fighting women. Lockhart's recorded memories of the Sheep Queen, however, depart dramatically from the factual story of Lucy Morrison Moore.

For example, in all of Lockhart's memoirs, she never mentions that Curtis Moore, Lucy's second husband, was always present, co-presiding over every meal. A gaunt, silent, humorless Vermonter, Curtis was clearly not the boss: the legend about Lucy giving him sheep before their wedding was true. (However, strychnine killed the mountain lion, and the children never mentioned being tied to sagebrush.) Lockhart must have seen that Curtis was extraneous to Moore's story and decided to erase him entirely, in order to emphasize Lucy's heroism. Lockhart similarly glossed over Lucy's first husband, Luther Morrison, who had not left her a widow until 1898, sixteen years after their journey from southeastern Idaho to Copper Mountain. Lucy had loved and depended on Luther's strength, ambition, and intelligence; he had managed sheep, built dwellings, and taken other jobs to help support the family.

Indeed, in the 1890s the Morrisons spent every winter in Casper, Wyoming, where the children could go to school. Luther built them a home downtown. In later years, perhaps even during the years Lockhart was visiting, Lucy wintered not in her sheep wagon but in Los Angeles.

Lavicy (real name: Lovisa) did not live in a sheep wagon even in the summer. She had a homestead cabin about a mile from Lucy's camp. That's where Lockhart slept. Lovisa herself at the time was a thirty-six-year-old widow, whom no other sources mention as dressing in pink. It was common practice for a sheep or cattle baron to ask an employee or a relative to file on a nearby homestead so as to acquire full title to strategic grazing land, signing it over to the baron as soon as he or she officially gained title. The Sheep Queen had lost a lot of her grazing territory to competitors using such unethical techniques; now she and Lovisa were striking back.

Lockhart never mentioned religion, but many Sundays Lucy and Curtis Moore descended Copper Mountain into Thermopolis for church. An exceedingly religious woman, Moore often noted that many biblical figures were shepherds, while none raised cattle. She was not misanthropic, nor vengeful toward legitimate homesteaders; in fact, she once said, "I like people, so I was glad when the country began to settle up." She lived in a sheep wagon on a desolate flat because she loved a nomadic life, and because she had feared cottonwood-laden streams ever since her first son had drowned in one so many years ago in Idaho. Nostalgia for the 1880s had nothing to do with it—in fact, she warned her daughter-in-law about the dangers of romanticizing the frontier past. She embraced change rather than fearing or hiding from it: when in the 1920s Moore started investing in Los Angeles real estate, she loved driving to her winter home in her fast new car.

So why did Lockhart recall the story differently? In part, she preferred stories that supported her opinions, and she tended to fudge facts (even in works labeled nonfiction) for dramatic effect. This tendency would increase in future years, even as publishers, critics, and scholars became more interested in the documentability of facts. But furthermore, in this case, the Sheep Queen refused to give out her full story. Wanting to write her own autobiography, Moore withheld from Lockhart the stories about her early experiences. Lockhart had to fashion her own legends out of rumor.

So we should not be surprised that in Lockhart's memories, the Sheep Queen was a little more eccentric, a little more persecuted, a little more dime novelish than she was in real life. That's what writers do. Similar dynamics had created the phenomenon of Buffalo Bill, which in many ways had driven the greater phenomenon of the cowboy West. Indeed, one could even argue that in creating alternative (feminist, sheepherding, atheist) fables of the West, Lockhart hewed far closer to the facts than had those who created the fables she was rebelling against.

The novel Lockhart wrote next, *The Fighting Shepherdess*, actually drew not just on the Sheep Queen but on Lockhart's entire career to date. The novel's opening scene, for example, recalls *Me-Smith*:

> While Kate hung the harness on its peg, Mullendore waited for her outside. "My! My! Katie," he leered at her as she came back, "but you're gettin' to be a big girl! Them legs looked like a couple of pitchfork handles when I went away, and now the shape they've got!"
>
> He laughed in malicious enjoyment as he saw the color rise to the roots of her hair; and when she would have passed, reached out and grabbed her arm.
>
> "Let me be, Pete Mullendore!" She tried to pull loose.
>
> "When you've give me a kiss." There was a flame in the muddy eyes.
>
> With a twist she freed herself and cried with fury vibrating in her voice, "I hate you—I hate you!"

Like Susie MacDonald, Katie Prentice is a feisty teenager. She doesn't know her father, and her mother, a roadhouse operator known as Jezebel of the Sand Coulee, laughs when Mullendore rips the girl's clothes off. Katie runs away to the camp of a traveling sheepman, who agrees to take her in.

Like Smith, Mullendore represents the flip side of the frontier hero. He is a successful trapper, but greedy and immoral—Katie scolds him for mistreating his horses. In a sad reversal from *Me-Smith*, Lockhart also telegraphs his wickedness by calling him a "half-breed." He's a mixture of Apache, Mexican, white—and perhaps African American, to judge from his reaction when Katie labels him with a nasty racial slur.

Also like Smith, Mullendore is taken from real life—at least in the method of a murder he commits. One night in 1909 Seth Arthur Ash had arrived at his Cody home, opened his door, and was shot in the abdomen. A charge of buckshot had been placed inside the house, its trigger connected by a cord to the door. Ash and a man named Bert Lampitt were rivals for the attention of a young woman named Dorothy Newton; Lampitt was arrested for Ash's murder but never brought to trial due to lack of evidence.

Unlike Smith, however, Mullendore is not the focus of this novel. After that opening scene, Lockhart quickly moves to establish a set of other characters: a self-important traveling orator, Major Stephen Douglas Prouty; an imperious eastern couple, the Toomeys; and their well-bred young nephew, Hughie Disston.

Major Prouty decides to found a town. Moments after his inspiration, he introduces himself to another character by saying, "You'll probably hear of me if you stay in the country. The fact is, I'm thinkin' of startin' a town and namin' it Prouty." When asked if his proposed site isn't a bit far from water, the Major responds with vague plans for a vast irrigation scheme.

Major Prouty, in Lockhart's satire, is Colonel William (Buffalo Bill) Cody, and the town he founds bears a strong resemblance to the town Lockhart savaged in *The Lady Doc*. It has soon filled with striving midwesterners, society-building busybodies, and lazy men eager to get rich off the ever-more-complicated irrigation project. But Lockhart is more gentle in this version, her satire less vengeful. Major Prouty is a fop, but as postmaster he quickly becomes irrelevant to both the town and Lockhart's story. The mayor is nicknamed Tinhorn (like Cody's Frank Houx), but his sneers at Katie are merely part of a town chorus. There's a laundryman-turned-banker, a plumber-turned-newspaper editor, and a man mockingly called "Gov'nor" (like Cody's George Beck). But they're all minor characters, sketched for a good laugh and then set aside, as if Lockhart had no need to obsess over them. Perhaps her time away from Cody, along with her literary success, had mellowed her. Perhaps she saw that the real-life Cody irrigation project had proved only marginally profitable, and she took pity on the town's boosters (though given her personality, this seems less likely). Or perhaps her editors clamped down on her tendency to twist the knife too far. But whatever its cause, this novel's tempered tone achieves an outstanding social satire. As the town of Prouty—founded on the major's vanity and propelled by those absurd dreams of irrigated wealth—fails economically, the boosters' schemes become ever more outrageous: to flood the desert for peppermint bogs, to dig up mollusk fossils for sale to schoolchildren, and "to take nitrogen from the air and sell it to the government!" On the level of the individual character, as well, Lockhart makes the most of quick sketches and incongruous comparisons: an old widow with frizzled hair on her temples resembles a mountain sheep; her eligible daughter so anticipates matrimony that "the sharer of it seemed to be of secondary importance to the fact."

Lockhart wrote the book during the eighteen months following her visit to the Sheep Queen, and widely trumpeted Lucy Morrison Moore as its inspiration and true-life model. But the first two-thirds of the book is more about Prouty than sheep. Its theme is ostracism.

The sheepman who rescues Kate is known only as "Mormon Joe." But he is not a religious man—indeed, the nickname seems absurd unless it is meant to signify ostracism and caste, alluding to the ways Mormons were cut off from most of western society. Mormon Joe is an alcoholic and survives by trying to stay away from the temptations of town, sticking to his sheep. Yet that self-exile prompts the town to mistrust him even more than they would the typical sheepman. The strivers of Prouty then ostracize Kate, who has far more working against her: she shows up at a ball wearing tacky homemade clothes, she is a sheepherder, her mother was a harlot, and she is assumed to be sleeping with Joe. When Joe is murdered and she inherits his sheep, she is shunned as the assumed murderer, and furthermore the banker calls in her loan because he believes she cannot run a sheep business. This subject matter—especially the ostracism based on prudish small-town assumptions about sexual behavior—Lockhart obviously knew well.

But she takes the theme one level deeper with the Toomeys, who occupy a good deal of the narrative. Quickly losing their cattle ranch through extravagance and mismanagement, the couple moves into Prouty town, where they fear being victimized by the snobbishness they once practiced. When Jasper Toomey decides to raffle off their silver punchbowl, his wife dreads what the neighbors will think, and then despairs that she is living her life according to such standards. Kate offers her a loan, and Mrs. Toomey then faces a dilemma: ostracism for poverty, or for associating with a woman of poor reputation?

Lockhart exhibits a perhaps-surprising empathy for Mrs. Toomey, while still letting her waffle back and forth, ultimately losing both Kate's and the neighbors' respect. The fault is not entirely in the Toomeys' character, Lockhart implies; it is in the social structure of the small town. "Poverty makes most people sordid, selfish, cowardly," Mormon Joe explains. "People who live without change in a small community grow to attach an exaggerated importance to the opinions of others. . . . When life resolves itself into a struggle for bare existence, it makes for cowardice and selfishness. In time the strongest characters deteriorate with inferior associates and only small interests to occupy their minds."

Kate tries to protest such cynicism, pleading that human nature must surely be sincere, kind, and disinterested. But that idealism leaves her vulnerable to the townspeople's cruelty. The book is thus enlivened by what appears to be the author's unresolved philosophical debate with herself. Who is at fault for such social ills—the characters, or their social milieu? Lockhart so effectively portrays the insecurity driving the Toomeys' behavior that the reader can project such insecurities to the other neighbors as well, so these minor villains develop the humanity so lacking in *The Lady Doc*. Furthermore, Lockhart does not limit herself to scorning the townspeople's pretensions. She also gets humor out of depicting the town's desperate economy and infernal wind—a rich mixture that makes the whole picture seem so much more true.

But Kate—idealistic, driven, proud, and wounded—is the undeniable star of the novel. Witness this scene with Hughie:

"I wanted to surprise you," he said regretfully.

"You have."

"You don't show it."

"Then I'm improving."

"I liked you as you were, Kate—warm-hearted, impulsive." He dropped the bridle reins and sat down beside her.

"That got me nothing," she replied curtly.

A shadow crossed his face.

"And you don't care for anything that doesn't get you something?"

"Absolutely not."

"That doesn't sound like you," he said after a silence.

"I'm not 'me' any longer," she responded. "I made myself over to suit my environment. I get along better."

"What has changed you so much, Kate—what in particular?"

She hesitated a moment, then answered, coldly:

"Nothing in particular—everything."

"You mean you don't want to tell me?"

"What's the use?" indifferently.

"I might help you."

"How?"

"In ways that friends can help each other."

"I've tried that," she answered dryly.

"You've grown so self-sufficient that you make me feel superfluous and helpless."

"A clinging vine that has nothing to cling to sprawls on the ground, doesn't it?"

Since he did not answer immediately, she reminded him:

"Better loosen your horse's cinch; he'll feed better."

Like Lockhart's other novels, this one had title troubles. She first called it *The Daughter of Jezebel*; in serialization it was "The Wolf Pack." But publishers finally settled on *The Fighting Shepherdess* to emphasize the final third of the book, in which Kate responds to Prouty's derision by becoming the Sheep Queen.

Here Lockhart shows how many technical details she learned from Moore: She shows Kate navigating the risks of winter range and fluctuating prices, deciding to buy coarser-wool Rambouillet sheep, operating a dodge gate that requires hair-trigger reflexes (a function that in real life Curtis Moore had performed, while his wife kept the tally), and vaulting fences that halt the superfluous Hughie. And she shows Kate losing her femininity because of it. Kate becomes brusque, imperious, and unforgiving. Her clothes are bedraggled and shabby, her face grimy. She reads only about sheep and puts no decorations in her wagon. Though all of her herders obey her, only one likes her.

In contrast to Lockhart's previous heroines Susie, Essie, and Nan, we feel Kate's pain. Lockhart lingers over this period in Kate's life, which lasts eleven years. You could call it an antifeminist portrayal: doing a man's work turns Kate (like Dr. Emma Harpe) into less of a woman, with no interest in beauty or romance. But such a political reading deprives the novel of its emotional power, which likely was Lockhart's chief intention. She wanted to show how the midwestern society-builders had hurt Kate, hurt her badly, caused her to build up emotional scar tissue that held her from full enjoyment of her life. With her independence and self-confidence, Kate would not submit to their idea of the social order. So they banished her, and she became more independent, but not necessarily more happy.

Despite his disappointment in her ever-hardening appearance and attitude, wealthy Hughie continually expresses his love for her. He will marry her and take her away. Kate knows that they have this sort of romantic novelist's true love ("It's like peeking into Paradise," she says of spending time with him), but when he asks her to give up being a sheep queen, he asks too much. "I've set myself a goal," she tells him, "it's in sight now and I've got to reach it. If I stopped, I know that the feeling that I had been a quitter when a real temptation came to me would gnaw inside of me until I was restless and discontented, and I would have a contempt for myself that I don't believe would ever leave me."

Lockhart has finally broken with the rules of contemporary fiction. Her heroine will not be satisfied by loving and marrying a rich man. She has her own agenda to accomplish, by herself.

Hughie's marriage proposal is not enough. Watching Pete Mullendore confess to Mormon Joe's murder is not enough. Mullendore's death is not enough. Kate meets her father for the first time—discovering him to be a wealthy, sophisticated man who was legally married to her mother at the time of Kate's birth (thus establishing her legitimacy), and who has been searching for Kate ever since—but that is not enough. Kate tops the market in Omaha, making a huge profit on her sheep. That comes close to being enough, but still isn't, quite. Kate uses that money, plus her father's support, to buy expensive clothes and reestablish her femininity. (Aged only twenty-eight, Kate can shed her Sheep Queen look far better than Lucy Moore could have—though eventually even for Moore, after a debilitating 1930 stroke, "the old fighting look seemed to become entirely erased from her face and her features assumed the soft, womanly look the Creator intended her to have in the first place"). But that isn't really enough either. Kate must have vengeance on Prouty.

Before her trip to Omaha to top the market, Kate finally submits to the request of the struggling Prouty bank, which now desperately wants her account. She does so with a plan: After her return, she demands to withdraw the full amount. And the bank doesn't have it. Would you rather fail, she asks, or give me control? The banker who had once shunned her must now submit and beg in vain for his job.

Money is her goal. She tells Hughie that money is the only weapon a woman can use. "Without it she's as helpless as though her hands were shackled and left a target for every one who chooses to throw a stone at her." She must succeed at business and acquire her own fortune, ideally at the expense of the rest of Prouty. You could say that Kate's belief in business exceeds even Bruce Burt's, because she's fully aware of the costs of choosing ambition over love.

Kate's final revenge comes with the irrigation project. Without knowing his identity, Jasper Toomey has met her father and tried to get him to invest. In a scene worthy of a drawing-room mystery, the town gathers for a dinner at which he will announce his decision. His first announcement, of course, is to introduce his stunning daughter, now making a grand entrance at the same ballroom where she was first humiliated. He then explains that the dam is a marginal moneymaker—he could take it or pass on it—so he'll leave the decision to her. She is able to make a lengthy speech reviewing her grievances, condemning Prouty's sorry behavior, rubbing their faces in it—and it is not enough.

Of course. Vengeance is never enough. The only path to true happiness is forgiveness. Perhaps Lockhart's editors told her that, upon reading an early draft. Or perhaps she could even see it herself. As she is speaking, Kate realizes, "This moment is a disappointment. Instead of the sweetness of revenge, I feel only indifference" because Prouty was not worthy of her quest. So putting a positive spin on it ("When failures have knocked me down, it is you, my enemies, who have given me the strength to pick myself up and go on"), she grants them the project. Her father then imposes some draconian conditions, keeping Toomey and his ilk from all but the barest of profits, and on the very last page of the book Hughie reappears, allowing Kate to claim that now that she knows both, love is more important than fortune.

The forgiveness and love help elevate *The Fighting Shepherdess* to Lockhart's finest work of fiction. But these themes are a tad perfunctory, as if Lockhart herself was more interested in the earlier Kate, the one who told

Hughie that forgiveness amounted to failure, the one who was so single-mindedly focused on setting and achieving her monetary goals.

⮌

In Hominy, Oklahoma, in May 1918, Lockhart chafed under the stern hand of her sister Grace Edgington. Grace ran a tight household, reminding Lockhart of an old-maid schoolteacher. When Lockhart started eating a meal before Grace gave the signal, Grace scolded her. Lockhart, visiting on one of her typical eastern journeys to publishers and family, wondered if she'd be able to survive a week under her sister's sharp tongue.

But Lockhart needed money. Grace's husband, Roy, was a banker. Knowing that she would have to touch Roy for a five-hundred-dollar loan was part of what was making Lockhart so grouchy. So was the weather: the humidity swelled her feet. And her age: she was now growing a beard, so long that even her uncle in Denver had noticed. She cut off the fuzz, sickened by the knowledge that she'd have to keep shaving for the rest of her life.

Lockhart was also grouchy because of her conflicting attitudes toward her home. She was alternately pleased and disgusted with Cody. "I don't think I'll be in Cody much any more," she wrote in the diary, "for it is a living death . . . fruitless . . . inane." Yet while she was in Denver a local reporter had interviewed her and praised her "breezy tolerance, gracious womanliness, looking nifty in tailored togs"—and Lockhart's first thought was the reaction that description would get in Cody. She wondered, too, if she was "coming into my own in Cody, getting my hold back that I had when I first came."

But she was having boy trouble. Waiting for her in Oklahoma were a letter and card from Orin B. Mann, a wealthy ranch owner from Meeteetse, thirty miles south of Cody. She was crazy about Mann but didn't know what to do about him. At times he seemed to thrust himself upon her, and at those times, she knew he was impossible. At times she would throw herself at him, and he would back away. He was a philanderer. He would never commit to any one woman. Yet she found herself dreaming of the phrase "Mrs. O.B. Mann." She found herself waking in the middle of the night, thinking of him, wanting him—or someone.

That someone could have been Jack Painter, who also had a letter waiting for her at Grace's in Oklahoma. He wrote that he was sweating blood on the Salmon. Or the someone could have been Valentin Di Colonna—an

Italian nobleman who in Cody preferred to go by the name "Bill Miller"—a soldier now off fighting in the war in Europe. His rather incoherent letter, sending a kiss, was also waiting for her at Grace's. Or it could have been Andrew Ross, another mining entrepreneur, president of a huge mine and a bank in Gilmore, Idaho. He was married, but unhappily so, and his letter, too, was waiting for her. There was no letter from Jesse Mitchell, a one-armed cowboy and poor correspondent, far less educated and refined than the others, but whenever Lockhart thought of him, she realized he was as sweet and devoted as any woman could ever ask for.

She was hungry for love and affection and sympathy, and in Oklahoma she didn't feel like she was getting enough from either family or friends. She felt alone and hoped that work might cure her blues. But could she work now? Would publishers like the manuscript she was carrying, the one she was calling "The Daughter of Jezebel"? She would show it first to her old editor at *Lippincott's*, Berg Esenwein, now a freelance consultant. He might give her something to hope for. She needed money, success. She might have to look for another newspaper job. She'd had some discussions in Denver with the *Post*. She would check out the Philadelphia *North American*. And maybe the *New York World*. If only her emotional state would let her work.

For these were not her only fears. Indeed they paled next to the big one. The big one that was now four days overdue.

Lockhart's train ride from Oklahoma to Philadelphia was a nightmare. She was a nervous wreck. She kept reviewing her argument with Grace. Grace had seen one of Di Colonna's letters in which he used words like "bitch" and "pimp." A *gentleman*, Grace insisted, would not write such a letter to a *lady*. Lockhart fumed that Grace could be so quick to condemn; she just wasn't experienced with this type of man. Though the son of a bona fide Italian count, Di Colonna lived a rugged outdoorsy life in Cody. Such earthy language was part of his appeal. But Grace responded with her list of other grievances—the table manners again.

Lockhart shot back. Grace was provincial and narrow. Grace was boring. Visiting her was as dull as waiting in a railroad station. She was interested only in her own family. Yet at the same time she was so cocksure and opinionated. By the end of the argument the sisters were not speaking.

Lockhart lay awake that whole night before her departure. As she later told her diary, she was worried that pregnancy would be a profound misfortune. At her age, in her position. How could she handle a baby? She would almost prefer to be suffering from cancer. During the night, unable to sleep, she became despondent almost to the point of suicide.

At no point in her worrying (which she expressed in great detail in her diary) did Lockhart consider terminating a pregnancy. She apparently found abortion repugnant. Her papers make only one mention of the subject, many years later, when she summarizes a conversation a prominent Codyite has with Dr. Frances Lane. He is telling Lane off, condemning her for years of alleged blackmail. She had, apparently, performed one or more abortions for him. Lockhart is not surprised that Lane performed this service—after all, she'd depicted Emma Harpe in *The Lady Doc* as an abortion provider, and she always wrote from experience. But she does use the incident to reiterate her opinion that Lane is a murderer. (Codyites never spoke publicly of abortion. But privately, those who knew of Lane's practice may have speculated: could this have been the source of their feud?) Given such attitudes, it is not surprising that now, on the train to Philadelphia, Lockhart would consider suicide before abortion herself.

Then, finally, she told herself that it was the atmosphere that was getting her down. When she got out of this deadly atmosphere, where the earth steamed like a vapor bath, she would get her grip back. Then she could face whatever would come.

But the morning after she arrived in Philadelphia, she was still so anxious her teeth were chattering as she set out to visit Dr. Henry Beatie. She would learn the worst, she was sure. The jig was up.

How could it be pregnancy? When she had escaped all these years? Back when she was younger, she had not always been careful.

The doctor asked how old she was.

She told him she was forty-seven.

He was astonished. Her period was off because she was experiencing menopause, he said. She didn't have to worry about "the other." He would give her a prescription to help regulate her flow, if indeed there was any flow left to regulate.

She breathed again and thought "the other" was horrible to her. This was the lesser of two evils. But it didn't help her despondency. Menopause was "the beginning of the end for me," she told her diary. She still couldn't quite believe it. She did "not see why anyone so healthy as I am should not have it for several years yet."

A month later she was at Winthrop Beach, outside of Boston. Esenwein had liked her manuscript, though maybe not quite as enthusiastically as he might have. H. L. Mencken had volunteered to read it. The esteemed publishing house Little, Brown wanted to see it. An agent was confident about selling serial rights, which would generate the five hundred dollars needed to pay back Roy's loan.

Early Monday morning she brought the manuscript downtown to the Little, Brown offices. She met with a curly haired editor named Jenkins. His face was mostly a mask, but she thought she saw a quick sparkle in his blue eyes.

The next day Jenkins sent a note: the novel gave "an excellent picture of the life of a sheep raiser" but it was too long, with the love interest insufficiently developed. Insecurity bugged Lockhart ("God! Have I wasted two years and a half of my life? It is like a death knell"), but she decided to solider on. She made plans to speak in person with Jenkins, and then to lug the manuscript over to another publisher, Small Maynard. She dreaded going back to Lippincott, where she was sure she would get turned down.

In person, however, Jenkins was even more discouraging. The book dragged out interminably, he said. It was humorless. It lacked climaxes for serialization. It felt padded for length. Then he told her what it should be like: B. M. Bower. Bower, he said, was a shining example of what a western novel and western humor should be.

"Bower," Lockhart despaired to her diary, "who is humorless and whose characters are of the screen." Maybe the manuscript *was* too long. But maybe Jenkins was an easterner who just wouldn't understand. "It seems illogical that I suddenly have become hopelessly dull with no merit whatever in my work."

But further delay would cramp her finances. She wrote to her father, asking for financial help until she placed the book. She considered selling her car in Cody. Since it looked like she would indeed have to take that job in Denver, she wouldn't need a car in Cody. Her father sent five hundred dollars, saying this was the money he'd been planning to send next fall, and she wouldn't get anything else. "God! If only O.B. would ask me to marry him and end all this worry and unhappiness but that is too much to come to me. I'm so scared of getting too old-looking before he sees me again. I wonder why it is that I'm a failure." Louise Closser Hale, her old classmate at the Moses True Brown school, was now not only a successful actress but also a well-published writer. The western writer William McLeod Raine had a story in the current *Popular*. It felt like machine fiction, she wrote. "I skipped gobs of it. I don't see how anybody who evades tediousness as much as I do can be tedious in their work as Jenkins said I was."

The insecurity probably hurt Lockhart's business dealings. She signed too quickly with Small Maynard. Mencken told a friend of hers that Moffat Yard was interested, and she later found out that Lippincott had been offended she never approached them. For the next several weeks, publishing friends advised her that she'd signed a bad contract. She'd even signed over the serial rights (after one agent told her the book was not as good *The Lady Doc*, she may have despaired that they were worthless), but did later get them back.

Still, success buoyed her spirits. Painter sent a congratulatory telegram, which also asked her to wire him some of her advance money. A new agent was much more optimistic about serialization. E. A. Grozier, her old publisher at the *Boston Post*, told her she would love the Denver paper, and once its publisher saw her "he wouldn't let me go out of the office without signing a contract." Her looks, in other words, were still holding up.

Lockhart returned to Cody in late July and spent the next month revising the novel, penning some new short stories, and conducting slow though positive negotiations with the *Denver Post*. She was surprised to see how many Cody people waved at her, called her "exuberant Caroline." She didn't feel so exuberant, fretting over her love life and old age. But, she told her diary, "s'help me, if my hand hasn't lost its cunning I'll make good on the *Denver Post*. And achieve the ambitious goal I've set for myself—to be the best known woman west of the Mississippi."

The year 1918 is the first for which Lockhart's full diaries survive, so we see in full relief her insecurities about her career and her love life. We see why she was able to create such bold (even overstated) dramas in her fiction: she viewed her life the same way. Each crisis was monumental, each setback devastating. Each disagreement generated an "enemy." Each enemy required a victory. From the diaries it would be tempting to conclude that starting in 1918 she became overwhelmed by fear, indecision, and petty jealousies. But two factors should guard against that temptation. First, she seems to have used the diaries as therapy, and we should thus expect them to portray her as more fragile and more anxious than a truly rounded picture might. Second, she was likely this overwrought her entire life—we just don't have the earlier diaries to show it. Indeed, some people believe that Lockhart or her surviving relatives destroyed the earlier diaries because they were so scandalous. Thus, her difficulties with men, for example, were probably representative of most of her midlife years.

O. B. Mann was a gentleman rancher, which is to say he didn't like to get his clothes dirty. He dressed neatly in dark trousers, white shirt, and tie, even on very hot days, and he was wealthy enough to have other people do the sweaty work for him. Born in Indiana in 1869, he had come to the Cody area as early as 1892, when he taught school along the Greybull River. He then went to work at the Pitchfork Ranch, one of the area's largest, where he rose to foreman before buying his own place. He'd been briefly married, but his young wife had died. Now he was courting Lockhart, but since Meeteetse was thirty miles away, he wasn't too regular about it.

Mann would ignore her for weeks. Friends would tell her how much he was seen in the company of his female cook. Lockhart would resolve to break with him. Then he would show up, they would spend a wonderful evening together, making her feel as content and happy as she ever had. Then he would return to Meeteetse and the cycle would start again.

One of the ways she fought back was by spending plenty of time with other men. Jesse Mitchell would come into town whenever he got a break from cowboying; during one visit he declared that he would do anything for her. Andrew Ross came for a quick visit in which he declared, "I'd murder for you!" Di Colonna continued to send amorous letters from Europe. After announcing that he was getting divorced, a man named Paul Richter started spending a lot of time with her. So did a man named Willie Altberger.

Lockhart had solidified a friendship with Willie and Maudie Altberger on her most recent visit to Philadelphia. They came to Cody to visit and ended up buying Lockhart's property in a subdivision southwest of town, building a cabin there. They were older, and wealthy, and Lockhart greatly enjoyed riding horses with them. Yet despite the admiration both had for Maudie, Willie found himself immensely attracted to Lockhart, and she found herself tempted to respond. He paid to install electric lights in her house. The two traveled to Montana to attend the annual fair on the Crow Indian Reservation. He would help wash her hair and massage her face. And finally one night in October, he told her he wanted to kiss her.

She turned him down, and eventually they repaired their friendship.

They would eat together and ride together; he would moon over her, and she would record his behavior in her diary. As she continued to brood over Mann, Altberger reassured her that she was so magnetic she could attract anybody she wanted.

She herself wasn't sure. In late October she told her diary, "[I] have a book coming out that one of the best editors in New York says is wonderful, $1440 in cash for serial [rights] that will boost me some, a position on the biggest paper in the West and the chance to make a reputation. An inheritance that will amount to more than I can myself take care of, three or four men in love with me . . . why should I be miserable over a selfish, evasive, disloyal excuse of a man like O.B.[?] But for the present, I am."

The small town of Cody wasn't used to a woman juggling three or four men at a time. Late in November 1918 some anonymous letters circulated— Altberger got one, Mann another—saying that Lockhart was the worst troublemaker in Cody. They were fools, the letters said. She had "roasted" Altberger; she roasted everybody. She would soon get him in trouble, and then kick him out. She would throw Mann up in the air once she had his money. She'd slept with more men than any of the girls at Cassie's, Cody's legendary whorehouse. Mann and Altberger both told her that the letters were of no concern. Her speculation as to the sender centered on several Cody women. But she didn't seem terribly worried. When she saw Mann's letter, the one that compared her to a whore, she said it was "too foolish to make me even very mad." At this point Lockhart was finally ready to take off for her new job in Denver, but that decision had been driven mostly by Mann's lack of commitment, rather than the attitudes of anyone else in Cody.

It takes no great leap of psychological insight to assert that Lockhart, like her heroine in *The Fighting Shepherdess*, was assuaging social rejection through career ambition. She wrote so herself in the diary. All year she kept reminding herself of her goals. "I've a kind of pride in winning big out in the West," she told herself in Boston. "I've made my boast that I would be the best known woman not only in Wyoming but in the West." Later on that trip, in New York, she fretted about returning to Cody: "I cannot waste my life there alone. It will be the ruination of my work and happiness."

The idea now was that Lockhart would replace Frances Wayne as the *Post*'s Denver-based female celebrity while Wayne went to Europe to report on the aftermath of the war. Lockhart would get her name in front of every newspaper reader in the West—thus helping to market *The Fighting Shepherdess*—and she could research her next novel while receiving a regular paycheck. She was already thinking about an Indian story, set in Oklahoma.

The problem with that plan came when she finally arrived in Denver.

~

In the grand atrium lobby at Denver's fashionable Brown Palace Hotel, Lockhart saw Edith Crane peering around purposefully. The lobby's gold onyx walls, cast-iron railings, stained-glass ceiling, and plush palms made it the favored haunt of well-to-do visitors as well as Denver society. As a celebrity journalist, Lockhart lived there. As wealthy visitors from a Cody-area ranch, Edith and Russell Crane were staying there. Then Edith spotted Lockhart and called her over. Lockhart knew the Cranes as cocky Cody socialites, part of the Lane-Beck crowd—once her friends, but now her bitter enemies.

Crane fussed over Lockhart, an indication that the power dynamics had somehow reversed. After only six weeks of writing for the *Post*, Lockhart was no longer shunned by the Cody crowd. Friends wrote her that *Post*s were snapped up quickly in Cody. In a speech at the Irma Hotel, one of Cody's bigshots said the town should be proud of her. Lockhart told her diary, "Guess I look like *somebody* to 'em now; and they know I can guy 'em if I want to. It is a deep satisfaction!"

Those first weeks in Denver were good for Lockhart's ego. Announcing her hiring on the front page, the *Post* wrote of "the brilliance of her intellect, the beauty of her vocabulary, and the tenderness of her heart." They told of her adventures and her femininity. They claimed she had turned down a spot on the *New York World* for the *Post*, because it was the paper read by both millionaires and sheepherders; it was the paper of the West. She was surprisingly nervous about her debut but quite gratified over her performance.

Ever competitive, Lockhart also took pleasure in topping Frances Wayne. "I can write circles around her," she told herself. In late December Wayne returned from Europe and apparently wasn't too happy that Lockhart remained on the staff as well. "She is a sharp-nosed, wrinkled dame for sure," Lockhart wrote in her diary. "She writes front page stories that nobody reads."

Lockhart's stories followed the mixture of styles she had perfected twenty years previously: interviews with prominent people (a judge, the governor, leading cattlemen) and oddballs (a bigamist, a lady bandit); tiny stories of everyday life (a breakfaster lays his last pancake atop his coffee cup, a homely man attracts female attention by borrowing a neighbor's child); and stories about nothing really in particular (how to tell if your Christmas gift was inappropriate; a list of enemies she'd like to run over with a tank). Many of the pointless, whimsical pieces were especially popular, with fans telling her, "You could make a story out of anything." But compared to her wide variety of assignments in Philadelphia, her Denver work demonstrates her narrowing interests. Lockhart took particular delight in old-timers and loved to write up half-invented dialogues with cowboys, sheepherders, and other Old West characters.

She also loved to mock Cody. For example, she suggested that as a punishment for war crimes, the Kaiser be shipped there. "He could go for a joyride thru Shoshone Canyon in 'Jedge' Walls' machine with the 'Jedge' at the wheel." Then he'd be forced to listen to Frank "Tinhorn" Houx (by now not just mayor but a failed gubernatorial candidate) deliver "one of his famous lectures on the evils of drink." As a last resort, "if he did not laugh himself to death, they could bring in the lady doctor to operate."

But satisfaction was short lived. She became aggravated when stories were buried inside the paper, botched by bad headlines or typesetting, or killed entirely. She wasn't making enough money, just fifty dollars a week, compared to the sixty-five dollars she'd made fifteen years previously in Philadelphia. She wasn't really getting anywhere. The work was inconsequential, beneath her talents. "I'm getting discontented more all the time," she told her diary in mid-February. "No fun, no exercise, no recognition of my stuff in the jumble of trash—it is wasted, lost."

She was also terribly lonely. Though she received numerous visitors—including the Altbergers (twice), stockgrower L. G. Phelps, an old beau from Albuquerque, Jesse Mitchell, and O. B. Mann—the only person she knew well in Denver was her Uncle Seward Woodruff, whom she found uncouth. These men who claimed to love her—why didn't they write more?

Mann's January visit was wonderful. "He was the sweetest ever," she wrote in her diary. "I believe he wants to marry me. We kissed each other at the station twice before everybody. We get along like two turtle doves, chummier than ever. I wouldn't be afraid to marry Ornery the least bit in the world. Once we got to know each other's ways and make allowances, we'd get along."

Then he didn't write—at least not enough to satisfy her—and she tried to steel herself: "O.B. I cannot count on and I am doing my best to bring myself to that realization to save myself from more heartache." One visiting friend told her Mann was "a knocker and tattle-tale and small in every way." Another called him a "sagebrush Lothario." But it didn't matter. She was infatuated. She kept dreaming of him and told herself to remember "that there was never a man, save [one], who would not have stuck to me had I retained *my* interest. I've always held them and when I am determined, as is the case now, and he is attracted, I ought not to worry over results."

Lockhart paced the floor of her hotel room one night in March. She cursed. *God damn him!!!*

It had been a good day. A Colorado movie producer had made a major offer for the rights to *Me-Smith*. He even suggested that Lockhart might make a good actress in one of her movies some day. Andrew Ross and Jack Painter had each written to say he loved her. Jesse Mitchell had written to say that he would come to Denver as soon as he got back from a cowboying trip. Her copies of the newly released *Fighting Shepherdess* were due to arrive shortly. Her father had sent thirteen hundred dollars, and she didn't think she would spend more than half of that before *Shepherdess* royalties started coming in. Then a Cody merchant named Harry Sanborn had called up, "like an old college chum," and offered to stop by with news of her hometown. The news he brought: O. B. Mann had gotten married. His young southern belle of a bride was named, oddly enough, Nan Lockhart.

Even later, when she wrote in the diary, her emotion was still raw. "God damn him, I hope he'll never know a day's happiness from now on. How could he come here and accept my love and mean to do this all the time? *O curse him!* What a snake! What a hypocrite! This is agony!"

She drank half a quart of Scotch that night, took two sleeping powders and a headache powder. She skipped work the next day, still feeling terrible. Mann had met Nan the previous winter and had probably planned ever since to marry her. This infuriated Lockhart. "Bad as I am, I couldn't go on making love to other men meaning to marry one." But knowledge of his cheating character did not ease the pain she felt at his rejection. A few days later, when she woke, she "heard the birds and saw the sunshine and felt like

I used to when I was a kid. I forgot I was old and homely and then suddenly, I remembered O.B. and it was like a hammer blow over the heart. I must realize that the younger woman always wins. That there is no hope."

She brooded most of the month. A visiting friend chuckled over "a big, strong, capable woman like me taking on so over a *boob*. Still, he is my own boob."

Eventually she braced herself. Friends reassured her that Mann was beneath her. She resolved to commit to the ever-loyal Jesse Mitchell. "That unpolished cowpuncher is a *man* all right." She asked him to accompany her to Oklahoma, where she would research her new novel. In fact, after a few days' visit in Denver, he headed there early to get the lay of the land while she took care of her affairs.

Leaving meant resigning from the full-time staff of the *Post*, a job she'd soured on anyway. They offered to publish her freelance work, and she promised to send them some. She continued talking with people in Hollywood, wondering if her path might eventually lay out there. But for now it was on to Oklahoma, where there was a situation that cried out for the Caroline Lockhart treatment. In a classic case of history marching beyond the frontier, oil had been discovered on the Osage Indian Reservation, and members of that formerly downtrodden tribe had suddenly become fantastically rich.

She sat in her room. She walked the streets. She waited. She cursed to herself. Would he ever show up? She could brain him, she thought—and then decided it wasn't Jesse Mitchell's fault that he had only a thimbleful of gray matter. His head, she decided, was solid ivory.

She was in Pawhuska, Oklahoma, center of the Osage reservation, and the one-armed cowboy was nowhere in sight. This was where they had planned to meet. She'd written to him saying that. But apparently he didn't even have the brains to go get his mail.

And yet she took some comfort in the fact that he was letting her down because he was stupid, rather than a two-timer like Mann. She sent Mitchell another letter, and it came back labeled "addressee unknown." She started worrying something had happened to him. If so, would she end up old and alone?

She'd spent four days looking for him in Tulsa, and now more than a week in Pawhuska. She was writing a bit because *Lippincott's* had asked for one of her breezy short stories, and writing made her feel good.

She was also receiving reviews and letters about *The Fighting Shepherdess*. In just three weeks it had already gone through five printings. An ad in
the *New York Tribune* called it "better than Zane Grey at his best." (She recorded that in her diary, followed by "Ugh! That tooth-pulling ass. My *worst*
is better than Zane Grey at his *best*.") A week later she received a review from
the *New York Sun*, commending the book's humor and detail. They found it
"extraordinarily good" and Kate "splendidly drawn" but added, "Just what
keeps the story from being a topnotcher is hard to say," concluding that it
was perhaps the harshness of the villains. She was more willing to accept
this analysis. Her response: "That seems to be the fault that keeps me from
success, my bitterness. So my life has made me."

Other reviews would match these sentiments. The *New York Times* wrote
tepidly, "This is an interesting story." The *New York Evening Post* called it a
"sprightly tale" but said her irony was juvenile and her characters only partially set forth. Some reviewers pointed out that Lockhart's novels were especially appreciated in the West. And a few, such as the *New York Tribune*,
absolutely loved it: "a work of striking originality . . . among the best fiction
of the year."

Friends' responses were more personal. One encouraged her to "forget
past discouragements and heartaches, you have reached the top to stay!" Another called it "literature," a distinction (as opposed to entertainment) Lockhart valued. Another said it "breathes your true self. Sometimes I really see
you in spirit as your reflections take shape in *The Fighting Shepherdess*."

But Lockhart, a woman of action, didn't spend much time sitting around
admiring her reviews. She was caught up in her new adventure. And if
Mitchell didn't arrive soon, she decided, she would just go on by herself.

Lockhart knocked at the door of the house. She found it a pretentious
house: two stories, red roof, dormer window, wide veranda, well-kept lawn,
iron fence and gate.

Nobody answered the door. There was no movement inside. Strange: she
knew the family was expecting her. She knocked again.

Unceremoniously, an Indian woman in a silk shirt, a black sateen skirt,
and moccasins came around the corner of the veranda. She had a very large
waistline and shiny black hair braided in pigtails. Lockhart recognized her
from the previous day: Mrs. Baconrind.

"Good morning," Lockhart said cordially.

Mrs. Baconrind did not return any greeting, but opened the door and called into the house, "Mattie!"

Lockhart followed. The interior rooms were furnished with velvet rugs and heavy oak chairs and tables. There were gilt-framed pictures on the walls; cut glass, silver, and china on the dining-room sideboard; a pianola and Victrola in the living room. There were also a half-dozen people, sitting on the floor against the wall, or lying on blankets. None of them had risen to get the door. A few women beaded moccasins, a few men smoked. Lockhart smelled tepee-tanned buckskin mingled with tobacco. It was the unmistakable odor, she thought, of Indians.

Mattie came in from the kitchen and inspected Lockhart.

"This is the new hired girl," Mrs. Baconrind told Mattie. "Show her where to go."

To do her research—to see the lives of the Osage from the inside—Lockhart had gotten herself a job as a servant. While in Pawhuska, she later wrote, she'd seen plenty of evidence of Osage wealth: new cars, silk shirts, high-heeled slippers, and even the patronizing attitude toward whites that whites usually had toward Indians. She was struck that few Osage wanted anything to do with whites, except as servants. Noting that each Osage received more than four thousand dollars in oil royalties a year (almost fifty thousand in 2005 dollars), she asked, "What do they do with it? What effect has money and education had upon these primitive people? What sort of a type is the combination producing?" Her verdict: they were "grossly fat, vain, arrogant."

Today we cringe at the stereotypes. Ever the social Darwinist, Lockhart believed in breeding and class, and so found the Osage lacking. In fact, she also dismissed the Irish servant Mattie: "there was on her face the stamp of bad blood, of low origin that was unmistakable."

Lockhart had gotten caught up in the racism of the times, and her failure to find humanity in the Osage may help explain why she would continually struggle in her efforts to turn these experiences into fiction. Confusing the issue was her relatively enlightened attitude toward the Crow and Blackfeet—and her pride in it. "The dirtiest, poorest member of either of those tribes looks like a 'regular fellow' to me beside the average Osage," she wrote. But then she'd never had to beg a Crow or Blackfeet for a job.

The Osage Indians, a tribe related to the Sioux, had once controlled all of current-day Missouri, northern Arkansas and Oklahoma, and eastern Kansas. Lockhart's childhood homes were in Osage County, Kansas. Before her birth the tribe had been confined to a reservation in southern Kansas, and in 1871 they were kicked off that land and moved to Oklahoma.

But compared to most reservations, the Osages' new home had two advantages. First, the tribe had bought the land for cash (from the Cherokees, using the proceeds of selling their Kansas reservation), rather than having it assigned by the federal government. So they were better able to resist allotment, the 1880s drive to turn Indians into individualist farmers by outlawing their communal land ownership. The 1887 Dawes Act forced most tribes to sell off reservation lands in homesteadlike parcels (many of which soon landed in white hands). But owning title to their lands, the Osage resisted allotment for almost twenty years—and when they did finally allot their surface lands, they kept tribal ownership of the mineral rights.

The second advantage was oil. First discovered in 1897, it didn't take off for twenty years. But when it did, each new oil lease generated royalties that were split among every enrolled member of the tribe. By 1917 each "headright" earned $2,719 (and a family might have multiple headrights). By 1925 a headright's annual take would be $13,400.

Today we might hope that the discovery of oil on Indian-owned lands would have produced a satisfying reversal of fortunes, in which Indians leapfrogged into twentieth-century leadership positions. But though the Osage governing council included many smart businessmen, most Americans at the time viewed the entire tribe as unjustifiably standing in the way of white wealth.

Many whites simply married Osage women for their money. Several later murdered their wives—indeed, due to complicated headright inheritance laws, some multiplied their riches by murdering numerous family members in order. Others used violence, in the tradition of the frontier outlaw, to rob folks of their cash. And some whites used legal and financial shenanigans to fleece Indians without violence. Reservation towns such as Pawhuska, Fairfax, and Hominy soon filled with lawyers who got themselves appointed as "guardians" of allegedly incompetent Indians, proceeding to decimate their accounts. In 1924 a federal probe indicted twenty-four of these swindlers, though they settled out of court.

Throughout the 1920s national correspondents came to report on this wild story. Most heaped scorn on the Indians. But in 1919 Lockhart was one of the first journalists to discover it. How had she heard about the oil-rich Indians? She'd seen them first-hand the previous spring. Her brother-in-law Roy was a banker in Hominy, the heart of Osage country.

There's no evidence that Roy Edgington himself was corrupt. He may have simply made loans to and accepted deposits from some of the area's more legitimate businessmen (oil pioneers J. Paul Getty and Frank Phillips were among the Osage leaseholders). One reason we don't know more about Edgington today is that during this research Lockhart actually avoided Hominy. She and Grace were still feuding—Grace had angrily returned some jewelry Lockhart sent in December. So Lockhart did most of her reporting from Fairfax and Pawhuska. She intended to act as independently as possible.

Lockhart lay in the tent as Jesse Mitchell crawled out early in the morning. He was going fishing. He hoped to catch a big drum fish. Half asleep, she could hear him getting ready. Before he left he came back into the tent to give her a kiss. She smiled at the notion that he wouldn't even go half a mile fishing without feeling the need to kiss her goodbye.

The evening before they had stood in front of the tent, admiring the sunset. She felt happy and satisfied. This shabby tent she'd bought from a freighter actually felt like home, with a table and boxes and a place for the fire. Mitchell had fixed the fire for her. He had cleaned up and was shaving regularly for her. He was always tender and chivalrous, wouldn't even let her carry a bucket of water. He called her "baby." He told her that he believed *The Fighting Shepherdess* would be not only her best book, but also her last. Its success would mean she wouldn't have to work any more and could devote herself "to doing what I like, cattle and outdoor living. I hope he is right."

The innkeeper in Pawhuska, who had befriended Lockhart, said that when Lockhart was gone Mitchell talked about her constantly, worshipped the ground she walked on. The innkeeper asked him if they would get married, and he said, "No, she is too far above me, but I can love her till I die."

They were camped near Fairfax, about thirty miles west of Pawhuska, not far from the Baconrinds' home. Her job there had not lasted long, of course. She hadn't liked washing dishes; she'd been sassy and disagreeable; she'd taken a night off to go to a dance with the prodigal Mitchell (who had finally arrived, unscathed). She'd worked another week for another family, complaining about the monotony, loneliness, hard work, and low pay. Then one afternoon while sitting on a stone wall with Mitchell, she came up with a brilliant idea.

It's not entirely clear what the idea was, but it involved spying on the Indians by camping nearby. She bought a car and a canvas tent. The car cost $350, which the salesman assured her she could easily recoup when she resold it. Even though the tent was ragged, in it she was far happier than she'd been at the Brown Palace Hotel, far happier than she'd been in ages. "I never knew what it was to be so protected and worshipped with such self-abnegation," she told her diary. Every day she would set her typewriter on a box and work on her writing. She felt her creative juices flowing. Jesse had secured another job with an Indian family, for both of them. And now he was off catching fish for her.

He did not return all day. She told herself not to worry: after all, he always told her not to worry. He was probably having troubles with the car, which had turned out to be a lemon. But in the late afternoon, as she was making new coverings for their pillows, a terrible nervousness seized her.

She walked up the road to the fishing hole. She saw the car there. A sickening fear came over her. She got closer, and the fear became more sure. She started running down the road. She sent a man for help, and some Indians came from the nearby village. "It was like a Belasco setting," she wrote, referring to a famous stage manager, "the blood red sun behind the trees and the Indians in their bright blankets running along the high, green bank shouting, 'Jesse, Jesse!' I laid down in the grass and cried, weak and perspiring with grief and horror of the future without my pardner."

The riverbank by the road was ten to fifteen feet high. Mitchell's clear footprints started down the embankment toward a small foothold just above the water. But the ground had caved in. In mid-May Salt Creek was at its raging peak. With just one arm, Mitchell was no match for it. Dragging the hole, rescuers recovered his body about 11:00 that night.

Lockhart explained to the authorities that she was his sister. She didn't want her name to get out; she didn't want to embarrass Grace and Roy Edgington.

Funny, the sheriff said: Mitchell had told somebody in Fairfax that she was his wife. And there was a bruise on his head, no water in his lungs. It added up to a pretty suspicious situation.

The county prosecutor came over from Pawhuska. Lockhart had to hire an attorney of her own. She also had to tell them who she was.

The attorneys turned out to be friends of Edgington. They thought the world of him. Once they knew who she was, they accepted her story. They even fixed the press account for her. The newspaper report identified Mitchell as her "chauffeur, cook, and helper." It noted that "she comes from a good family having relatives in this county who stand high in the community in which they reside. She is a writer of ability, being the author of a number of books, the latest being *The Fighting Shepherdess*."

Despite the tragedy, she lingered in Pawhuska another week. She met a traveling photographer who did portraits of Indian families. He invited her to ride along with him. Though she found him boring, she accepted. In fact, his vehicle aggravated her back, so she soon volunteered to let him drive *her* car. Though his lousy driving was hard on the car, she decided it was a pretty good stunt: another way to get in and see Indian families.

The photographer apparently didn't understand that she was just using him for her research. Three days after they met, he asked her to marry him. She found it ridiculous that he would expect her to give up her literary career to write letters for him, sew his buttons, collect his laundry. Hilarious— and yet heartbreaking. When Mitchell had suggested that she would give up her career for cattle and outdoor living, she had found the notion glorious.

Three days later she left Oklahoma for good. The trip had cost her one thousand dollars and the life of a man who was devoted to her. She found that the greatest loss. In retrospect, at least, she elevated Mitchell to Mann's equal: the only men who really captured her heart, the only men she ever could have married. Though in her immediate actions she did not appear to be mourning him, in her diaries it was a tragedy from which she might never recover.

She returned to Cody, where friends said the town seemed merrier with her there. Indeed, she arrived just after a party. Valentin Di Colonna had returned from the war. A hundred people met him at the train station, but two days later he had a more intimate welcome: dinner and drinks at the home of Caroline Lockhart. He asked if he could kiss her, and though she coquettishly refused, she was quite smitten.

She was torn again, in the pattern that recurred throughout her life. Men found her irresistible. Her ego desperately needed their attentions, and she continually filled her diary with insecurities about how men felt toward her.

1. As a young woman, Lockhart was beautiful, brash, and adventurous. Courtesy of Park County Historical Archives, Cody, Wyoming.

2. In Philadelphia Lockhart wrote a newspaper column under
the pen name "Suzette." Courtesy of Caroline Lockhart Papers,
American Heritage Center, University of Wyoming.

3. Main street of Cody, Wyoming, in 1907, three years after Lockhart arrived in the still-frontier town. Courtesy of Buffalo Bill Historical Center, Cody, Wyoming, P.5.1466.

4. Lockhart's first love, journalist-adventurer Andrew McKenzie,
preceded her to Cody. Courtesy of Caroline Lockhart Papers,
American Heritage Center, University of Wyoming.

5. John L. "Me" Smith fashioned himself as a "bad man," prompting
first Lockhart's attraction and then her mockery. Courtesy
of Buffalo Bill Historical Center, Cody, Wyoming, MS30.1.15.1.

6. Lockhart and Dr. Frances Lane were friends at one time,
when they acted together in a Cody minstrel show, probably around
1906. Courtesy of Caroline Lockhart Papers,
American Heritage Center, University of Wyoming.

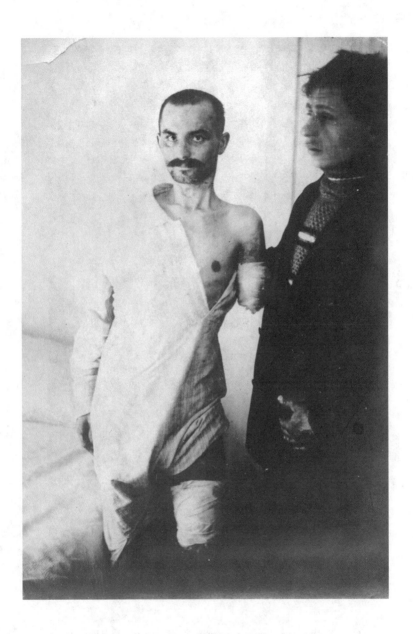

7. Injuries sustained by the young Austrian immigrant Marko Ferko
set Lockhart on a crusade. Courtesy of Caroline Lockhart
Papers, American Heritage Center, University of Wyoming.

8. An outstanding horsewoman, Lockhart also valued horses'
companionship. Courtesy of Caroline Lockhart Papers, American
Heritage Center, University of Wyoming.

9. Ever the character, Lockhart posed for this publicity photo with a bear cub even though her novels had little to do with bears. Courtesy of Caroline Lockhart Papers, American Heritage Center, University of Wyoming.

10. At age forty-eight Lockhart applied for a job as a maid
for a wealthy Osage family in order to get the scoop on their
lives. Courtesy of Caroline Lockhart Papers,
American Heritage Center, University of Wyoming.

11. In addition to founding the Cody Stampede rodeo, Lockhart's
energy led to the creation of this Gertrude Vanderbilt Whitney statue
of Buffalo Bill, a centerpiece of downtown Cody. Author's photo.

12. Flaunting Prohibition, Lockhart regularly entertained friends at a bar in her Cody home. Courtesy of Caroline Lockhart Papers, American Heritage Center, University of Wyoming.

13. Lockhart's boyfriend, Lou Ericson, shown here on horseback, was an exceptional jockey but found less success as a ranch manager. Courtesy of Caroline Lockhart Papers, American Heritage Center, University of Wyoming.

Dave Good

John S. Kirkpatrick

14. Dave Good (*left*) was the sort of genuine cattle hand Lockhart
had been searching for all her life. Courtesy of
Park County Historical Archives, Cody, Wyoming.

15. The L Slash Heart Ranch today. Courtesy of Kari Clayton.

But at the same time she could never fully believe that love would satisfy her.

How could she? In that era a woman getting married generally left her previous life to support her husband's life. Lockhart seems to have had some rather immature notions of love—Mann fed only her insecurities; Mitchell fed only her ego; neither seems to have produced the sort of magical joy we like to associate with true love. But even if she had found a genuine partner, a commitment might have marked the end of her opportunity to pursue her own fame. Marriage would have meant giving up her ability to choose what she would work at, where she would live, and whom she would hate. She wasn't ready to give those up. So after describing to her diary how manly and chivalrous was Di Colonna, this handsome younger nobleman, she nevertheless had to conclude, "What satisfaction I can extract from success and from money will be all there is in life for me."

If Lockhart had planned to go into exile in order to boost her popularity in Cody, the plan actually worked. She returned in the summer of 1919 to take up residence as the town's celebrity. She still had numerous enemies, including many religious people and associates of Dr. Lane. But Cody had been through hard times: Buffalo Bill died in 1917 in Denver, and Colorado officials bribed his widow into having him buried there instead of in Cody. Then in 1918 influenza struck the town (as it did worldwide). Schools were closed and public gatherings prohibited as officials struggled to contain the deadly epidemic. So by the following summer, the community may have been ready for a hero. With Denver and Hollywood laying accolades at Lockhart's feet, Cody joined the parade.

Negotiations continued for the movie version of *Me-Smith*. The producers even wanted to film it in Cody (building on the success of a non-Lockhart movie, *The Hell Cat*, which had been filmed there the previous summer). To rile up her enemies, Lockhart started circulating a rumor that it was actually *The Lady Doc*, not *Me-Smith*, that would soon hit the silver screen. The deal never did happen, but soon bigger ones were on the way.

In July Lockhart's representatives sold *The Fighting Shepherdess* to a production company headed by starlet Anita Stewart and mogul-on-the-rise Louis B. Mayer. She also got an offer from Douglas Fairbanks.

Fairbanks, the dashing actor-producer who had just formed the United

Artists Corporation with Mary Pickford, Charlie Chaplin, and D. W. Griffith, greatly admired Lockhart's work. He had all of her books on his desk. Raised in Colorado, Fairbanks was looking for a good western vehicle. Lockhart, he said, was the one western writer who could give him something original. She claimed that he had offered fifty thousand dollars for a humorous western screenplay, or ten thousand dollars for a story that his own writers could work into a screenplay.

Thinking about Fairbanks drew her attention away from the Osage. She'd been working on short stories set on the reservation—they did not flow easily, and she continued to struggle with them for many years—but Fairbanks expected her to produce something original. She realized the setting was all around her.

Russell and Edith Crane, the Cody society folks who'd started acting more friendly toward Lockhart in Denver, ran a "dude ranch" near Meeteetse. Russell would spend several months each winter in the East, recruiting rich people to come vacation at his ranch in the summer. With the world war having cut into European travel, the idea of seeing the great American West gained increasing appeal. In fact, the Cody area, located so close to Yellowstone Park, was becoming a major center of dude-ranching activity. Princeton graduate Larry Larom ran one of the world's most famous dude ranches up the valley of the South Fork of the Shoshone. Tex Kennedy, another ranch manager, often asked Lockhart if he could bring his dudes by to meet her. The industry provided a perfect setting for Lockhart's trademark clash of eastern and western values.

"Dude ranches"—operating entirely as resorts, with no revenues from cattle—had been around since at least 1905. But writers had generally shied away from portraying them. After all, readers of western fiction—like visitors to dude ranches—wanted romanticized versions of an *authentic* West. The dude ranch itself was not authentic, and the self-reinforcing standards of the cowboy novel kept sending writers back to the 1880s. So just one national author had ever published fiction set on a dude ranch: Caroline Lockhart.

In 1907 the *Red Book Magazine* published a short story called "The Dude Wrangler," advertised as a personally conducted tour of Yellowstone. In it Lockhart mocks an ignorant if likable westerner who tries to shepherd ten easterners through their Wyoming vacation. In 1909 she published another story, "Jim's Dude," in which a western wrangler falls in love with a visiting lady. Now Lockhart expanded the plot of the first story, while incorporating some humorous episodes from the second one.

At the beginning of the book, the future dude wrangler Wallie lives year-round in seaside resorts with his overprotective maiden aunt, whose fortune he will inherit. A painter and an athlete, he spends most of his time with his aunt's doddering friends, who call themselves "the Happy Family." (The label is Lockhart's dig at B. M. Bower, who calls her Flying U cowboys by the same name.) When cowboy Pinkey Fripp, returning to Wyoming from the war, stops in at the resort to visit an army buddy, he sets off a Roosevelt-style crisis of masculinity for Wallie. Wallie did not serve in the war, cannot ride a western bronc, and is shunned by a sprightly Wyoming native named Helene, as he laments here to an affable Pinkey:

> "Er—by the way"—Wallie's tone was elaborately casual—"what did she mean yesterday when she called me 'Gentle Annie'?"
>
> Pinkey moved uneasily.
>
> "Could you give me the precise significance?" persisted Wallie.
>
> "I could, but I wouldn't like to," Pinkey replied, dryly....
>
> "It is, then, an epithet of opprobrium?"
>
> "I can't say as to that," replied Pinkey, judicially, "But she meant you were a 'perfect lady.'"

So Wallie decides to break with his aunt and make his own way in the West. He files on a homestead, and the first half of the book covers his misadventures in dry farming. He buys a horse that is loco and a milk cow that is dry; he tries to walk in cowboy boots; he tries to cook prairie dogs using a rabbit recipe from a highfalutin cookbook. Homesteading dry farmers were precisely the newcomer element Lockhart hated in Cody (they were widely disparaged using the invented slur *honyockers*), but by making this one a well-bred easterner rather than a striving midwesterner, she is able to find sympathy for him. As he stubbornly holds on and learns the ways of the West, his problems become less of his own making. He drills for water but it comes up salty; the evil owner of the neighboring ranch lets his bulls out to trample Wallie's first wheat crop; before the fields can recover they are devastated by a hailstorm.

The overall effect is quite comic. As usual, Lockhart sets in opposition the upper-class East and the earthy West, with just enough respect for each to hold back the nastiness. Wallie and Pinkey have entirely different vocabularies, usually because they have entirely different experiences to name.

Lockhart noted in her diary that she tried to put a grin in every paragraph, and while she was often heavy-handed about it, that ambition did keep out some of the political rants that marred, for example, *The Man from the Bitter Roots*. Sacrificed to humor, however, is character and motivation. Wallie, Pinkey, Helene, the evil Canby, and the Happy Family are all drawn in absurd caricature. Wallie's decision to start a dry farm on a lonely homestead—despite wealth that would have allowed him to buy an already successful operation—has no justification, except that it's needed to serve the jokes. Likewise, Wallie's ability to transform himself into a westerner resides not so much in his stubbornness as in the requirement to set up jokes in the second half of the book.

At his nadir, Wallie's bad luck has reduced him to working for another rancher for wages. He and Pinkey have become a matched pair of broke and hopeless cowpunchers. Then they revisit Wallie's forlorn homestead and he gets an idea:

> "Pink," he said, solemnly, "why wouldn't this make a dude ranch?"
> Pinkey stared back at him.
> "Gentle Annie," he replied, finally, "I told you long ago you was good fer somethin' if we could jest hit on it. You're a born duder!"
> "Thanks! I feel as complimented as the fellow in the Passion Play who is cast for Judas Iscariot."

So in the second half of the book, the Happy Family comes to Wallie's dude ranch, and we again have a contrast of East and West. The dudes wear ridiculous clothes, run their horses too slow or too fast, carry their weapons to meals, and refuse to eat with the hired help. This last particularly infuriates the cook, whose revenge comes in the form of serving one woman wormy trout, getting another to swim in a leech-filled pond, sending a man down a snowfield on a holey toboggan, and baiting bears with bacon tied outside the dudes' tents. Since a cook is irreplaceable, Wallie can't fire him even though each episode drives away another dude.

The demise of Wallie's duding outfit provides comic satisfaction, since most writers would have been tempted to give Wallie a happy-ending success in his new career. But Lockhart's love for the old-time West gave her conflicting feelings about dude ranches. They provided employment for cowboys and other old characters; they revered outdoor adventure, frontier skills, and the bygone days; they brought in the well bred. But since the dudes were paying the bills, the westerners always had to toady up to money. In the end, Lockhart decides, this is unacceptable. In her own life the West had won its clash of values with the East—in her fiction it should too. So the novel concludes with Wallie and Helene (impressed by his new western manliness) turning his homestead into a sheep ranch. They hire Pinkey to run it so they can travel, stopping first at the seaside hotel where the Happy Family has gaily if improbably reunited.

Lockhart spent the winter of 1919–20 finishing *The Dude Wrangler*. But Douglas Fairbanks never followed through on his interest. Instead she published it as a novel with Doubleday, Page and Company. Doubleday had published Rudyard Kipling, Upton Sinclair, Joseph Conrad, and other famous literary figures. Lockhart's association with this esteemed house represented a high-water mark for her career as a novelist. But by the time the book came out, she had already embarked on a new adventure.

Throughout her years of publishing books, Lockhart always referred to herself as a newspaper writer. When introducing herself to the Sheep Queen, she said she wrote for newspapers. When she gave an occupation to the heroine of *The Man from the Bitter Roots*, it was journalist, not novelist. When she wrote in her diary about the flattering way a Boston friend had introduced her in a restaurant, it was that she was "the brightest newspaper woman in the U.S.A." She had never really left the world of newspapers. But now she would enter it on an entirely different scale.

Cowboy Publisher

The men met in Caroline Lockhart's living room, amidst the bearskin rug and the picture of Sourdough Sam and the shroud of John Barleycorn, a memento from a "funeral" for liquor at an eve-of-Prohibition party the previous summer. Wampus, Lockhart's pet wildcat, stalked through the room. The house, now more than sixteen years old, was starting to show some age on the outside. It needed paint and a new roof. But the interior was full of keepsakes of the West, her parties, and her travels. Lockhart herself exuded humor and vigor. Though she was almost fifty years old, her heavy blonde hair and shapely figure made her look thirty-five.

The men with her included Larry Larom, the influential dude rancher; Ernest Goppert, an ambitious young attorney; Sid Eldred, editor of the *Park County Enterprise*; Clarence Williams; and William Loewer. It was April 20, 1920, and the topics of their meeting included Cody and the frontier.

Like many western towns, Cody usually celebrated the Fourth of July with a rodeo. Area cowboys would show off their roping, riding, and bull-dogging skills. There were concerts, baseball games, and minstrel shows. The events were small and not necessarily held every year. But the previous year, 1919, a couple of other developments had coincided to make for a bigger celebration.

One was the coming of Prohibition, which began in Wyoming on July 1, 1919, and convinced event planners to move the party to June. The other was the spring opening of the increasingly popular automobile road from Cody into Yellowstone National Park, on June 21. Entrance Day, Cody called its celebration that weekend. An empty lot downtown was converted into a village called Slippery Gulch, with its own sheriff and "Justice of the Pieces," plenty of alcohol, and any number of gambling devices.

Entrance Day had proved so popular that now, at Lockhart's house, this committee was planning how to expand it. They didn't want to call it a *rodeo* (that "sounded like a dude word," Lockhart later wrote jestingly, "and besides we did not know how to pronounce it"), so they called it the Cody Stampede. They wanted to make it an annual event and return it to the Fourth. They wanted to bring in more and better rodeo competitors, professionals like champion bulldogger Pinkey Gist, who'd hooked up with Lockhart during Entrance Day and served as her model for Pinkey Fripp of *The Dude Wrangler*. They wanted to attract people from around the region and even dudes from the East, in the manner of Cheyenne Frontier Days, a popular tourist event at the other end of the state.

Larom came to the meeting at Lockhart's house because this was the sort of event his dudes would love to attend. Goppert came because he had ambitions for Cody as well as for himself. He may have been the one who noted that the Pendleton Round-Up—which vied with Cheyenne's as the West's most famous rodeo—had made the fortunes of an Oregon town smaller than Cody. Goppert had tried to push the idea of the Cody Stampede at the powerful Cody Club, but folks there had not volunteered to do much work on it. Williams came because he'd run Entrance Day last year with L. M. Prill, Eldred's predecessor. Loewer came because he could serve as the mayor of Slippery Gulch. Lockhart hosted the meeting because to her the Stampede represented the frontier.

The Stampede's publicity materials, authored by Lockhart, do not merely talk about a rodeo, a dance, or a celebration of the nation's birth. They say, "The old West, with its sports and feats of daring, has almost passed. Nearly everywhere the honk of the scissor-bill's tin lizzie has replaced the yip of the cowboy. . . . [*Scissorbill* was popular slang for a foolish, incompetent loudmouth; a *tin lizzie* was a Model T Ford.] Yet some of that old West that we love can hold a little longer, if we make the effort. And surely there is no more fitting place in America for exhibitions of cowboy skill and valor than right here in Buffalo Bill's town at the foot of the Rockies." She echoes Buffalo Bill in calling the event "a Wild West" (not a "Wild West show," which would be mere entertainment rather than an authentic reenactment). The Stampede has two purposes, she explains: keeping alive that "spirit of the West" and perpetuating the memory of Buffalo Bill.

At the meeting they formed a stock association to raise the money to put on the Stampede. As the organization's directors, these six individuals voted Lockhart to be their president.

Eight days later Lockhart felt like kicking up her heels. It was like school was out for the summer. She'd just finished up *The Dude Wrangler*, handing it off to her typist. The last chapter had come out well. Lockhart celebrated at a dinner with friends: the Altbergers and Dwight and Lizzie Hollister. Then after dinner Doc Bennett came over to her house.

It must have felt like a gathering of twin souls. Like Lockhart, William S. Bennett had recently returned from a trip. She'd spent March and early April in Los Angeles, where she'd been frustrated with the movie business. (Although she attended plenty of meetings about converting her other work to the screen, nobody took any action.) Bennett had spent four months in Colorado and New Mexico, meeting with capitalists and investing in oil wells. But both were back in town for good, they said. In the paper that day, Bennett announced that he was now planning to devote all of his time to his Cody medical practice.

Their similarities ran deeper. Just one year older than Lockhart, Bennett had also been raised in Kansas and Illinois. He'd also come to Cody in 1904, though he split his time between Cody and Meeteetse until 1909. He was slim and handsome, with dark hair and a dark moustache. Energetic and amiable, he was blessed with social graces. He'd been a state representative in Meeteetse and later served a term as mayor of Cody.

But, like Lockhart, his wild living had offended the conservative Cody society. He bought a car in 1913 and drove it fast. Too fast. He was known as "the fastest doc in the West." Nobody wanted to ride with him because he got in too many accidents. He also had financial troubles. In 1916 a bank sued him for defaulting on a loan. In 1918 he convinced several local men to invest with him in a Nevada mine, and they all lost their shirts. He carried on an increasingly public affair with Cassie, Cody's notorious madam. One day Bennett's wife, proud of a new dress he had bought her, ran into Cassie at the post office wearing the exact same dress. Mrs. Bennett packed up and moved to their son's home in Cheyenne.

Between his financial troubles and the community's disapproval, he was forced to sell much of his real estate, including the drugstore that had served as the base of his medical practice. Returning now, he leased a tiny office, but would end up moving both it and his residence several times in the next few months.

In this visit Bennett told Lockhart he had an idea. The *Park County Enterprise* was for sale, and he wanted to form a company to buy it. The company would include him, a couple of the paper's employees, an area rancher, and Lockhart. She told him she would do it.

Compared to the debates she had with her diary about the *Denver Post* job—or even about some of the failed movie deals—her decision to buy the newspaper happened remarkably quickly and effortlessly. She did no financial analysis. She spent little effort imagining what owning a newspaper would entail, or how she would get along with her fellow owners. She just decided to do it.

Perhaps the decision seemed easy. The fifteen-hundred-dollar price was split among five investors: Bennett, Lockhart, editor Eldred, printer Charles Conger, and Larom. Perhaps she understood that the decision had to be made quickly: the *Enterprise* was nearing bankruptcy. A year previously its owner had written to her in Oklahoma, asking if she had any ideas on how he could dispose of it. It had only gone downhill since, and once it entered foreclosure, it would be far more complicated to purchase.

Perhaps she remembered being part of a stock company of local Republicans that had started the competing *Park County Herald* about ten years previously. That effort had been much like the Cody Stampede was now: a few people doing lots of work while a larger number of "stock subscribers" did little more than put up some money and get their names in the paper. The *Herald* subscribers had eventually gotten tired of the deficits and turned ownership of that paper over to its editor, Len Leander Newton.

She and Bennett may also have been influenced by a desire to combat Newton's *Herald*. Though Newton liked the idea of the Stampede ("That letter of yours is worth about $50 and I am enclosing a check for same without stipulation," he wrote Lockhart), he was more interested in the future than the past. He was more interested in irrigated farming than dude ranches. He was a short man, exceedingly clean cut, with a wide, rather dour face under a large forehead. His pet initiative was good roads. The *Herald* was still Republican, as was most everybody in Cody, but it was decidedly Methodist. It favored Prohibition and disapproved of immorality. Within a year the *Herald* and its allies, citing moral issues, would force Bennett out of his position as county health officer (seeking to install Dr. Frances Lane instead), and eventually drive him completely out of town.

Finally, Lockhart may have also believed that the *Enterprise* would address two of her recurring concerns. One was the need for money. Newspaper work was the only way she knew to earn regular income, but she didn't want to go back to work in Philadelphia, New York, or even Denver. If she had to remain a journalist, why not in Cody? The other was her ambition. As her Denver experiences showed, success counted more to her when she could show it off *in Cody*. She needed the approval of people she knew; she needed a sense of personal victory over the specific enemies she had made there. Though Lockhart still sought nationwide fame, she increasingly believed that the road to such fame started in her hometown.

However, all of these motives were small and not terribly conscious. In her only significant diary entry about the purchase, she wrote simply and unironically, "I think I shall enjoy helping on this. It will give me a little power and prestige." It would be a way to combat Frances Lane, keep her profile up in town, remind her of what bigger fame would taste like. It might also stem Cody's evolution from wild frontier to stultifying civilization. Nevertheless, she expected to spend most of her working time on novels, movies, and short stories, and most of her spare time on the Stampede. As the sale closed on May 5, she believed that with some token support, Eldred and Conger would be the ones to revitalize the *Enterprise*.

Every time that spring that Lockhart went for the mail, it seemed there was another check. Checks rolled in for the Stampede: $100 from former mayor Jakie Schwoob, the $50 from Newton, $10 from Paul Richter, $20 from Russell Crane. There was even $10 from Lockhart's traditional enemy Blanche Gokel. There was $20 from Josephine Darte, one of Lockhart's wealthy Pennsylvania relatives. "Aunt Josie," who was actually two years younger than Lockhart, was recently widowed and planning an extended visit to Cody. Meanwhile, Lockhart also received a royalty check, $82, from Small Maynard. Even her tight-fisted father sent $200 to build a sleeping porch.

The Stampede raised more than $2,000. The organizers could spend $1,250 outfitting Slippery Gulch, now renamed Wolfville (slogan: "your night to howl!"). They were able to set up the rodeo with more than $550 in prizes, more than most area competitions, which meant they would attract good riders. Pinkey Gist would be back, he said, passing up a $1,000 event in Chicago because the Stampede president had asked him.

What's more, every time Lockhart went downtown—maybe to deposit another check—people smiled when they saw her. She couldn't get over it. "Everybody grins at me," she told her diary in amazement. "It seems incredible that I am the same person who used to walk and ride down the street without one friendly face to greet me." She believed Lane had been responsible for that—people used to know Lockhart only through her battles with the lady doc. But now she was the face of the Stampede. That met with their approval, and their approval gratified her.

Her Stampede preview articles ran every week. They got better and better, people told her. She wrote about all these stock subscribers, all these checks coming in. She wrote about the riders planning to participate, the dude ranchers reserving hotel rooms for their guests. She wrote about the horses—the Old West, after all, was all about horses—saying "the horse shall have equal show with its rider." She wrote of the great posters designed by Valentin di Colonna, now being hung all over town. She wrote of the dance pavilion and the orchestra that would play there. "There will be a bar where patrons may put their feet on the rail and tell the bar-keep why they can't get along with their wives, and other troubles." Best of all, she said, "A Wild Man, captured recently in the Bear Tooth mountain[s], will be on exhibition. He drinks hot blood and eats raw meat. His bite is poison. Visitors will be requested not to tease him."

She was nervous, despite the breezy tone. She would get up early, run all day. The event organizers worked like hounds. But there were rewards. People loved the idea of the Stampede. Many said they were planning to come. Charlie Bonfils of the *Post* almost came up all the way from Denver, and though he couldn't make it he ran a double-column story with "the handsome Caroline Lockhart" in the headline. Lockhart was tasting fame, on a small local level. She liked it very much.

"Ladies and Gentlemen!" In front of the grandstand at the beginning of her official welcome, Lockhart felt as nervous as a grand opera singer. The weather was all they'd hoped for: no rain and not too hot. Everything else, too, was all she had hoped for. The bucking horses were suitably wicked. Aunt Josie had come and the two women were getting along like turtledoves. Pinkey too had arrived, acting fond of her.

Over at the sideshow, the Wild Man was snarling, tugging at his rope, hammering in his rage on the fence with a shin bone. In real life his name was Bob Hopkins, and he was a retired dentist. But here Hopkins snapped at people with his gleaming teeth. At one point his "guard" pulled a six-shooter and shot a round of blank cartridges at the Wild Man's bare feet to make him dance. The shots came too close, giving Hopkins powder burns. Going off script, he took his shin bone and whanged the guard on the top of the head.

Riders had come in from as far as Miles City, Montana, which was 250 miles away and had its own noted rodeo. There were town folk with cars, and tourists, and people on horseback. More people were gathered in front of Lockhart on the stands than had attended all three nights the previous year combined. One box sold for $250. It was the biggest crowd ever assembled in Cody.

"The Cody Stampede of 1920 is now on," she called out to the crowd, then issued the celebration's slogan. "Powder River! Let 'em Buck!"

It was the best Wild West ever put on in a small town, said her wrap-up article, just as the committee had promised. And everyone gave the credit to Lockhart. But she went to bed with a heavy heart.

She'd really made good, she'd done something for the town. But she was alone. Pinkey would come by and act fond of her, but when other people were around he would act like he didn't care for her. In truth he was not a very attractive man—in fact, she reflected, he was a "homely uneducated little mutt"—yet she could not work her charms even on him. And O. B. Mann, with whom she was still carrying on despite his marriage, had written her that he would come if he could, but she hadn't seen him at all. In fact, the cheapskate hadn't even sent a check for a stock subscription.

Later in the week she found out Mann *had* come to the Stampede but had brought his wife. And Pinkey had slept with another woman every single night he was there. "The great Stampede is done," she wrote in her diary. "It leaves me, as most things do." But then she composed a funny story about it for the *Enterprise* and started planning her next party.

The following weekend Wolfville was full again, with folks dancing to a repeat engagement of the Red Lodge Orchestra. Her friends had come from throughout northwest Wyoming to see the movie *The Fighting Shepherdess* and party with the author afterward.

The movie was not very good. She'd seen it in Los Angeles, lamenting that they'd made a commonplace picture out of her story. This time she suffered in silence. For her the real test was whether she could pull off another function as successful as the Stampede. She was pleased with the results. They came, they danced, and they got introduced to her preferred candidate for state senator.

The primary election was coming up in August, and she had just the candidate in mind, just the sort the *Enterprise* needed to support, a fellow named Terry Barefield from the remote Elk Basin region. He was there at the party and she introduced him to everyone. She was flattered to be participating in politics. Three senatorial candidates had sought the support of the *Enterprise*. Bennett liked one of Barefield's opponents. He even drafted an editorial endorsing him, but she and Eldred squelched it.

Owning a newspaper put her fully into area politics. She was interviewing U.S. Senator Frank Mondell the following week. It would be a chance to score against those who had ignored her, to demonstrate her victory over a legion of enemies. The paper endorsed Goppert for county attorney ("Although young in the legal game he enjoys a considerable practice and is not afraid to speak his mind when the occasion demands"). The primaries were the important election, the place where they could distinguish themselves from the *Herald*, since both would support Republicans in November. She thought she was handling it well. When she heard that Jakie Schwoob had expressed fears that her involvement would hurt the paper politically, she wondered at what he could have meant.

Besides, she wasn't going to spend much time on the paper. She'd gotten a contract to write titles for a silent film. She was still working on her Osage stories. Her agent was trying to get her into the *Saturday Evening Post*.

"Am out of a job," Lockhart complained to her diary. "Finished my book and nothing more in mind." She'd sent off final revisions to *The Dude Wrangler*, as well as the silent film titles. It was now mid-August, there was nothing to do for the Stampede, and her writing was stalled. The Osage stories still didn't flow.

Aunt Josie was still around, and they were getting along wonderfully. But Aunt Josie had fallen in love. With Bob Hopkins, the Wild Man. It was serious, Josie said. He was going to get a divorce, support her as his wife. "It doesn't seem natural," Lockhart told her diary. "But she is infatuated with him beyond a doubt." Lockhart eventually decided that the relationship was a good thing—anything was better than the loneliness and emptiness of a life alone, a life like hers. "There is nothing more for me but success and money to look forward to. Power, I will have that. I think." Without love, she could find happiness only through work. Without work, now, she was miserable.

Andrew Ross came through for another visit. They met at the Lake Hotel in Yellowstone Park. But although Ross was crazy about her and spent lavishly on her, whenever they had more than a few days together he would get on her nerves. For example, he thought she had a big bother on her hands with the *Enterprise*. And he drank too much. She did not find him sexually appealing. She knew it would never really work.

When Ross left she went in to the *Enterprise* office and worked on the paper's makeup. The next day's paper, she decided, looked good. However, she had some real problems with Eldred as an editor. He'd made her mad in the very first issue they published together by running a story she thought was too long. How could new ownership improve the paper if it still had the same old editor? He seemed to have no idea of news value. One of the late June papers had been especially disappointing—especially compared with the *Herald*—but she'd been too busy with the Stampede to do anything about it. Some of the July papers had been better. But still, were they good enough to be associated with her name? Now she went to Eldred and told him that unless she had something to say about the conduct of the paper, her stock was for sale and she would end her connection with it. He seemed to back down, and by the end of August she was again pleased with the *Enterprise*.

But her candidates, including Barefield and Goppert, lost in the primaries. Then Bob Rumsey decided to run for state senator as an independent. Though they were friends, Lockhart didn't take much interest until the *Herald* attacked him in an editorial. This would be a good fight!

Except that Larom didn't believe in Rumsey's campaign. Bennett didn't either. The state Republican Party was pressuring them to fall in line. She wanted to run a letter from Dwight Hollister extolling Rumsey, and her fellow owners tried to convince her not to. She insisted. If they refused she would leave the partnership, make them run the paper by themselves. They relented, and Hollister's letter was published prominently. At a dinner party with the Hollisters and Rumseys, the rancher Bill Hogg told them that if she could be turned loose, she could have Rumsey elected in forty days. She beamed. They talked politics all night, and she loved it.

If only there weren't these difficulties with the other owners. If only Eldred wasn't such a jackass. In October he tried to sell the back page to the Democrats. She told Bennett if he did that she would quit. Eldred called her bluff, saying that he, too, would quit if he didn't get his way. If he quit they wouldn't get a paper out at all that week. They couldn't afford to lose him.

She relented, but the episode sealed her fury. In an attitude toward employees that would become familiar, she decided there had to be a way to circumvent Eldred, to get him out of the picture. She might wait until after the election and her next Stampede obligation, but then she would do everything she could to get him canned.

Arrayed in elaborate paint and warbonnets, the Crow Indian warriors waltzed and foxtrotted with women in evening gowns. Meanwhile, white men in their best duds danced with Indian women in blankets. The music was pierced by both cowboy yells and war whoops. Gus Thompson, an old-timer admired by both Crows and whites, performed an Indian stomp dance with two squaws at once. Simon Bulltail—dressed in a beaded vest, face painted with yellow ochre, eagle feathers in his hair—tugged at Lockhart's arm and pointed at her enemy Blanche Gokel. He wanted to dance with her. Gokel was willing, and Lockhart said that while they danced Bulltail was "so proud that he leaned backwards."

It was the first annual Cody Stampede ball, a fund-raiser at the Irma Hotel on October 28, 1920, with honored guests from the Crow tribe. Goppert hadn't thought the event would make money, but it cleared more than four hundred dollars. "We doubt if in Cody or anywhere else there was a scene more unique and picturesque," Lockhart wrote of the way the cowboys and Indians mixed. "There were no social lines, or color lines, when it came to that." One attendee called it the League of Nations.

Lockhart had brought to life her vision for Cody: wrapped in Old West imagery, full of unusual characters, and bereft of social pretensions. The Irma was decorated with saddles, chaps, boots, spurs, ropes, bridles, and quirts. Of course, people arrived by train and automobile, but when they entered the Irma they entered the realm of the horse. The word "picturesque" was one of Lockhart's favorite tributes, incorporating not just the West's landscapes but also the culture that inhabited it. The horse and its accoutrements represented an ideal world.

Because Indians had also ridden horses—because the Crows were renowned as some of the world's finest horsemen—they were an equal part of this nostalgia. Previous generations may have seen Indians as violent and savage, but Lockhart had come west late enough that they were primarily picturesque. She had no use for the Osage, who drove Cadillacs. But in paint that recalled their days as mounted warriors, she found the Crows glorious.

She condescended to them, and not only in the basic way by which we today understand the word *squaw* as derogatory. Her depiction of Bulltail's pride suggests that it is unwarranted. She has a matching picture of Fanny

Sits-Down-Spotted, "far from handsome and not too young," perspiring profusely through a foxtrot with a white local resident, her face filling with radiant delight when he bows and thanks her "as if she were the finest lady in the land."

But she did find them important, and she did treat them with some degree of humanity. She invited them to stay in her home. It may be a sad commentary on how they were treated by the rest of white society at the time, but the Crows admired her. They called her "Its-Be-Che-Loti" or "White Woman Chief."

In fact, the Crows came to the Stampede Ball only because she had made a special visit to Chief Plenty Coups at his home on the reservation a few weeks previously. She was accompanied by Bob Hopkins, Aunt Josie, and a man named Lou Ericson, who worked a ranch near Plenty Coups's home. After their successful plea to the Crow chief, they stayed overnight at the Charley Phelps ranch on Dryhead Creek, and Lockhart realized that she had a "case" on Ericson. "Mild, but sincere, so far as it goes. Why, God knows, but he attracts me and I do not fight it for it helps take my mind from O.B. He reciprocates with equal warmth and he is not a skirt-hound." She found him likable, affectionate, and thoughtful. He was a small man, good with horses, a jockey. He'd once ridden for the famed Copper King Marcus Daly. He liked outdoor life, and he treated her very well. After he returned with them to Cody, he would wait on her, as if she were somebody who needed to be looked after. Just two weeks after they met, she wrote in her diary that the two of them "got along like two old sour-dough pals."

Knocks came on Lockhart's door. She knew it was Ericson. The knocks came persistently, as if he knew she was there, had seen the lights on. But she wouldn't let him in.

Inside with her was O. B. Mann, the man she called "Orn'ry." She couldn't allow both of her boyfriends into the house at the same time. It would be scandalous enough if anyone knew that just one of them was there. As she had fallen into the relationship with Ericson, she noted to her diary that nothing would prevent it "but fear of talk and for that I just watch out." Cody remained a small town. Her situation with Mann was even more delicate due to his marriage. He told her he had hoped he could forget her and gloss things over after the wedding. But he couldn't. With her in his arms, he told her, it was living. When they were together, she believed he would come to her eventually. But for now their moments together had to be stolen.

She knew it was a bit crazy juggling two lovers—or three if you counted Ross. (Valentin di Colonna had recently moved away.) She knew that she should feel "cheap and contemptible," she told her diary. But she was nearly fifty years old and had never been married, might never be married, might never experience that sense of blissful domesticity that seemed to so sate her enemies. So, she wrote, she would take "anything to escape the torture of being unloved and lonely."

Ericson might be sore, she knew. She hated to do this to him. When she told him in November that she might go east for her annual winter visit, he cried. More than once. He said, "I'm not used to having anyone so good to me as you are." But Mann was the love of her life; Ericson was just someone who could take her mind off of Mann. (Though not entirely. One night with Ericson a few weeks later, she caught herself continually calling him Orn'ry.)

On this particular January night, if she was not terribly worried about her lovers' emotions, that may have been because she had other things on her mind. J. C. Emerson was due in the following day. She'd met Emerson in Denver, on her way back from the East. (She had indeed taken that trip, for the month of December. Bob Hopkins had come along, to meet Josie's family.) Emerson was a newspaperman. She'd finally gotten Bennett and Conger to agree with her that the *Enterprise* needed a new editor to replace Eldred. She'd recruited several candidates on the trip east. When she returned, even Larom, who'd been wishy-washy, agreed that Emerson sounded good. They told her to write to him, ask him to come.

Dwight Hollister had sounded Eldred out about buying his share. Eldred seemed intrigued, but he didn't yet know that his replacement was arriving on tomorrow's train.

Things moved slowly for the next couple of weeks. Eldred asked for one thousand dollars for his share. Emerson arrived and struck Lockhart as more chattery and inconsequential than she remembered. She wondered if she should have chosen her other candidate. But Emerson was in her camp. He was tickled with her stories. He told her people were calling her a genius. And, he said, the books showed Eldred to be a crook—or at best so hopelessly irregular that he might as well be. Financially, the *Enterprise* was in trouble. But this was only one of Lockhart's concerns.

"Hoped I would have a sheriff for breakfast!" Lockhart was writing in her diary one morning in February 1921. She'd been tipped off that Sheriff C. A. Davis and a deputy were staking out her house "—believing I *sell* booze!"

Wyoming had voted for Prohibition by a 3 to 1 margin (in Cody it was 3.5 to 1), and Davis's sheriff campaign had been endorsed by the *Herald* and its Dry, Methodist friends. But what sort of enforcement did the law require? On the one hand, Lockhart and her allies believed that Prohibition was intended to get rid of the saloon, but not liquor in private homes. If you wanted to buy liquor from a bootlegger, serve it to your friends, even drink out of a private flask at a public function such as the Stampede Ball, wasn't that still your personal freedom? The Drys, on the other hand, saw liquor as bad regardless of its source. They saw a slippery slope of permissions: from drinking at private parties to private drinking at public parties to public drinking parties. And indeed that was precisely Lockhart's vision for Wolfville: a public drinking party. But she was appalled that they might think that meant she *sold* booze.

So she prepared to greet the sheriff. She had Ericson set a forty-pound bear trap under her bedroom window. She bought plenty of birdshot for her shotgun. And she stayed awake drinking coffee most of the night. "I sure want to fill them full of shot," she wrote.

It was not an ideal time to spend a sleepless night. The paper was taking up more and more of her time. It was going pretty well—she felt like these articles were making the hit of her life in Cody—but she was increasingly disappointed in Emerson. His grammar was horrendous.

She was also spending a lot of money. She staked Ericson $250 to buy ponies for resale, reasoning that as more people came to Cody in search of the Old West, they'd create demand for horses that represented that West. She also bought Bennett's stock in the newspaper. His finances remained in poor shape, as did the *Enterprise*'s, so it's puzzling that she gave him $500 for a share that had been worth $300 ten months previously. Emerson told her *she* was the paper—Bennett had done little to improve it—but when Lockhart wanted something she was never one to dicker over price. While she could be cautious about her private life, even hiring an investigator to look into Ericson's background, her desire for control over the *Enterprise* was a different story. She even considered getting a $2,000 loan from Andrew Ross or Roy Edgington to buy all of the shares. But the paper was $50 in the hole and its auditor found Emerson as inefficient as Eldred. Lockhart started hoping

The Dude Wrangler would be a financial success—not to spend the money on herself, but to spend it on the paper.

She still tended to see the *Enterprise* through the eyes of a reader or writer, rather than a businessperson. Seeing the *Herald* ("looks like the official organ of the combined churches"), she vowed to beat it. Seeing people lining up to buy *Enterprise*s as soon as they came out, she believed she'd succeeded. Seeing a big news week, she prophesied a sensational paper and cried with disappointment at the layout of the final product. Seeing the county commissioners award their lucrative printing contract to the *Herald*—despite lower bids from the *Enterprise* and the *Powell Tribune*—she took it personally and decided to go after them.

A small town can be a very political place, especially if your business depends on it, and especially if you tend to see things in boldly dramatic terms. But her tip may not have been correct, or her enemies smarter than she thought. The sheriff never showed up at her house, and she'd spent the sleepless night in vain.

Lockhart was so mad she just went ahead and used the telephone. (The device was new to Cody and she didn't fully trust it.) She called up Ernest Goppert. Was she to understand that the Stampede Committee wanted to limit her to the publicity end of things?

They'd elected her president again this spring, and things had gone smoothly. But now, in June 1921 as they prepared for the second annual Stampede, she was feeling crowded out. She sensed that Goppert, along with William Loewer and Clarence Williams, resented her power. Nothing wrong with wanting it their way, she knew, but their way was not efficient, would not yield satisfactory results. Williams seemed to be behind it. She regarded him with a growing dislike. If Goppert wanted her out, she told him, then he could just buy twelve thousand dollars' worth of steers and collect twenty head of bucking horses on his own.

Lou Ericson and his brother Bud had already started for the reservation to buy the cattle. She'd done a lot of work for this Stampede, and she believed that everyone still gave her credit for the last one. She wouldn't be pushed aside now. She was in too deep.

She was in too deep on most of her Cody initiatives. Larom had come to her in March, said he suddenly needed cash, and asked her to buy his share for $450. She hesitated, because it tied up a lot of money, but finally agreed.

The paper also needed a new linotype machine, although she couldn't afford it. In early April, Eldred had finally settled as well: $350 for his share, plus $150 in back salary. He then left for New York City, stopping on the way to ask her to autograph one of her books for him.

Emerson was still dissatisfactory. She would lie awake at night cursing his trite phrasings. "Silent messages . . . grim reaper . . . God Almighty!" She tried to cut his salary, but he refused, finally saying that if she could find someone better and cheaper, she could go ahead and hire him. But meanwhile he was full of cheap sensationalism and exaggeration and didn't seem to get many local items, the social notes that made up so much of a country paper's news. For that he relied on her. He was, she told her diary in May, "the most hopelessly incompetent ignoramus that ever drew a salary" as an editor. She wrote to the other man she had recruited back east, but until he came she would have to wait.

In acknowledgment of the work she put in, the masthead started listing her as "assistant editor." In addition to local news, the paper started printing some of her feature stories, such as a piece on the Osage that had previously appeared in the *Denver Post*. It was becoming more and more Caroline Lockhart's paper, and she liked that.

But she still had to struggle with politics. One of the mayoral candidates, she'd heard, intended to "fix" the *Enterprise* if he got elected. So she had to ensure his defeat. Then there was the rumor that Marjory Ross was going to come out for mayor. ("A bird told us that Miss Marjory Ross is donning her running togs in preparation for a race for mayor," Lockhart wrote in the *Enterprise*. "Go to it, Marjory! May the best man win.") If it happened, friends said, they'd run Lockhart against her. "Ye gods," she wrote in her diary, "what if she should get it! And what is almost worse, what if I should get it!"

Folks had feared Lockhart would run the paper into the ground because she knew so little about politics. And she did realize that through her strong political stands she was making enemies. But she believed she was making friends too.

Money was the biggest problem, the biggest way she was in too deep. The bank told her the *Enterprise* owed $266 in back taxes. The *Herald* reaped easy revenues every week with the county printing. Meanwhile, she was buying the Stampede cattle herself. *The Dude Wrangler* was out and getting decent reviews, but a national recession meant slower sales than she would have liked. She wanted money, she had to have money; in her position, only money could give her power and independence.

It was around this time that she told her bootlegger to bring her a case of bourbon, at the cost of $110. She bought it as speculation for Ericson to sell, so that he could use the profits to buy a new hat, a suit, and boots.

On the telephone, Goppert reassured her: she was the president, she would run the Stampede. Williams was just sore over another matter. They could patch things up. It was exactly what she wanted to hear. In too deep? She was going deeper.

The front page of the *Enterprise* on June 29, 1921, made this announcement:

> Editors may come and editors may go, but, like the brook, the *Enterprise* goes on forever.
>
> The mantle worn by a long line of the august gentlemen who have assumed the grave responsibilities of this position for periods varying from twenty-four hours to six months, is now draped temporarily about the shoulders of Mr. Webb Adams of Thermopolis.
>
> Mr. Adams will need no introduction to the Old Timers of Park County as he has been a resident of this state and Montana for some years.
>
> He is the gentleman who in the recent election bet $5,000 that Hot Springs County would vote for the good roads bonds by a greater majority than any other county.
>
> We mention this not as a matter of news particularly but to appraise our citizens of the fact that he has $5,000.

Adams had called up Lockhart to recommend himself, and though she might not normally have listened, she had just fired Emerson—and a week before Stampede. "Nobody could be worse than he is," she figured, "and there is a chance that Adams may be better." When he arrived, however, Adams proved to be another chatterer, high on himself, full of nervous energy. She knew from the start he was not a long-term solution but asked him to stay through Stampede.

That event's final preparations turned out fine, just as she had wanted them. Not as many Indians came as she had hoped, but it still drew the biggest crowd in northern Wyoming. Financially it was less successful, losing three hundred dollars. She quarreled with Loewer and Williams about Wolfville and vowed that if she were president again, Williams at least would be gone.

Andrew Ross came for another visit and said he wanted her to go east and put on a Cody Stampede in Madison Square Garden, capitalized at two hundred thousand dollars. She knew she could put it over big. But he didn't actually have the money, because the bottom had dropped out of the mining market. Furthermore, she still found him physically unattractive.

Webb Adams turned out to be useless, "worse than Emerson and just as ignorant. $35 wasted. I am learning the game however so I can get out the paper if I have to." Indeed, Lockhart's self-confident style increasingly infused the *Enterprise*, with tidbits like this in the local notes: "Mrs. Lydia Peckham, we are informed, made the assertion that the plague of army worms visited only the wicked. The next morning Mrs. Peckham had lost her garden." Her other editorial prospect, S. A. Nock, would arrive by the end of the month. But meanwhile the paper was overdrawn.

In late July she told her diary, "This morning I awoke with the fact clearly impressed upon me that I am up against it financially. Through helping Lou [and] biting off more than I can chew in the *Enterprise* I have left myself with nothing to live on. I counted so strongly on selling my picture rights but quite evidently I was too optimistic." The bottom had dropped out of the moving picture market too.

An interior page of the *Enterprise* on August 10, 1921, made this announcement:

Introducing new editors to its readers has become one of the *Enterprise*'s favorite pastimes.

There is reason to believe, however, that with the coming of Mr. S.A. Nock of New York City, we are to be deprived of our weekly recreation of hiring editors.

Having proven to our satisfaction that he can write an obituary without referring to the "Grim Messenger," "Silent Reaper," or "Angel of Death," and about an accident without "Snuffing Out" the victim's life, we have taken him to our heart.

Nock was just a kid, she realized once he arrived, too inexperienced to be all that good as either a newspaperman or a businessman. She wondered if he was really worth the money she was paying him. But she did get a bit of time to work on her fiction, and she hoped he would grow into the job.

Meanwhile, a friend named Barry Williams (no relation to Clarence) had bought a racehorse and asked Ericson to be his jockey. After winning a race in Billings, they decided to take the horse south for winter races. She would miss Ericson, and he her. He didn't really want to go. He told her he would rather marry her and take up a homestead in the wild Missouri Breaks country of northern Montana. She wrote, "Guess it doesn't matter much what I do with the rest of my life now. It is only pride that keeps me from [running off with Ericson]." Barry Williams also bought her car. She put the $250 into the paper. Now she would get around on horseback.

She lay awake nights worrying over payroll. She started drinking alcohol to put her to sleep. The worry, the booze, and the sleeplessness made her look haggard, which depressed her further. But the paper was starting to look better, she thought. The work was starting to pay off. Newsstand copies always outsold the *Herald*. If she could just stick with it, she could make it a success.

Because of an episode in which Clarence Baldwin emptied his gun into a porcupine that had ambled into the pool hall, Lockhart called Cody's night marshal by the name "Hairbreadth Harry." She noted that Hairbreadth Harry's record-breaking arrest numbers were due to the large number of liquor violators he cuffed. Then in the fall of 1921, Hairbreadth Harry disappeared, taking with him an advance on his pay.

Lockhart had a field day. "Where is our wandering boy tonight?" asked one of her headlines. She mockingly reassured folks that he would return, since he had credit due at Len Leander Newton's store and had borrowed a hundred dollars from county commissioner Sanford Watkins. City officials weren't happy with the stories, but she considered herself at war with them. If she could entertain the masses by poking fun at her enemies, then life was good. And people did laugh at her stories. Then, much to everyone's surprise, Hairbreadth Harry reappeared. When he did, he called down the sidewalk at Lockhart. She pretended not to hear him.

Weeks later, after the November election, he finally tracked her down. He said he actually liked her. He wanted to tell her how much the mayor and other city officials hated her. They had gone in with the *Herald* to produce a circular denouncing her, which had been distributed in churches. They had broken into the *Enterprise* offices the night before the election and were seriously considering blowing up her presses with explosives. The mayor had even commented that it would be easy to "get" her some day when she was riding on her horse—though someone else had immediately told him he was crazy.

She got Harry to put his story in an affidavit. Then if Len Leander Newton ever sued her for libel, she would have ammunition for a countersuit. Someone else told her that Newton's partner, Ernest Shaw, was bragging that now that he'd succeeded in running Doc Bennett out of town, Lockhart would be next. It was a good old-fashioned newspaper rivalry. She blasted away at the *Herald*. Usually Newton blasted back.

But the financial crunch continued. She had trouble paying Charles Conger, who manned the newspaper's printing machines and was her sole remaining co-owner. Thinking that she was trying to squeeze him out, he dug in his heels, which only frustrated her further. She realized that she didn't much care for the way he made up the paper, always putting too much of the important news on the inside. It would be better if he would let her help.

They went to Hollister, the lawyer, and hammered out an understanding. She would give him his back pay—maybe by signing over one of her interests in the paper—and then lay him off for the winter. She was reluctant to take this step. She found him "competent and faithful though irritating." He was a puttering old man and she didn't really know what else he would do. But she didn't know how else to cut the paper's expenses.

Unfortunately, Conger didn't get the same message out of the meeting with the lawyer. He kept on coming to work, believing that his salary was about to start again.

In her memoirs Lockhart remembered a single day, a single issue of the newspaper, when the town came to a sudden realization. She had put a small box on the front page restating her position on the Eighteenth Amendment, and the papers sold like hotcakes. "The news quickly spread to the furthermost ranches: The lady editor was wet!"

Evidence suggests, however, that the process was more gradual. Papers had sold well throughout her ownership. ("The christers [churchgoers] are sore over our last issue—but we have sold all our papers, people are talking about us, and the old-timers, roughnecks and folks that cut ice are with us," she wrote in September.) The "small box" she put on the front page in late November 1921 was actually a large black-bordered column titled "As Seen from the Water-Wagon." But in its very first appearance it said nothing about Prohibition.

Like many newspaper columns, "Water-Wagon" mixed opinion and anecdote in an area set aside from the more objective news coverage. Lots of newspapers in that era ran such columns, and lots of small-town newspapers ran them on the front page. The only unique thing about Water-Wagon was the personality of its author: a tad nasty, wickedly funny, obsessed with the passing frontier, and exceedingly Wet.

The debut column was part of her publicity for the second annual Cody Stampede Ball. An accompanying news article highlighted the fact that there would be a cabaret show, Indian dances, an orchestra, and (tongue in cheek) "the United States Shimmy Inspector" to examine the dancers. It promised "a real party for real folks—the kind who have not yet had the spirit legislated out of them." The column told stories of Gus Thompson encouraging the Indians to come to the previous year's ball, noting that the recently deceased Thompson would be sorely missed. In other words—given Lockhart's penchant for writing opinionated, fanciful, personality-filled news stories—the column actually wasn't all that much different from the rest of the paper.

But over the next four to five years, the contents of the column did generally fulfill the message of its title (by going "on the water-wagon"—later shortened to "on the wagon"—you vowed that instead of alcohol, you would rather drink from the wagon that sprayed water on dusty streets). Lockhart coined aphorisms, such as, "It is an uphill business making people good by law." She summarized news of the national anti-Prohibition movement, including testimony from any experts who said the law was not working. She reported prices being charged for liquor in various parts of the nation. She outed stool pigeons and printed recipes for New Year's punch. Thanks in large part to the column, the *Enterprise* became known as "the Booze Sheet of Wyoming."

But she also used the column to showcase some of her tiny vignettes and witticisms, her humorous take on news far and wide. For example, in April 1922 she wrote, "While prosecuting a case in Omaha, Nebraska, Charles Kubat, assistant county attorney, gesticulated so vigorously that he dislocated his arm. The opposing attorney pulled it back into place for him. The defendant was convicted." And the following month she wrote, "Last week we had Lumbago or something equally terrible. At any rate, it hurt us to move, to laugh, or even to smile, and then some one drifted in and told us that T. P. Cullen was coming out for sheriff and nearly killed us."

"Comes now the plaintiff . . ." The petition shocked Lockhart. With the help of attorney Paul Greever—one of the fellows who Hairbreadth Harry said wanted to blow up her newspaper—Charles Conger was suing for dissolution of their partnership. The agreement he'd signed at Hollister's office was obtained by misrepresentation and fraud, he said. She'd wrongfully laid him off, he said, intending to deprive him of not only his livelihood but also his interest in the business. She wouldn't even let him look at the books.

She was unqualified, he said. She'd hired incompetent help. Her policies and writings were ruining the business, driving away subscribers by "sanctioning outlawry and ruffianism." Her articles were "vulgar, obscene, coarse, ribald, foul, and of such character to make the said newspaper unfit reading matter in the home." He'd worked years on the *Enterprise*, building it into a meaningful business, and she was driving it to ruin. She was also, he said, "an habitual drunkard, and has frequently . . . attempt[ed] to carry on the business and management of the said partnership while in a drunken and intoxicated condition."

That last charge was the most stinging. No coincidence that it came so quickly after the debut of Water-Wagon: now that she was publicly Wet, it would be easy for people to believe she was publicly drunk.

Furthermore, she *was* drinking herself to sleep most nights. Was she genuinely alcoholic? The diaries don't provide conclusive evidence either way. She never mentions drinking during the day or at the office. She does mention occasional hangovers, which might suggest that she did not always overimbibe. She also mentions occasional days when she did not take a single drink of alcohol—mentions them with perhaps a bit too much pride. Since she disapproved of others (especially her boyfriends) drinking too much, you could argue that she favored moderation in drinking. But you could also argue that she was deceiving herself as so many alcoholics do. Whatever their truth, she found Conger's charges explosive. They were just close enough to prompt some soul-searching. Worse, they were and just close enough to be devastating if widely circulated in such a small town.

Despite her fears, the charges didn't get out. It appears that Conger simply wanted free from the partnership. He'd offered to sell her his share—perhaps for the same five hundred dollars the others got—and she'd ignored him. He filed the lawsuit to give himself more leverage.

But Lockhart stubbornly refused to settle. She didn't need his share, of course: she had four and could outvote him. She didn't want to tie up any more money in another share. Furthermore, the lawsuit infuriated her. She decided she wouldn't even let Conger sell his share to someone else. She told him she would turn the paper around and someday his share would actually be worth something.

The charge of incompetence must have also rattled Lockhart, because again it came close to the truth. Though she'd written for newspapers for twenty-five years now, she'd never run one. She knew little of typesetting, printing, and makeup—not to mention keeping books and managing employees. She was learning, slowly, but still felt herself at the mercy of her editors and linotype operators.

The lawsuit didn't need to overtly state a common belief of the time: no woman could run a newspaper. Women might be able to write society news, but when it came to writing about politics or crime or sports—or when it came to the machinery-laden tasks of producing the physical product—newspapers were a man's world.

Although there were a few women editors and publishers around the country, almost all of them had inherited their newspaper from a husband or father. Even the celebrity and ambition of someone like Nellie Bly hadn't led her far beyond writing. Widowed by a wealthy industrialist, Bly tried to run a factory but went bankrupt, and as of this date was working as an advice columnist. All of Lockhart's quibbling with co-owners and obsessing over money and power had a very real and terrifying source: a society structured to render women powerless.

Occasional diary entries suggest that from Lockhart's very first involvement, part of her wanted to be the *Enterprise*'s sole editor and publisher. When Emerson arrived, she wrote that things were moving "to the end of getting rid of Eldred and installing myself there." A few months later she wrote, "It is fascinating to see what I can do with it, and make a success since I *have* taken hold of it." She believed such a success would give her an unassailable power base, offer local fame, and provide concrete evidence of her victory over the people she was sure wanted to get her.

But at the same time she would often wonder if it was a mistake to invest so much in a little newspaper in an out-of-the-way community. What about her ambitions for national fame? What about substantial power and wealth, such as that she could gain from a national bestseller or hit movie? The newspaper was a waste of time and energy and kept her from working on her fiction. "I am so sick of this God-damn paper," she wrote in her diary now that she had become so essential to its operation, "yet I cannot leave it in incompetent hands or sell it to people who will be enemies."

Likely she had not made up her mind. Her ambitions—fame, power, domestic bliss, and a cowboy lifestyle—conflicted. She was only starting to realize that she could never achieve all of them.

⌒

The second annual Stampede Ball took place in December at the Irma Hotel, spiritually and geographically the center of Cody. Sheriff Davis was there, which meant no booze was served—at least publicly. People who wanted alcohol, of course, still tried to find a way to drink it. Davis believed he had to try to stop them too. In January 1922 he stood in city court on the witness stand to explain.

He'd seen Bob Hopkins leave the building, Davis testified, and go to his car. Hopkins brought two other men with him, but they didn't get into the car. Instead they shut the doors again and walked to a back corner of the building. Suspicious, the sheriff and his deputies tried to sneak up on them but failed: the men ran away down an alley.

In the alley, Davis testified, he saw Hopkins hide a jug behind a rock. Running up, Davis stopped and looked at the jug: it was liquor. He thus brought charges against the three men for violating Prohibition. The *Enterprise* covered the trial on the front page.

It was a busy week in the courtroom, with at least three other liquor trials. In her Water-Wagon column, Lockhart noted that Mrs. P. A. Ingraham and Mrs. Lydia E. Peckham had come to one of the trials as spectators, bringing their knitting. The knitting particularly nettled Lockhart, who compared these two locals to "women of the French revolution who counted stitches while the heads of aristocrats fell." (When they protested the following week that they had merely come to lend backbone to the proceedings, Lockhart countered, "In spite of our best efforts, we have failed to learn whether the Judge or the Prosecuting Attorney drew the rick-rack edge for his nightie.")

She also claimed that at one of the trials she overheard someone say, "Yes, I know a couple of bootleggers, but they're on the jury."

At the Hopkins trial, after the sheriff told his story, one of Hopkins's co-defendants admitted he'd heard about a jug, a "community jug," but said he hadn't been drinking from it. He said he'd run away down the alley because he had "an antipathy to sheriffs." The second codefendant wouldn't even admit that much.

The *Enterprise* described Hopkins as "an honest, plain, industrious farmer," despite the fact that Lockhart now suspected he had married Josie only for her money, was fooling around on her, and had stolen liquor from both Josie and Lockhart herself. She would stick with family, especially when family was attacked by Prohibitionists. Hopkins was the final defendant to take the stand, and he echoed the first. He too had "an antipathy to sheriffs." He too had heard of "a community jug." Then, he said, as he was running down the alley, he saw a jug and leaned over to see if it really was that community jug people had been talking about. He saw that it was, and so he left it behind the rock where he'd found it.

"As further proof that it could not be his jug," the *Enterprise* noted, "Mr. Hopkins pointed to the fact that it was still half full."

The jury acquitted all three men. Indeed, none of the cases that week gained a conviction.

Lockhart wrote this amusing note in the middle of the *Water-Wagon* column on February 1, 1922:

> We have introduced so many editors to our readers since acquiring Park County's great moral uplift weekly that now that it is incumbent upon us to present another we find ourself at a loss for anything new to say by way of introduction. Therefore, we will state briefly that June Little has consented to add another to the responsibilities which are making him prematurely gray and round-shouldered, and he will fill this position until the New York Sun or Herald outbids us for his services. We trust that the public will treat Mr. Little with the respect and consideration due his age and experience.

June Little was the youngest, least experienced editor Lockhart had yet hired. But his father was a big publishing executive in New York, and the family had a ranch outside of Cody where June had lived since returning from a lengthy trip to the Orient the previous spring.

The Littles were part of a new Cody—drawn by scenery and vacation rather than a midwestern farm ethic. These new eastern immigrants were naturally drawn to the dude ranchers, who often came from the same social class. Lockhart admired them for their breeding, for their typical stand against Prohibition, and for the economic opportunity they represented.

Farming had not blossomed to the degree Cody's founders had hoped. "Dry" farmers, as Lockhart amusingly depicted in *The Dude Wrangler*, faced far too many obstacles to succeed without irrigation. While irrigated farms were more successful, they were rarely successful enough to pay the high costs of irrigation. Furthermore, although the dam had been built at Cody, most of the land it irrigated was far downstream, where the town of Powell had arisen to compete with Cody for farmers' dollars. Upstream, small cattle ranchers struggled because their numbers far overwhelmed the availability of range. Beef prices had plummeted in 1919-20, and many stockmen were wiped out.

Alternatively, tourism promised a boom. The railroad was building a new hotel at the depot for its passengers on their way to Yellowstone. Auto traffic was growing even faster. And most lucrative of all were dudes who would come spend a week or more on area ranches. Dudes seemed a natural fit for Cody: they were intrigued by Buffalo Bill, liked proximity to Yellowstone, and enjoyed an Old West atmosphere. Regardless of his editorial skills, June Little personified Lockhart's alliances in the fight to remake Cody as a cowboy town.

An early test of those political dynamics came later that February 1922, when the Stampede stockholders met to elect new officers. The battle lines were clearly drawn: Lockhart stood for the Old West of Buffalo Bill, who'd been quite a drinker himself. Williams, Loewer, and Goppert stood for progress, civilization, and Prohibition. All month the two sides gathered proxies for the vote on February 17. Lockhart went into the meeting confident and was not disappointed. "Well, the battle's over and I've licked 'em proper," she wrote in her diary the next day. "My supporters were out in force and they were a handful. . . . Loewer looked like a wildcat that was about to scream and spring over the seats at me. Goppert was nasty and showed up to very bad advantage."

But one election would not decide the issue. The Goppert faction tried again, through their other allies in the community. Marjory Ross urged the Cody Women's Club to pass a resolution demanding that management of the Stampede be turned over to another organization. The resolution failed. Ross then published a resolution in the *Herald* demanding that the Stampede be conducted "in accordance with law and order."

In the *Enterprise*, Lockhart shot back. It was not possible to conduct a Wild West "along the lines of the Chautauqua assembly," she said, referring to the staid educational forum that Cody put on each summer after the Stampede. "On the whole, the Cody Stampede is as orderly an affair as may be found anywhere in the country, and conducted in a fashion which is wholly satisfactory to everybody except the Meddlesome Marjories of both sexes." Then, typically, Lockhart made the debate personal and nasty. "We cannot but wonder where Miss Ross was that she saw so much during former Stampedes that she felt such a request necessary. We are very sure that Miss Ross was not insulted by any visitor, drunk or sober, for we are confident that Miss Ross is one of those women who could go anywhere in the world without fear of molestation from the opposite sex." That issue of the paper—which was also the first to use a new slogan, "The policy of this paper is to uphold the standards and perpetuate the spirit of the old West"—was one of their best sellers ever.

Marjory Ross also sat on the library board, where her actions apparently prompted a petition asking the library to reinstate Lockhart's books. The novels had been donated to the library but were now not available on the shelves. An open letter to the board, published in the *Enterprise*, said, "We would also appreciate it if you will tell us why these books were removed from the shelves just after Marjory Ross became a member of the board. We have been told that Marjory Ross says that if these books are replaced it will be 'over her dead body.' . . . we do not believe that the public should be deprived of something it obviously wants, and is entitled to, because of spite on the part of Marjory Ross."

No longer on the defensive, Lockhart was taking it to her enemies. But was it having any effect? She was devastated one day when she passed Frances Lane in a hallway at the Irma Hotel. Lockhart didn't know that Lane had just finished negotiations to put up a sign in the hotel, and was pleased with the result. All she knew was that Lane gave her a smirk as she passed. Lockhart saw the smirk as one of hatred and triumph. Triumph for Lane,

Lockhart was sure, meant a loss for herself. For the next several days—until she learned about the sign negotiations—Lockhart feared that her world was about to collapse.

"Pontoon Johnny" Burghman went to vote in the May 1922 city election. A droll, merry old-timer, he was a favorite of Lockhart and later told her this story with delight.

"Where do you live when in Cody?" asked the election clerk. It was an extremely controversial election, so she was trying to do her job thoroughly (*too* thoroughly, Lockhart believed).

"Here!" Burghman replied promptly. The voting was taking place in the town jail.

It had been a difficult few months for Lockhart. June Little was on his way to becoming a great editor, but in mid-March he told Lockhart he had to go visit his ill mother. Instead he went on a three-week drunk. Lockhart would have been happy to take him back, but his father grounded him on the ranch.

So Lockhart was editing the paper herself. It should have been the achievement of a longtime ambition. But instead it felt like indentured servitude. "I am no freer than I ever was," she grumbled. She hadn't been able to go east at all this winter. She was glad to get the full editor's salary, but with too little time to exercise, she felt herself getting fat. She was very happy with the newspapers she was producing, but they just weren't bringing in enough money. "I need clothes, a car, a linotype machine, house painted, [and] roof sheathed. I am going to seed, running down at the heels, and no way out that I can see."

She perceived the political situation to be ever more dire. Goppert was managing the reelection campaign of the mayor, apparently with the agreement that they would then crack down on the Stampede. Then in the fall Goppert would run again for county attorney—this time with the support of the *Herald* rather than the *Enterprise*—and Lockhart feared that the new administrations would truly succeed in driving her out of town.

Meanwhile, the "Newton Element" was trying to co-opt her issues. In response to her new slogan, the *Herald* agreed, "Perpetuity of the spirit of the West is a noble sentiment and should never be lost." But Newton defined that spirit as "the age old urge to do things . . . to build roads and bridges and construct railroads." Newton scoffed at those who thought "the spirit of the west means a carefree life, no regard for the rights and liberties of others, license to do things which in civilized communities would be taboo." He liked the legacy of Buffalo Bill as much as the next man, Newton implied—but you could endorse that legend without endorsing lawlessness and bad taste. "The Herald refuses to quarrel over the tourist business," he wrote, encouraging the town to "play up and use [Buffalo Bill] as a magnet to draw the east to the west."

On a day when her opponents were out of town, Lockhart, Dwight Hollister, and Bill Hogg rounded up a bunch of unregistered voters and took them to the elections office in the men's cars. The gambit was not enough to win the school board elections in early May, so for the city elections they turned up the heat.

Hollister and Hogg (along with others who moved in Cody society better than Lockhart did) convinced Dr. R. C. Trueblood, president of the influential Cody Club, to run for mayor under a platform that would "banish the strong factional feeling that exists at present." (In addition to cultural issues, the city was split over how to handle its waterworks.) Hogg and Harry Thurston tried to file last-minute candidacies for two council spots, but somebody tipped off the elections registrar to leave town and stymie their filings. Typically overdramatizing, Lockhart wrote in her diary, "Looks as if civil war might break out in the little burg. The enemy are counting on using force to prevent voting. We are lining up a few warriors, too. Goppert and Greever are just inexperienced fools enough to do something like that."

Trueblood indeed won the election, by a solid majority. Lockhart's news story painted the event in epic terms: "It was a battle between the normal, conservative citizens of Cody and the fantastical reformers . . . who have controlled the town for the past year. Tired of petty tyranny and persecutions, sick of character assassins, the people of Cody [spoke]. . . . Every cheap, dishonest, shyster trick that could be thought of was used by the reformers to defeat Dr. Trueblood, who represents the real business men and the sane, normal, well-balanced citizens of the town."

In her diaries she was even less inhibited. "We gave 'em such a licking as no political faction ever got before in Cody and Trueblood is mayor. They look sick and yellow. . . . I never was so excited in my life, and others said the same. . . . The vote was nearly two to one. It will strengthen the *Enterprise* and hammer home the fact that we must be recognized as a factor. I am tired but *tickled* beyond words. I never saw such real rejoicing—like people who have thrown off a yoke."

She had come to a thorough understanding of local politics, as a Water-Wagon analysis a few weeks later showed. High school students had chosen Presbyterian Rev. A. M. Shepperd to be their graduation speaker, but the school board, breaking tradition, rejected the students' choice and substituted a man from out of town. Lockhart wrote of the board, "Now Mr. Bell is a Methodist. Mrs. Len Leander Newton . . . is a Methodist. With the exception of Mrs. J.H. Van Horn the other three members of the board are the type that should be Methodists." Every Cody issue boiled down to this war of values.

It's a bit surprising that Lockhart would be such a crusader, since she had never before been terribly political. She had seen politicians as celebrities and as people who could boost her own power, but rarely as ideological symbols. But she had always been keen on injustice, and now she herself felt wronged by the zealous enforcement of Prohibition. So she saw minor city elections in terms of oppressed people throwing off yokes—and though that vision may strike us as overwrought, it apparently struck Codyites as having at least a ring of truth.

However, once Trueblood was in office, Lockhart showed little interest in *how* he governed. Elections were merely a battleground, and now she would search for a new one.

Gertrude Vanderbilt Whitney came from the sort of money Lockhart could admire. Whitney's father, Cornelius Vanderbilt II, was one of the richest men in America. Her husband, Harry Payne Whitney, was a polo-playing, safari-hunting heir to oil, tobacco, and banking fortunes. Just four years younger than Lockhart, Whitney too had chafed at the dull life of society summers on the Atlantic shore. She too was creative, ambitious, and frustrated by the confines in which upper-class women were supposed to keep themselves. Whitney decided to become not just a patroness of the arts, but an artist herself. By the late 1910s she became known as the most gifted woman sculptor in America; in 1919 she completed a memorial for victims of the *Titanic*.

Whitney met Lockhart in Cody, just a few days after the success of the third annual Cody Stampede, in July 1922. Lockhart had wanted her to come for the Stampede itself, to see Cody in its true western form, but Whitney had been delayed, and indeed stayed in Cody less than a full day. Lockhart showed her an empty space in front of the Irma Hotel, as well as some empty land west of town. Then she took her to Buffalo Bill's old suite at the Irma, recently restored, to meet with another civic committee.

Shortly after Buffalo Bill's death in 1917, still troubled that he had been buried in Colorado and not his namesake town, Codyites had started the Buffalo Bill Memorial Association to perpetuate his memory, perhaps through a historical monument or statue. They got the state legislature to set aside five thousand dollars for it. They debated a school or park but for many years took no action. Then Lockhart got involved.

Along with Arthur Little, June Little's father, who knew Whitney, she decided that Whitney should sculpt Cody's statue. (She did advertise for other sculptors; her favorite response came from a man in Hastings, Nebraska, who wrote that he had "modeled a figure of a farmer and two pigs out of lard at the Omaha exposition which was well spoken of by the Omaha Bee.") Lockhart wrote Mary Jester Allen, a niece of Buffalo Bill who lived in New York City, to enlist her help. Allen, busy with other projects, didn't pay much attention. But Lockhart kept sending telegrams and letters, urging Allen to reach out to Whitney. Finally Allen relented and met with the sculptor.

Whitney saw great potential in being the first to sculpt such a widely known hero as Buffalo Bill. She found him a distinctly American character, representing the frontier, its adventure and romance. She wanted to be part of this project.

Now, at the Irma Hotel, she told the committee of her vision. Buffalo Bill would be aged about thirty or so, when he was a scout and plainsman, before his theatrical career. He would be mounted on a "typical Western horse such as has been immortalized in the drawings of Remington and Schreyvogel." It would cost fifty thousand dollars.

The committee signed a contract that afternoon. In *Enterprise*s all summer, Lockhart wrote up the vision in glowing terms. "This statue will mean more to Cody than is yet realized," she wrote. "It will bring tourists who might otherwise use another of the Park entrances. It will be a Mecca for the thousands of hero worshippers throughout the world to whom the Colonel was a typical American."

To Lockhart, in other words, the statue would establish the town of Cody as the home of the romanticized cowboy. In Cody the West would not be about farming, or mining, or the process of establishing civilization in former wilderness. It would be a carefree man on a horse. Though located in the heart of the West, the statue was really born of the East. Whitney (an easterner), as trumpeted by Lockhart (a former easterner), wanted to retrace the images of Remington (an easterner) in lionizing the man who earned fame as an entertainer by giving easterners romanticized melodramas that claimed to be the spirit of the West. Horses, cowboys, independent romantics freely pursuing their happiness on the frontier—this was the West that Lockhart and Wister and Remington and thousands of others had sought and eventually enshrined in their art, even if they'd never really quite found it in life.

In the August Republican primary, Lockhart endorsed a reform ticket. She supported a Powell farmer named David Powers for county commissioner and Hollister's partner William Simpson for county attorney. To support former sheriff Henry Dahlem in his quest to retake that office, she ran articles criticizing the huge expenses of C. A. Davis, implying that Davis's efforts to enforce Prohibition used too much of the county budget. To support the Greybull rancher Thomas Osborne, she ran an unflattering picture of his opponent, incumbent county commissioner Sanford Watkins, and harped on Watkins's vote on the county printing contract. The commissioners had given that contract to the *Herald*, she reminded voters, despite receiving two lower bids. The *Herald* supported Watkins only because Newton made so much money on that cozy relationship. Of Newton, she said plainly, "If anyone ever gets him by the hind leg and pulls his nose and feet out of the trough[,] we can imagine how Len Leander will squeal when he feels himself going."

The voting did not go her way, in part because Newton was state committeeman, meaning he ran the county Republican Party. "We were whipped," she admitted to her diary. Powers did win, and Osborne came within eight votes of Watkins, but several sheriff candidates split the anti-Davis vote, and Goppert cruised over Simpson. Prohibition, it seemed, would still be enforced. But she wasn't ready to give up. She couldn't let Newton and Goppert win. Her revenge, she vowed, would come in the November general election.

First, however, she and Ericson took a vacation, on horseback through the Pryor Mountains just south of the Crow reservation. She called the trip "interesting and restful." Though she was gone only a week, coming back to the same old dreary house depressed her. She couldn't get over the contrast.

A few days later she wrote, "My little trip with Lou showed me how happy I might be in the right conditions."

⌒

Harry Wiard, Cody's town marshal, was standing in front of the Irma Hotel one afternoon in October 1922 when he noticed a couple of women of ill repute walk past. He decided to follow them, especially when they were joined by a man. The three went into the women's house, and Wiard, completing his shift, told his relief to keep an eye on them. Neighbors had been complaining about parties at that house.

Sure enough, it was a party. The relief man, Joe Davenport, and a buddy named Rex Spencer watched through a window for more than an hour. The three were drinking ginger ale highballs. The man was so drunk he was lurching and staggering. They called Wiard back on duty, and when the man left the house at midnight, Wiard followed him downtown.

You're drunk, Wiard said to the man, and I'm going to arrest you.

You can't arrest me, said the man, whose name was Galen Hodge. I'm a federal agent.

But Wiard was indeed going to arrest him. To do so, he put a hand on Hodge's shoulder. Hodge resisted, and they fought. After one of Wiard's blows broke Hodge's jaw, Hodge pulled a gun and fired it against Wiard's leg. Then Hodge brought the gun against Wiard's stomach, but Wiard wrested it away before it could go off again.

Hearing the shot, Spencer approached. Wiard deputized him to arrest Hodge. Hodge brandished a blackjack and ran away. But he stumbled and fell on the sidewalk outside the Irma, and Spencer was able to subdue him. Needing help, they telephoned for Davis, the county sheriff. But when Davis arrived on the street scene, he found a conflict. Wiard was asking him to arrest Hodge, but Hodge was asking him to arrest Wiard. Hodge really was a federal Prohibition agent, while Wiard worked for the town, where Mayor Trueblood was aligned with the Wet forces.

Davis sided with Hodge. He ordered Wiard to jail. Wiard refused. Davis took the whole crowd to a nearby building and called Dr. Frances Lane to attend to the men's injuries. She fixed up Hodge, but Wiard refused to let her look at him. So Davis dragged him to jail with an open hole in his leg. After an overnight stay and much legal wrangling, he was finally permitted to be confined at his doctor's hospital.

Hodge claimed that he had been undercover and that Wiard and Spencer had conspired to interfere with an officer in the performance of his duty. He said he was not drunk—that charge was absurd—and that Wiard and supporters had intended to lure him to an out-of-the-way place and kill him. Accordingly, the county attorney filed conspiracy, interference, and assault charges against Wiard and Spencer. Town officials insisted Hodge also be prosecuted—for assault, resisting an officer, and attempted murder—but did not succeed. Hodge eventually paid a fine for public drunkenness but kept his job.

Lockhart was predictably outraged. She noted that Wiard's nine-thousand-dollar bond was "$4000 more than Fatty Arbuckle's when he was held for murder." She quoted police sources elsewhere in the state who said Hodge was habitually drunk. The New York humor magazine *Judge*, likely at her prodding, noted that Prohibition officers were the only people in the country allowed to drink—indeed, the drunker they were, the harder they must be working. *Judge* recommended to town marshals everywhere that they never arrest any drunks, given the chances that they were actually gun-toting federal agents on the job.

The event took place just weeks before the 1922 election, in which Lockhart had been planning to endorse Democrats despite her paper's long-standing Republicanism ("when it comes to L.L. Newton's hand-picked candidates for county offices, whose nominations were secured by unfair and characteristically newtonish methods, that is another matter"). But Wiard-Hodge was so scandalous that her endorsements may have been irrelevant. Though Goppert won, Sheriff Davis and Commissioner Watkins were thrown out, replaced by Democrats.

The following month Lockhart wrote, "The one thing we regret about S.A. Watkins' retirement as county commissioner is that we shall no longer have occasion to print his [highly unflattering] picture." That mention being occasion enough, she printed it again.

Buried in the local notes of the *Enterprise* on November 29, 1922, Lockhart made this announcement: "Mr. Paul Eldridge of Dewey, Okla., arrived last week to join the *Enterprise* staff. Mr. Eldridge finished at Harvard last year and has since been employed on the Journal at Jacksonville, Fla." Paul Eldridge had grown up in northeast Oklahoma, where he knew the Edgingtons and may have even met Lockhart on one of her visits. However they met, he was corresponding with her even in 1918, before he started work on his masters in literature at Harvard. He had now completed that degree and hoped to accelerate his writing career on her newspaper.

Eldridge lasted only a month. But his short tenure was notable in two ways. First, she did not hire him as editor—that role was now hers. Second, he was profoundly affected by what he saw in Cody and wrote about it years later. It was, he wrote, "the Homesteaders versus the Cattlemen, the Scissor-bills versus the Old Timers. It was totally inclusive warfare with no decisive battle, no Waterloo, no Gettysburg to end it, but it was fun while it lasted." He described Lockhart as arriving at the office every day with "a smile on her face as she meditated mischief on her opposition or inquired as to their latest attack." He instantly found himself a foot soldier in that battle, "irrevocably committed, so far as the community was concerned, to a cause of which the day before I had been ignorant. . . . Armed not with a six-gun but a Remington portable typewriter, weaponed not with Sharps' buffalo gun but an intractable oldstyle K linotype . . . I rattled out my cattleman copy and launched my shells, as it were, at the Scissorbills. The Scissorbills seemed not to mind. There were so many of them, you know, and more kept coming."

Eldridge sketched these reminiscences as a sort of eulogy after Lockhart's death, which may help explain their nostalgic glow. They strike even the most casual reader as absurdly romanticized. Eldridge wanted to live in a Wild West, one that matched what he'd read in his literary studies. In the 1930s he'd written to Lockhart that his attitude was akin to a "worship of the West—the shining mountains, the lucid space, and the ghosts of the cowboys, the Indians, the buffalo hunters that almost visibly walked."

If he so worshipped the West, why didn't he stay? From Lockhart's perspective, she was soon writing in her diary that he was "as green as grass, a waste of money." From Eldridge's perspective, he never spoke of a reason. We can imagine that if pressed he might have noted that he went on to a career in academia, something not possible in Cody. Given the repressive nature of the times, he probably would not have talked about—but surely must have thought about—a more personal reason. He was gay. Small-town Wyoming was not an easy place to be a young homosexual. Especially when the only person you knew in town was your boss, and especially when your boss enjoyed publishing snide remarks about Frances Lane and Marjory Ross.

So Eldridge may not have stayed long enough to understand the dynamics of the town. He admired Lockhart, and he admired romantic interpretations of the West. So he grafted the two together. Lockhart and Newton may have been fighting over the enforcement of Prohibition and the awarding of county printing contracts, but since they were fighting in front of those glorious western landscapes, Eldridge saw the battles as mythic. He was hopelessly sentimental, in love with "picturesque trappers, sheepmen, cowmen, Indians and assorted outlaws." He wanted to be in a battle for them and against the shopkeeper and dry-farmer class that represented the end of the frontier, as they had throughout the American experience. Could there be a more noble fight? "I had a feeling that you couldn't hold back history," he wrote, "but [trying] was an unforgettable experience." In that attitude he well mirrored his mentor.

"All you have to say to the average easterner is that you live [in] or come from Cody, and he will begin a rapid fire of questions as to the wildness of the locality, the number of Indians in the vicinity and will want to know just how wild everything is out here." The speaker was Tom Ames, who owned a ranch up the South Fork of the Shoshone, near the Littles. He was addressing the Cody Club in February 1923 in what would prove an influential speech. A dude rancher, Ames sought more widespread support for his industry. For twenty years, he recalled, town leaders had tried to persuade immigrants from middle-western states that "Cody is no different from any town in Iowa." However, now it was time to break with that tradition, establish Cody as very different from Iowa. Cody, he said, should be a western town. "Big hats, blue jeans, and chaps are what the visitor is interested in seeing and such things are what induces them to linger longer while here . . . [so let's] give them what they want and keep their money coming in."

The problem, Ames said, was that Cody didn't really have anything to distinguish itself from any other town in Wyoming, except the name. Associating the name with Buffalo Bill, tourists came to Cody expecting to see the types of characters they'd seen in Buffalo Bill's Wild West. Although Cody had not come into existence until the late 1890s, long after the Crow and Shoshone Indians had been banished to their reservations, and although its reason for existence had been a dam to irrigate farms, Ames called on the town to invent a more picturesque history. "Cody should be more as it used to be, with more riders, Indians, big hats, etc., and a general wild and woolly atmosphere."

June Little, back for another turn on the *Enterprise* staff, wrote a column in support of the idea. "It doesn't take such a terrible bad man to wear a large hat," he said, "even you or I." By doing so, he suggested, Cody could gain the reputation of being wild without having to suffer any bad men. He even suggested building hitching racks and false-fronted buildings to make the town look more like an 1880s movie set, and hiring riders and Indians to parade up and down Main Street. The Indians would surely come cheap: just a calf a week.

This was, of course, the same message Lockhart had been promoting for years. She was the one who had first invited Plenty Coups and his Crows to Cody and had made them feel so welcome. She was the one who had pushed so hard the notion of the Stampede: the Fourth of July as a celebration not of America but of the Old West. She was the one who set up the Stampede Ball as an old-time costume party, and she was the one who was getting fed up with people who attended it dressed in their "store clothes and evening gowns." For the 1923 ball, she would write, "the Stampede Committee wants it to be a real Stampede ball with western folk in western clothes, bright shirts, gay handkerchiefs, high heeled boots."

It's easy to see why the dude ranchers pushed these concepts. The more that Cody could match their guests' visions of a western atmosphere (the more, in other words, it could be a Buffalo Bill Theme Park), the more money they would make. But why was Lockhart so keen on it? It wasn't a direct source of income. Rather, she gained great value out of living every day in that atmosphere that tourists could only visit on vacation. Every day, for her commute to the office, she put on boots, spurs, a divided skirt, and a Stetson, saddled up her buckskin gelding, and rode four blocks. Granted, she was too broke to afford an automobile. But plenty of people would have walked.

Lockhart had come to Cody to live in the Old West. When, almost immediately upon her arrival, progress took the town out of what she imagined as a blissful condition, she tried to re-inhabit it through her novels. Mixing big hats with realistic landscape descriptions, she had created an Old West that, though it was heavily romanticized, she believed was more authentic than Zane Grey's. Now she had a chance to create such a world not just in a novel but in real life. Unlike Eldridge, she seemed not yet aware that this amounted to trying to turn back history—or even trying to prop up an *imaginary* history—and that such an effort was necessarily doomed.

The following appeared in Lockhart's *Water-Wagon* column on March 7, 1923:

> Having purchased the interest of C. Conger, a job printer formerly employed in the mechanical dept. of the *Enterprise*, we now take considerable pride in the fact that we are its sole owner, and hope some allowance will be made if we toot our own horn a little.
>
> This paper was in the hands of a receiver when we acquired an interest in it a little more than two years ago. It was about to give its last gurgle and expire. It had a little advertising, no county or city printing, its subscription list consisted chiefly of persons who were dead, moved away, or had not paid since they first subscribed for the paper, while to look at its front page with poems entitled "Eternal Peace" and three column clippings from the Literary Digest as the leading news stories, was to weep.
>
> Since that time we have purchased all other interests, eliminated the dead ones (eliminating dead ones is our specialty) and added hundreds of live ones to the subscription list. The *Enterprise* is now the official city and county paper, receives its share of the local advertising, and for "Eternal Peace" we have substituted the Water-Wagon.
>
> In addition, we have reduced the mortgage against the paper to a minimum, purchased a $5,200 Intertype machine and bought a new building to put it in. In view of the fact that we had so little business training we did not know a day book from a ledger, and was so inexperienced in publishing a country newspaper that we tried to read the congressional record, we do not feel that we have done so badly, though we hope to do better when we are older.

Things really were falling into place. Lockhart had settled out of court with Conger, buying his share for three hundred dollars. The new building and linotype machine spoke to some degree of financial stability (though it would prove fleeting). In February, when the *Enterprise* and *Herald* both bid to do the county printing at the standard rate, recently elected commissioners Powers and Markham voted to give the job to the *Enterprise*. Furthermore, she had gained enough self-confidence to refer to herself as editor and publisher. Her articles, and indeed the newspaper as a whole, reflected her unique personality in grand style.

"Costs $1.00 to Kick an Editor," announced one headline. A man arguing politics with L. L. Newton had finally kicked Newton onto the sidewalk. Newton got Goppert to bring charges, and the judge levied a fine of a single dollar. (Newton subsequently appealed to a higher court and got the fine raised to ten dollars.)

"Hot Debate for Cody *Enterprise*," read another headline. It reported that a local women's club had informally debated which was a better newspaper. "The *Herald*'s champions declared that it was an advocate of good roads, catered to the farmer and had a high moral tone which made it a force for good in the community. The supporters of the *Enterprise* argued that they were fed up on good roads and farm articles and would far rather read what was happening in boot-legging circles; that they preferred to be entertained to being uplifted." But what tipped the scales was their delight in the unflattering picture of former commissioner Sanford Watkins. This being sufficiently newsworthy, Lockhart printed the picture again.

"Lawyer Takes Odd Fee; Left Hole in Floor," read another headline. The article noted that in the aftermath of a lawsuit, Goppert walked out of the Cody Hotel "tenderly clasping a bathroom fixture to his bosom. . . . It was not the bathtub, nor yet the lavatory, but an accessory found in all well appointed bathrooms." But not all stories were frivolous. The community had still not decided on the best way to enforce Prohibition.

At about dusk on June 25, 1923, a Nash touring car approached a lonely spot on Cottonwood Creek, north of Cody. Two men got out of the car and started loading it with boxes from a cache. Their names were Scotty Sherrin and A. E. Carey, and their load was forty gallons of moonshine. But they were not alone. Also concealed in the creekbed were J. T. McGonagle, a janitor at the courthouse, and another man named Harry Tipton. McGonagle and Tipton were armed with high-powered rifles.

Goppert and Sheriff William Loomis, following a tip, had driven out to Cottonwood Creek earlier in the day and discovered the cache. While Goppert stood watch, Loomis returned to town to deputize McGonagle and Tipton. Their instructions, repeated by Goppert before he returned to town, were to arrest the bootleggers, taking no chances with these potentially dangerous characters, but not to shoot unless fired upon.

Now, as Sherrin and Carey got back in the car to leave, Tipton stepped out and said, "God damn you—put 'em up!" Claiming that they saw the flash of two pistol shots despite the fact that it was not yet dark, Tipton and McGonagle then started shooting.

Inside the car, Carey hadn't heard the deputies say anything. He never saw a badge. He didn't even know anybody was there until he heard the shots. Still, he was tempted to obey the deputies and stop the car. But the bullets kept coming. He thought Tipton wanted to kill him.

"Christ!" Sherrin told him. "We can't stay here and be murdered!" Bullets broke the glass in the car's back windshield and whistled through the car. Sherrin dropped to the floor, and Carey pressed the accelerator. He tried to lie down on the seat, holding up just one hand to guide the steering wheel. The deputies reloaded and began firing again. (McGonagle later said he'd fired sixteen times.)

Another bullet came through the car, through the front seat, and through the spot where Carey's backbone would have been had he been sitting up straight. Since he was lying prone, the bullet caught his hip. "Kid, they got me!" he said.

So Sherrin got up and sat in Carey's lap to take the wheel. By this point they had come even with the deputies, so Tipton had an angle from the side, just fifty feet away. He shot through the window and into Sherrin's chest. The shot went through Sherrin's heart. His head dropped and he grew limp instantly, crumpling up on Carey's lap, slipping and pushing Carey's foot off the accelerator. The car swerved crosswise in the road.

Carey pushed Sherrin's body away and again slammed down on the gas. He soon got out of the deputies' range, blood streaming down his leg. He tried to stuff a handkerchief against the wound, but the rough roads kept jouncing it away. Losing blood through the sixty-mile trip to a friend's house in the town of Greybull, he got so weak that he could barely see.

The deputies, meanwhile, hitched a ride back to town and alerted the sheriff. Arriving in Greybull later that night, Loomis easily spotted a bullet-riddled Nash and arrested Carey at the nearby house.

In the paper, Lockhart was outraged. "It looks to the people of this locality as if human life was getting pretty cheap when any person with a nickel star pinned on him can go out and shoot and kill in the name of law and order without a warrant, for an offense which at most is only a misdemeanor." She called it cold-blooded murder and pinned it squarely on Goppert. It's not clear why she tried to give Loomis a pass, claiming that he'd been out of town all day, that Goppert alone had engineered the raid, that afterward Goppert "chortled" over his discovery of the cache. At Carey's trial the following spring, testimony showed Loomis was equally culpable. Perhaps, having endorsed him over Davis the previous election, Lockhart wanted to believe he was softer on liquor. More likely, she simply saw this as an opportunity to discredit Goppert, whom she now saw as not just a political opponent but a full-fledged "enemy" along the lines of Frances Lane.

When the article came out, Goppert immediately sent Lockhart a letter of protest. He accused her of libel, especially in the charge that he alone had set up the raid. Lockhart reported the following week that he had made the protest and she intended to be fair to him, but the whole scandal had exploded during the week before Stampede. "Next week when we have the time and leisure we will give Mr. Goppert's protest our attention," she wrote.

The 1923 Stampede did turn out a success—with more than eleven thousand dollars in receipts, it was not only the biggest event of its kind in the area but also financially viable—but Goppert couldn't wait. Five days later he filed a lawsuit against her. His popularity had suffered irreparable injury, he said, since the false charges in the article had fanned the "ridicule, opprobrium, criticism and hatred of the people of Park County." To repair his reputation and career from this libel, he demanded thirty thousand dollars.

Privately, Lockhart was gravely concerned. She'd long feared a libel suit, though she'd expected it to come from Newton. As the trial dragged out for more than three years, it became as big an albatross as the financial and time demands of the newspaper itself. "The ordeal of the [lawsuit] I dread," she told her diary in July of the following year, and then five months later, after more delays, "I should work but find it hard to do so with my libel suit in the air." Publicly, however, she was utterly unfazed. The *Enterprise* printed a story on the lawsuit, in which she continued to mock Goppert as "Park County's extremely active prosecuting attorney." Its final words: "Go your best, Mr. Goppert!"

In her memoirs Lockhart referred to Goppert as one of her favorite enemies, as if having an enemy—her father's wife Steppy, Dr. Frances Lane, and later her neighbors Edith Barry and Hank Lane—energized her life. Certainly the *Enterprise* over the next six months showed her in rare form.

In the same issue as the announcement of the libel suit—in fact, given far more prominent placement, at the top of page 1—was a story in which Goppert, mingling at Wolfville during the Stampede, demanded that the marshal arrest a man carrying a suspicious-looking sack. The bottles in the sack turned out to be full of soda. Lockhart titled the story "Gop Gets Pop in Raid on Car."

The following week she examined how other Wyoming papers had covered the libel story (a standard procedure in the days when editors gathered considerable material from "exchange papers"). The summary in a Casper paper called the *Oil Index* editorialized that Goppert seemed to be "playing the baby act"—so she titled this article "Here's Chance for Goppert to Sue Casper *Oil Index*."

In September she revisited the bathroom-fixture story, and in October she reported on some of Goppert's other hardware. A man had rented out his house for the summer, and Goppert had raided it for liquor. But when the landlord returned he found his hammer missing and raised so much hell with Goppert that Gop bought him a new hammer. In another case, she said, Goppert had taken a cream separator from a farmer, in lieu of his attorney fee, and was now trying to sell it. She consulted a moonshiner, who told her the cream separator could be turned into a very nice still. "Won't somebody step up and buy Mr. Goppert's cream separator?" she asked.

She printed stories of editors acquitted of libel charges—from places as far away as Albuquerque and even Peking. As county commissioner, David Powers—the quiet Powell farmer whom she had tepidly endorsed the previous year—started questioning the costs of Prohibition enforcement. The commission said it would no longer reimburse informants for the purchase of liquor, prompting another Goppert lawsuit, this one by the county attorney against his own county commission. When the case came up, Lockhart noted that added to the $5 charge in question was also $3.70 in costs and 28 cents in interest.

In the *Herald* Newton and Goppert charged that Powers's poor administration, rather than Prohibition enforcement, was emptying the county's finances. Powers responded with a stinging article for the *Enterprise*, laying out the county's bills and asking Newton to specify which ones he would renege on. "Will the fountain of wisdom that sits in front of the typewriter in the Herald office kindly forget the county printing contract for a few minutes and elucidate?" He also asked why the county should heed Newton's advice on any financial matter, given that Newton's other business, a general store, had just gone bankrupt.

Lockhart played up these charges—noting the Newton bankruptcy in her headline—and added a few shots of her own. "Before the last election we prophesied that if anybody ever got Len Leander Newton by the hind leg and pulled his front feet out of the trough where he has fed so long and bounteously, his squeals would be long and earsplitting. This was just what Messrs. Powers and Markham did to him when they took away his monopoly of the county printing and perquisites. . . . (Starting a mud fight is dangerous business, Len Leander; besides we have lived here nearly twenty years and very likely our memory is as good as your own.)"

Newton's alliance with Goppert redoubled her delight at skewering him. Noting that Newton was "much elated over the fact that we are being sued for defaming the character of E.J. Goppert," she concluded that between "being sued and being kicked, we really prefer the former. It cost a husky citizen only $10 to kick the editor of the Herald, whereas it will cost the prosecuting attorney many times that amount to sue the *Enterprise*."

Meanwhile, the committee to erect a statue of Buffalo Bill—with Lockhart still a major player—had run into big problems. That fall of 1923 they had to send an important emissary to Gertrude Vanderbilt Whitney in New York. The emissary's name was Smokey Groves.

Surprisingly, the crisis was not over money, despite the fact that Cody had raised less than 1 percent of the statue's price tag, which was now climbing toward a hundred thousand dollars. Lockhart had run big, fawning articles about how Cody's "Sammy Girls" (a women's organization that had supported servicemen during the World War) would lead the fund-raising, but in fact their efforts netted little actual funds. And although the committee had used the five thousand dollars from the state to purchase a large piece of land west of the county courthouse (which at that time was the west end of town), an architect employed by Whitney visited Cody and decided he didn't like that site. The statue, he said, needed to be in a landscape of native trees and sagebrush. He engineered the purchase, by Whitney herself, of a larger piece of land farther west, on a bluff overlooking the river. (Lockhart was delighted. In Water-Wagon she wrote, "Speaking for ourself, we are relieved to learn that the Whitney statue of Buffalo Bill is to stand in the sagebrush and not on a smug, velvet lawn shaded by neat rows of poplars reminiscent of Keokuk, Ia., or Lincoln, Neb.")

That land only increased the project's cost, which would eventually reach

$250,000. How to raise that money? Rather than wasting their time on the dusty western town, Whitney and Mary Jester Allen simply turned to people they knew in New York. They started another committee, the Buffalo Bill American Association, filled it with rich easterners, and held a fund-raising dinner at the Biltmore Hotel. In soliciting national money, they didn't talk about a commemorative local statue in northwest Wyoming. Rather, they spoke of Whitney sculpting an image of the nation's cultural values as represented by the cowboy Buffalo Bill. This statue, they suggested, would demonstrate the self-sufficiency and freedom that the frontier had uniquely bestowed upon the authentic American spirit. While such nostalgia for the cowboy as the ultimate American had already existed in the nationwide consciousness, the committee's work certainly promoted that view, helping to cement it as an expectation of the twentieth century—in large part because Lockhart had insisted on getting a statue of Buffalo Bill that she couldn't pay for.

Freed from the responsibility of raising money, Lockhart and her Cody cronies made few objections. The local committee held on to ownership of its land (no longer needed for the statue, it would many years later become a city park), while it let the national committee do most of its fund-raising work. "You started this very big thing," Lockhart quoted one of Whitney's employees saying, "and now they [the national committee] have assumed the task of finishing what you so gallantly began." In a sense it was a dream come true for Lockhart: with Buffalo Bill as the *nation's* hero, not just the town's, surely people near and far would have to pay attention to him, his hometown—and his promoter. No, the crisis didn't arise over money or meaning. Instead it arose over Buffalo Bill's horse.

When Whitney circulated a preliminary drawing, the Cody committee said the horse looked too eastern, too fat, "too much of the polo pony type." Buffalo Bill, especially as a young scout, would have ridden a more wiry, muscular range horse. Furthermore, "when a western horse is pulled up as sharply as the horse in the model, it bunches its feet to stop, rather than throwing them forward. The stirrup, too, is eastern rather than the larger leather covered stirrup of the western stock saddle." Lloyd Coleman, one of Lockhart's Stampede buddies, helpfully explained to an eastern reporter, "It's a society animal—and that won't do for Buffalo Bill. He's got to have a regular he-man horse."

So now they were shipping Smokey, a genuine western horse, to New

York City for Whitney to study. Coleman accompanied the horse and even posed on it for a film in Central Park so Whitney could appreciate how it moved. For Lockhart, as for westerners throughout the twentieth century, the authenticity of the details—the size of the horse—had become far more important than any interpretation easterners might apply to the history of the region.

Minor victories continued for Lockhart through the winter and spring of 1923-24. The Stampede Ball went well, and later Lockhart was reelected as the organization's president, with little controversy. The library board, with Goppert's wife picking up where Marjory Ross left off, got into a big mess: firing a popular librarian because she lacked credentials, then losing a credentialed librarian because they tried to meddle in her personal life. The commissioners finally fired the entire board, with Lockhart providing all of the embarrassing publicity she could. And at the newspaper Lockhart finally found an employee she thought she might be able to trust. In May—faced with a busy summer of the Stampede and a vacation with Ericson in the Pryors—she leased the operation to George Huss.

She still contributed a great deal of writing: Stampede publicity, Water-Wagon columns, and a good helping of political and local news. But having achieved her ambition of being editor and manager, she was able to let it go. Huss would take care of the books and supervise the weekly operations. Huss could run the paper without her if need be. She had found the pressure of unrelenting deadlines, the same work week in and week out, to be drudgery. She never had time to work on her stories for national publications, or on a new novel. Leasing the paper allowed her to re-inhabit those ambitions.

Furthermore, her plan had proved correct. By wresting the county printing contract away from Newton, she had broken him. First his store had gone bankrupt, and now he sold the *Herald* to his partner Ernest Shaw. Though she didn't much care for Shaw either, the intensity of the newspaper feud had been driven by her personal clash with Newton. With Newton leaving town (he bought a newspaper in Lander, 160 miles south), she could disengage a bit herself.

Or at least she convinced herself she could. She convinced herself that Huss could run a newspaper—could run *her* newspaper—to her satisfaction. He would last about six months.

Lockhart sat on her horse, listening to the 1924 Stampede program. Despite drizzle and cool temperatures, there were ten thousand people in attendance, the biggest crowd ever assembled in Cody. Many were rich easterners, attending the unveiling of Whitney's statue of Buffalo Bill. *The Scout*, thirteen tons in weight, had come to Cody on a railcar, after its initial viewing in Central Park in early June. It was twelve feet high and thirteen feet long, showing Buffalo Bill on a western horse, holding his rifle high above his head in signal to other scouts.

Consistent with the money that had funded it, the statue's dedication focused less on Buffalo Bill's connection to Cody and more on the way he symbolized America. It was not a shrine of a man or a town, but a "shrine of frontier patriotism." The Boy Scouts, who had been heavily involved in fund-raising, held a position of honor, and Lockhart had predicted that "inspiration to be strong men literally will surge into their hearts at that awesome moment, there to make its abiding place and mold their futures." Despite the fact that Lockhart, Whitney, and Allen, the driving forces behind the statue, were all women, the event became a celebration of masculinity.

Likewise, despite the statue's cowboy theme, the event celebrated modern civilization. An airplane circled above, and the *Enterprise* noted that it symbolized the progress of the West since Cody's time as a scout. But Lockhart watched that airplane from the back of her horse. It was her kind of progress, the sort that venerated the cowboy traditions. She noted that most of the speeches struck "that note of preserving what is left of the Old West." Specifically, Yellowstone National Park superintendent Horace Albright tied such preservation—in the form of Lockhart's Stampede—to the patriotism that drove the national agenda, saying, "Let us hold each year celebrations that will be so colorful and picturesque as to keep up our own interest in this conservation of the spirit of the old West, and also for the purpose of spreading to the people of every state of the union the feeling that this spirit of the pioneers must be preserved if America is to be home of the Americans and this nation the moral leader of the World."

It may not have been obvious to her at the time, but Lockhart's goal was nearly achieved. The town of Cody now stood for Buffalo Bill's Wild West, rather than his irrigation scheme. Its future would be increasingly tied to big hats and tourism rather than farming and midwestern progress. What's more, that future economy would thrive because of the cowboy's increasing nationwide profile. While still infused with the spirit of the *pioneer*—"the age old urge to do things" that L. L. Newton had admired—Americans through the twentieth century preferred to identify themselves with the spirit of the *cowboy*—brash, direct, thrill seeking, and disdainful of civilized refinement.

As Lockhart sat listening to these speeches, however, an even greater highlight awaited. Across the back of a horse came a card being passed to her. Opening it, she looked at the name on the card: G. N. Lockhart. Thinking it was someone with a similar name, she looked up at the stranger and said perfunctorily, "How do you do."

Then she saw his eyes and did a double take. Those black eyes belonged to her brother George. She hadn't seen him in thirty years. She wouldn't have recognized him without the introductory card. "We just shook hands like two Injuns without saying much," she said of that meeting, but it was obviously a profound one. George was her next-youngest brother, who had also rebelled against the family, traveling for most of his life in Mexico and the Southwest. He had recently married and settled in Tucson, Arizona; he and his wife had motored to Cody from California. They breakfasted with Lockhart the next day, and she reported the results to her diary with delight: she liked his wife very much; the reconciliation would make it easier for her to return to Kansas and reconcile with the rest of the family; "and George is the most interesting person I have met in a long time. Fascinating."

But all was not triumph for Lockhart. It was a huge weekend for Cody merchants, some of whom Lockhart felt competed too directly with the Stampede. Again the event was a popular success but a financial failure. "I suppose as usual I shall hold the sack," Lockhart told her diary. "It will be for me to sign notes and 'dig up.'" She was disgusted by what she saw as Cody's greed, graft, and selfishness. She wondered if it was worth giving her time and strength to a community that was giving so little back.

Ernest Goppert tried all autumn to take out an ad in the *Enterprise* detailing his record as county prosecuting attorney, in advance of November's election. But Lockhart refused to take his money. In late October, as the election drew near, she finally printed his slogan, "Me and My Record," in the paper. In fact, she used it as the headline for an entire news article.

Accompanied by a large, outdated photograph of Goppert in military uniform, the article said that in the previous election, "as now, he was running upon his record. At that time it was his war record. The uniform in which he was photographed was an obvious bid for the soldier vote. . . . Mr. Goppert's war record is very simple. When America became involved he was a law student at the University of Kansas. He was one of two or three members of a large class who did not immediately volunteer their services. Afterward he married and moved to Wyoming." (In fact, Goppert *had* served in the military, even if he hadn't enrolled "immediately." The picture was taken at an officers' training school in Kansas.)

In another article Lockhart admitted she'd turned down his ads, saying, "The *Enterprise* refused to print Mr. Goppert's record because it contained statements which were incorrect and misleading." He was trying to show that his office was a paying proposition for the county, but she conducted a study that she said proved otherwise. His calculations had failed to include payments to waiting jurors (as well as sitting jurors) as a cost of his office. It had also counted bootlegger fines as a benefit of his office, though by law those fines had to go toward the budget of the schools rather than the county.

Lockhart had taunted Goppert through almost every issue of the paper since he won the primary election in August—by an incredibly thin margin, she claimed, given that his youthful opponent "was practically unknown outside his social circle and . . . made no campaign to speak of." Later, hinting at the upcoming study, she wrote, "The prosecuting attorney sees something sinister in the fact that the *Enterprise* refused to publish his record even at his expense. Be patient, Mr. Goppert, keep your camisole on! We will get around to your record after a while, and it won't cost you a cent!" The week after her study, she ran another article also titled "Me and My Record." This one never mentioned Goppert's name, but said this:

> I am the republican candidate for the office of prosecuting attorney.
> . . . I am a modest man but I *will* say that I am the most learned, efficient, economical, honest, active, truthfully patriotic official that has ever filled the position I am seeking. . . . I am feared by bootleggers, who confess at the sight of me. I have a great nose for moonshine and can smell evidence three miles when the wind is right. . . . I love babies. I am a sterling young fellow. I am a wonder. I cannot write anymore because I have worn out all the I's on my typewriter.

Every single voter in the town of Cody cast a ballot on election day in 1924. Goppert lost by thirty-three votes.

At the 1924 Stampede Ball, again the Indian guests held a place of honor, their bright costumes making the evening's memories. As one attendee wrote, "Ladies in sparkling evening gowns rubbed shoulders with squaws in the varied colored blankets, or dancing with one or the other would be gentlemen in an ordinary business suit or a cowboy in full regalia, and mingling everywhere with that vast throng was Miss Lockhart in full leather trappings, a genial hostess to a gay ensemblage."

It was the fifth annual ball, now attracting hundreds of people every year from all over the region. Some came for the spectacle of Indians, including, this year, the "last living Custer scout," a Crow who had served as an advance scout for the ill-fated general almost fifty years previously. Others came out of curiosity about the event's reputation for wildness and lawlessness, though at least one said the reputation was overblown. And still others came to see its acknowledged queen, for whom leather trappings were not so much a costume as a quest.

If she seemed more genial than expected, that may have been because she was far less anxious. True, she had taken the paper's management away from George Huss (she said he "is silly and [has] no ambition or executive ability. Just a printer."). But a new man was coming from Raton, New Mexico, and she hoped he would make the difference. True, Carey had spent six months in jail awaiting his bootlegging trial. But the courts had rejected Goppert's attempts to confiscate Carey's automobile under wild charges that Carey and the Nash agent were both bootleggers who'd conspired to use the car in their criminal activities. And true, Sheriff Loomis had gotten into trouble for taking the prisoner Carey with him on a hunting trip, but that controversy was almost blown over. True, Goppert's libel suit was still hanging over her, but at least they'd gotten a change of venue. It would not be tried in Cody, where so many people had already formed their prejudices and where it would be such a huge public spectacle.

What really eased Lockhart's anxiety was money. She had just learned that her father was giving each of his children ten thousand dollars in liberty bonds. She was headed to Kansas later in December to get hers. She told her diary, "It means I can have a car, fix my house, pay Andrew [Ross] some, and breathe easy."

She'd always said that money made all the difference, and now it didn't really matter whether the money came from her own business success or from an inheritance. In fact, heiresses were far more socially acceptable than journalists or businesswomen. She saw it as a personal triumph. "It will be the biggest blow yet to my enemies when it seeps in gradually that I am a real 'heiress' and there is no chance of them ever seeing me 'broke' and my wing clipped by poverty."

Over the past several years, Lockhart had occasionally grumbled that only death would loosen her eighty-three-year-old father's hold on his purse strings. But now that he was still alive and being generous, she felt as if she'd won the lottery. "Papa seemed glad to see me," she wrote of the visit. "He is old, feeble, and deaf but still looked papa." She regularly reminded herself of the wonderful things she was doing with the money: repainting her house (and the adjacent one she rented out for income), reroofing the houses, buying a car and building a garage to put it in, buying clothes, taking a month-long vacation that included a visit to George in Arizona. What's more, she said, "For the first time since I bought into the *Enterprise*, the writing feeling has come back to me." Upon her return from the vacation, she added, "I am crazy [with excitement] to start my new book."

However, money proved only temporary healing. By May 1925 she was writing in her diary, "I am enjoying my car and it is fine to feel independent and go where I please. But that is all I have—independence—no affection or love or happiness." She still had the same set of boyfriends—Lou Ericson, O. B. Mann, Andrew Ross, Jack Painter—and the only change was that now all of them were broke. She was trying to pay back Ross not only to square her affairs but also because he needed the money since his mines had tanked. Painter couldn't scrap together a hundred dollars to prove up on his Salmon River homestead. Mann kept trying to sell his ranch and move to California. Ericson's brother had cleared out of the cabin they were building together on the reservation. ("My impecunious lovers!" she'd written before her ship had come in. "Wish I could get one once that wasn't perpetually hard up.")

And if she saw little hope among her lovers, she saw even less among her friends. Cody increasingly struck her as full of cowardice and double crossing. Sheriff Loomis was impeached for taking bribes from a bootlegger. Carey was finally pardoned, but only after serving the longest sentence ever for a liquor violation, thirteen months. Lockhart continued to fear that even if Goppert didn't win his libel suit, the trial would make a sustained public fool out of her. And although her latest editor-manager, a man named

Kelly, signed a one-year lease on the newspaper, within a month she found out that he was stealing from her. "God! It just seems as if everybody was out to beat me and there are no longer any honest people," she wrote in her diary. But where else could a single fifty-four-year-old woman go? She couldn't stand the East; she hated Los Angeles. She still loved the West of her cowboy dreams, and although many of its picturesque rituals had returned to Cody through the sheer effort of her will, they had not brought the Old West itself.

All of her worries were still around—the paper (with Kelly gone, she was running it again), the Stampede (this year's event was shaping up well, she thought), and the day-to-day attitudes of Cody's high society—so despite the money, she still found herself with too little energy to write. Worse, she now saw fewer opportunities to triumph. Len Leander Newton, Ernest Goppert, Frances Lane, and Marjory Ross were all out of official public life, out of reach of the *Enterprise*. Still, she tried to keep after folks. In mid-April, given the newsworthy event that Sanford Watkins had bought a new car and was rumored to be moving to California, she again ran his unflattering picture.

Goppert decided to put an end to it. He got Watkins to sign over ownership of the picture and strode into the *Enterprise* office demanding its return—along with his own, the one in military uniform. Huss (who'd continued working as a printer, and after the Kelly fiasco had again showed signs of managerial ambition) told Goppert they were busy, he should come back later. Having heard that line before, Goppert filed suit immediately. He demanded the pictures' immediate return and twenty dollars in damages—the low amount, apparently, so the case could be handled quickly and without appeal.

The *Enterprise* didn't shy away from the story. Under the headline "Gop has another tantrum," Lockhart summarized the case and added, "Then Mr. Watkins met our business manager and threatened to whip him if his name appeared in the paper, so we have had to oil up the office musket and get it ready for emergencies. This is the life!" Just one week later, the judge found in Goppert's favor.

Lockhart turned over the pictures, be she also ran a story claiming she would appeal. Since there was now news value, she illustrated the story. One caption said, "Sanford Watkins thinks this picture does not do him justice." The other, apparently referencing Goppert's complaint about the many sarcastic captions that had accompanied his mug, said, "Yuzl bjk xyqmlpa."

Blanche Gokel and Lockhart had been enemies for years. It's not clear what started the feud, though when the anonymous letters disparaging Lockhart's reputation circulated before she left for Denver in 1918, she wrote, "it bears every ear-mark of Blanche." Gokel owned the Cody Hotel, which Lockhart frequently referred to as a dump, and they had sparred in court in early 1923, just after Ames made his "Big Hats" speech. Lockhart had printed that Gokel served as a character witness in a divorce case. But that was untrue: the divorce had been settled without a trial. Gokel was so upset that she threatened to beat up Lockhart, so Lockhart tried to get her arrested. Testifying, Lockhart admitted that she didn't actually fear a physical assault, and that she and Gokel had exchanged about an equal number of insults. The case would have disappeared quietly except for being part of the newspaper war. Newton pounced on it, claiming that Lockhart generally "lied about men too chivalrous to give her what she justly deserves and in this instance when she has insulted a member of her own sex, she hides behind her own petticoats," and noting that the judge urged Lockhart "to temper her articles with some reasonable sense of justice and regard for the truth." As with Frances Lane, it seemed a personal battle, one that judges wanted to avoid.

Now, during the 1925 Stampede, their rivalry surfaced again. Lockhart was under her typical pressure in putting on the event. The longhorn cattle were coming from a new source, she was trying to boost attendance by getting the railroad to offer discounts, and she had to mediate a rivalry between two factions of Crow Indians. Then, during the middle of the Stampede, she ran into Gokel, who cackled and taunted her. Lockhart snapped. She walked back and spit in Gokel's face. Gokel ran after her, threatening to spit in Lockhart's own face and force her to actually fight. She grabbed Lockhart's hands as if trying to break her thumbs.

A deputy sheriff stepped in and eased Gokel out of the situation. But Lockhart was shaken. Days later she still called it one of the most unpleasant situations in her life. She was sure Gokel would attack her again, and she knew she could get no protection from the law. She asked Bob Hopkins to make her a blackjack (the same illegal weapon she had criticized Galen Hodge for carrying). Though Gokel soon left town for the summer, Lockhart still worried.

It was a fitting cap to the Stampede. The organization was almost out of debt and would surely make up the last deficit with the autumn ball. Visitors were enthralled, with one proclaiming, "You have the best horses, and I don't think your riders can be surpassed anywhere on the globe." But Lockhart was bitter. "It is my last," she told her diary. "I cannot imagine going through it again for any amount. Not one dollar was volunteered by the Cody merchants who profit most. It is not worth the time and strain it costs."

She decided to lease the paper to Huss again—month by month, this time—and head off on another pack trip to the mountains with Ericson. She had two months of "peace and healthy outdoor life." She started working on a novel again, and it went well. And then she came "back again to hell." Huss had made a mess of the paper. He'd lost the city printing contract to the *Herald*. His papers had been dull—actually she found the whole town dull—and the whole arrangement wasn't working. Huss said he wanted to buy the paper outright; then he said he wanted to quit.

It broke her up, physically as well as emotionally. She was on the verge of a nervous chill. She dreamed of buying a place near Ericson's, in the Pryor Mountains. It could be a headquarters for Lou, who had been so unselfish toward her despite being a bit overwhelmed by the work required on his own place. And it could be an escape where she could finish her book. But for now she reluctantly plunged back into life in Cody, calling it "a damned bowl of mush."

On the front page of the *Enterprise* on October 14, 1925, Lockhart made this announcement:

> With this issue, our great moral uplift sheet, the Cody *Enterprise*, becomes the property of Victor H. Abrahamson, who purchased the newspaper this week from its present owner. We have had our play out and feel that we must get down to work if we are to accomplish anything in our own field before we are in our dotage.
>
> Experience has taught us that one cannot do too many things well, and publishing a country newspaper is much like taking care of a teething infant or sitting up with a typhoid patient. It has its compensations and we have enjoyed ourself, and it is with something of regret that we see our child become the property of another, but time flies. Since this must be, there is no one to whom we would rather entrust its future than to Vic Abrahamson.

He has been in our employ and we feel that we know him well. We have found him honest, truthful, loyal and efficient—a man altogether worthwhile. Out of a vast experience with burglars, blacksmiths, ignoramuses and imbeciles whom we have hired under the misapprehension that they were editors, printers, or machine operators we feel that we are qualified to judge.

So, taking the office cat in one hand and S. A. Watkins' picture in the other, we hand him the key, and may God have mercy on his soul!

In fact, Lockhart's trust in Abrahamson was tepid at best—she'd rejected his previous offers to buy the paper, perhaps because he was brother-in-law to the *Herald*'s Ernest Shaw. But she had reached the end of her rope. At first Abrahamson and Huss proposed to run the operation together, but then Huss couldn't come up with the three-hundred-dollar down payment she required. Fed up with Huss, and believing Abrahamson could do as well or better on his own, she cut Huss out of the deal. With so much of the payment deferred, she had to be sure they wouldn't run the paper into the ground.

The following week Abrahamson ran his own announcement of the sale. With passages such as "Many people will regret to learn that Miss Lockhart has relinquished her interest in the *Enterprise*. With others it may be different," it announced his theme of fairness. He wanted to be fair, he said, with patrons, readers, community members, and the *Herald*. In a companion article he noted that Lockhart had a short-story contract with a magazine and intended to write another novel, but that she was leaving for Denver for an indefinite period "and will hereafter probably spend a good deal of her time in traveling."

Lockhart, meanwhile, wrote in her diary, "I am free after four years of such worry and distasteful drudgery as I never experienced before and hope never to know again! I could yell I feel so relieved."

Though she did not publicize her plans to buy a ranch near the Pryors, that was far more than just a dream. Even as she was negotiating with Huss and Abrahamson, she had asked a woman named Edith Barry to keep an eye out for available properties. There were a few, in part because the area was so inaccessible. That did concern Lockhart, but what she wanted was escape. Plus, the inaccessibility was what made a good-sized spread affordable. She was expecting another check from her father—perhaps two thousand dollars—that would cover the purchase price.

She spent only a few days in Denver, ordering dresses, hats, and a fur coat. She spoke with Uncle Seward, who seemed excited about the ranch. She enjoyed being leisurely and wrote of Cody, "It's a grand and glorious feeling to be able to pass up these honyocker shopkeepers if I want to with no fear of losing their business."

She had referred to her announcement of the sale as an obituary, and indeed it prompted mourning. "The newspaper fraternity of the state of Wyoming has suffered a distinct loss," wrote one editor. "Fearlessness is her chief trait, one generally lacking in the profession," said another. "The pungent breeziness imparted to the *Enterprise* by Miss Lockhart's imagination and style made it more than a novelty among newspapers," said a third.

Indeed, an era was over. By mid-November Abrahamson had dropped one of her slogans, "Everybody reads the *Enterprise*—even if they borrow it." By the next summer he would drop the other slogan about perpetuating the spirit of the Old West. His paper, while fair, was usually profoundly dull.

By the end of November, she had laid out $2,250 for a ranch known as the Wasson place. She felt it was the most desirable place available, so much so that she had tacked on the extra $250 to make sure she outbid another party. She wanted it badly enough that she didn't want to quibble and risk losing everything. There would be a lot more money involved in building it up to what she wanted—she figured $5,000 total. But "it is what I wanted all my life and there's damned few years left in which to enjoy the realization of my dream."

The realization of a dream: it sounds like the end of a fairy tale. Or at least the end of a western novel. After the protagonist defeats his enemies, he lives happily ever after on a cattle ranch. But even Lockhart didn't realize that buying a cattle ranch is only the beginning of one's adventures. Especially since the very next month, Vic Abrahamson got sick.

5

Cowboy Girl

From Cody, railroad tracks wound sixty miles east, through a desert pockmarked with irrigated Mormon farms, to a tiny settlement called Kane. At Kane the rails turned south, paralleling the Bighorn River. To the north a trail ran across badlands next to the river's deep canyon. Perched between the Bighorn canyon to the east and the Pryor Mountains to the west, it was the only available route north and had been used for tens of thousands of years. Fur trappers in the 1820s and 1830s had followed the Sioux and Shoshone rock cairns, though never with ease. In his account of the U.S. Army captain Benjamin L. E. Bonneville's 1832–35 journeys, Washington Irving described it as "a rugged and frightful route, emphatically called the 'Bad Pass.'"

Not much had changed in ninety years. An old-fashioned stagecoach ran north from Kane twice a week over arid, twisted, poorly vegetated terrain. With land to the north set off as the Crow Indian reservation, Bad Pass attracted little traffic. (The railroad, for example, detoured west of the Pryors.) Ten miles north of Kane, the trail crossed Crooked Creek, where a few ranches huddled. But no permanent settlements had arisen north of there until 1897.

When they did come, the first Euro-American settlers hunted gold and stole each other's cattle. Prospector Erastus Ewing built a ranch about ten miles north of Crooked Creek. About five miles north of Ewing's, farmer Link Hannon was caught stampeding some Crooked Creek cattle into the Bighorn Canyon in 1902. He may have been headed for Chain Canyon, a legendary spot where a rustler could put a fifteen-foot chain between two canyon walls to effectively fence in a huge, inaccessible basin. Hannon allegedly led the gang that made this area second only to Hole-in-the-Wall as a notorious haven for rustlers. Another five miles north of Hannon, civilization came in the form of an eastern-educated, half–Nez Perce Indian named Charley Phelps, who built a large ranch operation partly in the Pryor National Forest and partly on the Crow reservation. It was while visiting Phelps's three-story log cabin after meeting Plenty Coups that Lockhart had first fallen for Lou Ericson.

The Ewing-Hannon-Phelps neighborhood, hemmed in on three sides by the Bighorn Canyon, the Pryors, and the reservation, was known as the Dry-head. The name was translated from the Crow "Dry Skulls," referring to the bleached buffalo skulls that had once filled the area. From Kane, the Dry-head could be a full day's journey by horse or stage. That journey took you across the border into Montana; to get to the Carbon County seat of Red Lodge could be a three-day trip, either to Kane and by several train transfers or on horseback twisting around the nine-thousand-foot limestone peaks of the Pryors. Even in 1926, the Dryhead had never seen an automobile.

The area was hot during summer—often over a hundred degrees—and snowed in during winter. The wind often howled. When finally enough children lived in the area to establish a school, in 1916, it ran in the summertime, April to November, when kids had minimal battles through snow and cold.

Such inhospitability, combined with a lack of economically viable resources, meant that the Dryhead remained a pocket of frontier long after even Cody became civilized. "Doctor" Grosvener Barry promised riches to investors in his gold-mining and horse-breeding companies, but they proved as illusory as his medical degree. Barry and his wife, Edith, living about half-way between Ewing and Hannon, ended up taking in orphans for money. (One such orphan, Ruth French, claimed that she never received a single gift from the Barrys, was frequently beaten when her cooking fell short of their standards, and was told she was younger than her actual age, in an effort to delay the moment when she would feel old enough to marry and leave.) Farmers named Berky and Wasson each tried taking over Hannon's place, raising cattle and a few chickens and growing alfalfa on a tiny irrigated plot. But the location was too remote, the returns too marginal. By 1917 the Wasson family moved to the relative civilization of Kane, holding on to owner-ship of their Dryhead cabin until at last they met someone to whom isolation, inaccessibility, and a frontier atmosphere didn't sound like such a bad thing.

Inside the tiny log cabin on the Wasson place, in the summer of 1926, Caroline Lockhart wore a neat housedress that fitted tightly around her waist and bunched fuller above and below, an effect that reminded at least one observer of the shapely actress Lillian Russell. Her yellow braids were pulled back from her forehead in a pompadour and circled around her head in a sort of coronet. She had a cigarette in her mouth—limp, because she rolled her own.

She flipped pancakes on the woodstove for breakfast. After the meal she washed dishes, swept the kitchen, and started getting ready for the noontime dinner. After dinner there was more cooking and cleaning—clothes had to be washed by hand—plus preparations for supper. She might pick weeds or potato bugs in the garden, or clear years of accumulated trash out of the creek bed. Lou Ericson and a hired man named Henry Miller were cutting hay, and another hired man, a doddering sixty-five-year-old named Clay Jolly, chopped wood, hauled water, and tended to the chickens, milk cow, and a pig named Gop. Spending so much time taking care of the crew, Lockhart had little time to herself.

Lockhart may have owned the ranch, but she was also the only woman there. Cooking and cleaning were women's work. So despite her horsemanship, despite her perception of herself as of a higher class than her employees, despite the fact that the entire enterprise relied on the proceeds of her inheritance and marked the fulfillment of her dream, Lockhart did all of the thankless housework.

Paul Eldridge, for one, couldn't believe it: Lockhart had voluntarily entered "the laboring class." As he saw it, in Cody she had been a queen, if an embattled one. With her blackjack and the office gun, she'd been living a life akin to the (male) hero of a romantic western novel. Now she was a glorified dishwasher.

Not that haying was easy: it involved fourteen-hour days of backbreaking work. The men cut the hay, piled it, and some years used a horse-powered baler to wire it into cubes. "Lou is working hard, too hard. He is worn out at night. Runs his legs off: not a lazy hair in his head," Lockhart wrote in her diary in June. When the first cutting was done, Ericson and Miller went to work fixing up the cabin and outbuildings, which had been largely abandoned during the Wassons' later years. Then in late July they went back for a second cutting of hay.

Nobody was complaining, though—at least not at first. "L Slash Heart ranch: Here I am at last—happy as I ever expect to be, on my own ranch at last and in my own log cabin," Lockhart wrote in her diary upon arriving in June. The log cabin sat in a grove of cottonwoods, a hidden oasis on the barren Dryhead. Grass grew; birds twittered. A tiny trickle of water fed the cottonwoods, garden, orchards, and a nearby pasture that was flat enough to grow hay. To the south was a hillside covered in limber pine, to the north, a bare ridge; to the west, limestone palisades marching up the steep slopes of the Pryors. A few days later, despite all the housework, Lockhart wrote, "I still find it like a dream, this place, and hard to realize it is *mine*. Will even have a triangle to hammer on shortly to call the men to dinner. It is cool and lovely. I get up early and exercise more. Now if only I can get down to work I shall be content." She felt worn out but useful. And when in late July the joy of usefulness started wearing thin, she hired a cook.

Lou Tiffany Ketcham was a fifty-eight-year-old widow who had done some housekeeping for Lockhart in Cody. She was willing to come to the Dryhead. Though Ketcham could do most of the cooking and cleaning, Lockhart soon rediscovered the problem she had had with Ketcham in Cody: the woman really liked to talk. She would chatter incessantly through all of her chores. Lockhart, cooped up with her in the same two-room log cabin, might be freed from physical burden, but she still couldn't get anywhere with her writing. Between the excitement of the move, the housework, managing the operation, and being droned at by Mrs. Ketcham, Lockhart in her first summer at her literary retreat accomplished almost no literary work.

During the winter of 1925–26, between purchasing the ranch and moving there, Lockhart kept getting tugged back to Cody. Ericson stayed on the Dryhead to start fixing up the place, but Lockhart had to attend to obligations such as her final Stampede Ball, held in December 1925. She was still trying to get back the money stolen by her former editor Kelly, and she had Goppert's libel suit to worry about. Blanche Gokel was back in town, and Lockhart feared having to use her blackjack or gun on her enemy. With all the distractions, writing went slowly.

Her worst days came when Vic Abrahamson got appendicitis at the end of November, just six weeks after purchasing the paper. He'd been struggling—at first considering passing the paper on to Huss, then deciding to lay Huss off. Now that he was going to Denver for an operation, he would cut down to four pages per issue, less than half what she'd run. She found his paper "rotten—worse than the Herald." But to succeed, he needed the support of her enemies, which meant that he would never turn to her for help or advice. Still, she kept finding herself dragged into *Enterprise* concerns— and developing a disgust for the mess he was turning it into.

She considered taking the paper back from Abrahamson. She traveled to Casper and Cheyenne looking for an experienced editor-manager to whom she could give a lease with an option to buy. She even considered selling to a Democrat. But in the end she stuck with him as he regained his health.

She had similar concerns about her alliance with Ericson, especially when the neighbor Edith Barry wrote that he was telling people in the Dryhead that he was going to "get" the whole country. "He cannot seem to help lying, bragging, and babbling like a fool," Lockhart told her diary. But she may have just been venting, for she decided to stick with him, hoping that such sentiments reflected his pride in their ranch and his willingness to work hard for it.

In spring 1926, with her writing starting to flow a bit better, and her sentiments perceiving Cody as full of "liars and cheap crooks," two events propelled her fully out of her old orbit. The first was a conclusion to the Goppert lawsuit. Held in late April in the town of Worland, at the south end of the Bighorn Basin, the trial was one of the area's most popular entertainments in many years. Inside the courtroom, every seat was taken. Outside, spectators sat in trees, where they reminded Lockhart of a bunch of blackbirds.

She had feared being "nervous and stupid" on the witness stand, but afterward decided she had been "as cool as possible." She had feared being humiliated by Goppert's attorneys, but they didn't even cross-examine her. Goppert, meanwhile, spent a full day on the stand, and she felt that her attorneys' cross-examination "took the hide off him and left him raw and quivering."

After three days of testimony, the judge gave the jury forceful instructions: the deputies' shooting had been unlawful, he said, and they were guilty of involuntary manslaughter; furthermore, "every person who shall counsel, encourage, hire, command, or otherwise procure such felony to be committed is [equally] guilty." So the question the jury had to decide was the degree to which Goppert had engineered the raid. If he had played no part in it, only then had Lockhart libeled him.

The jury deliberated just a few hours. They found against Goppert and ordered him to pay Lockhart's attorneys' fees.

She found it such a major victory that she even tried to appeal the decision on the S. A. Watkins picture, the one suit where Goppert had beaten her, in order to kick him when he was down.

But she finally let it alone. She was willing to put her Cody fights behind her, as demonstrated in June when she agreed to a consolidation of the

Enterprise and *Herald*. The combined paper, though run by Ernest Shaw, would keep the *Enterprise* name—and she'd get fifty-six hundred dollars in cash. She told people she'd made money on the paper, though it's hard to say if the forty-one-hundred-dollar price difference reflected all her equipment and other investments.

Even Lockhart herself was surprised to find how easily she could leave behind her friends and relatives. Bob Hopkins, whom she was now calling the Big Pimp, treated Aunt Josie abominably; Lockhart despised not only him but also her for putting up with him. Uncle Seward died in a Denver hospital before she even knew he was sick. Within a year her father would also be dead—and so would Andrew Ross, from heart failure that she felt sure was brought on by his financial worries. O. B. Mann never left his wife. The Altbergers, frustrated with the problems of keeping good employees at their ranch, started looking to sell. Two of the Stampede's bigwigs, Jakie Schwoob and Dinty Moore, got married, and she didn't even get an announcement from either. But she didn't much care. "I am so uninterested in Cody anymore," she wrote in her diary in October 1926, after spending the summer on her ranch. And when she returned to town in the following month—to spend the winter in Cody, because the ranch was so inaccessible in winter—one of the first things she wrote in her diary was, "I want to get back to the Dryhead."

On the Dryhead, Lockhart had a plan. Ambitious as she was, she had not simply bought a retirement cabin, a place to retreat from the world. She would not fade into obscurity, at least not permanently. She continually fretted over how little time she had left to leave her mark, to build something that people would remember her by. Newspapers were too ephemeral; fiction—though still her favorite outlet—could falter because of mistakes by publishers or the fickle tastes of the public. Now she wanted a big ranch, and she embarked on several initiatives to get it.

One step was to file for a homestead. Arid and inaccessible, most of the Dryhead had never been homesteaded. Even in 1926 the federal government was still trying to give away this land. In fact, the homestead law had recently been changed again to help.

The original Homestead Act of 1862 had given 160 acres to a head of a family who made agricultural improvements and occupied the plot for five years. The Desert Land Act of 1877 had expanded the idea for lands too dry to support a family farm: you could buy up to 640 acres at $1.25 per acre if you irrigated some portion of that plot. The Stock-Raising Homestead Act of 1916 expanded the concept yet again: you'd be given 640 acres without even irrigating. All you had to do was just graze your stock on it and put up a cabin and some fences.

This progression reflected a progression of available land: well-watered homesteads were taken early, and later failures (such as the Kansas farmers who sold out to Lockhart's father) demonstrated the difficulty of farming some of the West's higher, drier terrain. So the act changed to keep the homesteading ideal in tune with realities on the land.

Actually, homesteading had never worked as idealistically as planned. As a homesteader, you might get numerous family members, each calling themselves a head of household, to file on adjacent parcels. You might not make the required improvements on all of them. But if you brought in the right witnesses, or bribed the right officials, or pulled strings with the right politicians who had enough clout with the bureaucrats, you could skate by. Busy with their own schemes, your neighbors might turn a blind eye to such apparently victimless fraud; it wasn't much different from cheating on your income taxes today. Most big livestock operators, including the Sheep Queen Lucy Morrison Moore, had violated at least the spirit of the Homestead Act in expanding their empires. And although we think of homesteading as a nineteenth-century phenomenon, Montana's boom came after the turn of the century, continuing into the 1920s; nationwide more than twenty million acres were patented from 1923 to 1927.

Lockhart was part of this last wave of homesteaders. She filed on a parcel just west of the Wasson place. Because a homesteader couldn't already own adjacent property (after all, homesteading was intended for the poor), she had Ericson listed on real estate documents as Wasson's buyer. When she went to Billings to file her homestead application, she brought along Lou Ketcham and Clay Jolly. They too filed homestead applications on parcels adjacent to the Wasson place.

Filing homesteads was a game you played with the federal government. You rounded up as many eligible friends and relatives as you could find—in the planning stages, Lockhart had even debated getting elderly Uncle Seward involved as well. Then you sat on the land and (in another tactic we don't hear much about today) delayed the actual patenting for as long as possible. Because once you owned your property, then you had to pay taxes on it.

When Lockhart and Ericson bought the ranch from Wasson, she paid $500 cash, with the other $1,750 to come after he proved up on his homestead. In other words, though the place had been inhabited for almost twenty-five years, seventeen of them by Wasson, he'd never officially taken ownership. A week after the sale, Wasson realized that the government wouldn't let him prove up if it knew he'd already sold. So the agreement was hastily changed: Ericson was *leasing* the outfit for $500; Wasson wouldn't sell until after he'd proved up. (In her diary, Lockhart admitted that since she liked the property so much, she'd be willing to pay the $2,250 just for the improvements and the right to take over the homestead claim, if anything went wrong with Wasson's patenting. But nothing did.)

The homestead filings were a well-thought-out component of Lockhart's land acquisition strategy. She also expected to buy lands and immediately started negotiating with a woman named Caldwell and a man named Howe, who each owned (outright) additional adjacent properties.

Meanwhile, though, she wanted to turn the home place into a showpiece. Though she enjoyed entertaining close friends, she had almost no visitors those first couple of years, because she had no place to put them. Hannon had built a single-story gable-roofed log cabin with a single interior wall, looking out on a tiny stream. An outhouse sat thirty yards downstream. Wasson had added three rundown log sheds built into a hillside: a bunkhouse, storage shed, and springhouse. The springhouse surrounded a spring that bubbled about five gallons per minute, providing not only water for Jolly to carry into the kitchen in buckets, but also a cool room to refrigerate eggs and dairy products. Refrigeration and on-site water were luxuries not enjoyed by most Dryhead settlers—part of what made this place so attractive.

The living quarters, however, were not up to Lockhart's standards. She soon had Ericson, Jolly, and other hired men add a large living room that she lined with bookshelves. They also built newer bunkhouses for themselves to live in. For the cattle and horses, they built a rectangular corral and livestock pen out of pine rails and juniper posts. They also built cabins on each of the homestead parcels (Lockhart's, Ketcham's, and Jolly's), since proving up required you to build a structure and live in it for five years.

Lockhart ran longhorn cattle on the four plots and occasionally on the unfenced government land that surrounded them. The hay they cut all summer would feed the cattle all winter. Longhorns represented a switch from her father's old preference for well-bred shorthorns, but this land was more rugged than eastern Kansas, and she wanted tough cows that would protect their calves against wolves and other predators. Fencing the ranch and homesteads—to keep her cattle from mixing with the neighbors' (and to keep the neighbors' from eating her grass)—was another gigantic, nearly endless task for her crew.

The final task, and the final component of her plan to develop the ranch, concerned the road. The old Bad Pass Trail had run right through the middle of the place, between the main house and the springhouse, across the creek and past the corrals. There wasn't much traffic—the twice-a-week stage, which carried the mail all the way to Phelps's Dryhead Ranch, plus an occasional foray by one of the dozen or so neighbors—but Lockhart wanted peace and quiet, a genuine retreat. She had her men reroute the road through the badlands to the west. As they fenced off the old road, she prepared to enjoy her isolation.

Carbon County's three commissioners stood looking at Lockhart's new road. They opened a bottle of Cedar Brook sour mash whiskey and everybody had a drink together, except the county surveyor. The surveyor, Lockhart thought, looked sober and grumpy. He pulled out his instruments and started measuring the grade of the new road. It was August 1927, and the county officials were here to settle a dispute.

Lockhart's neighbors didn't like what she'd done with the road, fencing off the old one and forcing them over this wild new trail. It was impassable, they said. The mail carrier, Jas Faust, said that if he had to use this new road, he wouldn't be able to get through and nobody would get any mail. Edith Barry had already written the commissioners several letters about Lockhart's improper fencing, and now her son, Claude St. John, drew up a petition about the road and got most of the neighborhood to sign it. They insisted Lockhart reopen the old road.

Lockhart hired an attorney in Red Lodge to persuade the commissioners that the new road was perfectly passable. Faust was exaggerating. In fact, this road was actually shorter than the old route. The two sides were at an impasse. The commissioners—likely resenting the long trip—had to come see for themselves.

The surveyor issued his opinion: the grade was steeper than it should be. It would have to be lowered. Lockhart sensed some disappointment—perhaps she'd oversold the new road. But the commissioners were cordial when they departed to interview the neighbors.

Ericson accompanied them briefly, and he later reported to Lockhart that they told him not to fence any more roads or he would get in trouble. They told him to leave everything as it was and let them do their work. She feared that Ericson, who could be argumentative and somewhat arbitrary in those arguments, had antagonized them.

But the real damage, she imagined, would have been done by the Barrys. They would have told the commissioners that the L Slash Heart was a losing proposition, that Lockhart was a tenderfoot about to go broke in the cattle business, and thus not worth listening to.

So she was worried when they came back the next morning. They seemed less cordial. Maybe, she hoped, it was only that they were sober. Furthermore, she hoped, the surveyor seemed more friendly now, and one of the commissioners—the only one who knew anything about ranching and country roads (the other two were merchants)—seemed to give her a look of approval. Another commissioner asked her if Mrs. Barry wasn't rather peculiar. All these signs were hopeful, but Lockhart must have known her case was sketchy. She decided she didn't want to bet a nickel on what their final decision would be.

In her first eighteen months on the Dryhead, she had crossed swords with most of the neighbors. The mail carrier, Faust, was a leading source of her complaints. For any sort of contact with the outside world—correspondence, financial dealings, supplies, even baby chicks for the henhouse—she depended entirely on the post. She thus seemed to especially resent the control a mail carrier had over her. The mail could be late, missing, or even stolen, and what could she do? When Faust moved away a few years later, she quickly transferred the resentment and complaints onto subsequent mail carriers.

"The Barrys" were another target, perhaps because they too represented control. Their ranch complex, Hillsboro, was the area's post office, and their Cedarvale Dude Ranch was, if not the cash cow Dr. Barry had envisioned, at least an occasional source of revenue. Grosvener Barry himself had passed away, but his widow, Edith, remained an irritant. She was a stout, determined-looking woman with dark hair pulled away from her face, emphasizing her sharp, narrow features and a seemingly permanent frown. It's not clear what exactly soured the two women on each other, to the point where Barry called Lockhart "Old Caroline" and Lockhart called Barry "Old Satan." Barry, five years older than Lockhart, had wealthy ancestors in Mississippi and Louisiana, and when they first met Lockhart admired her intelligence. Eventually, however, Lockhart came to share an opinion of several other Dryheaders that Barry was at best two faced, at worst downright evil.

Claude St. John, thirty-six, Barry's son from a previous marriage, now managed the businesses at Hillsboro. Lockhart found him a "consequential jackass" and soon nicknamed him Mushmouth. Also living at Hillsboro was one of the Barrys' adopted orphans, Eddie Hulbert, who had an excellent reputation as a blacksmith. Ruth French had escaped as soon as she could, marrying Bert Smith, a neighboring homesteader nineteen years her senior, in February 1926. Since they had little affection for the Barrys, the Smiths got along fairly well with Lockhart.

There was another man named Smith in the area, however: Joe Smith. ("Child, that's not his name," one of the Dryheaders told a woman who met him in 1929. "Everybody out here is named 'Smith.'") Slightly swarthy and with a decidedly murky past, he claimed to be of part Portuguese descent, though he spoke in an Irish brogue liberally peppered with the phrase "Be Jesus." (At the funeral of a fellow Dryheader to whom he had loaned money, as the body was solemnly lowered into the grave, he muttered, "Be Jesus, there goes my $150.") When Lockhart met him her first summer on the ranch, he gave her some of his moonshine and she told her diary, "I like Joe Smith although he is too fresh and talks too much for his own good. But I believe he is a good friend so long as he is treated right." He did some work for her, including building the claim shack for the Ketcham homestead. But somehow they turned on each other. Many years later he admitted to a neighbor that when he needed beef he would sometimes "help himself" to one of Lockhart's cows. Lockhart knew it, too, though she couldn't prove it in court—Joe Smith was a rustler.

There were a few others homesteading in the Dryhead, not necessarily aligned with either Lockhart or the Barrys. Dad Chesmore was an old buffalo hunter. Steve "Old Man" Colegrove and his son Charlie each had a place up higher in the Pryors, as did a family named Cook. A fellow named Burroughs occasionally worked for Lockhart. Philip and Alma Snell, whose relatives ran ranches in Kane and Lovell, had purchased the old Ewing place.

The Phelps and their five children ran both dudes and cattle on the Dryhead Ranch to the north. Some or all of these folks may have signed the Barrys' petition about the road.

It was important to them because they expected the Dryhead to follow the same historical course as the rest of the West: fill up and civilize. The road condition especially mattered because people now wanted to drive cars on it. The neighbors also resented Lockhart fencing off her three 640-acre homesteads because those lands had previously belonged to the government (that is, nobody) and were free for the grazing. It was the classic range war, cattlemen vs. homesteaders—with two major differences. First, it was happening in the 1920s rather than the 1880s. Second, roles were reversed: the wealthy, well-bred Lockhart was the homesteader, while the poverty-stricken Smiths (Joe, Bert, and Ruth) were the ones dependent on open range.

The situation could hardly sustain itself. The arid Dryhead couldn't support all these people's cattle. (That was, after all, why it hadn't been settled earlier.) The question was which few outfits would survive. When Ericson had boasted that he was going to get the whole country, he was mimicking Lockhart's views that she would drive all those honyockers out of there. (She was upset with him not for saying such things, but for saying them *to the honyockers*.) Like her father, she was going to watch everyone go broke and then buy up their land cheap for grazing. She was going to build an empire on the Dryhead. This was merely the first battle.

Two weeks after their meeting, a registered letter arrived from the commissioners. Its tone was formal and cold. It told her to fence both sides of the road—the old road. "I start in on a diet of crow," Lockhart said in her diary that day. "They have taken the first trick but I hope and mean that it shall be [their] last."

Bill Poole kissed Lockhart on the mouth. "Do you like me?" he whispered.

"More than that," she replied.

"I love *you*," he said huskily. It was May 3, 1928, and Bill Poole was a new man she'd hired in Cody six weeks previously. "It seems strange that a chap with so much intelligence, industry, and remarkable good sense never has made anything of himself but floated around the world like a chip adrift," she'd written then. "I've taken quite a shine to him. I could fall for Bill like a ton of bricks."

There was a problem, however: Lou Ericson. He was still working for her, managing the ranch. She'd juggled multiple boyfriends before, but never had they all been living together in the middle of nowhere. She knew Ericson was jealous, and she expected a showdown at any moment.

Lockhart's physical passion for Ericson seems to have ebbed, as it had for Andrew Ross, Jack Painter, and others. And though she still cared for him, she was increasingly exasperated by his drinking and his self-important airs. Even the idyll of her first summer on the ranch had been spoiled by his attitudes. Jolly told her that while Ericson was good with horses, he wasn't much of a manager. Joe Smith told her that he'd double-crossed everyone on the Dryhead. Over the course of that year she officially "bought" the ranch from him (since she had already filed on the adjacent homestead, it was now legal to own this place). Now, after almost two years in the Dryhead, she'd settled into a passionless routine, figuring that at age fifty-seven she was too old and hardened to again find love.

But then she found Poole. He was much younger than she, perhaps even in his thirties. (She apparently never learned his exact age, though she did conclude he was young enough to be her son.) He was a good hired man, and he said he would battle for her. Someone told her he'd once spent time in jail, but she glossed over that. She thought he could help her make a success of the ranch. She told him that, and they grew closer. But she tried to keep her feelings secret from the rest of her employees; she and Poole would sneak off into the bushes to kiss. She did not speak of it at all to Ericson.

A week after that first kiss, Poole told her he'd soon be hitting the trail. She was just stringing him along, he said. As she started crying, suddenly Ericson dashed up on the back of a horse, his eyes full of jealousy. She sent him away and called Poole into the house, where they reconciled.

A week later, on May 17, she told Ericson to leave. But he just kept on going about his business on the ranch. Over the next several weeks, the two men remained at swords' point, while Ericson tried to convince her she was making the wrong choice. He even got Ketcham to agree, but there was no changing Lockhart's mind.

On June 14 Ericson left, kissing her goodbye. "I've loved you for ten years," he told her. She had to fight back tears. She knew that as difficult as Ericson sometimes was, Poole might eventually turn out to be far worse.

The next day "a new chapter opened," she wrote in her diary. "Bill . . . came in my bedroom where I was. And, well, we are *real* pals, as we have wanted to be for weeks. He was very sweet and tender and delicate. I am convinced he worships me."

Ericson didn't go far. His brother still had their ranch on the reservation. In late June he came back, staying in the bunkhouse. He had a lot of gear to move out, and Lockhart needed him to help with the haying. Poole didn't like it much. At dinner on Monday, July 2, Poole told Lockhart that if Ericson didn't go the next morning, he would.

At about 6:30 that evening, the two men got into an argument in the bunkhouse. According to Poole, Ericson appeared to be packing up one of Lockhart's saddle blankets, and Poole accused him of stealing it. Specifically, Poole called him a petty larceny thief and then used a foul name reflecting on his mother.

According to Ericson, Poole spoke vulgarly about Lockhart, boasting about his intimacy with her. Poole told Ericson he would soon own the ranch. As their words heated up, Poole attacked the smaller Ericson with a heavy hammer and knocked him down. Ericson then escaped and ran into the main house.

In the house, Ericson found a 30-30 rifle and ran back outside with it. As he went through the new living room, Lockhart saw him and chased after him. She yelled for him to stop but he kept going. At the bunkhouse he fired once. He was about five feet away from Poole—so close that the blast blew chunks of flesh onto the ridge logs.

By the time Lockhart got out to the bunkhouse, Ericson was standing over the unarmed Poole with the rifle's trigger pulled to finish him off. She jumped in between them. Poole got knocked into a corner and looked up at her with a dazed expression in his eyes. Ericson lowered the rifle as she pulled Poole to his feet and dragged him toward the door. Before they got out of the bunkhouse, she was covered in his blood.

The wound was in his right arm. It was not dangerous except for the amount of blood he was losing—and the difficulty of getting him to a doctor. She laid Poole on a mattress from her porch and put the mattress in the back of a neighbor's truck. Then they started over the rough roads through the reservation to Billings. Poole lost blood continuously through the eight-hour trip, until they finally arrived at a hospital at 3:00 a.m. The doctor said that luckily no bones had been broken and no tendons cut. The primitive conditions had not poisoned his blood, and he might not even lose the arm.

But now Lockhart was stuck in the middle of haying season without her two top men. Of course, Ericson had to leave. She bought most of his gear so that he would have some cash to start over with—and then, after another tearful goodbye, she let him take a full load of that gear, just so that he would go. Poole remained in the hospital in Billings, but she couldn't see him much because she had to stay to manage the haying, and the publicity. The *Lovell (Wyoming) Chronicle*, nearest paper to the south, got hold of the story but didn't question her assertion that Ericson had acted in self-defense. If Poole had died, Lockhart reflected, more investigation might have been required, and Ericson might well have hanged.

Over the next year Lockhart settled into life on the Dryhead, despite—or perhaps fueled by—such emotional scenes. As in Cody, she may have even thrived on the conflict. Poole healed successfully but in coming months proved to be just as jealous and hotheaded a lover and manager as Ericson—indeed, perhaps more so, though Lockhart tried to see it as indicating the strength of his passion for her. Meanwhile, the neighbors' antagonism only strengthened her ambitions.

Hearing that Jas Faust wanted to buy land between their places, she decided to beat him to it. She bought the ranches of Nephi Robertson and B. F. Boice, gaining control of a few thousand acres. She could now claim "one of the largest cattle ranches in southern Montana." In what must have been a press release she sent to the *Enterprise*, she explained, "Miss Lockhart is a lover of the old west, and made her home in Cody for many years until the 'dudes' and the march of progress made this an altogether too citified atmosphere for her tastes. In the Dryhead country she has found just the haven which she desires and there her broad-backed whitefaces and long-horned dogies range the hills, and the drone of the motor car is unknown."

Such expansion meant selling some of the Kansas investments into which her family had put the rest of her inheritance, but she reasoned that she didn't really take an interest in what happened in Kansas. Besides, more money and property in the Dryhead would make an impression on the neighbors, "which means power and influence if they think you've got the dough." As at the *Enterprise*, she was up against the sexism of the era. Because she was a woman people saw her as weak. She needed money and power to show them otherwise.

She decided to live year-round at the ranch. She kept her houses in Cody, including one reserved for her weeklong visits three or four times per year. But with few friends there anymore, she always felt alone now in Cody. Even during the coldest days of winter on the ranch, "I sleep better than I have for years and wake up full of ginger." At times she even tried to convince herself that she was more content now than she had been in Philadelphia, when she was a celebrity in the spotlight.

While visiting Cody on the occasion of her fifty-eighth birthday, in February 1929, she went through some old letters and found herself in an oddly reflective mood. Over the course of her life she'd valued friendships too little, she decided. She was too "headstrong, super-sensitive, hitting back cruelly whenever offended." So how was it that so many men could have fallen in love with her? Especially when some of her female friends told her she lacked magnetism—but then they'd only seen her with men to whom she was indifferent. When she was interested in a man, she could usually inspire him to go to hell for her. "Always I aroused ambition . . . a feverish desire to succeed that was like my own tense eagerness. I always hurt them in the end but I guess they were no worse off for having loved me."

She looked through the letters to find out how it had happened. "They all speak of my beauty, my wonderful figure, my strange strong individuality and tremendous vitality—and independence." She counted up her lovers—fourteen in all—and reflected on how her tastes had changed. "There could be no greater contrast than between my first and last, Andrew MacKenzie with his brilliant mind—like Robert Louis Stevenson more than anyone else—sensitive, refined; and Bill—a yegg." (Popular slang of the era, *yegg* referred to a thief, especially a burglar or safecracker. Poole hadn't admitted to her that he was an ex-convict, but she'd apparently become sure of it.) Had she stepped down in social scale? Though she didn't answer the question, perhaps asking it was enough.

Another question she asked and did not answer concerned their hold on her. "O. B. was the only one who hurt me deep. The only one I wanted to marry. The most selfish and undemonstrative of them all. Curious! I wonder if there will ever be another?" Her passion for Poole had apparently cooled (though his jealousy had not). She expected that age would soon take what attractiveness she had left, and then he would lose interest. She figured he'd be the last—but then, she reminded herself, she'd said the same about Ericson.

Lockhart walked up behind the men's toilet—an employees' outhouse behind the bunkhouse—to look for Poole. Ketcham had seen him up there and said he was drunk. He'd stolen a keg of moonshine from behind Lockhart's dresser and taken it up there. He'd also taken her 30-30 rifle.

It was the end of June 1929, about a year since the last episode with the rifle. Poole had become increasingly jealous of Lockhart's attention to anyone. He was even jealous of Mrs. Clark, a guest from back east who'd arrived with her daughter two weeks previously. It was not yet time for haying, and Lockhart's three other employees—Jolly, Fred Burrows, and Tom Millich— were up at Jolly's homestead site, building an addition on his shack. The previous night Poole and Burrows had gotten into a fight that climaxed in Poole hitting Burrows in the shoulder with a horseshoe hammer. Burrows fled to Joe Smith's house, spent the night, and came back vowing to have Poole arrested.

Sure enough, on the hill behind the outhouse, Lockhart found Poole with the moonshine and the rifle. He was planning to shoot at the three men as soon as they returned from work. She asked him why. Millich had built a closet for her, he said. Burrows had capped the beer for her, he said. (They'd been making moonshine.) Jolly—well, there wasn't a clear reason to shoot Jolly.

"Then half sober," she wrote in her diary, "he blurted it all out. That his love for me was nearly killing him. That the feeling he had for me was more than love. That he had never found anyone like me. I was all he had, etc. I know it's the truth yet he insults me with every breath, uses filthy language and swears and slurs, doing everything but hit and I suppose it would come to that after a while."

She got him calmed down, and when the men returned he apologized all around. He told Burrows that he would pay for an x-ray on the shoulder, and so Burrows agreed not to have him arrested. (It would have taken a round trip to Lovell to swear out a warrant. Actually, Poole had no money, so what he was really offering was that *Lockhart* would pay for the x-ray.) But Burrows said he would no longer work at the L Slash Heart as long as Poole was there. Millich agreed, and even the faithful Jolly seemed to be leaning that way too.

Poole had to go, Lockhart knew. She dreaded how empty the ranch would be without him. She believed she'd learned enough about haying to oversee it herself—but how could she live without the attention of a lover? Two days later Poole rode off on his favorite horse, Whingding. She loaned him a saddle and bridle and gave him ten dollars in traveling money. He said he would sell the horse and send her the proceeds. As he rode away he did not look back.

But did she know how to manage the haying? That season's crop turned out poorly, though blame went to the departed Poole for the way he had watered it. Then through faulty figuring, Lockhart ended up overpaying her haying crew. Then she discovered they'd left the machinery a wreck. The hot weather dried up her barley crop. And she was fighting with the neighbors again.

In April she'd decided to buy Old Man Colegrove's homestead, up against the Pryors. It would give her ownership of nearly all of Davis Creek, which would eliminate many clashes over water rights. "Only Joe Smith's little place will be left," she wrote in her diary, "and that is of no consequence except that I would like to be rid of the skunk." She knew she was lucky to have the money to carry out her plans, where the rest of the Dryheaders did not.

Unfortunately, however, purchasing land did not necessarily give her control of it. For all of her rejoicing that the Dryhead was still a frontier, that meant it was far removed from law enforcement. Part of our never-ending fascination with any frontier is that it lacks moral institutions, from police departments to churches to insurance companies. With the coming of civilization, such institutions help reinforce property rights, and so our fascination with the frontier revolves around examining what people do when they have to fight for such basic rights with their own mettle. The frontier hero never just waits for the cavalry; he shows the strength of his character by seeking to right the injustice himself.

But that frontier hero is almost always a man. How could a woman enforce her rights if the neighbors didn't fear her? After all, they didn't care how much money she had, how many homesteads she bought. They knew they could always cut her fences.

Fencing was essential to Lockhart's plan for the ranch. She had started fencing in earnest in 1927, and fences as much as the road had caused the bad blood with her neighbors. Part of their frustration, obviously, was that this had once been government land, open range, and now she had cut them off from it. But part of it was that she fenced too much.

The rocky Dryhead soil did not easily accommodate postholes. Lockhart had neither the patience nor the manpower to dig enough postholes to string fences along each side of the road through her entire property. She just fenced across the road. Claude St. John told Ericson that they couldn't do that, it was a county road, but Ericson insisted they could. St. John told him he would cut the fence across the road, if he had to do so to get through, and a week later he did. Lockhart tried to have him prosecuted but discovered the law was on St. John's side.

Eventually she fenced along both sides of the road (and eventually she got her new road acceptably graded, rerouting traffic away from her house). She fenced in all her pastures. But her spread was so big she couldn't always keep track of the gates. Someone would leave a gate open, and the neighbors' cattle would file into her pasture and eat her grass—or worse, in the wintertime, eat the hay she'd put out for her cattle. Sometimes neighbors' cattle appeared in her pastures even when the gate was closed. And sometimes the pasture fences were cut.

For example, in 1928 while Poole was in the hospital after the Ericson shooting, she found Joe Smith's cattle in her pasture. The gate was closed; she knew he'd put them in there illegally. She went to the work of shooing them out. The next day her fence was cut.

What could she do? Once Poole returned, the neighbors seemed to respect or fear his temper. He was a wild card: suspecting the Barrys had butchered one of her calves, he butchered one of theirs. Suspecting Joe Smith had butchered a steer, he stole three of Smith's chickens. But now he was gone again. Her other men weren't strong or confrontational enough. In August one of them found a Lockhart cow with a Barry-branded calf. Obviously the calf had been illegally branded—and in such a bold and recognizable way that the crime would be easy to prove—but he didn't immediately drive the calf into a corral. After he told Lockhart and she sent him back to look for it, he couldn't find it. All summer she kept finding neighbors' cattle in her pastures. She kept missing cows and calves.

Meanwhile, Poole never sent her the money he owed. He wrote to tell her he'd sold the horse but didn't send any money. He told her he'd pawned the saddle for $10.50 but didn't send any of that money either. (Later she learned it was a $25 sale, not a $10.50 pawn. But either way, it wasn't his saddle.) He told her he'd gotten a cowpunching job and wanted her to send his chaps and boots by parcel post. She did so, but when she sent additional letters to that address, they kept bouncing back. He was a thief, she realized, "as yellow [and] low-down [a] skunk as ever stood in dirty socks." But she had no faith that the men who replaced him were any more honest, only that they were more timid.

Lockhart's spirits were boosted in the fall of 1929 with the arrival of a new foreman, Dave Good. Two years younger than she, he had the weathered face and skeptical squint of a cowboy who'd spent his life on the range, which he had. Born in eastern Nebraska to a family of fourteen children, he left home at age thirteen and worked the last of the big cattle drives in the late 1880s. For more than thirty years he bounced around the West, cowboying, until he filed on a homestead north of Cody and went into the cattle business with John Chapman, the rancher-turned-banker who had also financed Lockhart's *Enterprise*. It's not clear what exactly went wrong with the homestead or business, but by the fall of 1929 he found himself working with sheep. It was the utmost indignity to a cattle lover, so he was eager for a new job. He agreed to come to the Dryhead to care for the cattle all winter, but even before he arrived Lockhart was hoping it would be more permanent. She knew him as "a hand of the old school. We talk the same language, and I believe we are going to hit it off for I feel we like and trust one another."

Not up for another winter on the ranch, Jolly departed for Billings. Good suggested that in his place Lockhart hire Ephraim "Two Dog" Johnson, and he too proved a "peach. He is like a nice, neat, sensible old lady around the house and simply a wonder when it comes to looking after the pigs, chickens, and cow and doing the chores." Johnson, sixty-eight (the same age as Jolly), was also a Cody old-timer, and the presence of these two men seems to have stabilized the ranch. The winter after their arrival, Lockhart's diary entries focused less on her feuds with neighbors and more on her increasing attraction for Good.

He was attracted to her too, which made him want to stay. But he was surprised and concerned about the poor condition of the range. Soon after arriving he bought a load of cattle to winter and calve. But after getting to know the land better, he realized he'd overstocked. He pledged to stay through the winter, since they'd be a lot of work, but he said that as soon as the grass greened up he would move on to a bigger operation.

That would become one of Lockhart's recurring themes for the early 1930s: a sense that her ranch was too small. She now sought to buy adjacent ranchlands so as to run more stock. While she'd always hungered for a big place to show up the neighbors, now she also realized that she needed a big place to pay for itself. Quality employees such as Good and Johnson required decent wages, which required better revenues from cattle, which required more land. In December 1932 she calculated that she had 223 head of cattle but needed closer to 700 to make the ranch profitable.

As a cattle rancher, she was in the business of turning grass into beef. (If you were just going to let the cattle eat hay or other feed, you could do so at a feedlot—no need to take them all the way in and out of the Dryhead.) But the arid and overgrazed Dryhead never produced enough grass. You needed a great deal of land to feed enough cattle to pay the staff—and it was a vicious cycle because more land required more employees, more fences, and more potential clashes with the neighbors.

Two days after Valentine's Day of 1930, Lockhart was getting dressed in the morning when she heard Good approaching her room. As he rapped on the door, she slipped out of her bathrobe and told him to come in. He looked wild, as if he'd slept poorly. His white hair was standing up on end. "I can't stand this," he said desperately. "I can't stay here like this—I've got to quit!"

All winter they had edged toward a romance. He spent a good deal of time up at the Robertson place, about three miles away, where they wintered the cattle. But he came down for meals or camaraderie, sleeping in the bunkhouse. They kept eyeing each other. At Christmas she gave him a scarf; he loved it, and she liked how good he looked in it. It was all she could do that night to keep from touching him, touching his hands and his hair. If they ever kissed, she knew, they'd both fall madly in love.

But they didn't kiss. He kept pulling back. He told her he hadn't cared for a woman in twenty years, and he never expected to. She told herself that he was uneducated, unpolished, lower class. He didn't even have Poole's charm. But he was a *man*, she felt, in every way.

In early February she had asked him how much he loved her. He told her he would show her soon. She feared that meant a marriage proposal, since he had such oddly high principles, seemed to so idealize women. He told her one reason he'd left the sheep ranch was that he had once seen the owner's wife drunk. Lockhart didn't think she could marry him, given his lack of education. At least not until they knew each other better.

A few days later Johnson left for a brief vacation, and they had the ranch to themselves. She proposed that he join her in her bed. She'd never been so aggressive with a man, but felt she had to because he was so timid. He said no. He felt sad, he said, but word must not get out. He didn't want the neighbors to know. He kissed her and hugged her—and slept in the bunkhouse. She cursed his lack of guts. If he wouldn't take what he wanted, then she didn't want any part of him. She would invite back Bill Poole. But then Good relented, agreed to sleep in her bed, hold her in his arms. And nothing happened.

She couldn't believe it.

The following night was the same: they went to bed together but remained "virtuous." In the middle of the night they woke up, and she could sense the struggle he was having. It was tearing him to pieces. He finally told her he'd been a fool to keep going like this. He was going to stop, now. He'd never done anything undercover; he'd been raised to always tell the truth. If anybody accused him of being intimate with her, he had to be able to give an honest denial.

The Dryheaders talked scandalously about her, he said. He'd fought one of them already over it, and if anybody ever called him the names they called Ericson, that somebody would get killed. So from now on he was simply going to work for her, strictly business.

She was terribly hurt, but she said nothing. If that was the way he wanted it, she told him, that would be all right. But she did explain about Ericson, countering what he'd heard from Joe Smith. She hadn't given Ericson money to blow like a drunken sailor in town; he worked for every cent he got. They split their partnership after the first carload of cattle; after that she paid him wages just like everybody else. She asked Dave to do her one favor: stop visiting Joe Smith, who was the one who kept spreading such lies.

Then dawn broke and she saw that they were both lying in bed with their arms folded, "as if we were two strangers afraid of catching smallpox or getting lice." All that next day she tried to treat him as a hired man, just what he wanted. By the end of the day, she decided, "he looked ten years older, every line on his face seemed to have deepened, and when he sighed unconsciously it was almost a groan. At nine o'clock, he got up, gave me a glance lying on the couch, said good night and went to bed in the bunkhouse."

She cried and pulled out some moonshine to help her sleep. The world looked dreary. Life would be only existence. The ranch would be a prison. But she was determined not to weaken.

Now it was morning and he was saying he had to leave. "Can you ever forgive me for hurting you so?" he asked. Then he put his arms around her and cried. She couldn't believe it. He "sobbed! Hard-boiled Dave!"

He told her he couldn't get along without her. The situation was killing him. "You're a good woman," he said, "the best I've ever known! God love you!" Then he added, "I'll be jealous even of God if he did."

She told him he was not going to leave. He was going to stay, and they would be as happy as they could. ("Happy?" he responded. "I've never been happy and never expect to be.") She admired his honesty and pride, she told him, and if this was just an infatuation, "only a common little passion," they would be right to break it off. It wouldn't be worth the risk of scandal. But it was more, she said. And if the neighbors talked, so what? She told her diary, "To love and be loved is the only thing that makes life worth while. And life is getting so damned short."

That evening they sat together on the couch in the living room. Good said, "If I had—" Then he started again: "I would ask you to marry me, but I know you wouldn't look at me in that way." Lockhart hesitated, then said, "We don't know each other well enough." "No," he agreed emphatically. She was struck by the strength of his emotions, all of them. He might be a crusty old cowboy on the outside, but that hid a passionate soul.

That night they consummated their love physically—or tried to. Good, she was stunned to discover, was impotent. It made him humiliated, embarrassed, ashamed. He wouldn't talk about it. ("What the cause may be," she wrote in her diary, "I do not know, though I have heard that cowboys get that way from riding so much.") But she now understood his previous evasions. It was not just that he wanted to be speaking the truth when he defended her to the neighbors. He was terrified that she would turn away from him in disgust.

Clarence Curen stood at Lockhart's door, a six-shooter dangling in front of him. The Dryhead was a frontier all right, but even in the Dryhead men did not go around wearing revolvers. Especially not men like Clarence Curen.

He was just starting his homestead this summer, 1930. He struck Lockhart as having little money and less class. She called him "The Pill." A few years later she would write, "The most charitable thing a person can say about this man is that he is not well balanced." He'd spent the last six months living with Joe Smith while preparing his homestead. Now he and his wife were living there, in a shack along the road near the L Slash Heart.

Curen was one of a new wave of people arriving in the Dryhead in 1930 and 1931 who became Lockhart's "enemies." They earned her scorn largely because they sought to homestead on open government land (just as she had a few years previously). They interfered with her dream of controlling the whole country.

Another such enemy was Hank Lane. (It is merely coincidence, though an entertaining one, that her enemies on the Dryhead had the same names—Lane, Smith—as her enemies in Cody.) White haired, squinty eyed, and mustached, Lane—like many Dryhead men—often wore long-sleeved shirts and pants that bagged over shapeless hips.

One young cowboy described his first meeting with the "cantankerous old bachelor" this way:

> We get in the house and the first thing he does is dips into a large open-topped crock and pours two big glasses of chokecherry wine. Now when he's pouring this wine he strains the flies and crud out with a tea strainer. He then knocks the crud out of the strainer on a piece of firewood in the woodbox and rinses the strainer in the water reservoir on the cookstove. . . . [He] peels some spuds, then without washing them he puts them on to boil in water from the reservoir in which he'd rinsed the strainer. That place of his is sure dirty and he don't improve its looks one bit. If I hadn't been a little leery of his reputation I'd have left there in a hurry. I make it through supper and offer to help with dishes. He says there aren't enough to do and he just sets them plates on the step for the dogs to lick. I have often wondered if that might not have been all the washing they ever got.

Lane first appears in Lockhart's diaries as the likely perpetrator of a June 1931 fence cutting, for which she claimed the Forest Service was about to prosecute him. But nothing came of it. Later that summer even the more cautious Good decided that Smith, Lane, and Curen had been butchering Lockhart's stock all year.

Also arriving at about the same time was a man in his late twenties named Charles "Tuffy" Abbott. He first went to work for Lockhart, who knew and admired his in-laws in Kane. But she soon took to calling him "the Packrat" because of the way she felt he accumulated her stuff. He worked hard and by many accounts faithfully, but she could never bring herself to trust him. And in that mistrust, of course, she made dozens of tiny slights toward him, prompting him to take actions that deepened that gulf. One of the biggest such actions came in September 1931, when he staked out a homestead on land adjoining hers. "I am annoyed as hell but there is nothing to do about it but make it miserable for him so he will wish he hadn't done it," she wrote, and then proceeded to do just that.

On the afternoon that Curen stopped by, brandishing his gun, he was hoping to speak with Lockhart alone. "If you have anything to say, say it now, right here," she responded.

"I want you to tell me your side of what took place yesterday." Had she done so, she would have explained that she and Ketcham had gone to pick serviceberries, which required riding past the Curens' house on the public right-of-way. "Mrs. Pill," as she called Grace Curen, suddenly came out of the house shouting and screaming. Getting Ketcham to open the gate, Lockhart whipped her horses to get them past the woman, who then started throwing rocks at Lockhart's back.

Had she given that explanation, Curen would likely have responded that the reason his wife came out of the house so upset was that Lockhart was riding across their yard, not a right-of-way. He would have said that Lockhart quirted not only her horses but his wife. He would have accused her of spitting in his wife's face.

Lockhart would have likely denied such charges—not even in the diary, where she expressed the wish that she'd kicked in Mrs. Pill's teeth, did she claim any such actions. The entire altercation horrified her, "being mixed up with such scum. It is so undignified and makes me look ridiculous." She didn't want to even broach the subject—especially not to a man who came to her house brandishing a handgun. To his request that she tell her side, she responded, "I'll do nothing of the sort. I haven't anything to say to you at all. You are not welcome here, now get out." Then she closed the door in his face.

In general, though, things were going well for Lockhart. Of course she convinced Good to stay as foreman. They got along well together. On the rare occasions that he could perform sexually, she found him quite satisfying.

When he could not perform, he would hold her in his arms and caress her. On the job, he lacked business skills, she found, but was very good with the cattle.

Paul Eldridge informed her, much to her surprise and delight, that H. L. Mencken had published a new volume of his encyclopedic reference book *The American Language* in which he cited her vocabulary as "gorgeous and glowing." In a paragraph discussing novelists' use of local vernacular, he paired her with Ring Lardner and Sinclair Lewis. In the diary, she mused, "I thought he even had forgotten I existed—what a remarkable man—after all these years! I am more pleased by such a tribute from him than by anything that ever has been printed about me, except the assertion by a critic who said I had 'something akin to genius.' Oh, if only I could prove it yet!"

Domestic tranquility allowed her to think again about writing. Reading Edna Ferber's extremely popular novel *Cimarron*, she again couldn't help making a personal comparison: "She is better on plot but I have the humor she lacks." But contrary to previous years, Lockhart's jealousy of another writer was not entirely consumed with how they had received better publishing and marketing. "She is where I should have been," Lockhart reflected (a familiar sentiment), but then added insightfully, "if I had not let myself get side-tracked as I did when I took on the Cody Stampede and the *Cody Enterprise*."

She similarly commented on the trials and expenses of the ranch. "I thought I'd have quiet and peace over here, instead of which I'm upset constantly and cannot concentrate. What bad judgement I've shown in allowing myself to be sidetracked from my writing!"

Lockhart and Good sat at the kitchen table one day in October 1931. She was smoking a cigarette. Suddenly she noticed that he was looking hard at her. Her left eye watered and felt heavy. She figured the cigarette smoke was making things blurry.

Finally he commented on her appearance. The expression on the left side of her face had changed, he said. Ketcham agreed. Lockhart looked in the mirror and indeed it was true. Now that she thought about it, in fact, her lips felt queer and stiff.

A stroke, a slight one. "It passed over me like a shadow without warning and painless." She tried to minimize it at first, hoping that strangers would not notice anything odd about her face. But eventually she went to a doctor, who insisted she spend a couple of weeks recuperating in Cody. Marie Louise Hopper, a close friend from Philadelphia, had been visiting the ranch and now helped nurse her back to health. The droop of her face was indeed visible to strangers. She could laugh out of only one side of her mouth. But the doctor said her condition should iron itself out in about six months.

In a sense the stroke was good for her, because it pulled her away from the "sidetracks" of the Dryhead. Good and other employees (Johnson had returned to Cody) were able to run the ranch quite smoothly. Lockhart was able to write. She had published just one short story since coming to the ranch in 1926—a lesser output than she had accomplished even while running the *Enterprise*. But she had an idea for a new novel, and during the winter of 1931–32 especially, she threw herself into this project, which she called 18 *Karat*.

At the start of the novel, twenty-year-old Vance Galloway is ashamed by the way fellow cowboys are treating a disreputable woman. Manipulated by them and her, he agrees to a paper "marriage" to legitimize her young son, with the understanding that either party will dissolve the marriage as soon as they find a meaningful partner. He then drifts from South Dakota to New Mexico to Wyoming, where he comes across a comical group of cowboys at a ranch called the S Bar Bell. Rebelling against their foreman, who has insisted that they vote for his preferred political candidate, they instead quit, move to town, and persuade a buddy to defeat the candidate.

Meanwhile, Vance spends several months in the remote Bighorn Canyon branding stray cattle on behalf of the S Bar Bell's owner, who has taken a shine to him. Vance spends his free time communing with animals and contemplating his brief encounters with the beautiful sixteen-year-old tomboy Nellie Kent.

A fast-moving plot and plenty of colorful minor characters provide entertainment, though perhaps not as rich as that in Lockhart's previous work. For example, the evil ranch foreman is named Frank Spivey—so is he the same character as the villain in *The Full of the Moon*, or has the author merely reused the name? Sadly, the character is such a throwaway that one can't even answer the question.

Still, some of the other themes that Lockhart reuses here were quite admirable in their first incarnation and remain so even as pale imitations of themselves. The best example is Nellie. Like *Me-Smith*'s Susie MacDonald, Nellie is half Native American. (It's never made explicit, but her deceased mother must have been Osage.) Nellie also has career ambitions, insisting that she wants to *be* somebody, and like *The Fighting Shepherdess*'s Katie Prentice, she demonstrates the strength of character it takes to accomplish such ambitions. When her wicked stepmother informs Nellie that Vance is already married, Nellie runs away into the desert, where she has an extraordinary encounter with a misanthropic trapper.

The book then fast-forwards twenty years. In its second half, the town of Haller has boomed with prissy midwesterners obsessed with Prohibition. All of the S Bar Bell's comical cowboys now work in town at more modern jobs: auto mechanic, dairyman, dude rancher. When their old buddy is defeated in the primary election, they seek a new anti-Prohibition candidate to run in November as an independent.

Their choice, of course, is the reluctant Vance, who has inherited most of the S Bar Bell and works diligently on his cattle herds. Meanwhile, who should appear at this moment on the dude ranch but Nellie Kent—grown up, successful, and never married. Nellie, it turns out, had been a journalist before inheriting huge oil royalties from her mother's estate, so now she buys a run-down newspaper with the intention of promoting Vance's candidacy. The novel then completely recapitulates Lockhart's time on the *Enterprise*—incompetent editors, ladies attending liquor trials and compared by the author to knitters of the French Revolution, the shooting of a bootlegger who then drives away stuffing a handkerchief in the hole in his hip—compressed into three weeks and culminating in a heavy-handed, obvious happy ending. Coincidences abound: Spivey, who had been revealed at the end of part one as a rustler, is now revealed as also a federal Prohibition agent and as the father of Vance's "wife's" son, while the rumrunner he kills is her current common-law spouse. Meanwhile, intentionally oblivious to the political campaign, Vance does not even meet Nellie until the final scene, when they rediscover their eternal love.

Such a plot summary doesn't do justice to Lockhart's style, breezing through a large number of lively happenings in a way that makes the book quite readable. And again, Lockhart has done some unusual and admirable things: what other novel of the time—much less a western—so venerates a single, career-oriented, thirty-six-year-old woman? As with Katie, it is clear that Nellie's end-of-novel marriage will not dampen her feisty independence. Additionally, if you know nothing about Lockhart's actual struggles, Nellie's newspaper adventures are enjoyable. The opponents she always called, in capital letters, "the Better Element" are filled with delicious hypocrisy, and the cowboys speak in the rich local vernacular that Mencken so admired.

But particularly interesting today is how Lockhart depicts the ruination of the West. The evils of what might be called the "New West" (though Lockhart's text never uses that phrase) include onerous federal regulations; big ranches increasingly carved into tiny patches of weeds; rich, clueless outsiders moving in and ruining things; politicians stealing elections with underhanded, last-minute charges; lives devastated by illegal narcotics; and a homogeneity of development in which new towns look like anyplace else, "exchanging the picturesque for the commonplace." Look at that list again—it's exactly what twenty-first century westerners deride as the problems of the New West.

In other words, while most authors of cowboy novels were riffing on Owen Wister and Zane Grey, creating ever-more-fantastic gunfighter fables, Lockhart put her finger on the actual—and enduring—tension behind the development of the West. To her, the *true* westerners are independent spirits who distrust government, love seeing livestock in wide-open spaces, and prefer ornery characters to idealistic community-builders. Seventy years later the specifics differ slightly: federal regulations typically concern the environment rather than Prohibition, the devastating illegal narcotic is methamphetamine, and the clueless outsiders are derided as Californians rather than midwesterners. But the philosophical debate remains: individual vs. community, libertarianism vs. regulation, ornery independence vs. neighborly likability.

Lockhart thrived on the writing. "I am getting back into my old form somewhat," she told her diary in January 1932; in February, "I am writing like one inspired upon the second half of my book with which I anticipated so much trouble." Later that month she wrote, "I do not understand it. My brain has cleared and all my old zest for writing has come back to me." She was delighted that her old editor at Doubleday wanted to see it, and in March she sent it off to her friend, freelance editor Berg Esenwein, for polish. She dreamed of success to match that of Ferber and Fannie Hurst (who was then known as the world's highest-paid short story writer). "It would be like the climax of a story, if in addition to the $5,000 [inheritance] I get next January, I should bring out a book that made a killing after all my despondency and worry—and such a disappointment to my enemies!" Indeed, she got a little too caught up in the grandeur of what she was doing, at one point musing, "It might be that I am writing the *Uncle Tom's Cabin* of Prohibition."

She spent the month of April away from the ranch, having the manuscript typed and attending to affairs in Cody. When she returned it was like she was coming out of a fog—and suddenly seeing a cliff in front of her. The man she'd left in charge of the ranch had scratched her phonograph records and run down the batteries playing the radio. He'd snooped through the house and was wearing Mrs. Ketcham's hat. He'd done little of the work he was supposed to. She fired him and refused to pay him. He threatened a lawsuit, and she told him to have at it. Then before he left he attacked one of her other employees. She screamed at him and ran for her gun that always hung on the wall.

The gun was missing. (She later discovered that Good had it.) The only thing she could see was a rubber boot, so she grabbed that and threw it at him. It missed, and the confrontation finally dissipated. But she discovered other things missing, such as a Charlie Russell print and an old Indian blanket. Lots of hay was missing—they'd run out in February though they'd expected to last until mid-April—and she now realized it was because a neighbor had been stealing it. She had to buy more, which was expensive. She'd been unable to rent her house in Cody and was now in red at the bank. "I swallowed my pride," she wrote in her diary, "and asked Marie Louise for the $500 she offered to loan me last winter, and Roy [Edgington] for $500 on very personal note." She saw nothing but failure and humiliation ahead.

April 1932 was, after all, the middle of the Great Depression. The 1920s had been boom years for much of the country, but not the rural West. Agricultural prices fell after World War I and never bounced back as much as expected. Drought struck all of the Great Plains through the 1920s. Cattlemen finally came to appreciate the extent to which the range had been overgrazed for the last forty years. Across Wyoming, 101 banks failed in the 1920s (only 27 would fail in the 1930s). But now adding to those struggles of the 1920s were the difficulties of the rest of the country in the 1930s. Prices were dropping again; banks everywhere were tottering. Some sheepmen found that the money they got for their sheep at the market barely paid for shipping them there.

You could see it as a temporary condition, an opportunity to buy land and cattle cheap. If you got big enough, you might become bulletproof: impervious to economic conditions or neighbors or drought. But that meant you had to have an independent source of revenue to pull you through. Lockhart again found herself hoping for her book to make money so it would finance one of her sidetracks—though from experience she now knew how unlikely that was. Lockhart looked forward to the five-thousand-dollar inheritance (from a deceased uncle named Lute) that Aunt Josie assured her would be paid out in January. But could she hold on even that long?

Doubleday liked the book. But they wondered if she could come up with a better title than "18 Karat." Ketcham left for Nebraska to care for her ailing mother. Lockhart was a bit glad to be rid of her chatter, but ran through a succession of new employees looking for a decent cook. And every time she fired one, she'd have to fill in with the housework herself.

In late May, Good reported that the cattle were already starting to lose weight, though May was typically a wet month with grass flourishing and cows packing on the pounds. He told her that the L Slash Heart was so strung out that it required too much labor—it would break her in the end. He suggested sacrificing her three most recent acquisitions: renting the Robertson land to Tuffy Abbott and letting the two Boice pastures go back to grass.

Lockhart agreed. She was sick of this farming, she said (referring to the growing of alfalfa for hay on those properties). When she came out to the Dryhead, she hadn't wanted to be a farmer. She'd wanted a literary retreat. The rich alfalfa had changed her mind, but now the drought had withered it, and they needed a new plan.

Good suggested she sell out. But where could she find a buyer? She didn't think she could recoup half of what she'd put into it. He suggested she cut down to 150 longhorns and turn the place into a dude ranch. She was appalled.

Cattle prices might go up, she told herself, and grazing land would follow. She and Good decided to throw all their cattle into the mountains this summer, on the open government range. That would give them fewer calves next winter, because their bulls would be servicing everybody else's cows. But they hoped their cattle would eat out all of the feed and thereby starve out the neighbors. They could use the Depression to grab the entire Dryhead.

In late June she went out to Billings to do some business. On the way back she went through the Dryhead ranch (Charley Phelps's old place, now under new ownership). There, "slick fat cattle stand to their knees in grass." And when she got to her own place, she saw "rocky ridges, bare hills and flats . . . interspersed with tufts of short grass[.] It made me heartsick. For the knowledge of the terrible mistake I have made in investing my inheritance in such a country, and no way of getting it out, came to me as clearly as if someone had suddenly pulled a blindfold from my eyes."

And even that wasn't the worst of it. In July they found fence cut on her former Colegrove property, with dozens of the neighbors' animals grazing there. In August the fence along the lower Boice property was cut for more than three-quarters of a mile. "This damned place sure is souring whatever I had of sweetness in my nature," she wrote.

She held on through the fall, borrowing money and steeling resolve. Her editor suggested a new title for the book: "Cowboy's Luck!" She found that "too terrible for words." Saying that she would never consent to such a title, she made a counteroffer: "Blue Smoke."

They came back with another idea: "Old West—and New." They told her time was running out and made her acquiesce to it on the spot. But for the next several days she kicked herself for giving in. "It's flat and uninteresting—sounds like a historical or a descriptive book," she told her diary; and then a week later, "How can they be so *stupid* as not to realize that it is no title for a *novel*? I am deeply resentful and there will never be another published by them, at least unless I can choose the name myself."

In late January a letter arrived from a bank in Wilkes-Barre, Pennsylvania. It informed her that she would get nothing from Uncle Lute's estate. The letter she wrote in early February to her Cody banker was "the hardest I have ever had to write[,] but the one I probably will have to write to Roy will be worse. The future sure looks dark—I can't see any in fact."

Later in February 1933 she got another letter. This one came from the Government Land Office. It was rejecting her homestead application.

⁀

The lawyer showed Lockhart the registered letter she'd sent him. Its seal had clearly been broken.

She'd written to the lawyer, Guy Derry, to help with the homestead. He told her not to worry: she would get a chance to speak at a hearing that would be run much like a trial. Both sides would present witnesses. She started lining up support: Bob Hopkins, Two Dog Johnson, and some of the neighbors. One, she recorded in her diary, "says he will lie like a horsethief for me. Which will help." Another, a newcomer named Carl Abarr, said he would get his brother to get a "relinquishment" from Clay Jolly (who had the weakest case) so that at least Jolly's homestead would remain controlled by Lockhart's friends.

She had responded to Derry with the registered letter, and then decided to go into Billings herself. And he'd shown her that somebody was tampering with her mail. They took it to the postmaster, who agreed.

Lockhart had long complained about the mail service, which came through the Barrys' post office at Hillsboro. Her mail was late, she said, and tampered with; sometimes it was missing. Just the previous summer she'd prodded federal authorities to investigate, but they'd turned up nothing. Now here was proof that she wasn't just paranoid.

But she couldn't parlay this tampered letter into another investigation. It was just like the confrontation she'd had with Mrs. Curen, where forces of justice also moved too slowly: when she filed a criminal complaint, the Curens cross-filed, and the only result was that the three of them had to sign an agreement saying they would behave. Similarly, in her fight with Joe Smith over water rights, she'd finally taken him to court, and even gotten a trial date—but now she was too busy with the homestead hearing and had to temporarily drop the suit. She'd written to the famous detective Joe Le-Fors—who'd helped the big Wyoming cattle ranchers beat the rustlers back in the legendary range-war days—but his response had basically demanded to know how much she could pay.

Between the drought and the economic conditions, the Dryhead feud was heating up. Her enemies, Lockhart saw, intended to beat her out of her homestead land in order to drive her under completely. If her land went back into open range, they could better survive.

Old West—and New came out in April 1933. She liked the cover; she hoped it would sell well. But she already suspected that it lacked "some of the freshness and rigor of *Me-Smith*, *The Fighting Shepherdess*, and *The Dude Wrangler*." Paul Eldridge suggested that she should have kept it all in the Old West and showed Vance Galloway succeeding through his own initiative, rather than Nellie's. Of course, it was a little late for constructive criticism, but Lockhart also believed Eldridge was wrong—that wasn't the book she had wanted to write.

Several of her other correspondents, including her sister Grace and Grace's daughter Sylvia, called the book "interesting." She knew that was damning with faint praise. A few days after she complained about it to her diary, she received "a letter from Miss or Mrs. Spear [who] says *Old West and New* is 'very interesting.' My God! Who else?"

The response of most professional critics was little better: reviews were generally tepid, somewhat kind, but very short. For example, the *New York Times* wrote, "It is the publisher's rather than the author's intention that this book should provide a comparison between the old West and the new. The sociological aspect of the tale is almost negligible. On the other hand, it makes quite an efficient Western yarn." Vindication, perhaps—nobody liked the title—but hardly cause for anybody to go out and buy the book. (Indeed, the public had lost interest in cynical views of heartland life. The small-minded "Babbittry" that Sinclair Lewis and H.L. Mencken had condemned was sufficiently vanquished that even Mencken's star was fading. Mencken soon reinvented himself as a good-natured memoirist, but Lockhart was not there, yet.) Doubleday told her to expect royalties of about $250. Given that she felt she'd labored seven years on the book, and was thousands of dollars in debt, it hardly felt like a triumph.

The homestead hearing was delayed until October 1933. Meanwhile, Lockhart had a new cook—and a new rival for her foreman's affections.

As at the *Enterprise*, Lockhart always had trouble finding good employees for the ranch. The summer of 1932, her first without Ketcham, she'd had three different cooks, none of whom lasted more than a month. It was a tough job, of course: you were stranded out in the middle of nowhere, always under the boss's thumb; you had to be amiable but not too chatty; you had to cook great food but not waste too much. ("She is a wonderful cook but needs a grocery store on one side of her and a butcher shop on the other," Lockhart said of one employee.)

Lockhart had first tried to get a male cook, since a woman was so socially disruptive. But few men were willing to do such housework, and certainly none to Lockhart's satisfaction. During the winter Lockhart could do most of the cooking herself, but in April 1933, as more employees arrived for the spring farming chores, she hired a nineteen-year-old girl named Ellen.

Ellen was amiable, but Lockhart noticed she took an interest in Good. Good didn't seem to be responding much, until one night in June when Lockhart "caught a smile and look exchanged between them that made me about half-sick." She dreaded the thought of losing Good's love (with characteristic overstatement she told her diary that it "would be the culminating tragedy of my life"). But she was so haunted by her own declining looks that she was sure it would happen.

Finally she confronted her lover. The result, she recorded in her diary: "If anyone but Dave had told me I was wrong in my suspicions I would have not believed it, but he is not a liar nor a hypocrite and his astonishment seemed so genuine that I could not doubt him. He was so broken up and said he thought I did not like his work."

The reassurance didn't hold. The whole summer, every time Good looked at Ellen, Lockhart became convinced he was two-timing her. Apparently she dared not fire the girl on such flimsy evidence, but she spent a great deal of energy concocting schemes to drive Good and Ellen apart. When the detective Joe LeFors arrived, she found him "an inconspicuous little man who likes to talk about himself." But she still tried to set him up with Ellen. Maybe Ellen would get pregnant, she hoped, and that would end Good's affection for her. She regularly snooped in Ellen's diary, and once lied to Good that from the diary she'd learned Ellen had syphilis. During their fitful happy times, she wondered if marrying Good might take away temptations, "but most people would think I have married beneath me after all these years. But perhaps that isn't so important if we are happy over here as we should be. The idea both scares and attracts me."

In late August she laid off Ellen and a boy named Pat who'd also been chasing after the young cook. She and Good drove them to Billings, where they learned that the bottom had completely fallen out of the cattle market. "There is no feed, no money, and everyone is prophesying a terrible winter," she wrote. It had been another summer of drought and grasshoppers. More fence had been cut. The only good news was the result of a lengthy approval process for a loan from an institution Lockhart did not really understand (her first diary entry mentioned "the Regional Bank—whatever that is—at Helena"). It was a regional branch of the Federal Reserve Bank. The federal government—which had earned her scorn for propping up Cody's irrigation project, and was now earning it again for Franklin Roosevelt's support of people she called deadbeats and chiselers—would give her the money to save her ranch.

Two days after they returned from Billings, Good told her she "would *drive him away* if I did not stop accusing him of being in love with [Ellen]. I said, 'Dave, I believe you, *I will, I will!*' But it continues to nag at me" as it would for the rest of her life.

The homestead hearing took place in the office of Gustave Reimer, an attorney in the small town of Bridger, forty miles closer to the Dryhead than Billings. Though Reimer ran the proceedings, the decisions (on all three homesteads—Lockhart's, Ketcham's, and Jolly's) would be made by a regional Land Office bureaucrat, based on the transcripts of the session. Still, the hearing had all the drama of a full trial. For example, at one point the prosecutor asked Lou Ketcham if she was aware of the penalty for perjury.

Ketcham slumped in her chair, an indication to some of those attending the trial that she was indeed aware of the penalties, and was indeed aware that she deserved them. Nevertheless, Ketcham insisted that she had lived on her homestead from March to November every year from 1926 to 1931. It was about a mile walk from the L Slash Heart, and she would get up early every morning, in order to walk to work with Baldy the dog at her side. She would have breakfast ready by 6:30 or 7:00 a.m., for an average of about five people including herself.

Ketcham knew that the law required her to live on the homestead for six months every year. That's why she had walked there every night until the snows got too deep. She also knew that the law required her to make improvements on the land. That's why she was so devastated by all of this fence cutting. She was a poor woman, she explained, and had to pay herself for these trips from her mother's bedside in Nebraska to testify. (She'd also shown up in May, not having heard that the hearing was postponed.)

Lockhart made a similar argument. She had walked a half-mile every day from the ranch to her homestead after breakfast, wrote there all day and returned to the ranch for supper. (Clay Jolly confirmed that when he occasionally passed the shack, "She had that rattle machine of hers going.") After supper she'd go back to the homestead shack to sleep, except perhaps when the weather was really bad.

But no witnesses had ever visited her at her shack, ate meals there, or stayed overnight. Charles Howard, a mail carrier, said that when he made his regular rounds, smoke from the homestead shack's chimney was thick and heavy, as if she'd just started a fire—because she knew he was coming. Claude St. John said he had seen her arrive at the shack just before the mail carrier to start such fires. Several witnesses testified that when they passed the shack early in the morning or late at night, they never saw smoke nor lights nor any other signs of habitation. Joe Smith said he'd seen cows coming out of the shack. He also said that the only person who had ever slept in Ketcham's shack was a man paid by Lockhart to build fence there.

The government's investigator, who had conducted interviews on a trip to the Dryhead, was particularly skeptical. He said of Lockhart, "When interrogated as to the platform [on which the cabin was built], she was extremely vague in identifying the size of the platform, and what is more strange of a woman, the size of the rug which she claims covered the platform." He noted that though she was supposedly living at the homestead, she had added three rooms to the Wasson place.

"I didn't expect to live indefinitely on the rock pile," Lockhart responded, explaining that investments in the Wasson place were for the future. Her attitudes were changing now that she realized the poor quality of range, she testified, and the homesteads probably hadn't been worth filing on—"as I know now. It wasn't worth the cost of improvements, if that is what you mean." But even if she wouldn't do it again, she *had* done it, she said. She had followed the law—she'd even asked the government land agent in Billings if she was performing up to snuff, and he gave her the OK—so she deserved to gain ownership of the land.

St. John said Lockhart had not followed the law. He'd told the inspector, "Both Ketcham and Jolly are old people, with no livestock and no means. The improvements on their claims were placed thereon by workmen employed by Lockhart, the lands were fenced with the Lockhart lands and were grazed by Lockhart cattle. Neither Ketcham nor Jolly are now in the country, or in the employ of Lockhart." Ketcham and Lockhart had both spoken of the thousand dollars Lockhart had promised to pay Ketcham once she proved up. All of this violated the law.

Jolly's case was the most outrageous. His homestead was three miles from the ranch bunkhouse, and he freely admitted he had not spent every night there. He'd only visited on weekends. Derry tried to argue that residence was a matter of intention, that Jolly resembled other poor unmarried men who work somewhere else during the week in order to make money to put into their plot of land. But the homestead law clearly required physical occupancy, and even Derry knew Jolly's was a lost cause.

The poverty of Jolly and Ketcham was used as evidence against them—and so was the wealth of Lockhart. The inspector reported that "Miss Lockhart is reputed to be a woman of considerable means" and that the L Slash Heart "is the best ranch in that country." Lockhart continually hid her financial worries from her neighbors (and even most of her employees), believing that in order to have any power, she had to appear to be rich. But such appearances lent credence to the Dryheaders' claim that she was running a giant land scheme rather than eking out a homestead. Her deal to front Ericson as Wasson's buyer was fraudulent, they said; all along she'd intended to gain control of the entire country.

Not true, Lockhart said. "My job is writing books and the last thing I had in mind when I came into the Dryhead was filing on land or engaging in the cattle business." According to this testimony, she'd once taken a trip into the Dryhead to see the scenery and visit friends on the reservation. During that trip, she said, her hired driver Ericson had asked for a loan to buy the Wasson place. He promised he would pay her back with money from his mother's estate. But just a few months later, admitting there was no money from the estate, he defaulted on the loan and she ended up owning a ranch she had never seen.

She was lying. But so, she believed, was everybody else. A petition had been circulated against her homestead, signed by Edith Barry, Claude St. John, Clarence Curen, Joe Smith, Eddie Hulbert, Ervin Howard, Phil Snell, and F. W. Blythe—but nobody would admit to circulating it. (St. John admitted he'd mailed it, but claimed rather lamely that he'd done so because he just happened to find it sitting on the table in the post office.) The previous spring Hank Lane had tried to prove up on a homestead of his own, and Lockhart knew he had lied as well—along with his witnesses, including Joe Smith. St. John had once earned a homestead too—on land adjacent to his spread at Hillsboro, in a scheme resembling the one he was accusing Lockhart of conducting—and he'd boasted that he'd never spent a single night there. Joe Smith was utterly untrustworthy: he'd been caught red-handed butchering other people's beef; he had boasted of wintering his cattle on Lockhart's hay and stealing wire from her fence. LeFors told her he had "never in all my experience seen so many unprincipled, conscience-less scoundrels congregated in one small community."

For days after the hearing, she lamented that rather than mounting a defense, they should have simply rested their case—and had each of the opposition witnesses arrested on the spot for perjury.

All winter they waited for the decision by the hearing officer. Derry assured Lockhart that she and Ketcham didn't have to worry. But she continued to quarrel with Tuffy Abbott, whom she was now calling a "lantern-jawed thief." She would hire him to work for her, be happy with the result, but accuse him of filching too many supplies. She continued to fret over Good's alleged affair. Everybody continued to worry about money. Even the Dryhead Ranch, which Lockhart had so envied just eighteen months previously, was now in rough financial shape; if she had the money, she suspected, she'd be able to take over all their leases on the reservation.

Bob Hopkins died, leaving Aunt Josie alone to run her own ranch north of Cody. Lockhart was too bitter to find much sympathy: "They will learn what I have been up against," she told her diary.

Lockhart and Good had a discussion about marriage.

"Would you be skeered?" she asked.

"No. We might get along better." Then he asked if she would be.

"Kinda." Only public opinion held her back, she said again. It was an odd statement for someone who defied it so frequently in her life. But she felt that if news got out that she had married her hired man, they would become objects of ridicule. His fine qualities, his character and principle "would be overlooked in the criticism." Might that ridicule and criticism be worthwhile if they would end the gossip that surrounded their current relations? She thought about talking it over with someone like Aunt Josie, but then dismissed the idea since "Dave's so much more of a man than Bob Hopkins ever was that they are not to be mentioned together."

If she refrained from talking even to Josie, one of her closest relatives, she shared even less with anyone else. That spring Paul Eldridge wrote her a letter that discussed the effects of that silence:

"Inscrutable" was the [word] I was reaching for when I suggested that it was your "unfathomability" that made you perpetually intriguing to your female neighbors. You would make a wonderful heroine for a novel, there are so many unexplained gaps between your achievements that would make any motivation possible. Newspapering. Silence. And then a book like *Me-Smith* that simply knocks one off his feet. Silence. And then *The Fighting Shepherdess*, say. And both of them produced out of the incredible, dismal monotony of Cody, like oases in the desert. The contrast hits one as does that of your intellect fraternizing with Squaw Smith or with . . . the Sheep Queen of Copper Mountain. And then you in the Dryhead. Sophistication set upon Davis Creek, and eating its meals with "Two-dog" Johnson.

She had reason to be especially inscrutable with Eldridge. By now any sharing of her feelings would have chiefly involved disgust. When he came to visit the following January, she swore to herself that he would never be back on her ranch again. She had somehow learned he was gay. In her diary she wrote, "There is no doubt but that he made one of his dirty breaks at Dean before he left, although Dean did not say so in so many words." She checked with relatives in Oklahoma and learned that Eldridge "was definitely let out of [his job at a] school because it was practically common knowledge that he is a sexual pervert. I can't understand how a person of intelligence should so wantonly jeopardize his position and friendships and career like that." But since they never talked, she never learned.

Now spring was coming again and she started to dread the summer. Ranch life was proving to be less than she'd hoped for. With all of the hired help, she'd be stuck again in the kitchen.

In May 1934 the news came. They lost the homesteads. Derry said he was shocked and disgusted. He also said that the national Land Office in Washington still had the opportunity to overrule the Billings office. He filed the appeal and told her to bring on as much political pressure as she could find.

Indeed, she lined up Wyoming senator Joseph O'Mahoney, former Wyoming governor Nellie Tayloe Ross, LeFors, and Cody luminaries including banker Fred McGee. It may have been the search for addresses that sent her rummaging through old financial records. "God! how I curse my foolishness when I look at the stubs in my checkbook and see the amounts I have written for that pinhead, Lou Ericson, and that thug, Bill Poole. How could I ever have been so easy and soft. A perfect damned fool. I would be ashamed to have anyone know how I handed it out. And both of them liars, traitors, rattlesnakes. . . . The greenest dude in the world could scarcely have done worse."

In May, Good told her he thought she was up against a losing proposition. He did not think she could make it at the L Slash Heart. Therefore, he said, he was willing to work without wages. He needed a bit of money for some personal obligations and expenses, but after that he didn't care if he died a pauper. The man she called Davey Spotted Horse told her he admired her courage and determination to succeed in the face of so many obstacles. And that, she decided, was some reward for her struggles.

It was not easy. One night that summer, after a couple of drinks in Billings, Good shared some of his concerns. She told her diary that he "blamed me because I fall out with one man after another . . . saying that none have liked me. He disregards the fact that I fall out because they are either shirks, incompetent, or disloyal." On this occasion his dire predictions about the ranch's future struck her as accusations. She tried to turn them back on him. "I have told him time and again to hire and fire and manage on his own, but he does not do it. . . . He has little executive ability and shrinks from responsibility, I think."

Yet imagine the responsibility of making her dream succeed. In September he wanted to ship their cattle to Omaha, but she wanted to try Chicago, and that's where they went. The price proved a disappointment. In November a man offered to buy her house in Cody for two thousand dollars, but she tried to hold out for three thousand. They'd gotten halfway home before Good convinced her that two thousand would feed every hoof she had all winter, and by the time she tried to pursue the deal, the man had backed down. They reversed typical gender roles: Lockhart held tight on the purse strings while Good felt more empathy, particularly toward employees. When she fired a man in December, Good encouraged her to pay the man a disputed $4.11 "so that he wouldn't go off sore and do a lot of talking, so I did it though I know it won't make any difference for he is a *rat* in every possible way. . . . No wonder Dave hasn't anything saved. People would just take it away from him if he had a fortune."

Good may have been frustrated to feel that he had no control, but you could say the same about Lockhart. From Helena, three hundred miles away, the Regional Bank had ideas on how she should manage her ranch. At one point the bankers suggested she cut down her herd to 40 head. "I must sell cattle to pay my debts and then I will have no source of income," she griped. After an inspector visited, the ceiling was lifted to 225. But cattle and hay kept going missing—probably from the neighbors' thieving, though possibly from her own mistallies. The Pill took lumber and logs from one of her properties. And in the spring of 1935, things started vanishing from her house.

It started with a derringer pistol, missing from her dresser drawer. Next a half-bucket of brown sugar was gone from the storehouse. Then a little microscope disappeared from a shelf in the dining room. The scope showed up after a search, but two weeks later four large boxes of matches went missing.

The thefts appear to have nagged at Lockhart because she half-suspected she herself was at fault. She was now sixty-four years old, and both her memory and her eyesight (she now wore thick glasses) were starting to slip. She felt that only clothes could offset her declining looks, but she could not afford the trips out to buy them.

But her ambition remained. That winter she tried to swing a deal to lease the Dryhead Ranch and take over its leases on the reservation. She also started thinking about a new writing project. "I want to write a book of the present and of what I have known and felt myself since living in here," she told her diary. "Put in all my experiences and grief. I want it to be a masterpiece."

Despite her fears, and despite continued drought, the ranch limped along. Her creditors let her slide a bit. In May 1935, a year after the previous decision, she learned that the Land Office commissioner in Washington had approved the two homesteads. Though the prosecution appealed to the secretary of the Interior, so far political pressure was working. In August her cattle brought far less than she'd hoped, but nevertheless topped the market. (It was an honor when your cattle got the best price of anyone at the sale, implying that your breeding and management were better than your neighbors'.) A new "choreboy" arrived who would prove to be a long-lasting employee. He was, in fact, another old man, a "conceited old cuss . . . a downright contemptible old fart," as one visitor described him, named Ed Pickering. "Pick" spent some of his time working on additions to her house. He built another new wing for her bedroom/office and constructed sheds and other outbuildings from the remains of Ketcham's claim shack.

Lockhart started investing more in horses, heavy draft stock, in which she took a greater interest than cattle. She bought a wind-powered battery charger to give her dependable power by which to listen to the radio.

The Curens became friendly, admitting they had been overly influenced by the Barrys' vicious talk. Lockhart hired each of them to do a few chores. In March 1936 she won the appeal on her homestead. The ruling was sympathetic to the neighbors' charges—"The appearances are that the ranch was the claimant's home and that residence on the homestead was merely colorable"; "The deal with Lou Erickson appears questionable"—but noted that nobody could prove she hadn't slept in the claim shack.

That summer three carloads of her cattle again topped the market in Billings. She sent a press release to the newspaper and then sent the clipping to New York literary columnist Christopher Morley, who reprinted it warmly, commenting, "At this rate Miss Carrie should be able to afford to write another book. We need it."

Her diaries through these years provide occasional glimpses of a woman coming to terms with life. Topping the market brought her satisfaction, proving her worth as a rancher, validating that she had succeeded in this man's game. When she found time to write, that activity generally made her happy, and she seemed to be continually relearning the lesson that she needed to hire great domestic help so that she herself could spend time writing. (Never finding such an ideal employee, she also continually re-forgot the lesson.) And she developed with Good the most enduring, most committed romance of her life. Intellectually incompatible, they couldn't talk about much other than the L Slash Heart. She still found him too accommodating, and he still found her too jealous. But they both did love the ranch, and the country, and the lifestyle—and they were able to build their relationship on that.

However, these are merely glimpses of satisfaction. The diaries also show a woman consumed with anger at her own powerlessness. She had not yet won her battles.

Though the days of the big Texas cattle drives were now fifty years in the past, Good and his men did have to drive the cattle from the L Slash Heart to a railhead most autumns. Movies show cattle drives as the most sublime of western experiences, but Lockhart herself did not join in on them. A drive in 1936 may suggest one reason why.

This year in September they took some cattle to market, and in October took the rest to a winter pasture Lockhart had leased from O. B. Mann. She'd run into Mann the year before in Cody, and he'd again sobbed that she was the only woman he'd ever cared for. She was quite delighted to find she felt nothing for him anymore. She was committed to Good. But she and Mann continued to correspond, and in August he promised her a pasture where she could winter her cattle, with hay at ten dollars a ton. It was a great relief to her, though she puzzled at a September letter in which he started changing his prices: twelve dollars per ton for new hay, nine dollars for old hay, plus four dollars an acre for pasture. Remembering that "he had distinctly said that the pasture went with the hay at $10 a ton," she decided to ignore the letter and send him a five-hundred-dollar down payment on three hundred tons of new hay.

It was a bit of a risk. She didn't know where she was going to find the money to make the rest of the payment. She also feared the Regional Bank: they could make trouble because she didn't have a formal contract with Mann, and they also didn't like cattle crossing state lines. For this reason she hurried Good off with the cattle. She put together the camp outfit for Good and his crew of Irma Curen (the Pills' daughter) and another man.

Three days later she got a letter from Mann. The pasture absolutely did *not* go with the hay, he said. If she wanted to negotiate she could come talk to him. But meanwhile he was returning her check.

She toyed with doing nothing. Good would descend on Mann with 368 head of cattle, and Mann would just have to live with it. But she decided that wasn't fair to Good. So she asked Mrs. Pill's brother to drive his car after the cattle with a message.

At that point Good was in the town of Cowley, Wyoming, several miles southwest of Crooked Creek. He hadn't slept in forty-eight hours. He was desperately worried about the cattle, and he was sweating out a cold. But he allowed the messenger to bring him back to the ranch. After a few hours' sleep, he and Lockhart set out together. Since they apparently had no place to winter the cattle, they would have to get rid of them.

Good had left the cattle in a small field near Cowley. But due to a short-age of rail cars, they were unable to ship from there. They investigated truck-ing the cattle to Billings, but that would have cost an extra thousand dollars. Feeling stuck, Lockhart agreed to sell the cattle to two Cowley-area men. The market had fallen; these steers brought 20 percent less than had the ones she'd shipped in early September. Days after the sale, she discovered that Good hadn't followed up with a simple comparison between the num-ber of cattle sold and the number they left the ranch with (he was waiting, he said, for *her* to do it). When they finally counted, they were thirty-four head short—a loss of another twelve hundred dollars.

She spoke with Cody attorney Milward Simpson about suing Mann for breach of contract. Mann, she reasoned, should have to pay for the money she'd lost by selling in Cowley. But Mann responded that she'd misunder-stood him, that this fiasco was damaging him too since he still hadn't sold his hay, and that she'd gotten out of the cattle business by her own act, not his.

A month after the first conversation, Simpson told her that he'd just remembered that he also represented Mann. He couldn't sue his own client. In her desperation Lockhart even went to Ernest Goppert, though she eventually retained E. E. Enterline, her primary attorney in her suit against Gop. Enterline finally informed her that the law required a contract in writing, and she fumed that a man's word couldn't be trusted.

Throughout 1937 her feuds continued to proliferate. In May she wrote, "I can't get it out of my head that my enemies are cutting my fences and driving my stock into or out of my pastures, rustling, etc. If they are not doing this, they want to, and are only waiting for the proper moment."

Carl Abarr continually kept his sheep on his brother Merle's land—the former Jolly homestead, which Lockhart had leased from Merle. Even after she hired Enterline to get a judge's opinion, and even after Abarr agreed to abide by that opinion, he stubbornly kept putting his sheep and cattle where he wanted to. He was so determined that she decided somebody—such as the Barrys or Hank Lane—was egging him on, promising to back him if there was any trouble. Even after several trips to Red Lodge finally convinced the sheriff to come in and arrest Abarr, he simply paid a fifty-dollar bond, came back to the Dryhead, and put his stock back on Merle's section.

She finally decided to take matters into her own hands. It was mid-August, unbearably hot, and drought was drying up springs all over the country. Abarr was away, doing some work for his brother-in-law. Lockhart slipped behind the hills with a flour sack full of Kreso-Dip, a foul-smelling chemical used to clean lice off sheep. Hoping that nobody saw her, she headed to Abarr's spring. Unfortunately, the Kreso-Dip turned milky when poured into the water itself, so she just sprinkled it around the edges in hopes that the smell would keep the sheep from drinking.

She didn't want to kill anything, just make the sheep so thirsty that Abarr would have to put them somewhere else, preferably farther away from her land. But it had no effect that she ever heard of. Two days later they went into Bridger to try a lawsuit against Abarr and discovered that Abarr had lined up Joe Smith and Claude St. John to testify for him. She had no confidence in her lawyer's ability, especially against such a formidable lineup, so she quickly withdrew the complaint and filed a different one, hoping to exhaust Abarr's finances with all these trips to the courthouse.

But two could play at that game. Abarr's lawyer filed a continuance himself, and by the time the case came up in October, somehow the deputy had failed to serve the proper subpoenas. Each trip to Bridger was also costing her twenty-five dollars, so she finally agreed to drop the case in exchange for a promise that Abarr would keep his sheep off her land.

Meanwhile, several other Dryhead-area ranches were also missing cattle, including the Cooks, Moncurs, Strongs, and three Indians on the reservation. Rumor had it that Hank Lane was heading a cattle-rustling ring.

One of Lockhart's employees that summer was a man named Ben Taylor. She felt that he'd started out as a hard worker, but St. John and Tuffy Abbott had turned him against her; he stuck around only because he was smitten with her new cook. In one of their trips to Bridger, Good bet Taylor that he couldn't eat three full pounds of hamburger, with trimmings, in one sitting; though he fell twelve ounces short, Lockhart found the entire episode disgusting. She also believed Taylor was a communist. When another employee was bucked off his horse, injuring his back so badly that his eyes rolled back in his head, they lugged a mattress out to where he lay, took him home on it, undressed him, and laid him flat. Lockhart said they should let him sit for a few hours and get over the shock ("it wasn't like a tick or a snakebite that needed instant attention . . . and I thought quiet was the best until we found out"). But Taylor thought he should go to the hospital in Billings at once. That, Lockhart said, "shows me what he is—a *radical*, a typical Red agitator whose first and only thought was to make me pay well for the accident." When the injured man indeed started feeling better, she felt vindicated. (He later admitted he'd had several previous back injuries; the following week they had him x-rayed and the doctor said he was fine.) By the fall she was calling Ben a "loud-mouthed hoodlum" and a "born criminal at heart [who] would do *anything* for money."

So she gave him a chance. "I made him a proposition when we settled up and he jumped at it but whether he will carry it out is something else. I told him I was *not asking* him to do this, but Hank Lane's *ears* were worth $100 apiece to me. He said he would get 'em."

There's only one way to get a man's ears: kill him. She knew she was putting out a contract on Lane. "This may be the worst thing I've ever done in my life," she told her diary. And she was worried. But not about the moral aspects of taking a man's life—she was just worried about whether they could get away with it. "It's not eliminating a brute that upsets me," she told the diary the next month, "but only that there is a big risk involved if he [Taylor] pulls a boner."

In late October Lane was arrested for rustling. Deputies found three hides on his place. Lockhart had offered a two-hundred-dollar reward to anyone who solved her rustling cases, so if the hides were hers she would have to pay the reward. Which would be better? To rely on the uncertain deal with Taylor, with all of the risk and nervous strain? Or to pay the same amount to see Lane behind bars? The law had let her down so continually since she'd come to the Dryhead—could she trust it now? Either way, she would need two hundred in cash, which she had her brother Bob (who ran the family lands back in Kansas) send to her in tens.

Fences kept getting cut. Lockhart's eyes deteriorated. Ketcham demanded the thousand dollars she'd been promised for her homestead. In late November, Lockhart made a trip to Cody and Billings. She visited Aunt Josie and her new husband. She saw an eye doctor who informed her that her right eye was diseased and neglected and would require medical attention. And one evening she saw Ben Taylor.

He explained his plan: to rent a horse in Billings, ride to Lovell and then up into the Dryhead, past Lockhart's to Lane's. It would be well over a hundred miles, the biggest chunk of it on a highway (hard on the horse's feet), with few places to stop for feed or shelter. It would take at least three days; he planned to ride only at night. He would use cyanide—easier and less risky than a gun. He would write to her before he left so that she could leave the area while the act was being done, then meet him in Billings for the payoff.

She found it strange to be sitting in a quiet room, calmly discussing a homicide. But she later told her diary, "My nervousness and cold feet are gone. When I weaken, I think of the way that monster [Lane] hobbled his horse with barbed wire around its flank and hind legs until it died by inches, and then chopped another horse with an axe, and beat another's head to a pulp and nearly dead it staggered back to the barn and died. Nothing is too bad an end for such a devil as *that*."

Such was her empathy for animals that she almost wrote Taylor, after the meeting, to remind him to turn loose any stock that Lane had tied or penned, so they wouldn't starve to death after their master's murder. The murder itself didn't concern her at all. "Thinking of all the problems the neighbors have caused me over the years, I wish Ben could wipe out the whole caboodle." She gave him a thirty-dollar check for a down payment.

What exactly makes a place "the frontier"? You could use an economic definition: when the timber was cut and the crops were planted in northwest Illinois, Joe Lockhart left for Kansas where he could still find untapped resources. Or you could use an accessibility definition: the Swiftcurrent River mining camp of Altyn, Montana, was so far from the nearest railroad, shopping district, or government outpost that folks had to rely on themselves. Or you could use a personality definition: when confronted with a problem, residents of a place such as the Dryhead were always ready to resort to violence.

Around the time of Lockhart's birth, "the West" and "the frontier" became synonymous. Throughout her life Americans became fully vested in a mythology that married the huge landscapes of the West to the "regeneration through violence" (as one scholar puts it) that represented this frontier nature of the national character. Perhaps the greatest hunger for such myths came from the West itself. The romantics who had come to the frontier (perhaps even originally seeing it as an economic or self-reliant frontier) soon fell in love with a set of stories and interpretations that called them cowboys, that allowed them to brandish six-guns and talk of vigilantism. They reinvented themselves in the image that Owen Wister had given them.

Lockhart was a prime example. She had come to the frontier as a romantic in search of adventure. The West was the latest backdrop—after Labrador and Paris and the bottom of Boston Harbor—for her stories about herself. But as she fell in love with western trappings—the landscapes, the horses, the men who gritted their teeth through pain—she adopted this cowboy myth as her own. In her first book, a subplot mocked Wister's depiction of the cowboy and schoolmarm; in her last book, calling her hero a cattleman was sufficient to establish his heroism.

She had taken to the frontier in all of its definitions, and yet never gotten the fulfillment they promised. She came to Cody to revel in its remoteness, but civilization kept trying to catch up with her. She came to the Dryhead to reap the economic opportunity of a land not yet developed into cattle ranches, but she ran up against the land's limits on economic expansion. And then she came to a realization—surprisingly slowly, given her longtime immersion in the myth—that the way to solve the problem of her weakness in the face of the lawless Dryheaders was through violence. She had to take the law into her own hands. She had to stand up for her own rights.

Of course, it's tricky business, trying to enact a myth in real life. As a wealthy rancher trying to squeeze out the homesteading neighbors—and, in frustration, ultimately deciding to have one of them murdered—did she more resemble one of her cowboy heroes, or one of her evil villains?

She never saw Ben Taylor again. He simply cashed her thirty-dollar check and failed to follow through, knowing there was nothing she could do about it. The next spring he wrote to her, saying he felt justified in cheating her out of the money because she had promised him a job painting her houses and then not delivered. (Not surprisingly, she disagreed. Regarding the thirty dollars, she told her diary, "It was *weak of me* to let him have it and serves me damned good and right.") In fact, with the Depression still on and jobs scarce, Taylor became increasingly desperate, writing again to urge Lockhart to hire him back the following summer and deduct the thirty dollars out of his wages. But she was done with him.

Life went on, much the same as it had for years. She spent a couple of months in Cody that winter and felt productive in her writing, but by April told her diary, "I am ready to go back" to the Dryhead. And when she arrived she felt it was nice to be *home*.

Lockhart kept worrying over money but gradually scaled back her operation and—in part thanks to additional money coming in from her family—worked her way out of debt. In 1938 her cattle again topped the market in Billings, and she rejoiced over how Codyites and Dryheaders would react to that news on the radio.

Kate "Steppy" Lockhart died and gave her interest in the family ranch to Lockhart's youngest brother, Bob, the only sibling still in Kansas. (His descendants own the ranch to this day.) George had already died; the will gave Grace five hundred dollars and "my step-daughter, Caroline, $1." A month later Dr. Frances Lane died of pneumonia at age sixty-four, and Lockhart wrote in her diary, "Curious that two people I have hated most and for so many years should kick off so close together. I really have no one to hate now but O.B. Mann, feel lost!" She believed those two women were roasting in hell, and found satisfaction that she was still here on earth. But she did not reflect on exactly why she had so hated the lady doc.

Ruth French Smith, the orphan who had married the first homesteader she could find in order to get away from the Barrys, was now left alone again upon the death of her husband, Bert. Though their homestead now housed a post office for the farther reaches of the Dryhead area, she had a four-year-old daughter to support—and, by one account, just twelve cents to her name.

After the Curens split up, Ruth married the Pill, but two months later he too dropped dead. Lockhart tried to get Ruth on welfare, but she wouldn't take it, instead working at the post office and doing housekeeping for Lockhart.

Good, Lockhart felt, still had inordinate admiration for the girls who worked as cooks and ranch hands. But in October 1938, coming back from a cattle drive, he bought her a gift of some silk bedspreads and tablecloths from a traveling salesman in Lovell. She bawled him out. It wasn't silk but cotton, "peddler's trash . . . the cheapest kind of stuff, made to sell to boobs." He was so ashamed of his failure to please her that she couldn't stay upset at him.

In 1939 she completed her next novel, the one about the Dryhead, and sent it to her editor Harry Maule at Doubleday. But he sent it back. There could be several reasons for the rejection. This was the first time in several books that she had not worked with the editor Berg Esenwein to improve the manuscript before sending it to the publisher. She also, just before mailing it off, complained to her diary that she seemed to have lost a few pages. Her sight and memory problems may have made the unedited narrative difficult to follow.

More substantially, *Old West—and New* had not sold well, and publishers always rely on previous sales in measuring their enthusiasm for a new book. Furthermore, the poor sales could be traced directly to Lockhart's refusal to follow the by-now-established western formula. Publishers wanted books about the West to be gunfighter-oriented thrillers, and Lockhart would not write such a book.

In this manuscript, a southern woman named Judy St. Clair moves to the West with her husband, who claims to be a miner, and an adopted girl named Letty. Judy turns out to be a counterfeiter and murderer who hates Letty because Letty's mother had once stolen Judy's true love. Typical of Lockhart, the work features lots of dialogue with regional accents, especially Judy's *Ahs* and *youahs*. But despite the novel's unquestionably modern setting (Letty's father dies on the *Lusitania*, in 1915, just before her birth), the novel doesn't feel very twentieth century. Indeed, its caricatures give the book a romanticized Old West flavor—but without gunfights. So it ends up being not quite a western, not quite a romance, not really funny enough to be humor, and far too predictable, melodramatic, and shallow to be meaningful literature.

Again it is based on real-life people: Judy St. Clair is Edith St. John Barry. Lockhart had traveled all over the region to find dirt on the Barrys to incorporate into the novel; she continually insisted that Edith was a real-life counterfeiter. But where in previous novels her character assassinations were tied to insights about changing social conditions, no longer was Lockhart in the forefront of a New West. Instead, she and her neighbors had escaped to a place where they rehashed visions of the Old West (visions many of them had gained from movies and dime novels). Certainly somebody could have made interesting sociological insights into such a community, but Lockhart was too close to it. Like many writers, she was best when one step removed from her setting: *The Man from the Bitter Roots*, set in Idaho, was written in Honduras and Cody; *The Fighting Shepherdess*, set at the Sheep Queen's, was written in Cody; *Old West—and New*, set at the Cody paper, didn't come together until she was on the Dryhead. Had she left the Dryhead, this novel too might have coalesced into a valuable portrait of a western subculture. But she would not leave the Dryhead.

The reason Maule officially gave for his rejection was that the manuscript was too confusing. It had too little action, too many characters, too much detail without enough payoff. Ever the optimist, Lockhart inferred that he was suggesting a rewrite to solve such problems. "I know he is right about everything," she told her diary about Maule's comments, "but the question is, can I *do* it?" At age sixty-eight, with failing eyes, did she have the stamina—and did she crave the attention—enough to put in the work of editing this manuscript into something readers would enjoy?

Lockhart had begun her career with a firm market orientation: she wrote whatever her editors at the *Boston Post* told her to, because that was what readers wanted. Now she had progressed to the other end of the spectrum: she wrote what entertained her. Lockhart's satisfaction increasingly came in the process of writing (where her enemies always got their comeuppance), rather than any riches or fame in publication. She knew rewriting and editing were valuable—she now cited *The Fighting Shepherdess* as her best book "because it is the most finished. . . . It took me two years to finish it and I rewrote it three times." But compared to the creative self-indulgence of writing, she found the discipline required for rewriting far less appealing.

Meanwhile, feuds with Carl Abarr, Hank Lane, and the Barrys continued. In July 1939 she was untying a wire that Abarr had hitched to her fence despite the fact that she had ordered him not to. He shot at her with a rifle. In one version she told later, the shot took her hat off and spooked her horse. In another version, she calmly finished the job of untying the wire, then rode slowly off. In a third version, the shot went in front of her horse, which threw her. By one account she shrugged off the incident as just part of living on the Dryhead; by another account it so haunted her that she never rode horseback again.

After thirteen years, Lockhart's feuds on the Dryhead were becoming something like legend. There started to be multiple versions of each story, many of them influenced as much by classic conceptions of heroes and myths as by actual events. Even more confusing: the mythmaking wasn't just taking place after the fact, but before.

Pete Spragg, a slim, soft-eyed, raw-boned seventeen-year-old, was helping on a cattle drive from Kane into the Crow reservation in the early spring of 1936. Some of the calves were so young that they couldn't walk that distance themselves, so he drove a sugar beet truck carrying them. The trail was still so gnarly that at some spots horses were required to pull the truck up hillsides, and at other spots the men had to take off its dual tires because they were too wide for the cliff-side road. After delivery the crew decided to take the truck back via the longer but safer route west of the Pryors.

Spragg said he wanted to take two days and go back through the Dryhead. His colleagues teased him that he just wanted to visit the young widowed postmistress Ruth Smith. In fact, he felt the long single-day trip following the truck would abuse his horse, but rather than start a confrontation about it, he accepted their teasing and went his own way.

Toward evening on the first day of his trip, Spragg came to the Lockhart place. It scared him a little, because he'd heard the woman was a hellcat on wheels, but he'd also heard the ranch was a beautiful spot, and he wanted to see it. When he stopped in, Good invited him to supper, as was that era's rural tradition. Good took Spragg and his horse to the barn, where Spragg took off the horse's saddle so her back could dry. Good approved: "I sure do like to see a man take care of his horse before thinking of his own wants."

With the horse set, they went into the house. Lockhart was cooking. It was still early spring, and she had not yet hired a summer cook. Spragg recalled, "She shook hands just like a man and got right up close a looking me over and said, 'I like to see what I'm feeding.'"

She was, he described, a heavyset woman wearing a muumuu-style dress, shapeless and dingy gray. "It sure did make her look like a drab old lady." Her forthright stare had done little to ease his anxiety, but he eventually realized that she was nearly blind. "Her glasses were so thick they made her eyeballs look like teacups."

He was especially impressed with the ranch house. In the new living room, a davenport, an overstuffed easy chair, and a wooden rocker sat in front of the fireplace. The walls boasted mounted heads of African animals (tiger, gazelle, springbok) and an eighteen-inch-wide snakeskin running two-thirds of the length of the room. Navajo rugs covered the floor. Gas and kerosene Aladdin lamps provided illumination, since she preferred not to wear down the wind-powered battery for lighting. From the living room, "you had to walk through the kitchen, Dave's bedroom and the cook's bedroom" to get to the study where Lockhart conducted business. This was also her bedroom, with a white china pitcher, washbowl, and bedchamber pot next to a steel bed covered in quilts and blankets. Both her bedroom and the living room were newly constructed of attractively varnished logs, but the old rooms between them—the original Hannon homestead—remained in their original condition. At the time the only modern item Spragg saw in those rooms was a kerosene-powered refrigerator; soon she had Pick build a shed to house it, so as to retain the kitchen's old-timey appearance.

She wouldn't even update the kitchen floors. They had huge gaps between the floorboards, which—authentic though they may have been—allowed in mice. To stem the mouse problem, she kept two bull snakes. "She had them named," Spragg recalled, "and claimed she could tell them apart. . . . I had one name for both of them, and have used that same name for other things I have a strong dislike for." Some time later one of her hands killed one of the snakes; he was immediately fired. In general Spragg found the L Slash Heart "picturesque." Perhaps because of that attitude, and because he lavished care on his horse, Lockhart took a shine to him.

Spragg developed a keen eye for Lockhart's cooks. He later recalled, "That's the only way I can remember the years in there. Virginia was '38, Hazel was '39, and I think Marjorie was '40." During the summer of 1938, he found Virginia so cute that for the first time in his visits to the ranch, he offered to dry the dishes after dinner. That October he was in the Dryhead on his nineteenth birthday, so they stretched him out over a bench for Good to whip him with his chaps. Lockhart and Virginia cooked him a great big dinner, including both cake and a steamed pudding known as son-of-a-gun-in-a-bag. After dinner they gave him gifts: from Virginia, a set of monogrammed handkerchiefs, and from Lockhart, a picture of herself with Buffalo Bill on horseback. Good soon fell asleep in the easy chair, and Lockhart later halted the conversation when the news came on the radio. (It wasn't exactly the after-dinner activity he and Virginia had in mind. "This cowboy had plans that beat [Lockhart's] all to hell. But after the effort she put into my birthday I would have been some kind of a louse to have refused.")

The next day he and Good went out to move cattle, along with a hired hand. Spragg didn't think much of the men Good hired. "If a man had read a couple of western books and could talk, he could convince Dave he was a top hand." The talker would often start his job wearing "fancy inlaid multicolored boots, all shined up so they looked like a freshly painted circus wagon. When they got canned, usually within a month[,] those boots would sure be a sight, all scuffed up from the rocky terrain and the red dirt. . . . A lot of young fellows didn't realize that 90 percent of most cowboys' work was just plain menial labor." Spragg was one of the few who would do that menial labor. He believed in the values behind the big hats. He resembled Lockhart's cherished "old-timers" far more than people two or three times his age.

Good did occasionally hire quality help, Spragg recalled, but neither good hands nor bad lasted long. Spragg blamed it on Pickering: "he was always telling Dave or Miss Lockhart what everyone was doing, and a lot of the times it was a plain damn lie. . . . The better the hand, the more old Pick tried to get rid of them, because he knew the poor help wouldn't last long anyway. He told me his job is what kept the ranch percolating."

The following year Spragg didn't much care for Hazel, but in 1940 he fell hard for Marjorie. "That summer those cows of ours [in the Dryhead] sure did require a whole bunch of looking after." In September, after a cow kicked Good off the top of a truck cab, breaking his hip, he drove himself into Billings, where a doctor confined him to the hospital for a month. So Lockhart asked Spragg to help take her and Ruth's cattle to market. They trailed the steers north to the town of Pryor, where they loaded them on stock trucks for Billings. Then Spragg took Marjorie to her family's home in Bridger, where she needed to complete one more year of high school.

Marjorie jilted him that winter, so in the spring of 1941, when Lockhart suggested he come in and meet her new cook, Spragg found the first chance he could get to make the thirty-eight-mile ride. Just before getting to the house, he stopped out of sight to brush dust off his clothes and wipe his face with a bandanna. He knocked on the door and, when it opened, "there stood a scraggly-toothed Chinaman complete with pigtail and old-fashioned quilted suit." Lockhart and her crew found the joke hilarious.

Spragg recalled thinking that "75 miles of riding was a long damned ride for their entertainment." But overall he liked Lockhart, and he knew that she liked him. "With her it didn't seem like there was any middle ground," he recalled. "You were either her friend or her enemy. . . . Miss Lockhart was very, very conservative in her business dealings. In fact, I would class her as downright tight. But in my dealings with her over a period of years, she never beat me out of one penny. When they were in a bind and she asked me to work for her for a few days at a time, I'd have gladly done that in return for the hospitality they had shown me, but she always paid me. In our early dealings she could have taken advantage of this young cowboy, who in actuality was just a pistol-assed kid. Miss Lockhart was not only educated, she was a very intelligent person who could comfortably talk to a beggar or a professor, each at their own level." But his experiences with her "proved my feelings that a lot of people think they can take advantage of a lone woman in any kind of dealings."

Furthermore, he said, she was deceived by her employees. Not only did Pick talk down about the hired hands, he also spread rumors about the neighbors. "Two-thirds of what he told her was plain BS." Good, too, was at best a poor judge of neighborhood gossip—"he'd tell her everything he heard" regardless of how reliable the source. In fact, Spragg believed, it went even beyond that: "He always said, this gate was open, that gate was open, the fence was tore down here or there. When I was working over there two or three times he told her outright lies just to keep her agitated."

It didn't take much to agitate her. She often gave the appearance of thriving on the rivalry and hatred, craving more of it. But Spragg's report that the two of them "kept her in constant turmoil" suggests that perhaps what she needed was someone not only loyal and trustworthy but also forgiving and discreet—a calming influence to tame the Dryhead wars.

❧

The year 1942 blew in cold and nasty. Snow fell two feet deep, with drifts even higher. Wind blew fiercely from the southeast; temperatures dropped to twenty and thirty below. Good was in Denver, where he intended to have an operation. Lockhart felt bored, lonely, and anxious.

Pick was there with her, and two boys, Oscar and Dick Thompson, were taking care of the cattle over at the Robertson place. But as the cold continued to clamp down, Lockhart got grumpier. She was mad at Oscar and Dick because they wouldn't go get the mail. "They all seem like such sissies after Dave and Pick. Old Pick would go for the mail if he had a horse." But when Pick looked for a horse in the pasture he could not see one.

When the Thompsons didn't come down to the main house for Sunday dinner on January 11, she was grumpier—she'd spent all morning cooking, and then had to eat in glum silence with Pick. She'd given the boys a strip of bacon and several jars of beef, but now when she looked in the storehouse rafters, she saw not the two sides of bacon that she remembered hanging there, but only one. She asked Pick, who agreed: there used to be two. She decided Oscar and Dick had stolen the other side, taken it up to the Robertson place to waste. She'd trusted them, and now she was both angry and disappointed. But she had to hide those emotions until Good got back, because she couldn't lose their services tending her cattle.

Good had been complaining for years about his stomach and bladder. He feared he had cancer. Just after Christmas he had seen a doctor in Billings who insisted on treatments or an operation. He felt he would get better medical care in Denver, so she paid him five hundred dollars in back wages and he drove to Cody and got on a bus. But he should have been there a week by now, and she was anxious for his letters.

On Monday, finally, with still no horses in sight, Pick decided to walk to the post office. He brought back three letters from Good. They were written in dull lead on thin onionskin paper, which made them very hard to read—and Lockhart's eyesight made them worse. She could only make out a few words in each. She showed them to Pick—who was also concerned about Good's health—and he couldn't do any better.

The Thompsons came in on Tuesday to ask for butter and two more pounds of coffee. She could barely speak to them. She was so upset, and they didn't seem to care at all. They didn't offer any information about the condition of the cattle, or any excuses for missing Sunday dinner. They didn't even ask about Good. Oscar especially seemed impudent—and not just to Pick but even to Lockhart—and she could barely stand it. Later Pick told her that instead of working they'd probably been out hunting.

Today Oscar Thompson remembers Lockhart as an incredibly difficult person to deal with. "One day you'd be the greatest guy in the world. The next day you'd be just the lousiest person she'd ever met." It seemed to him that during all the time she spent alone, supposedly writing, she was just "thinking up how the world was treating her." Good and Pickering had to just go along with whatever paranoid fantasies she had dreamed up. (Obviously he'd never stolen any bacon.) Good told Thompson it was part of her character and vocation: "These people who write—these authors—they have to do a lot of dreaming and imagining."

But to Thompson, she simply was not a nice person. "She had a little income. And that's hard country. Everybody in there was doing the best they could to make a living. But she lorded it over them, calling them honyockers." They were poor people struggling through the Depression. And rather than being thankful for all of her money, she accused them of stealing from her.

During those bleak early months of 1942, with winter pouring into the Dryhead, Good gone, and the radio bringing news of German and Japanese advances in the war, Lockhart contemplated leaving the ranch. She and Good and Pick were getting too old to manage it. "I could be comfortable, well-dressed, and look far younger than my years if I could care for myself properly." But she had always moved *to* someplace, to a new adventure. When he returned from Denver, cancer-free, Good said maybe she should go to Europe or somewhere that would similarly appreciate her intellect. But she had always wanted to come to the West. And now she was here. Even at age seventy-one she was not yet willing to step down. "Would I ever be contented as here with nothing to do and my eyesight so poor?"

The back pages of a local paper ran this item on December 13, 1944:

> The announcement of the engagement of Miss Laura Mauch of Powell, Wyo., to Dave Good, of Dryhead, Montana, has caused a considerable stir in their respective communities since Miss Mauch is only 19 and still a schoolgirl while Mr. Good frankly admits he will be 72 his next birthday.
>
> They plan to be married when school closes next spring but whether it will be a formal church wedding or a simple ceremony before the Justice of the Peace they have not yet decided.
>
> The romance began when Miss Mauch resigned her position at the Klindt rooming house in Powell and applied for a job on Caroline Lockhart's L Slash Heart ranch in Dryhead where Mr. Good has

been cattle foreman for many years. Owing to the help shortage Miss Mauch was taken on to assist in the hayfield where her handiness with a pitchfork soon won the foreman's admiration and respect. Admiration and respect quickly developed into a warmer feeling, with the above result.

Miss Mauch is of Russian-German parentage and one of 17 children. While Mr. Good does not hope to equal or surpass the achievement of his father-in-law, who is 66, he nevertheless is looking forward jubilantly to a happy family life. He has a wide circle of acquaintances in Wyoming and Montana who will wish him well in his somewhat startling matrimonial venture.

It sounds like an April Fools' joke, and newspapers may have been hesitant to pick up on it. (A few years earlier a newspaper had reprinted Lockhart's whimsical story about Dryhead boys opening a "rattlesnake canning factory" as if it was actual business news.) But it was true. After all of Lockhart's paranoia about Good's romances with employees, now one had actually come to fruition.

Lockhart dismissed Mauch as a "husky" girl with "no more morals than a guinea pig." Her foul language, Lockhart claimed, disgusted the men on the crew; even old Pick thought of quitting. In September Lockhart fired the girl—in time for her to return to her senior year of high school—but that didn't help matters on the ranch. Now Good wore "a face as long as a saddle-rope." He said he didn't intend to leave the L Slash Heart, but Lockhart didn't believe him. Besides, if he got married but didn't leave, she would have to rehire Mauch, which she had no intention of doing.

In the past Lockhart had frequently juggled multiple lovers, but now that she was the one being juggled, it was apparently much more difficult. Her diaries after 1942 no longer survive, so it's unclear how far she and Good had drifted apart, and how personally she took his fulfillment of what she had previously imagined as a tragedy. In letters to friends, she claimed that she was simply concerned about how Mauch would treat him, and how his mooning for her ruined him for ranch work. In one letter she wrote, "A lovesick old man is a ridiculous spectacle and, somehow, pitiful. (I look to see him come out in a zoot suit next in his efforts to appear youthful.)" While avoiding the subject of her own emotional attachments, she acknowledged that on the ranch it would be impossible to find a man with the honesty and experience to replace him. Instead, she wrote, she wished "some nice, comfortable woman, who could cook" would catch him on the rebound. "I would be fixed" because she could coexist with such a woman on the ranch.

Visitors of the era recall that Good lived primarily in the "Crow's Nest," one of three guesthouses in the compound. But Spragg, for example, also referred to the bedroom next to Lockhart's as "Dave's bedroom." It was surely in part a fifteen-year-long fiction, since she had never acknowledged even to employees that she and Good were romantically involved. But Good also spent many nights, even during the heat of their passion, up at the Robertson place; like many old bachelors, he never invested much in any room where he slept.

Eldridge believed that in the fall of 1944 Good had decided to marry Mauch and told Lockhart that he intended to leave the ranch after the wedding. That's what prompted her to send the article to the paper—but she didn't tell him she was doing it.

Instead, one night when she was in the kitchen, she heard a grunt from the living room that sounded almost like an "Ouch."

Good came into the kitchen and said, "Did you write this piece about me?"

"Why not? It's news and you told it to me yourself."

There was a long silence. Good stared at the toes of his boots. Then he said sourly, "It ain't goin' to happen."

But whatever had driven him and Mauch apart would remain forever a secret.

Earlier in 1944 Lockhart had traveled to Baltimore to have her eyes examined by experts at Johns Hopkins. When she came back to the Dryhead, she took an airplane—all the way to her ranch. A private pilot from Bridger ferried her the final leg. She developed a landing strip just west of the house, and after that her trips to Billings and Cody became a bit more regular. Returning from the Baltimore trip, she also stopped in Chicago to meet a new friend, a restaurateur and cowboy aficionado named Jay Adler.

The Dryhead thinned out during World War II. Many young men entered the service rather than taking up a remote homestead. Several old homesteaders moved to more urban areas, where jobs were plentiful. They typically sold their land to the surrounding cattle ranchers. Lockhart, for example, officially bought Merle Abarr's homestead in 1942, along with Dad Chesmore's place. But most of the other places sold to larger ranchers from the Lovell area, who used the Dryhead as summer pasture. Many of these ranchers were Mormon, and Lockhart bore them prejudices typical of the day ("I take a dim view of Mormons as a rule," she wrote in one letter). As usual, she believed that they showed their lower-class breeding in their treatment of animals. In November 1945 she wrote to Adler, "Yesterday a bunch of Mormons went through with 500 head of cattle pastured at the Phelps ranch and they left a heifer in the lane that was paralyzed in the hind quarters and couldn't get up. I wanted Dave to put her out of her misery but he said it was agin the law without their permission."

But thinning out the country meant thinning out her enemies. Tuffy Abbott sold his homestead. So did Joe Smith. In February 1946 Hank Lane was arrested for rustling. In the winter of 1947–48, the Barry home burned to the ground. (Edith Barry's family heirlooms were lost, but the Barrys were able to continue living in other buildings on their compound.)

It would be interesting to see Lockhart's diaries for this period: did she feel that by hanging on in the Dryhead she was winning over her enemies? One of the odd dynamics of remote homesteading was that the "losers" often went on to much easier, more productive lives. Quitting the homestead might have been seen in the neighborhood as an act of cowardice, but if it meant moving to a promising career in a growing metropolitan area, it could prove to be a smart move. Those who held on to their homesteads saw themselves as "winners," but by some standards—such as having indoor plumbing—they comparatively suffered. Their victory was in their stubbornness itself, rather than any riches it brought.

If Lockhart gained victory over her enemies, in most cases it was of this nature. She was more stubborn. Furthermore, in most cases her "enemies" were not even aware of an ongoing contest. Lockhart seemed to understand that she was a bit irrational in seeing her life this way. But in almost every case there was a genuine clash, a true incident, an actual competition for resources that she blew into a feud. Hank Lane, Joe Smith, and the Barrys really were competing with her for range and survival on the Dryhead—and they probably rustled cattle and cut fence to do so. Ernest Goppert and Len Leander Newton really had sought to regulate Lockhart's personal life; Kate "Steppy" Lockhart really had served in the always-antagonistic role of stepmother. At this point in Lockhart's story, as the enemies fade away, we can see the way Lockhart had fit them into dramatic roles: the way they once antagonized her, the way that energized her to pursue important ambitions, and the way she childishly devoted attention to the battles rather than the ambitions. Their roles in her life follow a certain logic. There's only one exception: Dr. Frances Lane. Lane is gone and Lockhart no longer obsesses over her, but the doc's role in Lockhart's life is an enigma.

In the 1940s Lockhart did make peace with folks from earlier in her life. A childhood friend from Sterling, Illinois, came out to visit—the first Sterling friend she'd seen since leaving more than fifty years previously. Roy and Grace Edgington also came to visit, and the two sisters finally buried the hatchet. (Grace, however, did temporarily convince Lockhart that she'd been born in 1870 rather than 1871.)

She revised her Dryhead novel and boasted at one point of doing a third rewrite. She variously titled it "That Wicked Woman," "The Witch of Willow Creek," "Black Widow," "The Madam," and "Two Black Sheep," but publishers continued to reject it. She also contributed the "Dryhead News" column to the Red Lodge newspaper, mirroring the role of many older women in outlying districts: compiler of social notes. Of course, Lockhart's notes had their own unusual view of life:

> Ever since he went to the mat with a skunk that turned on the tear gas, Dave Good of the L-Slash Heart ranch, Dryhead, has been a lonely man, avoided by his friends and shunned by his neighbors.
>
> Hearing a ruckus in the chicken house at midnight, Dave grabbed his pants, a flashlight, and shotgun and ran to the trouble spot. He located the skunk, busy with his killings, by the flashlight but how to hold his pants, the flashlight, and use the shotgun at the same time presented a serious problem. Good solved it by dropping pants and shotgun and going after said skunk with a club he located.

Similarly, at the end of a list of Dryheaders' responses to President Roosevelt's wartime call to recycle rubber, she noted, "The writer of the deathless prose appearing in this column contributed her reducing girdle thus, so to speak, giving her waistline to her country."

In September 1948 Lockhart sat down to write a letter to Jay Adler, who had recently visited. Things had calmed down between Good and herself—

within months of Mauch's departure she said he was back to being him-self—but now some unnamed incident had brought her again to the end of her rope:

> The main difficulty is in getting someone to take Dave's place, some-one with experience and who has the guts to face a hard winter in here. When it comes to cattle he knows his stuff but outside of that he is and has been a detriment. The place has run down ever since he came as he has no system, no sense of order, and no management. As I told you the neighbors say he has cost me fifty or a hundred thousand dol-lars but this is an exaggeration of course but I would say it has cost me at least thirty thousand by following his advice in the matter of selling etc. Whenever we differ he flies into one of his senseless rages so I have let him have his way against my better judgement. He has cooled off somewhat but it is only an armed truce. . . .
>
> Inside I think he hates me so much that you put your finger on it when you said that he doesn't like anybody who likes me. He 'back-bites' me to my guests and tries to prejudice people against me with whom I have only business dealings. I suspected this for a long time but only knew for a certainty since this all started. He seems sane enough ordinarily and it is only now and then when he's been drink-ing or in a rage that what he is underneath comes out. Then he talks like a lunatic. He is the strangest person that I or anyone else ever met. A dual personality.
>
> When alone here he complains about the work and when I man-age to get help he runs them off. Heretofore I have thought he prob-ably was right but since I have begun to notice I see that it is largely his fault. He expects a man who has been here 24 hours to know as much about the place as he has learned in 20 years.
>
> You say you think I should sell and take life easy but I am here solely because it is home to me and I like it. The money end of it doesn't cut any ice though as a matter of pride I want to make it a financial success. Nor do I want to be driven to sell by Dave against my will.

To outsiders, it had long seemed that only Good's competence and incred-ible capacity for hard work kept the L Slash Heart afloat. Even today most folks assume that Lockhart could not have run the ranch herself: she didn't treat people well enough, didn't know enough about cattle, wasn't a ranch manager. (In other words, she was a woman.) She'd always relied on boyfriends—Ericson, Poole, and then Good—to run the ranch, without ever really comprehending their tasks, just signing the checks and driving away any of the other competent employees who might have helped them make a success of the place.

But her letters to Adler show a woman both smarter and less powerful than this standard view. Smarter: she did know something about ranching. As Spragg noted, it was Good, not Lockhart, who hired most of the drugstore cowboys. And one of the better hands, known only as Craig, wrote to Adler that same year about his departure from the L Slash Heart: "Old Dave made a damn fool out of himself several times in front of me and knew it and knew that I knew it too. He also knew I think that I knew those big stories he told all the time weren't true. . . . There are people like him and nothing will ever change them so the best thing a person can do is forget about them." Could it have been Good, rather than Lockhart, who drove away the talented employees, made the poor decisions that frittered away her fortune, and spewed the venom that ruined their relationship?

After writing to Adler, Lockhart wired her nephew Joe Edgington (Grace's son), getting him and his wife to come for a month-long visit. Edgington had spent a couple of teenaged summers on the ranch and had liked Good. At first he "couldn't believe that I had not exaggerated the situation," Lockhart later explained to Adler, "but changed his mind before he left. He resented Dave's disrespectful manner to me and told him as much." The strategy worked, as Good's behavior improved fitfully over the autumn, and when he left in December for a two-month trip to California, she wrote, "I haven't asked him but think he is figuring on coming back as he is not taking all his 70 years' gatherings. He has simmered down and been like himself lately. Perhaps learning he isn't indispensable has something to do with it."

It's dangerous to take this line of reasoning too far. To view Good as an incompetent villain is as wrongheaded as viewing him as a saint. Craig may have been angling to replace Good as foreman; other employees who complained to Lockhart had probably infuriated Good (probably through laziness) and knew it was him or them; the neighbors who told her how much he had lost her were almost certainly the same ones she'd been feuding with for decades. Yet the poignancy of these letters is that for all of her knowledge of what was actually happening on her ranch, she had little power to do anything about it. Where could she turn for an independent, authoritative view on the competency of a ranch manager? Where could she find a better one? As Spragg said, "a lot of people think they can take advantage of a lone woman." Spragg was thinking of people like Tuffy Abbott, whom he disliked, but he could as easily have been describing Ericson or Poole or perhaps Craig or Pick. Lockhart knew a few things about Good for sure. One was that he was honest. Since he had her best interests at heart, she could forgive his business mistakes (if indeed they were mistakes, if any of the available choices could have made money during those years of drought and Depression). Another was that he was a tireless and devoted worker, with the wisdom of an outdoor life polished to a certain honor and dignity. Even if their romantic relationship had waned, even if he was increasingly hard to get along with, she felt she owed him great loyalty, for the simple reason that he was what she had been searching for all her life: an old-time cowboy. The poignancy is heightened in hindsight, as it appears that his ever-more-erratic behavior had a physiological cause.

In 1949 Lockhart made the reluctant decision to sell nearly all of her cattle. She would continue to live on the ranch, with the garden, milk cow, and chickens, but lease her pastures to neighboring cattlemen. "I hate to sell," she wrote a friend, "as I wanted to try out that Brangus bull and I like my bossies a lot but I've decided, so that's that." Too few quality employees; too little hay or other feed; too many grasshoppers (this had been one of the worst summers yet). Cattle had become a "nuisance." As with the newspaper, you could argue that Lockhart had achieved her ambition—she'd become a successful rancher—and was able to let it go. It wasn't that she saw herself as slowing down. She just wanted to put more effort into her writing. "I am working like mad making alterations in my book," said the same letter, "and I take sadistic pleasure in cutting it as I now see plainly that it is too long and too much detail."

Her ambitions were still powerful, and she kept fixing up the L Slash Heart, installing a grand new fireplace in the main guest cabin. But she was coming to grips with age. "If only I were younger and had help," she wrote to Adler the following month, "I'd buy this whole country to the reservation line and get shet of the entire caboodle [of Dryheaders]. . . . Dryhead deserves the bad name it always has had but in the old days they did their stealing on a big scale where it took guts."

There were signs that, at age seventy-eight, she should leave the Dry-head for a life with less strain and more conveniences. Good still worried about his health and the ranch's condition. Someday he would wear down, and she felt she needed to consider him in her decision making. And since she still owned the house in Cody, it seemed obvious that she should return there. But she dreaded it—both the leaving home and the returning to a town she barely knew anymore.

The winter of 1949–50 was another cold one. Adler sent lemons and grapefruit for Christmas, and Lockhart took them to bed with her so they wouldn't freeze in the kitchen. One day during the coldest spell—thirty be-low night after night—Good took an inspection tour around the house and found a hole at the head of her bed. With only slight exaggeration, he told her he wouldn't have noticed it if he hadn't seen the cat going in.

That March she entered one of her despondent periods. Her book had been rejected again, by Scribners this time. Worse, she could see their point: the end seemed fatuous even to her, and she couldn't figure out how to fix it.

She told Good how blue and discouraged she felt over her writing.

"Why don't you quit?" he said.

"And do what?" she responded.

"Well," he said, "there's lots to do here: You could pull weeds!"

In July she sold the place. Bud DeVoss, a former employee, was willing to give her the fifty thousand dollars she wanted for it. She could also take her time about moving all of her stuff. "I could cry this minute at the thought of leaving but there is nothing else to do in the circumstances," she told Adler. "I know I shall hate living in Cody but won't spend more time there than necessary" between trips to exotic places.

By November 1950 she had fully relocated to Cody. She returned to the large house from which she'd departed twenty-four years previously, and Good moved into an apartment in back of the adjacent rental. He paid no rent, could come and go as he pleased, and even had his own Jeep to drive. He was a great deal of help in the move, but she was rather surprised to hear him say that he hoped to continue to receive his one-hundred-dollar-a-month salary in addition to the room and board. The salary, he expected, would be for waiting on her around town. But she believed she'd be able to do everything by telephone—and, she believed, he would be difficult to get along with.

There were few people left in town that she knew—and fewer still that she wanted to associate with. But, she told Adler, "I'll admit I am enjoying the luxury of steam heat, telephones, baths, and the mail brought to the door instead of hiking up that hill to the mail box twice a week." The floors creaked, the curtains were old, and her bed was a wire chain matrix supporting a single mattress that sagged in the middle. But still, the comfort was miles ahead of the Dryhead.

In January she heard that DeVoss had moved out. Winter in the Dryhead was too cold; he was staying with in-laws down on Crooked Creek. She expected that neighbors and passersby would pick the ranch clean. In February she admitted that DeVoss had not yet made the ten-thousand-dollar down payment on the ranch. He and his brother had a government contract to do flood control work on the Missouri River—and now his brother had been drafted. So he was putting the L Slash Heart back up for sale, at fifty-five thousand dollars. In March she got the ranch back. In April she sold it again, for the same terms: fifty thousand dollars, with ten thousand down and the rest at 5 percent. The buyer was Ike Tippetts, a Lovell Mormon who had already bought many other Dryhead properties, including most of the land directly north of Lockhart's. That pasture had little water, so the acquisition was good for him. She said he'd always treated her fairly—and, of course, she was never the type to look back.

"It wouldn't surprise me if there wasn't a picket-line in front of my house when the book comes out," Lockhart wrote to Adler. After an eighteen-year gap, Lockhart was being published again. It was not, however, her new Dryhead manuscript; it was a reprint of *The Lady Doc*. And it was not coming from a big New York publisher; she paid for the reissue herself.

Even while she still lived out on the Dryhead, booksellers told her that *The Lady Doc* continued to sell well. They urged the new "pocket-book" publishers to come out with a new edition. When that failed, they suggested Lockhart do so herself. Thus, she claimed, it was a business proposition: the bookstores would buy from her, and she could print 650 copies for two thousand dollars. At other times, however, she came close to admitting what townspeople suspected: she was doing it for fun, to tweak Cody's high society and recapture her high profile of bygone days. She even circulated a "key" that listed the novel's fourteen major characters and the historical residents they represented.

The books sold well—she made her investment back—but didn't cause the stir she'd hoped. She found few old-timers left in town anymore, and, actually, the ones who were left had an oddly forgiving nature. When the widowed Ernest Goppert got remarried, he invited Lockhart to the reception. Personal feuds, it seemed, could be buried—except for Lockhart and Lane.

She made some new friends, including Eloise Stock, whose husband was making a lot of money in oil, and Dorothea Nebel, a literary-minded Lovell-area ranch wife. She mentored Lucylle Moon Hall, a local ranchwoman who had run her own dude ranch before getting married in 1927, and was now writing a column for the *Enterprise*. (Hall was honored to be working with her favorite childhood author—she remembered reading *The Dude Wrangler* as a girl and laughing so hard the foreman's wife came out to see what was the matter—though she did say that by now Lockhart was "odd as Nick's nightcap.") Lockhart received occasional visits from old friends in Philadelphia and New York. With some sadness, however, she realized that she was now too old to do much traveling herself. "It is a chore even to dress to go to the bank to attend to business," she wrote to Adler, "and I refuse all invitations for the same reason."

Instead she continued to write. She continued to revise the Dryhead novel and also tried reworking *Old West—and New*. She understood that she needed to update these novels for modern readers, but literary trends baffled her. Reading James Jones's award-winning *From Here to Eternity*, she found it "a fascinating story of army life but the last word in nastiness. I can't see that the filth adds to it." Norman Mailer's *The Naked and the Dead* was not much better. By contrast, Nicholas Monsarrat's best-selling (though now largely forgotten) war novel *The Cruel Sea* she found wonderful but a tad discouraging since "it makes my efforts seem so puny that I fair blush at my conceit in thinking I could write."

Frustrated with fiction, she returned to some shorter magazine pieces. She profiled Carrie Hurlbut, a goat-loving hermit who lived outside of Meeteetse with a huge collection of books, in a piece that was empathetic rather than funny. National magazines rejected it. They also rejected her stories about Link Hannon's days of stealing horses in the Dryhead, the 1913 hunting trip of "Spend a Million" Gates, and an old bootlegger named Poker Nell. She did find homes for most of these stories (several in the Sunday supplement of the *Denver Post*, more than thirty years after she'd left their full-time staff). But in general her magazine work now suffered from the same problem as her fiction: her tales of stubborn individualists were wildly romanticized, but her romanticism didn't conform to the prevailing cowboy mythology.

She also spent a good deal of time managing her money and household. With proceeds from the sale of the ranch, continued family income from Kansas, and the appreciation of her various investments, her assets grew at one point to two hundred thousand dollars, "invested in loans, stocks, tenant houses, etc.," she wrote to Adler. "So many people seem to think that because I have no one but myself to support, it doesn't matter too much whether they return what they borrow or not. But as a matter of pride I don't figure on being an easy mark so it's not too often that they get away with it but it takes a lot of my time." One of her favorite loans was to a young couple trying to start a small cattle ranch up the Southfork: a chance to help create a real-life Vance Galloway.

She also sold or gave away many of her old mementos. She sent Adler some mountain sheep horns, saying, "'Squaw' Smith (Me-Smith) gave them to me a long time ago. I forget whether he said he killed the sheep or stole them. Probably the latter." She asked thirty-five dollars for "an old buffalo rug upon which Chief Plenticoos insisted upon sleeping when he came to visit me. . . . I hate to part with my Indian keepsakes but I have no room for them and just keep them in my trunks."

She especially contemplated her relations with Indians—indeed, she seemed to pay more attention to Native Americans now in reflection than she had when she lived just a few miles from the reservation. "Yesterday we went over to the reservation," she wrote to Adler, speaking of herself and visiting Philadelphian Marie Louise Hopper, "and put up the stone I had made to mark the grave of Other Buffalo. She was one of Chief Plenticoos' wives and my crony. It was a desolate spot and we had trouble finding it. The old Indians I haven't seen for 30 years knew me as soon as they saw me. They looked forlorn and down at the heels and I could have wept at the change in them. It's a lasting shame and disgrace the way the government has treated the Indians."

She had lots of complaints about the government. "We have become a nation of spendthrifts and grafters, in my notion," she began one rant to Adler. Another said, "How do you feel about the [Senator Joe] McCarthy feud?

I'm for him myself and think if there were a few more with his courage we would be better off." Labor unions and blacks also came in for criticism, and she was continually dismayed at people who collected "gimme checks" from the government. Despite the fact that she no longer wanted to pay Good, she was absolutely devastated when he applied for a seventy-five-dollar-a-month government pension.

In 1954 she got a new pet. It arrived via airplane. It was very cute, she reported, but not as housebroken as she'd hoped. It was a skunk, specially descented, and she named it Whiffy.

Lockhart worked hard at reconnecting with her wider family. Grace and Roy came to visit, as did their daughter Sylvia Crowder, now grown and with a family of her own. Lockhart even looked up a cousin in San Diego she'd never met and sent the woman a plane ticket. They got along delightfully. One summer Lockhart agreed to host Crowder's daughter Caroline Sue, a high school sophomore, for a solo visit of several weeks. Lockhart and Good met Caroline Sue at the airport and took her to the fledgling Buffalo Bill museum, which had sprouted in the park once purchased for the statue. They hired a young injured cowboy to drive the girl around Yellowstone, invited the Nebels to come over and bake cookies, and took Caroline Sue to a drive-in movie. Lockhart and Good were comfortable companions, Caroline Sue remembers, with little tension between them. Lockhart didn't get out much—she was heavy and slow moving—but friends came to visit. She enjoyed little home rituals such as the tradition, every evening before retiring, of taking some beer and Limburger cheese.

She was still writing. Lockhart would spend hours at the typewriter while Caroline Sue wandered around on her own, or pored over the scrapbooks of articles by Suzette. (Partly inspired by them, Caroline Sue went on to major in journalism in college.) "She was a lovely lady," Caroline Sue recalls, "loving and generous in her particular way. She always took an interest in me, and my schooling. My mother just adored her. . . . She was a forthright and prickly woman, who said what she thought. That Lockhart [family] temper was still around. But when I knew her she wasn't vindictive or bitter."

Friends encouraged Lockhart to finally set aside her novels and write her memoirs. Nobody really knew all the things that had happened to her, all her experiences in Boston and Philadelphia, the explorations of a bygone West. When she'd arrived in Cody, she'd venerated the "old-timers," but now all of them were gone and she was one herself. Her own stories came to represent the hallowed cowboy past she'd once admired in others. What's more, she represented a link between cowboys and culture. Eldridge—who had continued as a loyal friend and faithful correspondent—continually expressed astonishment at the accomplishments of her career and wanted to know, for example, how and why she had decided to write books.

She hesitated. "It may all be wasted work as the younger generation don't seem interested in anything but cars, gadgets, movie stars, TV, and their own inconsequential doings," she wrote Adler. She thought it'd be better to "rewrite some short stories and bring them up to date. That doesn't leave much spare time." What's more, she added in a puzzling mixture of absurdity and insight, "I have such a horror of old people who reminisce that I've never talked about myself and consequently nobody knows what I've seen and done. I may over-rate myself but I do think that if I had had someone to advise and steer me right I could have gone to the top. I had such wonderful opportunities and through ignorance and inexperience brushed them off. But that's water over the dam."

But she did go back through "some of my scrapbooks and little pen-pictures of people I have met [that] might be of interest." She apparently planned the memoir not with any formal outline but as a tour of interesting characters she'd known. To compose it, on any given day, she would sit down at the typewriter, roll in the backside of an old piece of paper, and recall an episode.

She recounted famous people she had interviewed in Boston and Philadelphia, such as freethought orator Robert Ingersoll, boxer Gentleman Jim Corbett, and financier Jay Cooke. She reviewed her trip to Paris for the 1900 World's Fair. She recalled the fire in Honduras that had burned her manuscript. Her memory may have been failing, because she told several of the stories more than once.

Or perhaps she simply enjoyed telling the stories, reviewing her life. To an occasional visitor she might show pictures, say, of a young blonde girl on a first-generation bicycle or in a first-generation diving suit. That was a way to tell the stories. And here was another way, for an audience that was always waiting: her typewriter. Her various memoirs on the beginning of her journalism career, for example—now all boxed together in her archives—cover many of the same scenes, using much of the same language. It was almost like she wanted to repeat these stories in order to make them true—especially since some of them were demonstrably false. She almost always claimed that she got the *Boston Post* job at age seventeen, walking into the editor's office and coming out with an assignment to interview the circus freaks. She almost always suggested that she came to Cody because of Buffalo Bill's fame, never because of Andrew McKenzie's love. She often reviewed her time working as a maid for the Osage chief Baconrind, and never mentioned the following week, when her boyfriend drowned and she was briefly accused of his murder. Indeed, she never mentioned any lover. She may have decided that she needed to whitewash her life for the prudish small-town audience she saw all around her (especially since she herself was disgusted by the frank discussions of sexuality in contemporary literature). To today's readers, however, the omissions, and the white lies she must tell to accomplish them, give her memoirs a sense of unreality. This is not a woman telling the truths of her life, trying to explain herself. Rather, it is the journalist-novelist—accustomed to telling the stories of others, exaggerating the facts to turn people into heroes and villains—now applying those tools haphazardly to episodes of her past.

It is, undoubtedly, an old woman's right: to tell stories of her life that put herself in the best light. In these memoirs Lockhart becomes something of a cowboy girl: raised on a southwest cattle ranch, stifled in the East, exploring the West on her own. She is an adventurer, a horsewoman, and a stoic hero. She is perhaps at times foolish, such as when she buys a run-down newspaper all by herself, but the memoirist gives a tone of comic nostalgia to it all: who could believe, in these glorious modern times, the sorts of challenges that faced a person in the Old West?

No story did Lockhart repeat with more frequency than that of her feud with Dr. Frances Lane. She would cover the same territory: Marko Ferko's abominable care, the government investigation, Ferko's lawsuit, and *The Lady Doc*. Today in the archives, you can look at numerous copies of the same story, typed, sometimes edited in pen, and set aside; you can visualize an old woman lost in her reminiscences, writing stories in which she vanquishes her enemies.

You imagine her, too, lingering over the pictures. A portrait of Sourdough Sam hung in her living room, in a "museum" of remembrances of the Old West. Her scrapbooks contain dozens of pictures of the Dryhead: her log cabin. The Pryors. A lone juniper against the limestone palisades. The big cottonwoods below the cabin. The living room. The corrals, from above.

Trees and hills and badlands, fences and corrals, horses. You imagine her seeing all these things, seeing them as the West, seeing herself as the cowboy in the West. Seeing her home.

In one of the memoirs, she tells the Lady Doc story a little bit differently than she had in the others. The new material starts with her discussion of the government investigation into the Lane-Bradbury hospital, as she recalls that "those of the townsfolk who had criticized the hospital and its doctors most strongly [before the inspection began, now] had reversed themselves completely." We see some of the bitterness sneaking through: when she went after Lane she thought she had had the blessing of the town, thought she was speaking for everybody. It wasn't so much that she cared nothing for public opinion, but that she had misjudged it. "All hope," this memoir continues, "that the facts I had presented would clear me of the charge of personal animosity toward these doctors—and Lane in particular—faded as I read [the government report]. And to this day there are many who still believe it." The public backed away; her friends believed the government instead of her. She felt betrayed. No wonder she kept pursuing the crusade.

Perhaps spurred by this slightly-more-confessional tone than she'd taken in other drafts of the story, she now continued, "I think rather that my feeling toward her was one of disgust as I knew her to be, not a hermaphrodite as some contended, but a sexual pervert. I learned this when upon an occasion we shared—at her insistence—a lower berth in a Pullman. She made advances to me that no one could possibly misunderstand and after that our friendly relations cooled perceptibly. Up to now, I never have mentioned this incident."

It was homophobia that fueled her hatred of Lane. The same sentiment fueled her hatred for Marjory Ross and nearly ended her friendship with Paul Eldridge. Her homophobia was both reinforced and repressed by the era: she didn't think she knew anybody who approved of homosexuality, but then she didn't know anybody who talked about it. Lane and Ross never talked about their love. Eldridge never talked about the cowboys in the bunkhouse. Lockhart simply assumed that everyone else was—or should have been—as sickened by such behavior as she was. And so she apparently figured that any woman of Cody who admired Lane must have had an affair with her. Any man who tolerated Lane was at best a wimp and at worst a "pervert" himself.

That's one of many ways to interpret this passage of the memoir. She'd "never mentioned this incident"—maybe that was because she was just now inventing it, like she was inventing her first interview assignment with Boston's circus freaks. Perhaps this was her latest slander against her mortal enemy, a final arrow she'd invented to put in her quiver. Or maybe she'd twisted it in her memory: maybe it was Lockhart who made the advance, finally submitting to a deeply suppressed desire, and it was Lane who rebuffed it, to Lockhart's never-ending shame. After all, homophobia and homosexual desire are tightly interwoven. But taken at face value, the passage rings true. (Most of the incidents she invented for the memoirs came from early in her life; her depictions of Cody are slanted but essentially verifiable.) Again, you can imagine Lockhart lost in her memories at the typewriter, suddenly recalling the horror of that Pullman berth. She need not have been the initiator: perhaps she simply felt her body responding in a way she did not want to be right.

I like to imagine another image tacked on to that one: this was the *last* time Lockhart wrote up the vignette of herself and the Lady Doc. (None of the manuscripts is dated, so it's impossible to tell.) When she had confessed the source of her hatred, when she had disgorged that pearl, she was free. She could complete the transformation of the last decade of her life: from a woman consumed by ambition and embittered by the untrustworthiness she saw in everyone around her, to one content to live out the last years of her life in a dusty house on a back street of a town in the middle of nowhere.

"Let me introduce myself," said the voice from the box in Lockhart's bedroom. She was surrounded by Dave Good, a woman named Betty Lou who was renting the adjacent house, and a bunch of kids from the neighborhood. The kids—"little monsters," she called them playfully—would yell and quarrel and fight, a dog would bark, and Whiffy the skunk would run hither and yon. Lockhart had acquired the first television set in the neighborhood, and everyone was gathered to watch. "I'm Hopalong Cassidy," the voice continued.

Created as a rough-and-tumble young cowboy at about the same time that Lockhart was creating *Me-Smith*, Hopalong Cassidy in Hollywood had become a teetotaling middle-aged do-gooder. In the early 1950s the sixty-six Hoppy movies were recut to show on television; Lockhart and her troupe watched this cowboy story.

In it, Hoppy is thoroughly scrubbed, clean shaven, and dressed all in black. He rides an all-white horse. He belts his well-creased slacks high across his waist. He never goes anywhere without his clean black cowboy hat, or without his dual-holster gun belt. He quite frequently wears his spurs indoors. The only work he ever seems to perform is a lazy cattle drive, always with a backdrop of scenic mountains and majestic music. He is friendly, patient, even tempered, good humored, and asexual. He regularly erupts in a warm, honking, throaty guffaw. There could be nobody more trustworthy. Frequently the plots involve strangers—often helpless women—who hesitate to trust him.

"You can trust me," he says to a wounded girl in *Devil's Playground*.

"I can trust no one."

"That's unfortunate. But you'll feel different in the morning."

The Hoppy movies are set in a simple world, a child's fantasy world, magical and surreal. Stepping into a western landscape is like stepping through the looking-glass, into a Wild West anybody can find tame. It is tame because Hoppy will always protect you. It is tame because cowboys are the world's most avuncular men, wearing modified Batman costumes, and all you have to do to be happy is to trust one.

In Lockhart's earlier years, a western book or movie would prompt her to complain about the author's incompetence, the importance of a realistic portrayal, her own relative merits, and the injustices that had eclipsed her star. But she watched Hopalong Cassidy peacefully. She didn't get upset at what it had to say about cowboys, or the West, or her career. "You would laugh," she wrote warmly to Nebel about the menagerie gathered in her bedroom, but only because of the way their eyes were glued to the screen. "The programs are mostly horrors," she wrote to Adler, "but I suppose they will get better later on."

Epilogue

One day in the late 1950s, Dave Good stepped out his door to see the world, dressed only in his pajamas and a Stetson hat. Despite his years of fear about stomach cancer, his mind went before his body did. He forgot the names of his friends; he quarreled with most of them. Lockhart tried to move him into her guest room, but the care he required proved too much. (By one account, he so threatened her that she had to start carrying a gun.) He moved into a rest home, where he lived to the age of ninety-one.

Aged eighty-eight herself, Lockhart found a new boyfriend. His name was Vern Spencer, and he was a much younger man—in his sixties. Tall, black eyed, balding, and black haired, with a tanned, leathery face, he too was a Cody old-timer, a former hunting guide and bodyguard for Buffalo Bill. He now lived in a shack down the alley from her. One of the final remaining photographs of Lockhart is at the head of a Fourth of July parade in 1960, riding in the back of a car with Spencer and another old-timer. The parade marked the opening of the Cody Stampede, which had become Cody's biggest annual event. (It remains so today, in a town so infused with cowboy character that it describes itself as the rodeo capital of the world.) In the picture all three old-timers wear cowboy hats and gaze at the camera. Lockhart's hair is swept away from her heavily wrinkled face. Her facial hair is trimmed and her neck wattles are covered by a filmy scarf. Her thin lips are set squarely, though not unhappily—peacefully.

In the spring of 1962, the ninety-one-year-old Lockhart became ill and went to the hospital. She stayed for three months, eating only when the ever-attendant Spencer fed her, and shriveled to ninety pounds. Finally on July 25 she went to sleep for the last time. Her niece Sylvia Crowder wrote, "She was really ill only with the burdens of so many years, and dying released her to go on and on, adventuring, as she loved to do." Lockhart had requested no funeral, though Crowder, Dorothea Nebel, and Eloise Stock organized a small private memorial.

The aftermath was sad. The Crowders found things missing from the house that should have been there; they had to assume that Lockhart with her hazy memory had given them away. Spencer accused them of mishandling her papers and mementos, though he may have merely been jealous that the bulk of her estate went to family. He did get to keep some of her ashes. The rest were scattered by plane, following her wishes, over "the most convenient peak."

Lockhart's obituaries—published only in Cody and Billings—outlined the framework of her life, taken from the stories she had told during her last decade. With so many old-timers already gone, there was nobody left to speak with independent authority on the quality of her writing or the value of her ideals. Her own stories were both vague and self-congratulatory, all the nuance polished out of them in the way she thought the market wanted. When applied to her own life, this technique made her seem out of touch with her own experiences, uninvested in the motives for her most extreme actions, more of a publicity hound than a pioneer. Yet they were all anyone had to judge her by. Her novels remained out of print, and an important set of scrapbooks and documents (including the revelation of the source of her hatred for Lane) remained unavailable to the public until 2001.

The Dryhead continued to empty of people. In the late 1960s the federal government built a dam on the Crow Reservation, backing up the Bighorn River into a seventy-mile-long lake at the bottom of its deep canyon. The federal government bought up most of the land around the canyon, including the old Lockhart and Barry places, to be part of a National Recreation Area. A road was paved from Lovell to a boat ramp called Barry's Landing, three miles short of Lockhart's ranch. Despite the blacktop, it remains one of the more remote recreation spots in the remote state of Montana, generally used only by powerboaters on summer weekends. When they go home, the Dryhead reverts to being less populated than it was when Lockhart arrived.

As a writer, Lockhart remained undiscovered. In the years after her death, bolstered by feminism, many readers rediscovered the work of early twentieth century women writers such as Willa Cather, Edith Wharton, Kate Chopin, and Sarah Orne Jewett. But this movement was chiefly interested in enduring literary quality, and Lockhart did not fit. Other critics rediscovered the western, gave credit to Owen Wister, and found in Zane Grey and Louis L'Amour if not literary quality then at least meaningful, well-constructed representations of the American self-image. But this movement was chiefly interested in mythic narratives and questions of masculinity, and Lockhart did not fit. More recently, critics rediscovered female westerns, celebrating Helen Hunt Jackson, Mary Hallock Foote, and B. M. Bower. But this movement was chiefly interested in countering the cowboy worship of male writers, and Lockhart did not fit.

As a historical personage, too, Lockhart faded. Though feminists became interested in women of the West, many sought stories of oppression: women dragged west against their will, enslaved by their husbands' adventuring spirits. Lockhart did not fit. Some feminists looked for heroes among middle-class political activists such as Dr. Frances Lane, and again Lockhart did not fit. Some sought women who, ahead of their time, embodied racial tolerance, political progressiveness, and a cultural sophistication that brought the West out of its campfire-tale past. Lockhart, emphatically, did not fit.

Through the 1970s a Cody historian named Lucille Patrick worked tirelessly to transcribe Lockhart's 1918–42 diaries and interview her Dryhead neighbors. But Patrick was horrified by what she found: the affairs, the elitism, the feuds, the murder contract. Her 1984 book *Caroline Lockhart* (written under the name Lucille Patrick Hicks) confirmed local legends that Lockhart was a monster.

Meanwhile, on the Dryhead, National Recreation Area employees pondered what to do with the old Lockhart ranch. After years of neglect the buildings had fallen into disrepair. But it was an intriguing historic restoration project, a pretty site representing a bygone way of life. Seeking details on how it looked during Lockhart's ownership, NRA employees interviewed people who had been there.

In September 1990 they went out to the ranch with Pete Spragg, the cowboy who had once fallen for Lockhart's cooks, now seventy-one years old. As they toured the buildings, he told them stories of the old days. He also discussed the unsavory character of some of the Dryheaders and the ways he felt their input had unfairly skewed Patrick's book ("Reading that book is just like a jury being allowed to hear the prosecuting testimony, but not being allowed to hear the defendant's testimony in a trial").

The transcript of Spragg's interview has a fascinating give-and-take. Everything's quite friendly, but the NRA employees keep trying to guide the conversation back to practical issues such as the locations of walls and furnishings, the presence of chickens or turkeys, the daily routines of a remote 1930s ranch. Spragg, however, veers off into pronouncements on reputation ("She was really a very successful woman in ways—before human nature would accept the woman as being successful"), and stories, such as the next-to-last time he visited the ranch, in March 1943. He brought his young wife and six-week-old son. That night a heifer was born, and at breakfast Lockhart announced that "little Pete" was now a stockman, since she was giving the baby this calf. She wanted Big Pete to raise the calf and her female offspring, saving the money for Little Pete's education. But Big Pete got drafted and, after the war, left ranching. He forgot about the calf until one day not long before Lockhart's death, when she sent him a note to come get Little Pete's bonds. When she'd sold out her stock, that heifer and her two calves had a special L-P brand, and the money from their sale had gone into bonds in Little Pete's name.

Long into their time on the Dryhead, Spragg and his interviewers finally get to a topic of mutual interest: livestock. "She had some mighty fine horses," Spragg begins, and then goes into a lengthy discussion of breeds, gaits, origins, and uses. As he then launches into the ways she experimented with cattle breeding—whiteface, angus, brangus—you'd think he was talking about any rancher, not one who was so often dismissed for her gender.

This discussion thus provides Spragg's greatest testament to the woman, more convincing than the stories or the pronouncements or the condemnations of her enemies. Because in admiring her cattle and horses, he honors her own ambitions. Of all of them—fame, fortune, literary reputation, and domestic happiness—perhaps her most cherished was the one he acknowledges she achieved. To run an Old West cattle ranch. To be a cowboy girl.

ACKNOWLEDGMENTS

I have been blessed with not only the opportunity to pursue this fascinating story but also much help along the way. My biggest thanks go out to Lockhart's previous biographers: Necah Stewart Furman's meticulous *Caroline Lockhart: Her Life and Legacy* provided numerous fruitful avenues for research, and Lucille Patrick Hicks's lively *Caroline Lockhart: Liberated Lady* added dozens of priceless anecdotes. Additionally, a wider community of folks interested in Lockhart gave me welcome and encouragement, especially David Dominick, Frank Boyett, and Chris Finley.

The Montana Committee for the Humanities and the Matthew Hansen Endowment at the University of Montana School of Forestry provided small grants at key moments to help my research. Clark Whitehorn and Annie Gilbert Coleman helped guide me through the relevant scholarship. Research thanks also to my interviewees, including Caroline Sue Dowling, David Dominick, Lucille Patrick, Oscar and Jane Thompson, Gene and Dorothy Spragg, and Ramona Warren. I relied on numerous libraries, archives, and museums—often small, rural, unheralded ones—and I'd like to make special thanks to those people who preserve local history and genealogy. Folks who trace the lineage and write down the stories of local individuals are some of history's most valuable yet underappreciated contributors. Finally, thanks to the following for going out of their way to help with research: Angie Hazelswart, Leslie Shores, Mary Robinson, Betty Obendorf, Henry Boyle, Liza Nicholas, Victoria Lamont, Rhonda Spaulding, Janie Dollinger, Charlene Porsild, Terry Buckaloo, Ava Bretzik, Cathryn Clayton, Ellen Knight, Jeannie Cook, Linda Fagan, Mary Scriver, Bud Webster, Art Kidwell, Julia Kanellos, Denny McAuliffe, Rich Furber, my colleagues on the WriterL listserv, and the incomparable Bob Moran.

I was moved by the support and encouragement of many people, including especially Paul and Jackie Clayton, Cathy Clayton, Gary Ferguson, Chasmo Mitchell, Mark Sherouse, and the following reviewers: Sue Hart, Frank Boyett, Mark Spragg, David Dominick, Dave Stauffer, and Sue Bury. (Of course, all mistakes that remain are my responsibility.) For publishing advice, I thank Clark Whitehorn, Dawn Marano, Chuck Rankin, and Nancy Jackson. At the University of Nebraska Press, I'd especially like to thank Elizabeth Demers, who first committed to the project; Heather Lundine, who gave it life; Ann Baker, my editor;

Annie Shahan, who designed the book and cover; and Kate Salem, who coordinated publicity. Thanks also to my freelance copyeditor, Jeanée Ledoux.

During the research and writing of this book I met, wooed, and married the love of my life, Kari Clayton. Her brutal edits have improved this book immeasurably; more important, her vivacious spirit gives my life the magical joy that Caroline Lockhart never found.

NOTES

The notes below discuss my sources for the facts of the story. Because Lockhart tended to overdramatize, scholars who are extremely cautious may be advised to be skeptical about some of the events and dialogue she claims to have witnessed. But I believe the following factors mitigate in favor of trusting these recollections: (1) Lockhart always worked from experience; for a fiction writer she had a remarkably limited imagination. (2) If I could disprove anything, I either highlighted that fact or kept it out of the book. In my research I was continually surprised at how many of Lockhart's doubtful statements were fully supported by circumstantial evidence. (3) Memory is a tricky thing for any of us—not necessarily trickier for Lockhart than for someone less colorful. The notes will indicate that certain passages are probably exaggerated, but one could say the same about almost any autobiographical account.

ABBREVIATIONS

BBHC Buffalo Bill Historical Center, Cody, Wyoming

BCNRA Bighorn Canyon National Recreation Area, Lovell, Wyoming

BP   *Boston Post*

CE   *Cody Enterprise*, including the *Park County Enterprise* prior to 1921 (at Park
County Library, Park County Historical Archives, or Buffalo Bill
Historical Center)

CL   Caroline Lockhart

CLC   Caroline Lockhart Collection, American Heritage Center, University of
Wyoming, Laramie, Wyoming

CLD   Caroline Lockhart's diaries. The originals are at the American Heritage
Center; photocopies are at the Lockhart-Furman Collection; and a brief typed
transcript is in the Lucille Patrick files at Park County Historical
Archives. (Most, though by no means all, of the diaries are excerpted in Hicks,
Caroline Lockhart.)

ES   *Eskridge Star*, Public Library of Eskridge, Kansas

JAP   Jay Adler Papers, SC1299, Montana Historical Society Library

KSHS Kansas State Historical Society Archives, Topeka, Kansas

LFC   Lockhart-Furman Collection, MS30, Buffalo Bill Historical Center, Cody, Wyoming
MHS   Montana Historical Society Library, Helena, Montana
OCC   *Osage County (Kansas) Chronicle*, Kansas State Historical Society Archives
OCP   *Ogle County (Illinois) Press*, Public Library of Polo, Illinois
PB   *Philadelphia Bulletin*
PCHA   Park County Historical Archives, Cody, Wyoming
PCL   Park County Library, Cody, Wyoming
SG   *Sterling (Illinois) Gazette*, Public Library of Sterling, Illinois
SPL   Public Library, Sterling, Illinois

PROLOGUE

3   *village, called Altyn*: "Copper Is King," *Swift Current Courier*, September 1, 1900, MHS.

3   *the richest and biggest*: "Copper Is King."

4   *across the summit*: *Dupuyer Acantha*, August 29, 1901, MHS.

4   *spry old man*: CL, from an untitled manuscript quoted in Dominick, "Introduction," 14. This old-age memoir of Lockhart's is not entirely reliable; for example, nowhere else is McNeill called "Sourdough Sam." It may have been her pet nickname for him, or it may have been a detail she later fabricated to improve the story.

5   *rough trail*: CL, "Girl in the Rockies," *Lippincott's*, August 1902; and "Granite Park Chalet Guest Information" brochure (September 2003).

5   *long-legged sorrel*: CL, from an untitled manuscript quoted in Dominick, "Introduction," 16. Subsequent quotes in this section are from the same source. My experience on the trail suggests Lockhart's account is perhaps overdramatized but basically true. For example, for horses slipping over cliffs, see Guthrie, *First Ranger*, 81.

1. BORN ON A HORSE

9   *Joe Lockhart*: Information about Lockhart in Illinois comes from the following sources: Carroll County real estate records for 1855–1930, Mt. Carroll, Illinois; Ogle County real estate records for 1855–1930, Oregon, Illinois; photo reproduced in Furman, *Caroline Lockhart*, center spread; Muster and Descriptive Rolls, Seventh Illinois Cavalry, Company B, Illinois State Archives; Thiem, *Carroll*, 137; Worster, *River*, 52; OCP, various issues 1869–73; 1870 Carroll County census, p. 96, Lanark Public Library, Lanark, Illinois.

10   *Sarah gave birth*: Caroline always gave her birthplace as Eagle Point, which is the name of the Woodruffs' neighborhood. So she may have been born at her mother's parents' house rather than at her own parents' house in Elkhorn Grove, which is quite close though separated by a county line. No record of the birth exists, and Hicks (*Caroline Lockhart*, 1) suggests Lockhart was born in 1870. But the 1870, 1875, and 1880 census data back up Lockhart's claim that she was born in 1871.

11 *Wakarusa*: Information about the Lockhart farm comes from the following sources: 1875 Kansas census, vol. 56, p. 10, KSHS; West, *Growing*; Kathryn Adam in Armitage and Jameson, *Women's West*, 95.

11 *largest mule*: "Local Notes," OCC, February 7, 1878.

12 *I was born on a horse*: Vern Spencer, quoted in Culpin, *Caroline Lockhart Ranch*, 1.

12 *Burlingame*: Information about the Lockharts in Burlingame comes from the following sources: OCC, various issues 1878–82; Kansas tract books and county real estate records, 1840–1930, KSHS.

12 *A children's party*: "Local Notes," OCC, March 6, 1879.

13 *terms and prices reasonable*: Advertisement, OCC, May 20, 1880.

13 *Our earliest recollection*: "Lockhart," *Burlingame Enterprise*, May 16, 1912, provided by Linda Fagan.

13 *I lived in a Western town*: CL, "My First Proposal," BP, undated in CLC 2:6.

14 *the word "cowboy"*: Information on cowboys, ranching, and homesteading comes from the following sources: Jordan, *North American*, 267–75; Worster, *River*, 338–39; Meinig, *Shaping*, 164–67; Malin, *Winter Wheat*, xii; Bowden, "Desert Wheat," 194–96; Wrobel, *Promised*, 53–58.

16 *Who's that boy*: CL, "My First Proposal." Since Lockhart was writing to entertain, this account is probably not the strict truth. (For example, she claims she was thirteen, but at that age her school was in Illinois, not Kansas.) But she was in her mid-twenties when she wrote it, close enough in time to have accurately remembered numerous details.

17 *didn't care about*: CL, *Man from*, 12–13.

17 *Paperback novels*: Information on novels and gender comes from the following sources: Sullivan, *Our Times*, 210–16; Johnson, "Memory," 501; Slotkin, *Gunfighter*, 145; Slotkin, *Fatal*, 87 and 307; Etulain, *Telling*.

18 *If you wear*: CL, untitled memoir, LFC box 1.

18 *thought the frontier no place*: Adler manuscript, JAP folder 7.

18 *Sterling*: Information on the Lockharts in Sterling comes from the following sources: Wallace, *Past and Present*, 1385; Gale, "Woman Author"; Bayliss notebooks 178 and 250, Sterling Historical Museum, Sterling, Illinois; 1885 Kansas census, Burlingame, p. 50, KSHS; Sterling directory 1883 and 1887–88, SPL.

19 *natural writer*: Ward, "Writer."

19 *nose for news*: "Famous Author." The Crawford, Clark, and cake episodes are from the same source.

20 *Captain Mortlake*: Information on William F. Cody's theatrical career, including quotations from contemporary critics, comes from Sagala, *Buffalo Bill, Actor*, 38–52, 67, 242–47, 345.

22 *Bethany College*: Information on the now-defunct school comes from the following sources: Mrs. Augustus Wilson, untitled, 141–43; Greene, "Sisters of Bethany." Remember the name "Prouty"—Lockhart did.

22 *Few knew she was ill*: "Death of Sarah Lockhart," *occ*, September 6, 1888. Additional information on the Lockharts at this time comes from the following sources: "Local Notes," *occ*, October 4, 1888, and January 3, 1889; "Sarah Lockhart," *ocp*, September 15, 1888; CL, untitled memoir, CLC 1:10, folder 4.

23 *My feet sunk deep*: CL, untitled memoir, CLC 1:10, folder 4. Subsequent quotes from Lockhart in this section are from the same source.

23 *formation of a proper character*: *Catalogue of the Officers*, 12 (italics in original). Additional information on Lockhart's Pennsylvania years comes from the following sources: Ava Bretzik (Asa Packer Mansion Museum, Jim Thorpe, Pennsylvania), personal communications with the author, April 2004; Moss, "Brief History."

24 *With cousins and aunts*: CL, "My First Proposal." The subsequent story of the proposal ("Sa-ay, do you know") is from the same source.

25 *I learned to make Vassar fudge*: CL, untitled memoir, CLC 1:9.

25 *that I guessed I'd have to*: CL, untitled memoir, CLC 1:10, folder 4. Subsequent quotes from Lockhart in the remainder of the chapter are from the same source.

26 *Kate Reed*: The wedding gets brief mention in *sG*, March 14, 1890; the obituary is in *es*, December 16, 1937, in CLC 2:6.

2. STUNT GIRL

31 *There is not a city*: CL, "The Boston Girls' Innocent Bohemia," *bp*, March 1, 1896, CLC 2:4. Subsequent quotes in this section are from the same source.

33 *My enthusiasm for a career*: CL, untitled memoir, in CLC 1:10.

33 *Rosedale*: "Rosedale," unsourced clipping in CLC 2:6. The play opened in Boston in May 1893.

34 *came out of clear sky*: CL, untitled memoir, in CLC 1:10, folder 6.

34 *Nellie Bly was making*: CL, untitled memoir, in CLC 1:10, folder 4. It may be that Lockhart minimized her years in the theater to imply that she'd been directly inspired by Bly's famous trip, rather than entering the field five years later.

34 *A newspaper of the early 1890s*: Information on this era's journalism comes from the following sources: Kroeger, *Nellie Bly*; Teachout, *Skeptic*; Ross, *Ladies*; Staples, *Bay State's*, 11–18; *bp*, February 11, 1894, at the Boston Public Library.

35 *Cub in*: CL, "Stage-Struck Girls," *bp*, undated, CLC 2:6. Subsequent quotes in this section are from the same source, with original spellings. Most of the clippings in Lockhart's scrapbooks lack dates, and the 1890s *Post* is not indexed, so I have made my best guess as to the order of their publication.

38 *Fancy Slippers and Shoes*: Advertisement clipped in an unpaginated scrapbook, CLC 2:6. The clippings are undated but clearly disprove the stories Lockhart told in her late-life memoirs about getting the job based on a single interview.

38 *Her stunts included*: All of the articles mentioned in these two paragraphs are collected in CLC 2:4 and 2:6.

38 *If the boat had not been*: CL, "A Sail Boat during a Blizzard," *bp*, undated, CLC 2:4.

38   *I felt very happy*: CL, untitled memoir, in CLC 1:10, folder 4, p. 23.

38   *McKenzie*: Information on McKenzie is from the following sources: CL, untitled memoir, in CLC 1:10, folder 4, p. 23; "M'Coy's Fight," unsourced, undated, CLC 2:4; "First of the Season," unsourced, undated, CLC 2:4; "A.C. M'Kenzie, Writer, Dead," unsourced, undated, CLC 2:5; Ellen E. Knight (Winchester, Massachusetts, Historical Society), personal correspondence with the author, January 10, 2003.

39   *Hunting for the Festive Rabbit*: CL, "Hunting for the Festive Rabbit," unsourced, undated, CLC 2:4.

39   *William Woods*: "Apologize!" and "Woods Is Sorry," both in BP, undated, CLC 2:6.

40   *Champion Fat Boy*: CL, "Champion Fat Boy of the World," unsourced, undated, CLC 2:4.

40   *freaks on display*: CL, "Museum Boardinghouse," BP, undated, CLC 2:4. In her late-life memoirs Lockhart claimed, incorrectly, that the museum freaks assignment served as a sort of interview/test for *Post* employment.

41   *Buffalo Bill*: CL, "She Rides a Broncho," unsourced, undated, CLC 2:6. Subsequent quotes in this section are from the same source.

42   *now only in the south*: Garceau's essay in Basso, *Across*, 163; see also Frantz, *American Cowboy*; and Etulain, *Owen Wister*.

43   *Now, I want to go*: CL, "Lost in the Fog," *(Boston) Sunday Post*, July 7, 1895, CLC 2:6.

45   *furriner*: CL, untitled memoir, CLC 1:10, folder 6, pp. 30–33.

45   *He is thinking of his life*: CL, "Her Bucking Broncho," BP, undated (but datelined Naskeag Point July 20), CLC 2:6.

46   *There is no vocation*: Cahoon, "Women." Subsequent quotes in this section are from the same source. To me, Cahoon's article reads as if she relied entirely on a single stunt girl. See also Kroeger, *Nellie Bly*, 180–92, 223–24, and 250.

47   *sold his story to the* Watchman: CL, 1898 diaries, CLC 1:17. Additional information on Lockhart's travels comes from the following sources: John E. Wilkie to CL, July 5, 1900, CLC 1:6; Hicks, *Caroline Lockhart*, 14–16; photo of Galloway (remember the name—Lockhart did), CLC 1:5; Dominick, "Introduction," 14; Furman, *Caroline Lockhart*, 18–19; CLD, February 25, 1929.

48   *Ava Willing*: CL, untitled memoir, in CLC 1:10.

49   *correct, conservative*: Ross, *Ladies*, 518.

49   *the maddest, gladdest*: Mencken, *Newspaper Days*, ix.

50   *believes she has been bewitched*: CL, "A Young Girl under a Spell," PB, undated, CLC 2:4.

51   *Iky Segerman's*: CL, "My Dear Newsboys," PB, undated, CLC 2:4.

51   *Any time that you are out*: CL, untitled, PB, February 13, 1903, CLC 2:4.

51   *William Jennings Bryan*: CL, "Suzette Makes the Trip through Delaware with William Jennings Bryan," PB, undated, CLC 2:4.

51   *I was not tired*: CL, "Suzette Trying Her Hand at Cigarmaking; Finds It Rather Pleasant than Otherwise," PB, undated, CLC 2:5.

52   *stout colored woman*: "Suzette's Stories of Everyday Life," PB, undated, CLC 2:5.

53   *Paris*: CL, "'Suzette' Finds Paris and Parisians Not All Her Fond Fancy Painted," PB, July 14, 1900, CLC 2:4.

53   *Ferdinand Peck*: CL, "Suzette Sees the Lafayette Statue Unveiled by Americans in Paris," PB, undated but datelined Paris July 5, CLC 2:4. Additional information on Lockhart in Europe comes from the following sources: CL, "Suzette Sees the Passion Play and Admires Its Fervent Dignity," PB, undated but datelined Oberammergau July 23, CLC 2:4; CL, "Suzette Takes a Plunge in the Surf in a Bathing Suit She Doesn't Approve Of," PB, undated but datelined Ostend Sept. 13, CLC 2:5.

53   *danced up and down*: CL, "Suzette Has an Experience with a Typical Paris Cabman," PB, undated but datelined Paris September 8, CLC 2:4.

54   *we had pigs feet*: CL, "The Sign That Failed," unsourced, undated, CLC 1:11. See also the 1900 census cited in Furman, *Caroline Lockhart*, 21.

54   *There are women of brains*: CL, "Uncle Jerry Roth's Bill to Tax Spinsters Arouses Indignation in True Womanly Hearts," unsourced, undated, CLC 2:4.

55   *Jack Painter*: Information on Painter comes from the following sources: PCHA biographical files; Carrey and Conley, *River*, 174–75; Hicks, *Park County Story*, 166; Hicks, *Caroline Lockhart*, 575–77; Furman, *Caroline Lockhart*, 47–50.

55   *I have a plan*: Undated note preserved in CLC 2:6.

55   *Walnuts and Wine*: Various clips, CLC 2:4, 2:5, and 2:6.

55   *Her Maiden Name*: CL, "Her Maiden Name," *Lippincott's*, June 1901, 745–55, CLC 2:6.

56   *Minz*: Note preserved in CLC 2:6.

56   *The Cowboy Girl*: Unsourced, undated, untitled clipping, CLC 2:4.

3. COWBOY NOVELIST

59   *went over the boulders*: CL, "A Girl in the Rockies," *Lippincott's*, August 1902, CLC 1:5. Additional information on Lockhart in Montana comes from the following sources: CL, "A Train Robber Makes a Call on Suzette in Her Rocky Mountain Home," unsourced, undated, but probably *Lippincott's*, CLC 2:4; Dominick, "Introduction," 15; St. Mary's township 1900 census data, MHS; *Swift Current Courier*, September 1, 1900. It's difficult to analyze how much of Lockhart's Altyn stories are fiction, since the points of comparison (Lockhart's other accounts of her trip) also may be partially fictionalized. I believe the cabin (see Guthrie, *First Ranger*, 80) and dialogue were real, but the train robberies were not. Lockhart herself may not have cared for the literal "truth" so much as she cared to equate horseback stories of adventure with the West. Regarding the frontier, I am especially indebted to the work of Richard Slotkin.

61   *I'm going to see my grandma*: CL memoir quoted in Dominick, "Introduction," 19–21.

62   *Do they live*: "Suzette Visits Grandma Mountain Chicken," unsourced, undated, but probably *Lippincott's*, CLC 2:4. Additional information about Lockhart's time in Blackfeet country comes from the following sources: Lamont, "Native American," 385; Henry Paul Boyle (LaMott's grandson), personal communication with the author, September 25, 2003; Jack Holterman, "Carrasco," in *1998 Blackfoot Genealogy*, 402–4. Spellings of LaMott vary.

63   *dog licked his cold face*: CL, "Straight as a String," unsourced, undated, CLC 1:5 (for the beginning of the story) and 1:6 (for the end).

63   *literary novelists*: Lamont, "Writing," 87.

64   *Miss Lockhart*: Unsourced clippings, likely from CE, October 19, 1904, collected in a scrapbook belonging to Agnes Chamberlain and quoted in Hicks, *Caroline Lockhart*, 26. Additional information on Cody comes from the following sources: Furman, *Caroline Lockhart*, 37–42; Hicks, *Caroline Lockhart*, 26–40; Hicks, *Park County*, 15 and 52; Patrick, "Three Women," 1–11; Bonner, "Buffalo Bill"; Rosetta Greenfield, "Lockhart House—Research," Lockhart file, PCHA; Andrew McKenzie postcard in CLC 2:5; "A.C. M'Kenzie, Writer, Dead," unsourced, undated clipping in CLC 2:5; Beck biographical files, PCHA.

65   *spent the winter*: "Local Notes," ES, April 13, 1905.

66   *a typically frontier town*: CL, untitled memoir, CLC 1:10.

66   *I like this country*: "Young Wyoming Girl Is Creator of Me-Smith," *Denver Times*, May 18, 1912, quoted in Furman, *Caroline Lockhart*, 41.

66   *Suzette Tells about the Man Hunt*: CL, "Suzette Tells about the Man Hunt and Hold Up at Cody," unsourced clipping datelined Philadelphia November 13, CLC 1:11. Subsequent quotes from Lockhart in this section are from the same source.

67   *The artist, in the course*: Mary Hallock Foote, quoted in Casey Bush, "Artist-Author Mary Hallock Foote and Her Angle of Repose," Oregon Cultural Heritage Commission, 2003, http://www.ochcom.org/foote (accessed May 10, 2005).

67   *Suzette Goes on a Hunt*: CL, "Suzette Goes on a Hunt with Buffalo Bill," *Philadelphia Press*, February 5, 1905, CLC 2:6. Information on Codyites' attitude toward Buffalo Bill comes from the following sources: Harvey, *General Historical Survey*, 34; *Northern Wyoming Daily News*, August 27, 1953, in JAP folder 6.

68   *Cody has gone plumb*: CL, "When Autymobile Struck Town," reprinted in Hicks, *Caroline Lockhart*, 34–36.

69   *pretty good riders*: Leaphart diary, July 28, 1905, quoted in Susan Leaphart, "Montana Episodes: Wheelmen in Yellowstone, 1905," *Montana: The Magazine of Western History* 31, no. 4:48–49.

70   *The Second Star*: CL, "The Second Star: A Mormon Story," *Lippincott's*, June 1905, in CLC 1:5. Other stories mentioned in this section include "His Own Medicine," *Lippincott's*, October 1905, CLC 1:5; "Gustave Hinkle: Martyr," *Lippincott's*, June 1907, CLC 1:5; "Stag Hound Bill," *Lippincott's*, March 1905, discussed in Yates, *Caroline Lockhart*, 11.

71 *Doc's Beau*: "Doc's Beau," *The Railroad Man's Magazine*, October 1906, CLC 1:5.

71 *as your own*: "The Woman Who Gave No Quarter," *Lippincott's*, February 1907, CLC 1:5 and 1:11.

71 *If Harrison had had a brain*: "The Pin-Head," *Lippincott's*, October 1908, CLC 1:5.

71 *I'll sell this dudin'-outfit*: "The Dude Wrangler," *The Red Book Magazine*, November 1907, CLC 1:5.

72 *John L. Smith*: Information on Smith comes from the following sources: *Billings (Montana) Gazette*, June 16 and 17, 1926, and February 23, 1926; John Clayton, "The Trials of John L. Smith," *Montana: The Magazine of Western History*, fall 2004; CLD, February 25, 1929; Smith photo, LFC box 1, folder 15.

72 *Smith is somewhere near*: CL, "Cody's Bad Man Runs to Escape a Few Stones," undated, unsourced clipping, CLC 2:4. As literal nonfiction, the piece strains credulity; it's likely one of Lockhart's half-invented sketches. Subsequent quotes in this section are from the same source.

73 *I'm a killer*: CL, *Me-Smith*, 17. Subsequent quotes in this section are from the same novel. For background on the novel, see clippings in CLC 2:5, including *New York Times*, February 12, 1911.

74 *humor and dramatic force*: *New York Times*, March 19, 1911, CLC 2:5.

74 *It is a story of a cowboy*: *New York Globe*, March 11, 1911, CLC 2:5.

75 *Red-blooded realism*: Information on Wister and early 1900s literature comes from the following sources: Basso, *Across*, 1–6; Slotkin, *Gunfighter*, 83, 104, 156–60, 179; Johnson, "Memory," 497; Etulain, *Owen Wister*, 33; Etulain, *Writing*; Etulain, *Telling*, 77; Frantz, *American Cowboy*, 158.

76 *In fiction that country*: *Review of Reviews* (New York), June 1911, in CLC 2:4.

77 *in some wonderful way*: *Birmingham News*, March 25, 1911, in CLC 2:5.

77 *It is worth noticing*: *New York Tribune*, March 5, 1911, in CLC 2:5. For mixed-blood heroines, see Yates, *Caroline Lockhart*, 17–18; the most famous was Helen Hunt Jackson's *Ramona*.

77 *Bertha Muzzy Bower*: I am especially indebted to the work of Victoria Lamont; see "Writing," 139–57. Other information on Bower comes from the following sources: Engen, *B. M. Bower*; Davison, "Author"; and Houston, "Introduction." Engen (vii) makes the claim that publishers actively masked Bower's gender; later sources counter that it was not a cover-up. However, given contemporary critics' reactions to Lockhart (frequently discussing her gender, without mentioning Bower), it seems to me that indeed the effect of Bower's publisher's actions was widespread ignorance that she was a woman.

78 *Mary Hallock Foote*: Information comes from the following sources: Lamont, "Writing," 79–97 and 114; Miller, *Mary Hallock Foote*; Foote, "Maverick," from *The Cup of Trembling, and Other Stories* (1895); Foote, "In Exile," from *In Exile, and Other Stories* (1894).

79 *Frances McElrath*: Information comes from the following sources: Lamont, "Writing," 36–67; Frantz, *American Cowboy*, 161.

79 *legitimacy*: Lamont, "Writing," 146–50.

79 *Once upon a time*: *Boston Globe*, undated, in CLC 2:5. The publicity photo is in the same scrapbook. See also "Young Wyoming Girl Is Creator of Me-Smith," *Denver Times*, undated (though Furman cites it as May 18, 1912), CLC 2:5.

80 *Marko Ferko*: Information on Ferko is from the following sources: D. W. Cole to H. N. Savage, Department of Interior supervising engineer, April 8, 1908, copy in CLC 2:1 (Lockhart or a friend apparently retyped several letters so as to have a record of them, and I have fixed some misspellings in these unedited drafts); "Marko Ferko Damage Suit," undated, unsourced clipping in CLC 2:6; affidavits quoted in Dominick, "Introduction," 37–46, and also summarized in Furman, *Caroline Lockhart*, 53–58; various unsourced, undated clippings, CLC 2:5; CE, June 25, 1909, quoted in Hicks, *Caroline Lockhart*, 659–60. Ferko's name is variously spelled Ferco, Furko, Marco, and so on.

80 *His escape from*: Cole to Savage, April 8, 1908.

80 *What about the leg*: "Marko Ferko Damage Suit."

82 *a piece of wool*: Affidavit quoted in Dominick, "Introduction."

82 *Well, I've got it*: CL, "Back of this petition . . . ," an undated, untitled, unsourced manuscript in CLC 2:1, which is surely Lockhart's draft of the introductory material to the *Denver News* exposé.

82 *youngish and not ill-looking*: CL, untitled memoir, CLC 1:10. Information on Lane comes from the following sources: Lane biographical file, PCHA; "Cody Community Mourns Death of Pioneer and Physician, Dr. Frances M. Lane," an undated, unsourced obituary in CLC 2:6.

83 *Before publishing anything*: "Copy of Letter from the Mayor of Cody, Wyoming, to the Denver News," November 18, 1907, typescript in CLC 2:1. For the *Billings Gazette*, see Patrick, *Best Little*, 118.

84 *I know we all missed you*: John Wilkie (on federal letterhead) to CL, February 19, 1908, April 18, 1908, and June 1908, CLC 1:6 and 2:1.

84 *they offered the best facilities*: Cole to Savage, April 8, 1908.

84 *never yet heard a single complaint*: S. L. Wiley to J. Ahern, March 30, 1908, copy in CLC 2:1.

84 *alleged troubles and dissatisfaction*: Letter from Lane-Bradbury hospital, date obscured, copy in CLC 2:1.

84 *The Reclamation Service whitewashed*: CLD, January 9, 1933.

85 *Marko Ferko . . . is suing*: "Doctors Face Damage Suit," unsourced clipping datelined Cody, February 7, CLC 2:6.

85 *that witnesses had left*: "Marko Ferko Damage Suit."

85 *For nearly two years*: "Doctors Face Damage Suit" (with original spellings).

86 *Yes, we went at night*: "Much Interest Is Shown," undated, unsourced clipping in CLC 2:6. Subsequent quotes in this section are from the same source.

87   *No author to-day*: Untitled, undated, unsourced clipping, CLC 2:5.

87   *The publication this fall*: Clipping from *Bookseller, Newsdealer, and Stationer*, October 1, 1912, CLC 2:5.

87   *Dr. Harpe arose*: CL, *Lady Doc*, 17–18. Subsequent quotes are from the same novel.

87   *abortion*: Information on abortion, satire, homosexuality, and interpretations of *The Lady Doc* comes from the following sources: Yates, *Gender*, 44; Teachout, *Skeptic*, 177–78; Yates, *Caroline Lockhart*, 12 and 23–24; D'Emilio and Freedman, *Intimate Matters*, 122–30; Boag, "Sexuality."

89   *the first unambiguous delineation*: Yates, *Caroline Lockhart*, 23–24.

90   *a disappointing story*: *New York Life*, May 1, 1913; *Detroit Journal*, December 6, 1912; *New York Sun*, October 12, 1912; *Philadelphia Press*, October 5, 1912; all in CLC 2:5.

91   *One could get*: Hicks, *Caroline Lockhart*, 48.

91   *a modern Jean d'Arc*: CL, memoir quoted in Dominick, "Introduction," 45.

91   *authoress of Me-Smith*: The Cody quotes are from the *Park County Herald*, November 15, 1912; *CE*, November 13, 1912; and *CE*, March 13, 1912; all in PCL.

92   *The Lady Doc I hail*: *New York Town Topics*, February 16, 1914, CLC 2:5.

92   *He's come from far*: Grey, *Riders*, 8. Subsequent quotes in this section are from the same novel. Additional background information comes from the following sources: Slotkin, *Gunfighter*, 212–17; Tompkins, *West*, 157–77; Gruber, *Zane Grey*.

94   *Let me out*: CL, *Full of the Moon*, 79–80. Subsequent quotes in this section are from the same novel.

95   *she was a snob*: Hicks, *Caroline Lockhart*, 38.

96   *The situations are impossible*: Reviews quoted from the *Minneapolis Journal*, April 7, 1914; *Chicago Journal*, March 21, 1914; both in CLC 2:5.

96   *uncouth and disrespectful*: CLD, April 7, 1898, in CLC 1:17.

97   *as for the young lady*: *New York Times*, March 1, 1914.

97   *Jack Painter*: See source note at page 55 in the previous chapter.

98   *Honest, now*: CL, "The Wildest Boat Ride in America," *The Outing Magazine* 59, no. 5, February 1912, 515–24, CLC 1:7. (It's reprinted in full in Carrey and Conley, *River*, 30–44.) "Pizen" is poison. Subsequent quotes in this section are from the same source, which strikes me as quite factual, not fictionalized. Additional information on Lockhart in Idaho is from the following sources: Jones, "Salmon River"; Furman, *Caroline Lockhart*, 68–73; Hicks, *Caroline Lockhart*, 575–77.

102 *I am trying to*: Quoted in *Montgomery Advertiser*, February 2, 1912, in CLC 2:5. The snapshots are also in CLC 2:5.

103 *Hi there*: CL, "Washing Out a Pin for Father," *Philadelphia North American*, August 27, 1911, CLC 2:5.

103 *passed through Elk City*: "The News of Elk City," *Idaho County Free Press*, November 14, 1912, quoted in Furman, *Caroline Lockhart*, 183. Additional information on Lockhart's travels comes from the following sources: J. Berg Esenwein, *Studying*

the Short-Story, in CLC 1:13; clippings about Kingston (Joe Lockhart's sister Isabelle Darte lived there) in CLC 2:5; "In the Bitter Roots," playscript in CLC 1:7.

104 *Miss Caroline Lockhart, who sprang into fame*: Jeannette Gilder, *Chicago Tribune*, March 21, 1914, in CLC 2:5.

105 *wanton slaughter*: CL, *Man from*, 31. Subsequent quotes in this section are from the same novel.

107 *It is my misfortune to have*: CL, "Honduras Report Conjures Pictures of Other Revolts," *Denver Post*, undated, CLC 2:6. Additional information on Lockhart in Central America comes from the following sources: "Miss Lockhart in Search of Material," CE, December 24, 1913, quoted in Hicks, *Caroline Lockhart*, 52; Humphrey, *Moon*; Langley and Schoonover, *Banana Men*; http://www.unitedfruit.org/chronology.html (accessed May 19, 2005); Berman, *Moon*; Furman, *Caroline Lockhart*, 73.

107 *They must have had a fire*: CL, untitled memoir, 69–70, CLC 1:9 (I have fixed some misspellings in the unedited draft).

107 *It's disheartening*: "Suzette Loses Novel in Ocean," PB, April 5, 1914, CLC 2:5.

108 *it is one of the best*: "A Chat with You," *Popular Magazine*, undated but probably August 4, 1915, CLC 2:5. The other reviews cited immediately below come from the following sources: NYC *Bookseller*, November 15, 1915; *Grand Rapids News*, December 22, 1915; *Boston Evening Transcript*, November 17, 1915; unsourced, undated; *Boston Globe*, November 20, 1915; *Chicago Continental*, December 16, 1915; *Philadelphia Evening Telegraph*, December 23, 1915; all in CLC 2:5. Additional information on the movie comes from the following sources: http://www.imdb.com and http://www.afi.com (accessed May 13, 2005).

109 *Marjory Ross*: Information on Ross comes from the following sources: CE obituary, December 30, 1964; http://lcweb2.loc.gov/service/mss/eadxmlmss/eadpdfmss/2003/ms003077.pdf (accessed May 12, 2005). Furman, *Caroline Lockhart*, 51, citing interviews with various Codyites, describes Ross as "small [and] attractive." Some legal documents spell Ross's name Margery, but I will follow Lockhart's and most other Codyites' lead in using Marjory. Fees ("Introduction") has already in print characterized Ross and Lane as lesbians, but I nevertheless tread on their privacy with much regret and unease.

111 *She was sixty*: CL memoir quoted in Dominick, "Introduction," 25. Subsequent quotes in this section are from the same source, except for "Get off," which is quoted in Furman, *Caroline Lockhart*, 77. (Furman, *Caroline Lockhart*, 77–81, and Hicks, *Caroline Lockhart*, 58–60, apparently rely on slightly different versions of the memoir.) I have fixed some misspellings in the unedited draft.

113 *fancy fruits and jellies*: Walker, *Stories*, 39–40. Writing in 1936, Walker (a woman herself) said, "Being a woman, she was naturally taken advantage of by her working men."

113 *fighting face*: Walker, *Stories*, 41.

114   *I like people*: Morrison, untitled, 68. Additional information on Moore's life comes from this memoir by the Sheep Queen's daughter-in-law, which is based on her own contemporaneous diary, as well as a lifetime of knowledge of the Morrison-Moore clan—qualities Lockhart's memoirs lack. See also Milek, *Hot Springs*, 58–62.

115   *My! My! Katie*: CL, *Fighting Shepherdess*, 4. Subsequent quotes in this section are from the same novel. You may recall the real-life S. S. Prouty, a trustee at Lockhart's Topeka high school.

116   *Seth Arthur Ash*: Background information on Ash and Dorothy Newton, who later ran her own sheep ranch and may have served as an additional model for Kate, comes from the following sources: "S. A. Ash, Manager of the Western Drug Co., Assassinated," *Cody Stockgrower and Farmer*, December 10, 1909, PCHA Ash files; "Wyoming Editor Recalls Murder of Grass Creek Oil Worker," CE, February 4, 1942; Gretchen Kuiper, personal correspondence with the author, September 15, 2005.

120   *the old fighting look*: Walker, *Stories*, 41.

122   *I don't think I'll be in Cody*: CLD, quoted in Hicks, *Caroline Lockhart*, 89–90. Subsequent quotes in this section (as well as much additional background) are from the same source, pp. 87–92. Additional information on Grace and family relations came from Ramona Warren, interview by the author, Eskridge, Kansas, April 22, 2003.

124   *the other*: CLD quoted in Hicks, *Caroline Lockhart*, 89–90. For abortion, see CLD, May 24, 1934.

125   *an excellent picture*: Jenkins as quoted by CL in CLD, quoted in Hicks, *Caroline Lockhart*, 96. Subsequent quotes and additional information in this section are from the same source, 91–103 and 148. Mencken scholars can find no record of Lockhart but note that not all of his prolific correspondence survives. Lockhart uses no pronoun to refer to Bower, so it's unclear whether she knew Bower was female.

127   *I'd murder for you*: CLD, October 21, 1918. Additional information on O. B. Mann comes from the following sources: Furman, *Caroline Lockhart*, 86; Hicks, *Caroline Lockhart*, 565–66.

128   *[I] have a book coming out*: CLD, October 27, 1918.

128   *too foolish*: CLD, November 27, 1918.

128   *I've a kind of pride*: CLD, July 8, 1918.

128   *I cannot waste my life*: CLD, July 13, 1918.

129   *Guess I look*: CLD, January 22, 1919.

129   *the brilliance of her intellect*: "Boy, Howdy! Meet Caroline Lockhart, New Star for Post," *Denver Post*, December 2, 1918, in CLC 2:4.

129   *I can write circles*: CLD, quoted in Hicks, *Caroline Lockhart*, 133. Subsequent quotes in this section are also from CLD, dated as follows: January 22, 1919 ("wrinkled dame"); February 27, 1919 ("anything"); February 11, 1919 ("no fun, no exercise"); January 14, 1919 ("sweetest ever"); February 5, 1919 ("heartache"); January 22, 1919 ("knocker" and "Lothario"); January 14, 1919 ("never a man").

130　*He could go for a joy-ride*: CL, "Why Fuss over Kaiser?" *Denver Post*, December 29, 1918, quoted in Furman, *Caroline Lockhart*, 95–96. Lockhart's other *Post* articles are mentioned in Hicks, *Caroline Lockhart*, 133–46 and/or collected in CLC 2:4 and 2:6.

131　*Lockhart paced*: Hicks, *Caroline Lockhart*, 142–45. The suggestion that Lockhart act is in CLD, December 23, 1918.

131　*like an old college chum*: CLD, March 9, 1919. Subsequent quotes in this section are from the same source, dated as follows: March 9, 1919 ("God damn him"; "bad as I am"); March 12, 1919 ("no hope"); March 18, 1919 ("my own boob"), and March 24, 1919 ("unpolished").

133　*better than Zane Grey*: CLD, April 4, 1919. Lockhart's diary for April 12, 1919, misquoted the *Sun*; I used the original clipped in CLC 2:4. Subsequent quotes in this section are from reviews clipped in the same source. Additional information on Lockhart in Oklahoma comes from the following sources: Hicks, *Caroline Lockhart*, 147–51; CLD, March–April 1919.

133　*forget past discouragements*: Quoted in CLD, March 27, 1919, and March 30, 1919.

133　*Mrs. Baconrind*: CL, "Getting Atmosphere," a manuscript in CLC 1:9, reprinted in Hicks, *Caroline Lockhart*, 609–15. Subsequent quotes in this section are from the same source. Especially compared to Lockhart's diary entries, the piece engenders my skepticism. Though probably correct in broad outlines, it likely played (even subconsciously) to societal stereotypes of Native Americans. For context on the Osage, see Terry P. Wilson, *Underground Reservation*; and McAuliffe, *Bloodland*.

136　*to doing what I like*: CLD, quoted in Hicks, *Caroline Lockhart*, 152.

136　*No, she is too far*: CLD, May 25, 1919. The subsequent two quotes are from the same source.

138　*chauffer, cook*: *Fairfax (Oklahoma) Chief*, May 18, 1919, reprinted in Hicks, *Caroline Lockhart*, 155–56.

139　*What satisfaction I can extract*: CLD, June 13, 1919.

139　*Douglas Fairbanks*: "Noted Cody Authoress Receives Big Offer from Doug Fairbanks," CE, July 23, 1919, reprinted in Hicks, *Caroline Lockhart*, 172. Using terminology common to the era, the article refers to screenplays as "scenarios." Lockhart was the source for this story; her monetary figures are absurd.

140　*Dude ranches*: My claim that no author had published dude-ranch fiction before Lockhart is based on a search for stories with "Dude" in the title in the comprehensive database at http://users.ev1.net/~homeville/fictionmag/ (December 8, 2004). That's far from foolproof, but Yates (*Caroline Lockhart*, 36) leans toward the same conclusion.

141　*Epithet of opprobrium*: CL, *Dude Wrangler*, 35. Subsequent quotes in this section are from the same novel.

143　*Brightest newspaper woman*: CLD, June 26, 1919.

147   *Caroline Lockhart's living room*: Information on Lockhart's role in the *Enterprise*, Stampede, and 1920s Cody comes from the following sources: CLD, 1919–26; CE, 1920–26; Furman, *Caroline Lockhart*, 109–43; Eldridge, "Woman"; Boyett, "Booze Sheet"; Nicholas, *Becoming Western*.

147   *Rodeo*: CL, untitled memoir in CLC 1:10, p. 1.

148   *The old West, with its sports*: CE, May 5, 1920.

149   *the fastest Doc*: Murray, "Dr. William Sabin Bennett."

150   *That letter of yours*: CE, May 12, 1920.

151   *I think I shall enjoy*: CLD, May 6, 1920.

151   *Everybody grins*: CLD, June 12, 1920.

152   *the horse shall have equal*: CE, June 2, 1920.

152   *a Wild Man*: CE, June 16, 1920.

152   *the handsome Caroline Lockhart*: CLD, July 4, 1920.

153   *The Cody Stampede of 1920*: CLD, July 5, 1920.

153   *homely uneducated*: CLD, July 6, 1920.

153   *The great Stampede is done*: CLD, July 8, 1920.

154   *Although young in the legal game*: CE, July 28, 1920.

154   *Am out of a job*: CLD, August 6, 1920.

154   *It doesn't seem natural*: CLD, August 5, 1920.

156   *so proud that he*: CE, November 3, 1920. Subsequent quotes about the ball are from the same source.

157   *Mild, but sincere*: CLD, October 24, 1920, and November 8, 1920.

157   *but fear of talk*: CLD, October 27, 1920.

158   *cheap and contemptible*: CLD, February 15, 1921.

158   *I'm not used to having anyone*: CLD, November 23, 1920.

159   *Hoped I would have a sheriff*: CLD, February 17, 1921.

160   *looks like the official organ*: CLD, February 11, 1921.

161   *Silent messages*: CLD, March 31, 1921.

161   *the most hopelessly incompetent*: CLD, May 22, 1921.

161   *A bird told us*: CE, February 9, 1921.

161   *Ye gods*: CLD, May 4, 1921.

162   *Editors may come*: CE, June 29, 1921.

162   *Nobody could be worse*: CLD, June 21, 1921.

163   *worse than Emerson*: CLD, June 30, 1921.

163   *Mrs. Lydia Peckham*: CE, June 29, 1921.

163   *This morning I awoke*: CLD, July 26, 1921.

163   *Introducing new editors*: CE, August 10, 1921.

164   *Guess it doesn't matter*: CLD, August 8, 1921.

164   *Where is our wandering boy*: CE, October 12, 1921. See also Dominick, "Introduction," 53–54.

165 *competent and faithful*: CLD, November 20, 1921.

165 *The news quickly spread*: CL, untitled memoir, CLC 1:10, folder 6, p. 106.

166 *The christers are sore*: CLD, September 18, 1921.

166 *Water-Wagon*: CE, November 26, 1921.

166 *It is an uphill business*: CE, June 21, 1922. I was skeptical that she coined the aphorism until realizing that C. S. Lewis gets credit for coining "You cannot make men good by law"—in 1952.

166 *While prosecuting a case*: CE, April 19, 1922, and May 31, 1922.

167 *Comes now the plaintiff*: File 890, Park County Closed Civil Cases, quoted in Boyett, "Booze Sheet." (I am especially indebted to the work of Frank Boyett.) Information on female publishers comes from the following sources: Kroeger, *Nellie Bly*, 305–64; Ross, *Ladies*, 458. The scant record of independent female editor/publishers before 1950 includes Mary Ann Shadd Cary and Ida B. Wells.

168 *to the end of getting rid*: CLD, January 16, 1921, and March 2, 1921.

169 *I am so sick*: CLD, October 16, 1921.

169 *women of the French revolution*: CE, January 26, 1922, and February 1, 1922. All Hopkins trial information comes from these two issues.

170 *We have introduced so many editors*: CE, February 1, 1922. I have fixed some misspellings in the original.

171 *Well, the battle's over*: CLD, February 18, 1922.

172 *in accordance with law*: CE, March 1, 1922. Lockhart quoted the *Herald* before launching her response ("Chautauqua," etc.).

172 *We would also appreciate it*: CE, April 19, 1922.

173 *"Pontoon Johnny"*: CE, May 10, 1922.

173 *I am no freer*: CLD, April 14, 1922. "I need clothes" is from the following day.

173 *Perpetuity of the spirit*: *Herald* quoted in Nicholas, *Becoming Western*, 48–49.

174 *banish the strong factional feeling*: CE, May 3, 1922; CLD, May 8, 1922.

174 *It was a battle*: CE, May 10, 1922; CLD, May 12, 1922.

174 *We gave 'em such a licking*: CLD, May 12, 1922.

175 *Now Mr. Bell*: CE, May 31, 1922.

176 *modeled a figure*: CE, January 4, 1922. For the story of the Whitney statue, I am especially indebted to the work of Liza Nicholas. See also "History of the Buffalo Bill Memorial Association" in MS 58, series VIA, box 15, folder 1, BBHC; Mary Jester Allen, "Colonel Cody's Dream of a Pioneer Center—a Reality," *Annals of Wyoming*, January 1942.

176 *typical Western horse*: CE, July 12, 1922.

176 *This statue will mean*: CE, May 10, 1922.

177 *If anyone ever gets him*: CE, August 23, 1922; CLD, August 26, 1922.

177 *interesting and restful*: CLD, September 7, 1922, and September 8, 1922.

179 *$4000 more*: CE, October 18, 1922.

179　*when it comes to L.L. Newton's*: CE, November 1, 1922.

179　*The one thing we regret*: CE, December 27, 1922.

179　*Mr. Paul Eldridge*: CE, November 29, 1922. Information on Eldridge comes from the following source: Hicks, *Caroline Lockhart*, 333, 335, 357, 570. Again, I would have preferred to tell this story without invading the late Eldridge's privacy, but Hicks has already published the material outing him, and his sexuality will help us understand Lockhart's all-consuming hatred for Frances Lane.

180　*the Homesteaders versus the Cattlemen*: Eldridge, "Woman." All subsequent quotes from Eldridge, except the one noted below, are from the same source.

180　*worship of the West*: Eldridge to CL, September 19, 1948, CLC 1:9.

180　*as green as grass*: CLD, December 9, 1922.

181　*All you have to say*: CE, February 14, 1923. Little's article is in the same issue; Lockhart's commute is described in Boyett, "Booze Sheet," 1. See also Nicholas, *Becoming Western*.

182　*store clothes and evening gowns*: CE, November 28, 1923, quoted in Nicholas, *Becoming Western*, 45.

183　*Having purchased the interest*: CE, March 7, 1923.

184　*Costs $1.00 to kick*: CE, May 2, 1923, April 18, 1923, May 20, 1923.

185　*God damn you*: CE, June 27, 1923.

186　*Next week when*: CE, July 4, 1923.

186　*ridicule, opprobrium*: CE, July 11, 1923.

186　*The ordeal*: CLD, July 20, 1924, and December 31, 1924.

186　*Park County's extremely active*: CE, July 11, 1923.

187　*Gop Gets Pop*: CE, July 11, 1923, and July 18, 1923.

187　*Won't somebody step up*: CE, October 17, 1923.

187　*Will the fountain*: CE, October 10, 1923.

188　*Before the last election*: CE, October 24, 1923.

188　*much elated*: CE, November 21, 1923.

188　*Speaking for ourself*: CE, July 18, 1923. Her quote from Whitney's employee is from the same source.

189　*You started this*: CE, April 2, 1924.

189　*too much of the polo pony*: CE, October 17, 1923. Nicholas, *Becoming Western*, especially 50–65, discusses the statue's meaning and the controversy of the horse.

191　*shrine of frontier*: CE, July 9, 1924, and June 18, 1924.

191　*that note of preserving*: CE, July 23, 1924.

192　*How do you do*: CLD, July 20, 1924. "Hold the sack" is from the same source.

192　*Me and My Record*: CE, October 22, 1924, and October 29, 1924.

193　*was practically unknown*: CE, August 27, 1924, quoted in Boyett, "Booze Sheet," 33–36; October 29, 1924.

194　*Ladies in sparkling*: CE, December 31, 1924, quoting the editor of the Lovell newspaper.

194 *is silly*: CLD, November 19, 1924. The subsequent quote ("It means") is from the same source.

195 *It will be the biggest*: CLD, February 1, 1925.

195 *Papa seemed glad*: CLD, December 31, 1924, February 1, 1925, and March 6, 1925.

195 *I am enjoying my car*: CLD, May 25, 1925.

195 *My impecunious lovers*: CLD, August 19, 1924.

196 *God! It just seems*: CLD, April 5, 1925.

196 *Gop has another tantrum*: CE, April 22, 1925, and April 29, 1925.

197 *it bears every ear-mark*: CLD, quoted in Hicks, *Caroline Lockhart*, 129.

197 *lied about men*: *Herald* story reprinted in Hicks, *Caroline Lockhart*, 192–93.

198 *You have the best horses*: CLD, July 15, 1925.

198 *peace and healthy*: CLD, September 21, 1925, for all quotes through "a damned bowl."

198 *With this issue*: CE, October 14, 1925.

199 *Many people will regret*: CE, October 21, 1925.

199 *I am free*: CLD, October 16, 1925.

200 *It's a grand*: CLD, October 17, 1925.

200 *The newspaper fraternity*: CE, October 28, 1925, and November 4, 1925.

200 *it is what I wanted*: CLD, November 13, 1925.

5. COWBOY GIRL

203 *a rugged and frightful*: Washington Irving, *The Adventures of Captain Bonneville* (1837), chap. 23. Information on the Dryhead comes from the following sources: CLD, 1926–42; Bearss, *Historic*; Harvey, *General Historical*; "Cultural Landscapes Inventory"; Eldridge, "Woman"; CL, letters to Jay Adler, JAP; Spragg, manuscript and oral history. Layout and Davis Creeks have changed names several times in the last hundred years; for simplicity's sake, I use current names. Ruth French's story, which may be exaggerated, is in Hicks, *Caroline Lockhart*, 593.

205 *the laboring class*: Eldridge, "Woman," quoted in Hicks, *Caroline Lockhart*, 570–71.

205 *Lou is working*: CLD, June 28, 1926.

205 *L Slash Heart ranch*: CLD, June 23, 1926, and June 25, 1926.

206 *rotten—worse than the Herald*: CLD, November 29, 1925.

207 *He cannot seem*: CLD, January 22, 1926.

207 *liars and cheap crooks*: CLD, January 26, 1926.

207 *nervous and stupid*: CLD, May 1, 1926. Boyett, "Booze Sheet," 48, quotes the judge's instructions; no trial transcript exists.

208 *I am so uninterested*: CLD, October 23, 1926, and November 3, 1926.

213 *consequential jackass*: CLD, August 13, 1927. Additional information on Dryheaders and homesteading comes from the following sources: Bearss, *Historic*, 383–87; Hicks, *Caroline Lockhart*, 208, 584–94; Worster, *River*, 338–40; Merrill, *Public*

Lands, 43–44; Gates, *History*, 496–97 and 516–29; Rufus Snell oral history (February 22, 2000, untranscribed), tape 2, side B, BCNRA; miscellaneous NPS documents collected in the "Lockhart Research Notebook," BCNRA; Culpin, "Caroline Lockhart Ranch," 20.

213   *Be Jesus*: Hicks, *Caroline Lockhart*, 581, 578, 592.

213   *I like Joe*: CLD, August 7, 1926.

214   *I start in on a diet*: CLD, August 25, 1927.

214   *Do you like me*: CLD, May 3, 1928, and March 28, 1928.

215   *I've loved you*: CLD, June 14, 1928, and June 16, 1928.

217   *one of the largest*: "Western Writer Adds Additional Acres to Large Ranch Holding," undated, unsourced clipping, CLC 2:6.

217   *which means power*: CLD, January 13, 1929.

217   *I sleep better*: CLD, December 1, 1928.

218   *headstrong, super-sensitive*: CLD, February 23, 1929. Subsequent quotes in this section are from the same source, with original spellings.

219   *Then half sober*: CLD, June 29, 1929.

220   *Only Joe Smith's*: CLD, April 21, 1929.

221   *as yellow [and] low-down*: CLD, September 2, 1929.

222   *a hand of the old school*: CLD, September 26, 1929. See also "Dave Good, Cody Old-timer Dies Monday," CE, April 15, 1965; Hicks, *Caroline Lockhart*, 232–33, 284–89, 572.

222   *peach*: CLD, November 19, 1929. See also Johnson testimony, Lockhart homestead case, LFC box 2, folder 4.

223   *I can't stand this*: CLD, February 16, 1930, and February 17, 1930, cover these dramas and her reflections on impotence.

225   *The most charitable thing*: CL to Fred Johnson, May 15, 1934, quoted in Hicks, *Caroline Lockhart*, 583.

226   *cantankerous old bachelor*: Spragg manuscript, 139–40. I have fixed some misspellings and standardized verb tenses in the unedited draft. See also Hicks, *Caroline Lockhart*, 220–21; Trails and Tales Historical Committee, *Trails*, 662.

227   *I am annoyed as hell*: CLD, September 15, 1931.

227   *If you have anything*: CLD, July 25, 1931. For Curen's account, see Curen testimony, Lockhart homestead case, LFC box 2, folder 4. Lockhart always spelled the word *savisberry*, but I have used today's standard spelling.

228   *The American Language*: Mencken, *American Language*, 270; CLD, March 8, 1930. Oddly, given that Mencken cites her explicitly as a fiction writer, the example he references is nonfiction, a 1918 *Denver Post* article. Later Eldridge would claim that Mencken's text also referred to Lockhart as "one of the four best humorists in America." (See Hicks, *Caroline Lockhart*, 571.) But it does not, and given that Mencken scholars can find no other trace of Lockhart in his papers, we have to assume that Eldridge was mistaken.

228 *She is better on plot*: CLD, April 2, 1931, and August 15, 1930.

228 *It passed over me*: CLD, October 15, 1931 (note that Hicks, *Caroline Lockhart*, 309, has mistranscribed the stroke).

231 *exchanging the picturesque*: CL, *Old West*, 212. See also John Clayton, "'New West' Is an Old Concept," *Denver Post*, February 4, 2001; Yates, *Caroline Lockhart*, 37–40.

231 *I am getting back*: CLD, January 22, 1932, February 6, 1932, February 14, 1932, February 7, 1932, and February 6, 1932. Obviously the novel was nothing like *Uncle Tom's Cabin*, in either quality or impact. Even by the time it was published, Lockhart understood that, and she would likely be furious at me for excavating such an embarrassing quote.

232 *I swallowed my pride*: CLD, April 30, 1932. See also A. Dudley Gardner, "Continuity and Change: The Great Depression [in Wyoming]," http://www.wwcc.cc.wy.us/wyo_hist/Depression.1.htm (accessed April 12, 2005).

233 *slick fat cattle*: CLD, July 1, 1932, and September 9, 1932. Phelps had sold the Dryhead Ranch, which was now going by the name of the Antlers Ranch.

234 *too terrible for words*: CLD, October 5, 1932.

234 *It's flat and uninteresting*: CLD, October 16, 1932, and October 27, 1932.

234 *the hardest I have ever*: CLD, February 4, 1933.

234 *says he will lie*: CLD, February 11, 1933.

235 *some of the freshness*: CLD, April 12, 1933.

236 *a letter from Miss or Mrs. Spear*: CLD, May 20, 1933, and May 16, 1933.

236 *Efficient western yarn*: *New York Times Literary Supplement*, November 9, 1933, 776, LFC.

236 *She is a wonderful cook*: CLD, July 4, 1935.

236 *would be the culminating tragedy*: CLD, June 9, 1933, and June 16, 1933.

237 *an inconspicuous little man*: CLD, July 8, 1933, and August 13, 1933.

237 *There is no feed*: CLD, August 24, 1933, and March 23, 1933.

237 *would drive him away*: CLD, August 26, 1933.

238 *She had that rattle machine*: Jolly testimony, Lockhart homestead case, LFC box 2, folder 4. Subsequent quotes in this section are from testimony in the same folder.

240 *My job is writing books*: CL, letter restating her case on appeal, quoted in Culpin, "Caroline Lockhart Ranch," 19. LeFors is quoted in the same source, p. 23. See also CLD, June 8, 1933, and October 20, 1933.

240 *lantern-jawed thief*: CLD, December 22, 1933.

241 *They will learn*: CLD, March 4, 1934.

241 *Would you be skeered*: CLD, March 15, 1934.

241 *"Inscrutable" was the [word]*: Single page of a letter enclosed in CLD, March 28, 1934. It's not signed or dated, but the context makes clear that Eldridge is the author.

242 *There is no doubt*: CLD, January 3, 1935, and January 22, 1935.

242 *God! how I curse*: CLD, May 28, 1934.

243   *blamed me because*: CLD, July 22, 1934.

243   *so that he wouldn't go off*: CLD, December 15, 1934. In January 1935 Good offered another man a twenty-dollar severance.

243   *I must sell cattle*: CLD, September 23, 1934. Lockhart's debt to the Regional in this era fluctuated from five thousand to eighty-four hundred dollars.

244   *I want to write*: CLD, November 27, 1934.

244   *conceited old cuss*: Spragg manuscript, 129, 146.

244   *The appearances are that*: T. A. Walters, first assistant secretary, Department of the Interior, "Adverse Hearings Dismissed" report, March 12, 1936, LFC box 7, with original spellings. *Colorable* here means intended to deceive. Hicks, *Caroline Lockhart*, 671, quotes Morley.

245   *he had distinctly said*: CLD, September 17, 1936. See also Hicks, *Caroline Lockhart*, 367–78.

247   *I can't get it out of my head*: CLD, April 26, 1937.

248   *it wasn't like a tick*: CLD, August 18, 1937, September 2, 1937, and October 18, 1937.

248   *I made him a proposition*: CLD, October 18, 1937.

249   *My nervousness and cold feet*: CLD, November 22, 1937.

250   *regeneration through violence*: Numerous scholars have written about the meaning of the frontier; again I'm indebted to Richard Slotkin. This phrase is the title of the first book in Slotkin's four-part history of the frontier.

251   *It was weak of me*: CLD, May 12, 1938.

251   *I am ready*: CLD, April 17, 1938.

251   *my step-daughter, Caroline*: CLD, December 29, 1937, and January 25, 1938.

252   *peddler's trash*: CLD, October 15, 1938.

252   *Judy St. Clair*: CL, "That Wicked Woman," unpublished 333-page manuscript in CLC box 1:10. Lockhart's papers include at least two versions of this novel, undated and with various titles.

253   *but the question is*: CLD, May 31, 1939.

253   *because it is the most finished*: "Spirit of Old West Dying Fast, Says Montana Woman, Author of Western Stories," undated, unsourced (though apparently Billings), CLC 2:6.

253   *He shot at her*: Hicks, *Caroline Lockhart*, 485, 672; Oscar Thompson, interview by the author, October 18, 2004. Given Lockhart's bad eyesight, I'm skeptical that it was a gunshot directed at her. The bad eyesight would also be a good reason to stop riding.

254   *I sure do like*: Spragg manuscript, 113. Subsequent quotes from Spragg are from the same source, except the recollection of the cooks and the claim that Good lied to Lockhart, which are from Spragg's oral history. Spragg's manuscript notes that *Chinaman* was a common reference in those days, and he does not mean to be derogatory; I have fixed some misspellings in the unedited draft. Spragg was not related to the Wyoming writer Mark Spragg.

258   *They all seem like*: CLD, January 9, 1942.

258 *One day you'd be*: Oscar and Jane Thompson, interview by the author, October 18, 2004. Subsequent quotes in this section are from the same source, including Oscar's recollection of Good's remarks. See also Hicks, *Caroline Lockhart*, 538–43, 557, 677–78.

259 *I could be comfortable*: CLD, January 30, 1942.

259 *The announcement of the engagement*: "Local Ranch Woman Announces Engagement of Her Employees," December 13, 1944, unsourced, CLC 2:6. (Hicks, *Caroline Lockhart*, 558–59, reprints it from *CE*; other papers ran it as well. Though not bylined, it's obviously written by Lockhart.)

260 *no more morals*: CL to Jay Adler, September 24, 1944, and October 20, 1944, JAP.

261 *some nice, comfortable woman*: CL to Mrs. Kerper, December 22, 1944, CLC 2:1. The "Ouch" episode is from the same source.

262 *I take a dim view*: CL to Adler, May 1955 and November 21, 1945, JAP.

263 *Ever since he went*: "Dryhead News," various undated, unsourced clippings, CLC 2:6.

264 *The main difficulty*: CL to Adler, September 9, 1948; "Craig" in Jordan, Montana, to Adler, February 20, 1948, JAP.

265 *couldn't believe that I had not exaggerated*: CL to Adler, October 8, 1948, and December 28, 1948, JAP.

266 *I hate to sell*: CL to Dorothea Nebel, August 8, 1949, LFC.

266 *If only I were younger*: CL to Adler, September 8, 1949, JAP.

267 *Why don't you quit*: CL to Adler, March 24, 1950, JAP.

267 *I could cry*: CL to Adler, July 24, 1950, and November 2, 1950, JAP. Additional information on Lockhart in Cody comes from the following sources: letters to Adler in JAP; David Dominick, interview by the author, February 16, 2003; Caroline Sue Dowling, telephone interview by the author, October 26, 2004.

268 *It wouldn't surprise me*: CL to Adler, November 18, 1951. The "key" is reprinted in the 2003 edition of *The Lady Doc*.

269 *odd as Nick's nightcap*: Cody Country Cattlewomen, *Sisters*, 30; CL to Adler, December 1955.

269 *a fascinating story*: CL to Nebel, June 13, 1951, and January 18, 1952, LFC.

270 *invested in loans, stocks*: CL to Adler, February 1956.

270 *"Squaw" Smith*: CL to Adler, October 20, 1946, June 28, 1951, and undated but likely summer 1955, JAP.

270 *We have become a nation*: CL to Adler, undated but likely summer 1955, and April 5, 1954, JAP.

271 *She was a lovely lady*: Dowling telephone interview.

272 *It may all be wasted work*: CL to Adler, undated, and April 5, 1954, JAP.

274 *those of the townsfolk*: CL, undated, untitled memoir beginning "Almost 50 years later," box 2:1, CLC, p. 25. Lockhart used the term *morphodite*, a comic slang pronunciation of *hermaphrodite*; today's preferred term is *intersexed*. I have fixed some other misspellings in the unedited draft.

275   *Hopalong Cassidy*: CL to Adler, May 1955, JAP; CL to Nebel, undated, LFC; *Devil's Playground*, 1946. We don't know which Hoppy adventure Lockhart was watching, but in almost every feature he's dressed the same, laughs that laugh, and at some point says, "Let me introduce myself, I'm Hopalong Cassidy."

EPILOGUE

279   *She was really ill*: Sylvia Crowder to Jay Adler, July 29, 1962, JAP.

280   *the most convenient peak*: Kathryn Wright, "Forever with Mountains, Winds and Water," undated *Billings Gazette* clipping, CLC 1:9. *The Lady Doc* was reissued in 2003. The CLC's second accession was purchased in about 2001.

281   *Lucille Patrick*: CE, March 21, 1984.

281   *Pete Spragg*: Spragg manuscript, 134, 150; Spragg oral history, 40, 38. I have fixed some misspellings in the unedited drafts.

BIBLIOGRAPHY

"Altyn." *Dupuyer Acantha*, August 29, 1901 (see also September 19, 1901, and October 10, 1901). MHS.

Armitage, Susan, and Elizabeth Jameson, eds. *The Women's West*. Norman OK: University of Oklahoma Press, 1987.

Basso, Matthew, et al. *Across the Great Divide: Cultures of Manhood in the American West*. New York: Routledge, 2001.

Bearss, Edwin C. *Historic Structure Report and Historic Resource Study, Ewing (Snell) and ML Ranches, WY, and Hillsboro, MT*. National Park Service, March 1974.

Berman, Joshua. *Moon Handbooks Nicaragua*. Emeryville CA: Avalon Travel Publishing, 2002.

Blackfeet Heritage, 1907–1908. Browning MT: Blackfeet Program, n.d.

Boag, Peter. "Sexuality, Gender, and Identity in Great Plains History and Myth." *Great Plains Quarterly* 18, no. 4 (1998): 327–40.

Bonner, Robert E. "Buffalo Bill Cody and Wyoming Water Politics." *Western Historical Quarterly* 33, no. 4 (Winter 2002): 433–53.

Bowden, Martyn J. "Desert Wheat Belt, Plains Corn Belt." In *Images of the Plains: The Role of Human Nature in Settlement*, edited by Brian Blovet and Merlin Lawson. Lincoln: University of Nebraska Press, 1975.

Boyett, Frank. "The Booze Sheet of Wyoming vs. the Christer Contingent: Caroline Lockhart at the Cody Enterprise." University of Montana research paper, 1987, provided (along with some research notes) by the author.

Cahoon, Haryot Holt. "Women in Gutter Journalism." *The Arena* 17, no. 88 (Boston, March 1897): 568–74.

Carrey, John, and Cort Conley. *River of No Return*. Cambridge ID: Backeddy Books, 1978.

Catalogue of the Officers, Teachers, and Students of the Moravian Seminary for Young Ladies. Bethlehem PA: Moravian Publication Office, 1889.

Cody Country Cattlewomen. *Sisters of the Sage: Histories of Cody Country Ranchwomen*. Cody, 1998.

Culpin, Mary Shivers. "Caroline Lockhart Ranch: Bighorn Canyon National Recreation

Area." Regional Historic Preservation Team, Rocky Mountain Regional Office, National Park Service, October 1981. Copy at PCL.

"Cultural Landscapes Inventory: Caroline Lockhart Ranch." Lovell WY: Bighorn Canyon National Recreation Area, n.d.

Davison, Stanley. "The Author [B. M. Bower] Was a Lady." *Montana: The Western History Magazine* 23, no. 2 (Spring 1973): 2–15.

D'Emilio, John, and Estelle B. Freedman. *Intimate Matters: A History of Sexuality in America*. New York: Harper and Row, 1989.

Dominick, David. "Introduction to Caroline Lockhart." Undergraduate essay, Yale University, 1959.

Eldridge, Paul. "Woman on Horseback." Unpublished essay in LFC.

Engen, Orrin. *B. M. Bower*. Self-published, 1973.

Etulain, Richard. *Owen Wister*. Boise: Boise State College Western Writers Series, 1973.

———. *Telling Western Stories: From Buffalo Bill to Larry McMurtry*. Albuquerque: University of New Mexico Press, 1999.

———, ed. *Writing Western History: Essays on Major Western Historians*. Albuquerque: University of New Mexico Press, 1991.

"Famous Author Once Attended Central School." *Sterling Daily Gazette*, December 4, 1936.

Fees, Paul. Introduction to *The Lady Doc*, by Caroline Lockhart. Cody WY: Wordsworth Publishing, 2003.

Frantz, Joe B., and Ernest Choate Jr. *The American Cowboy: The Myth and the Reality*. Norman: University of Oklahoma Press, 1955.

Furman, Necah Stewart. *Caroline Lockhart: Her Life and Legacy*. Seattle: University of Washington Press, 1994.

Gale, Paul. "Woman Author Begins Parent-Teacher Movement." *Sauk Valley Sunday*, March 26, 2000.

Gates, Paul. *History of Public Land Law Development*. Washington DC: Public Land Law Review Commission, 1968.

Greene, Peggy. "Sisters of Bethany to Hold Alumnae Reunion Here." *Topeka Daily Capital*, October 25, 1953, 14A.

Grey, Zane. *Riders of the Purple Sage*. New York: Harper and Brothers, 1912. Reprint, Roslyn NY: Walter J. Black, 1938.

Gruber, Frank. *Zane Grey: A Biography*. Roslyn NY: Walter J. Black, 1969.

Guthrie, C. W. *The First Ranger: Adventures of a Pioneer Forest Ranger, Glacier Country, 1902–10*. Huson MT: Redwing Publishing, 1995.

Harvey, David. *A General Historical Survey of the Pryor Mountains*. Billings MT: Bureau of Land Management, September 1974.

Hicks, Lucille Patrick (see also Patrick, Lucille). *Caroline Lockhart: Liberated Lady*. Cody and Cheyenne WY: Pioneer Printing, 1984.

———, ed. *The Park County Story*. Dallas: Taylor Publishing, 1980.

Houston, Pam. Introduction to *Lonesome Land*, by B. M. Bower. Lincoln: University of Nebraska Press, 1997.

Humphrey, Christopher. *Moon Handbooks Honduras*. 3rd ed. Emeryville CA: Avalon Travel Publishing, 2003.

Jameson, Elizabeth, and Susan Armitage, eds. *Race, Class, and Culture in the Women's West*. Norman: University of Oklahoma Press, 1997.

Johnson, Susan Lee. "A Memory Sweet to Soldiers: The Significance of Gender in the History of the American West." *Western Historical Quarterly* 24 (November 1993): 495–517.

Jones, Larry, et al. "Salmon River Navigation." *Idaho State Historical Society Reference Series* 774 (1983), http://www.idahohistory.net.

Jordan, Terry. *North American Cattle Ranching Frontiers*. Albuquerque: University of New Mexico Press, 1993.

Kroeger, Brooke. *Nellie Bly: Daredevil, Reporter, Feminist*. New York: Times Books, 1994.

Lamont, Victoria. "Native American Oral Practice and the Popular Novel; or, Why Mourning Dove Wrote a Western." *Western American Literature* 39, no. 4 (Winter 2005): 368–93.

———. "Writing on the Frontier: Western Novels by Women, 1880–1920." PhD diss., University of Alberta, Edmonton, 1998.

Langley, Lester, and Thomas Schoonover. *The Banana Men: American Mercenaries and Entrepreneurs in Central America, 1880–1930*. Lexington: University of Kentucky Press, 1995.

Larson, T. A. "Women's Role in the American West." *Montana: The Magazine of Western History* 24, no. 3 (Summer 1974): 2–11.

Limerick, Patricia Nelson. *The Legacy of Conquest: The Unbroken Past of the American West*. New York: W. W. Norton, 1987.

Lockhart, Caroline. *The Dude Wrangler*. New York: Doubleday, Page, 1921.

———. *The Fighting Shepherdess*. Boston: Small, Maynard, 1919.

———. *The Full of the Moon*. Philadelphia: J. B. Lippincott, 1914.

———. *The Lady Doc*. New York: J. B. Lippincott, 1912.

———. *The Man from the Bitter Roots*. Philadelphia: J. B. Lippincott, 1915.

———. *Me-Smith*. Philadelphia: J. B. Lippincott, 1911.

———. *Old West—and New*. Garden City NY: Doubleday, Doran, 1933.

Lukas, J. Anthony. *Big Trouble*. New York: Simon and Schuster, 1997.

Malin, James C. *Winter Wheat in the Golden Belt of Kansas*. Lawrence: University Press of Kansas, 1944.

McAuliffe, Dennis, Jr. *Bloodland: A Story of Oil, Greed, and Murder on the Osage Reservation*. San Francisco: Council Oak Books, 1999.

Meinig, Donald. *The Shaping of America: Transcontinental America, 1850–1915*. New Haven CT: Yale University Press, 1998.

Mencken, H. L. *The American Language: An Inquiry into the Development of English in the United States.* 2nd ed. New York: A. A. Knopf, 1921. Reprint, Bartleby.com, 2000, http://www.bartleby.com/185/ (accessed May 6, 2004).

———. *Newspaper Days, 1899–1906.* New York: A. A. Knopf, 1941. Reprint, Baltimore: Johns Hopkins University Press, 1996.

Merrill, Karen R. *Public Lands and Political Meaning: Ranchers, the Government, and the Land between Them.* Berkeley: University of California Press, 2002.

Milek, Dorothy Buchanan. *Hot Springs: A Wyoming County History.* Basin WY: Saddlebag Books, 1986.

Miller, Darlis. *Mary Hallock Foote: Author-Illustrator of the American West.* Norman: University of Oklahoma Press, 2002.

Morrison, Nell R. Untitled manuscript constituting the majority of a book authored by Bob Edgar and Jack Turnell, *Lady of a Legend.* Cody WY: Stockade Books, 1979.

Moss, Florence. "A Brief History of Asbury Park," http://asburypark.net/info/history.html (accessed May 4, 2004).

Murray, Ester Johansson. "Dr. William Sabin Bennett: The Rise and Fall of a Pioneer Doctor." *Annals of Wyoming* 61, no. 1: 39–46.

Nicholas, Liza. *Becoming Western: Stories of Culture and Identity in the Cowboy State.* Lincoln: University of Nebraska Press, 2006.

1998 Blackfoot Genealogy, Treasures, and Gifts. Browning MT: Blackfeet Tribal Business Council, 1998.

Pascoe, Peggy. *Relations of Rescue: The Search for Female Moral Authority in the American West, 1874–1939.* New York: Oxford University Press, 1990.

Patrick, Lucille (see also Hicks, Lucille Patrick). *The Best Little Town by a Dam Site.* Cheyenne WY: Flintlock Publishing, 1968.

———. "The Grand Tour of the Infamous Dryhead Country." Manuscript, Lockhart file, PCHA.

———. "Three Women of Cody." Manuscript, Lockhart file, PCHA.

Ross, Ishbel. *Ladies of the Press.* New York: Harper and Brothers, 1936.

Sagala, Sandra. *Buffalo Bill, Actor: A Chronicle of Cody's Theatrical Career.* Bowie MD: Heritage Books, 2002.

Slotkin, Richard. *The Fatal Environment: The Myth of the Frontier in the Age of Industrialization, 1800–1890.* Norman: University of Oklahoma Press, 1985. Reprint, 1994.

———. *Gunfighter Nation: The Myth of the Frontier in Twentieth-Century America.* New York: Harper Perennial, 1992.

Spragg, Merwyn "Pete." Oral history transcription, September 11, 1990, pp. 1–43, BCNRA.

———. Untitled manuscript, n.d., pp. 112–53, BCNRA.

Staples, Barbara. *The Bay State's Boston Post Canes: History of a New England Tradition.* Lynn MA: Fleming Press, 1997.

Stewart, Elinore Pruitt. *Letters of a Woman Homesteader.* Boston: Houghton Mifflin, 1998.

Sullivan, Mark. *Our Times*. Vol. 1, *Turn of the Century*. New York: Scribners, 1926, 1971.

Teachout, Terry. *The Skeptic: A Life of H. L. Mencken*. New York: HarperCollins, 2002.

Thiem, E. George, ed. *Carroll County—a Goodly Heritage*. Mt. Morris IL: Kable Printing Company, 1968.

Tompkins, Jane. *West of Everything: The Inner Life of Westerns*. New York: Oxford University Press, 1992.

Trails and Tales Historical Committee. *Trails and Tales South of the Yellowstone*. Billings MT: 1983.

Walker, Tacetta. *Stories of the Early Days in Wyoming: Big Horn Basin*. Casper WY: Prairie Publishing Company, 1936.

Wallace, Joseph. *Past and Present of the City of Springfield and Sangamon County Illinois*. Chicago: S. J. Clarke Publishing, 1904.

Ward, Harold. "Writer Caroline Lockhart Was Former Sterling Girl." *Sterling Daily Gazette*, n.d., CLC 2:6.

West, Elliott. *Growing Up with the Country: Childhood on the Far Western Frontier*. Albuquerque: University of New Mexico Press, 1989.

———. *The Way to the West: Essays on the Central Plains*. Albuquerque: University of New Mexico Press, 1995.

Wilson, Mrs. Augustus. Untitled article, *Parsons' Memorial and Historical Library Magazine* 1 (1885): 141–43.

Wilson, Terry P. *The Underground Reservation: Osage Oil*. Lincoln: University of Nebraska Press, 1985.

Worster, Donald. *A River Running West*. New York: Oxford University Press, 2001.

Wrobel, David M. *Promised Lands: Promotion, Memory, and the Creation of the American West*. Lawrence: University Press of Kansas, 2002.

Yates, Norris. *Caroline Lockhart*. Boise ID: Boise State University Western Writers Series, 1994.

———. *Gender and Genre*. Albuquerque: University of New Mexico Press, 1995.

INDEX

irrigation. *See* dams

Jackson, Helen Hunt, 78, 281, 292
Jewett, Sarah Orne, 78, 89, 280
Johnston, "Liver-Eatin'," 61, 72
Jolly, Clay: as employee, 205, 215–19, 222; homestead of, 209–10, 234–35, 238–40, 247
Judge magazine, 179

Kennedy, Tex, 140
Ketcham, Lou Tiffany: as employee, 206, 215, 227–28, 232–33, 236; homestead of, 209, 238–40, 244

Labrador, 47
La Ceiba, Honduras, 106–8, 253, 272
The Lady Doc (1912), 87–92, 102–3, 124, 139, 273; comparisons to other books, 118, 126; reprint of, 268
LaMott, Jennie, 61–62, 73–77, 103
Lampitt, Bert, 116
Lane, Frances: as doctor, 80–87, 124, 130, 150, 178, 281; and early friendship with Lockhart, 67–68, 83; and *The Lady Doc*, 87–92, 110; as Lockhart enemy, 83–92, 97–98, 139, 151, 172–73, 186, 196; and post-death influence on Lockhart, 251, 263, 273–75. *See also* Ferko, Marko; Ross, Marjory
Lane, Hank, 186, 226, 240, 247, 248–49, 253, 262
Larom, I. H. "Larry," 140, 147–48, 150, 155, 158, 160
LeFors, Joe, 235, 237, 240, 242
legitimacy (for writers). *See* authenticity, for writers
Lehigh University (PA), 23–24
lesbians. *See* homosexuality
Lewis, Sinclair, 88, 228, 236
Lexington MA, 39

Lippincott's magazine, 3, 55, 59–64, 77, 132; publishing house, 73, 79, 96, 109, 125–26
Little, Brown (publishing house), 125
Little, June, 170–73, 176, 181–82
local color (literary trend), 70–71, 78–79
Lockhart, Caroline: as actress, 26–27, 31–34, 37; appearance of, 3, 16, 33, 69, 103, 122, 147, 164, 204, 254–55; birth of, 10, 286; Buffalo Bill Cody and, 41–43, 64, 67–68, 116, 273; childhood of, 11–27; death of, 279–80; and doctors, 22, 71, 80–92, 124; drinking of, 164, 167, 224, 271; education of, 12, 16–18, 23–27; horsemanship of, 5–6, 12–13, 33, 41–42, 69, 205; as journalist, 3–6, 31–56, 60–62, 66–69, 143–200, 263, 288–90; as memoirist, 271–75; and men, 16–18, 47–48, 63, 122–24, 127–29, 154, 158, 218; money and, 121–22, 130, 150, 161–62, 194–96, 217; as novelist, 56, 62–64, 73–80, 87–92, 94–97, 102–9, 115–26, 139–43, 229–36, 252–53, 263, 271–72; pets of, 24, 147, 255, 271, 275; as pathbreaking woman, 5, 47, 87, 89, 100, 168; politics and, 81–87, 91, 153–55, 161, 164–65, 171–75, 177, 187–88, 192–93, 270–71; pregnancy scare of, 123–24; as publisher, 149–200, 268; as rancher, 204–67, 282. *See also* Cody, William F. "Buffalo Bill": statue of; di Colonna, Valentin; Ericson, Lou; Good, Dave; horses; Lockhart, Joe: parsimony of; Mann, Orin B.; marriage; McKenzie, Andrew; Painter, Jack; Poole, Bill; Prohibition; ranching: hardships of; Smith, John L.
Lockhart, George (brother): childhood of, 11, 16, 18, 22–23; rebellion of, 26–27, 31; and reconciliation with Caroline, 192, 195, 251

Wharton, Edith, 63, 78, 280
Whitney, Gertrude Vanderbilt, 175–77, 188, 191
Wiard, Harry, 178–79
Wilder, Laura Ingalls, 11–12, 25
Wild West (show), 21, 148, 172, 181
Wilkie, John, 83–84
Williams, Barry, 164
Williams, Clarence, 147–48, 160, 162, 163, 171
Willing, Ava, 48, 52
Wister, Owen: career of, 31, 41, 74–79; influence of, 92–95, 105, 112, 177, 231, 250, 280
women: as artists, 31–33; as authors, 3, 63, 77–80, 109; as journalists, 3–4, 34–35, 50; as publishers, 168; as ranchers, 12, 117–21, 205, 217–23, 245, 265; and relationship to power, 18, 113, 139, 257, 265–66, 276, 281; snobbery of, 25, 56; as stunt girls, 3–4, 35, 41, 45–47, 50; in the West, 11–12, 18, 60–62, 65–66, 69–70, 94–97, 220, 281. *See also* Lockhart, Caroline; Moore, Lucy Morrison; Whitney, Gertrude Vanderbilt
Woodruff, Seward (uncle), 122, 130, 200, 208, 209
Woods, William, 39–40
working class, 81–88, 113, 134, 166, 205

Yellowstone National Park (wy): as economic force, 65, 140, 147, 171, 191; Lockhart's visits to, 154